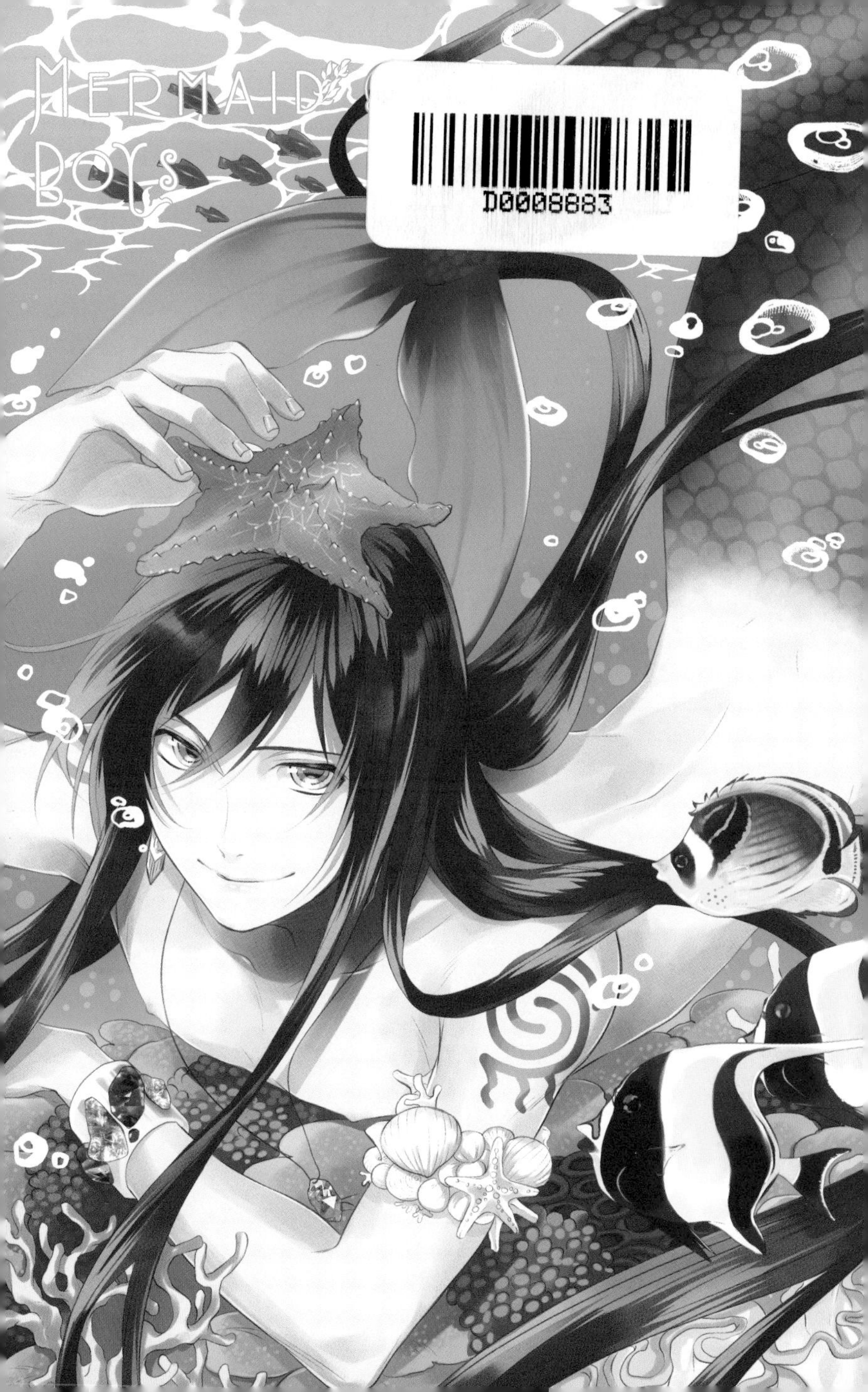
MERMAID BOYS

MERMAID BOYS

2

contents

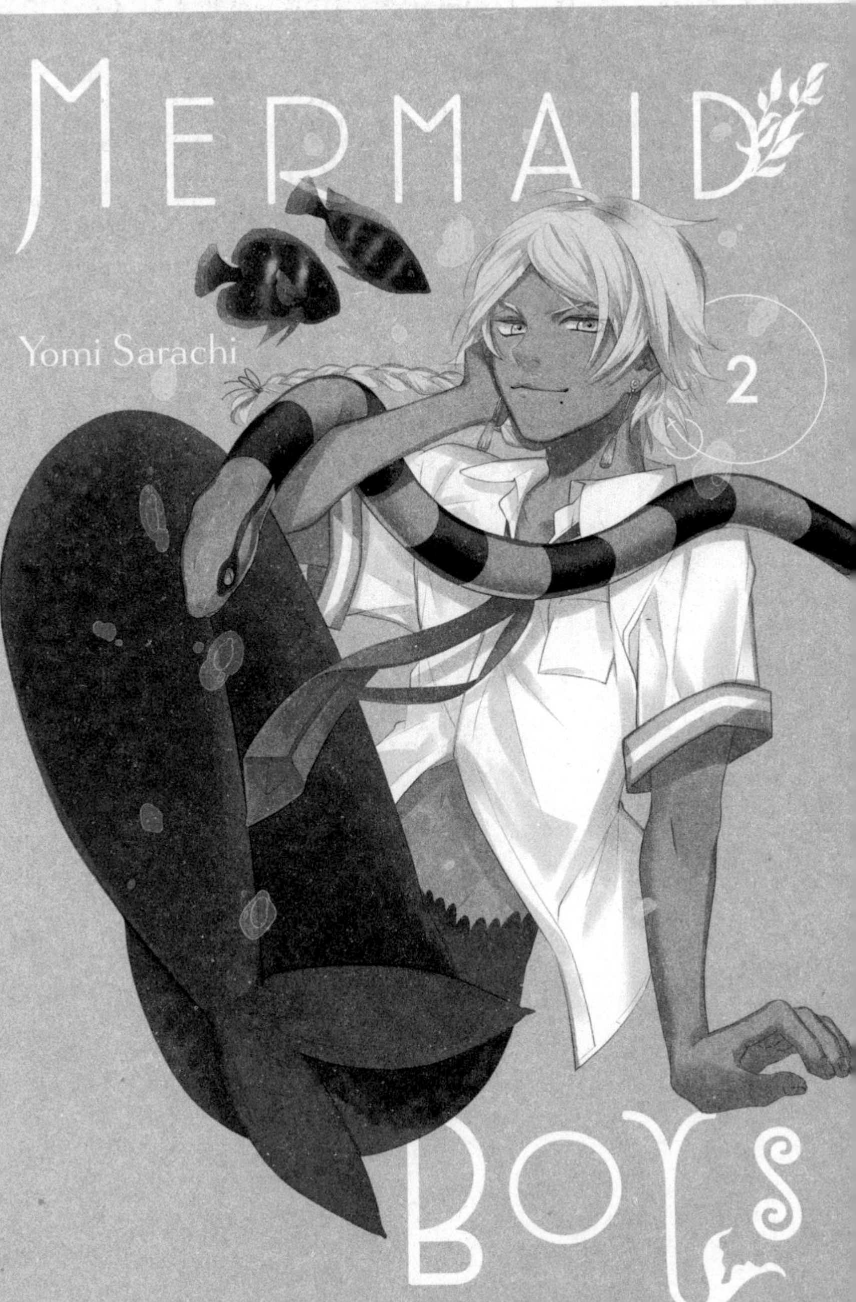
MERMAID
Yomi Sarachi
2
BOYS

MERMAID BOYS

CHARACTERS & STORY

A merman prince falls in love with a human girl—

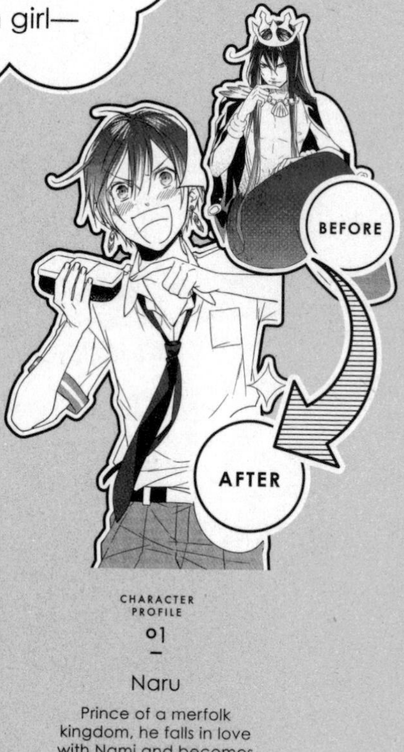
BEFORE
AFTER

CHARACTER PROFILE

01

–

Naru

Prince of a merfolk kingdom, he falls in love with Nami and becomes human, thanks to magic! He's very curious and a bit full of himself.

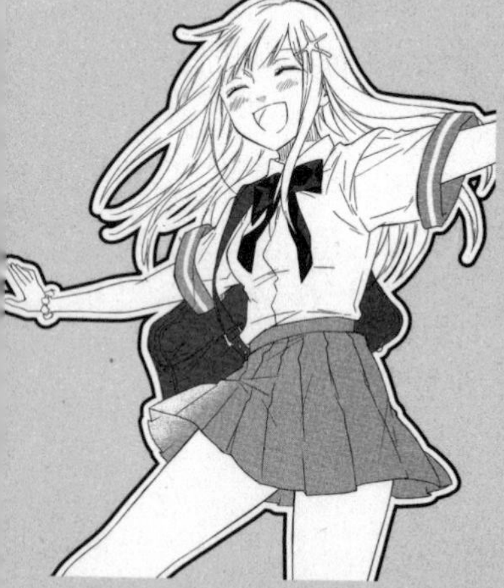

CHARACTER PROFILE

02

–

Nami Sakuragai

The high school girl Naru fell in love with. She's a hard worker who has inherited the inn her father left her. She's got beautiful legs.

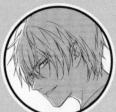

CHARACTER PROFILE 03

—

Mellow

The sorcerer who turned Naru human. What's the scheme he seems to be plotting...?

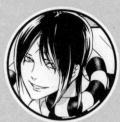

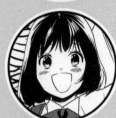

CHARACTER PROFILE 04

—

Arashi

Nami's childhood friend. Does he like Nami?

CHARACTER PROFILE 05

—

Ryou

Nami's other childhood friend. He gave up his sense of taste to become human.

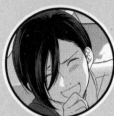

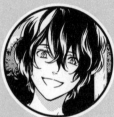

CHARACTER PROFILE 06

—

Natsuko

Nami's classmate. She's a hard-core romanticist.

CHARACTER PROFILE 07

—

Hikaru

The property manager who lives with Nami. He's like an older brother to her.

STORY

Naru is a merman prince. He falls in love at first sight with a human girl, Nami, and asks the sorcerer Mellow to turn him human so that he can meet her. In exchange, he has to give up his good looks and make an intimate connection with her within one year, or else he'll turn into sea foam!

Though he ends up living at Nami's house, his natural born smugness pushes Nami's buttons, and the fact that he keeps showing up buck naked makes Nami downright despise him...

At school, Naru realizes that a classmate named Ryou is also a former merman! Ryou tells Naru that the reason he got legs was to kill a certain human!

Meanwhile, back in the land of merfolk, why is Mellow getting ready to send off another merman to the human world!?

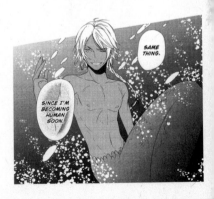

SAME THING.
SINCE I'M BECOMING HUMAN SOON.

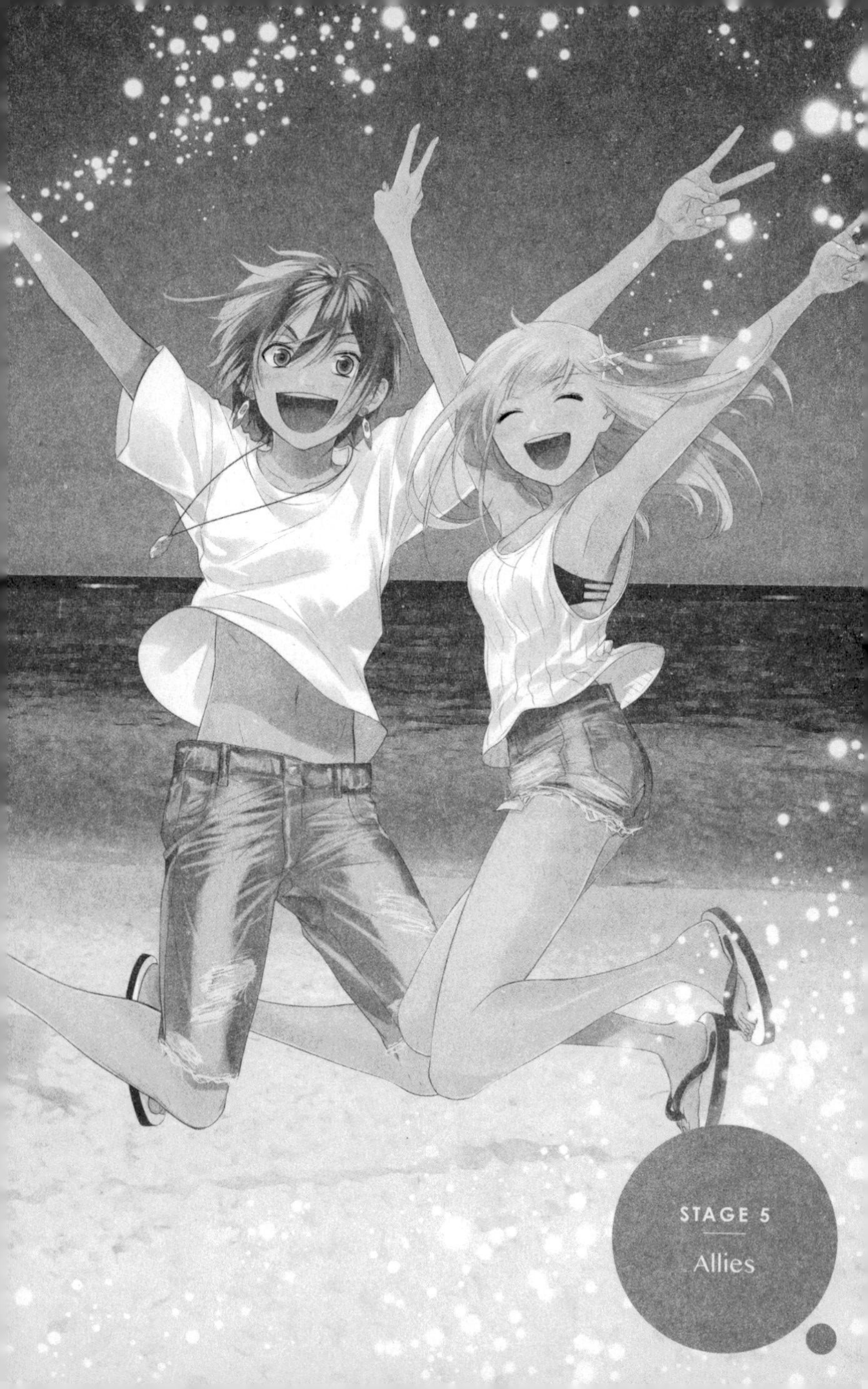
STAGE 5
Allies

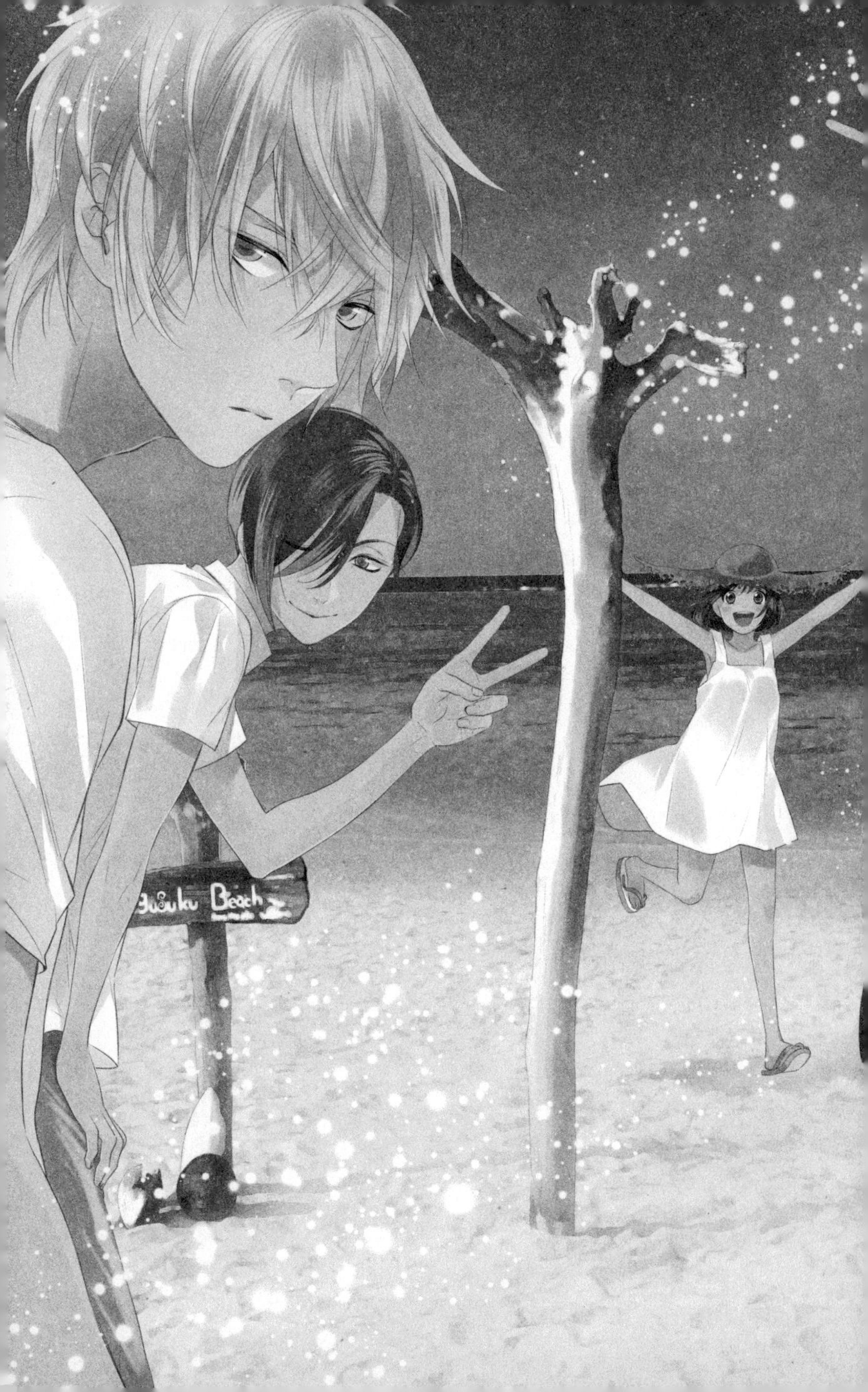
Gusuku Beach

MERMAID BOYS

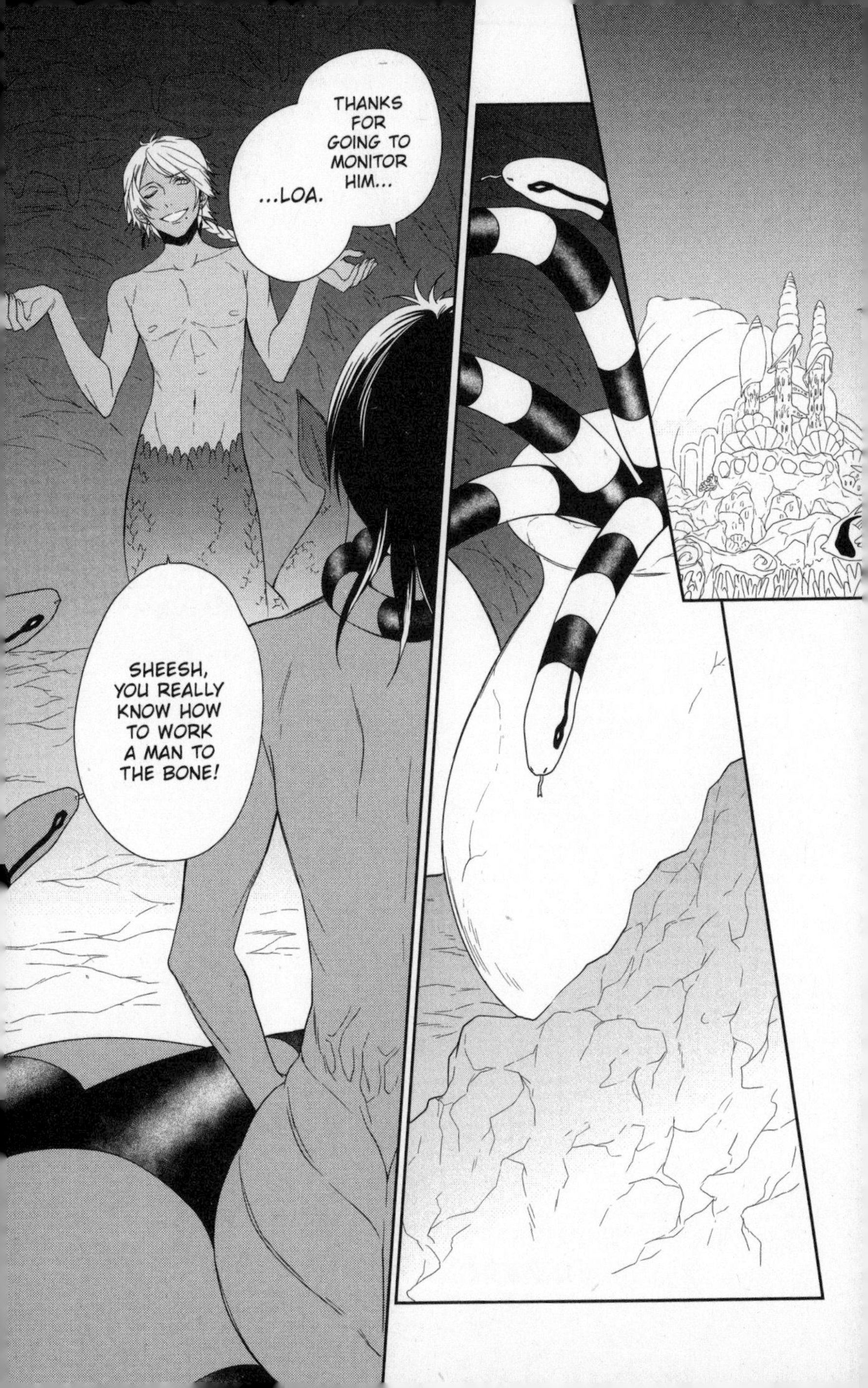
THANKS FOR GOING TO MONITOR HIM...
...LOA.
SHEESH, YOU REALLY KNOW HOW TO WORK A MAN TO THE BONE!

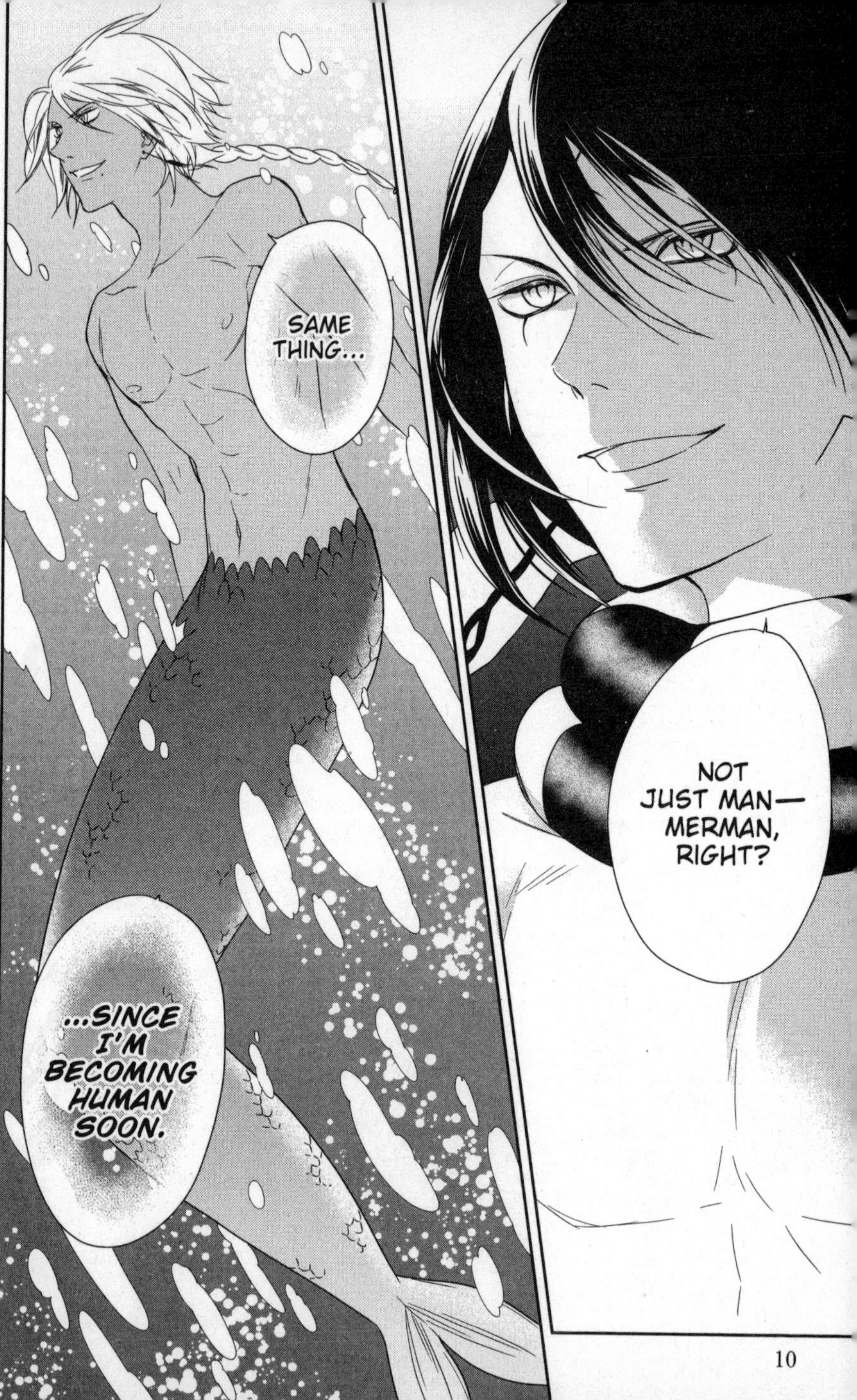
NOT JUST MAN—MERMAN, RIGHT?
SAME THING...
...SINCE I'M BECOMING HUMAN SOON.

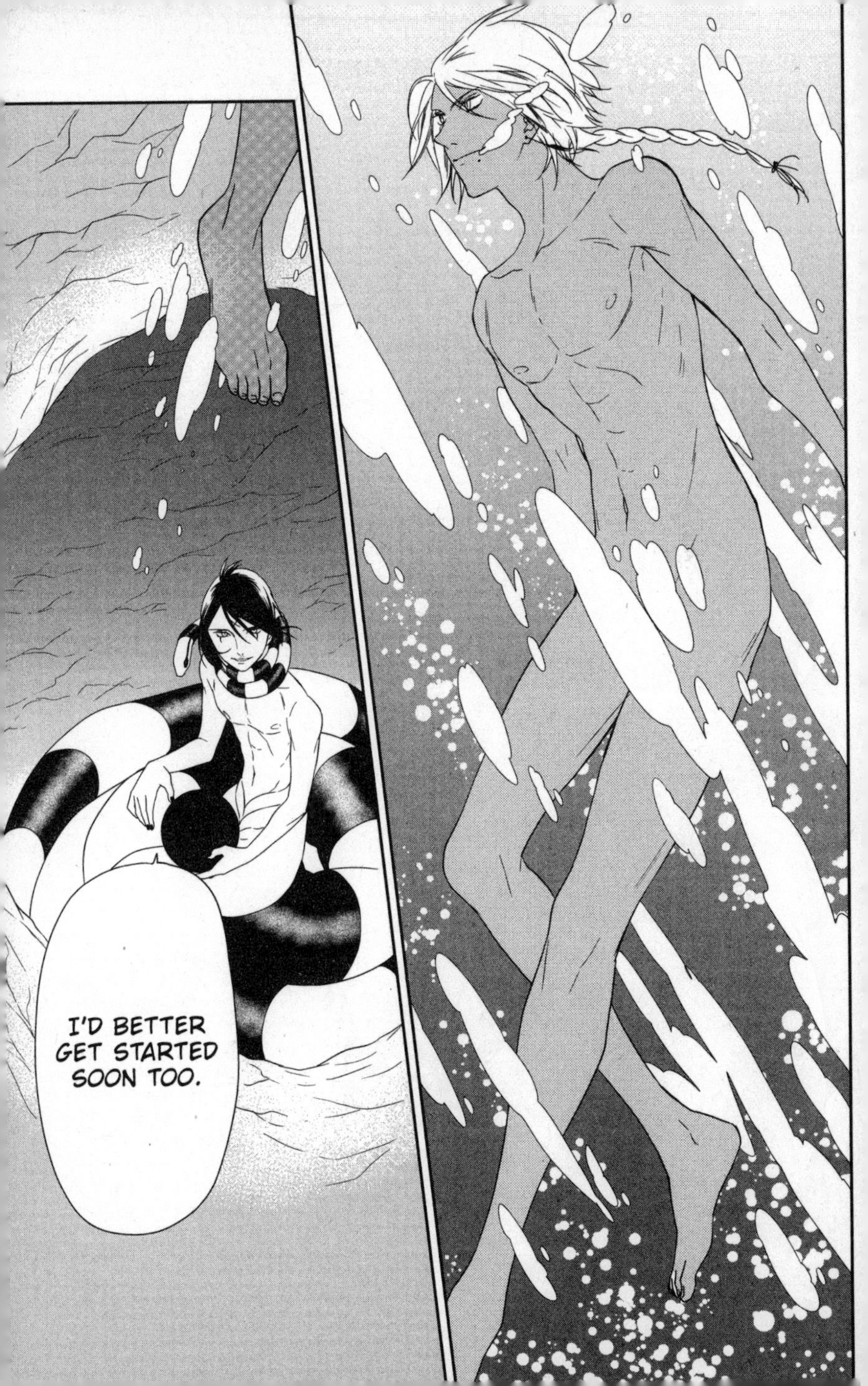
I'D BETTER GET STARTED SOON TOO.

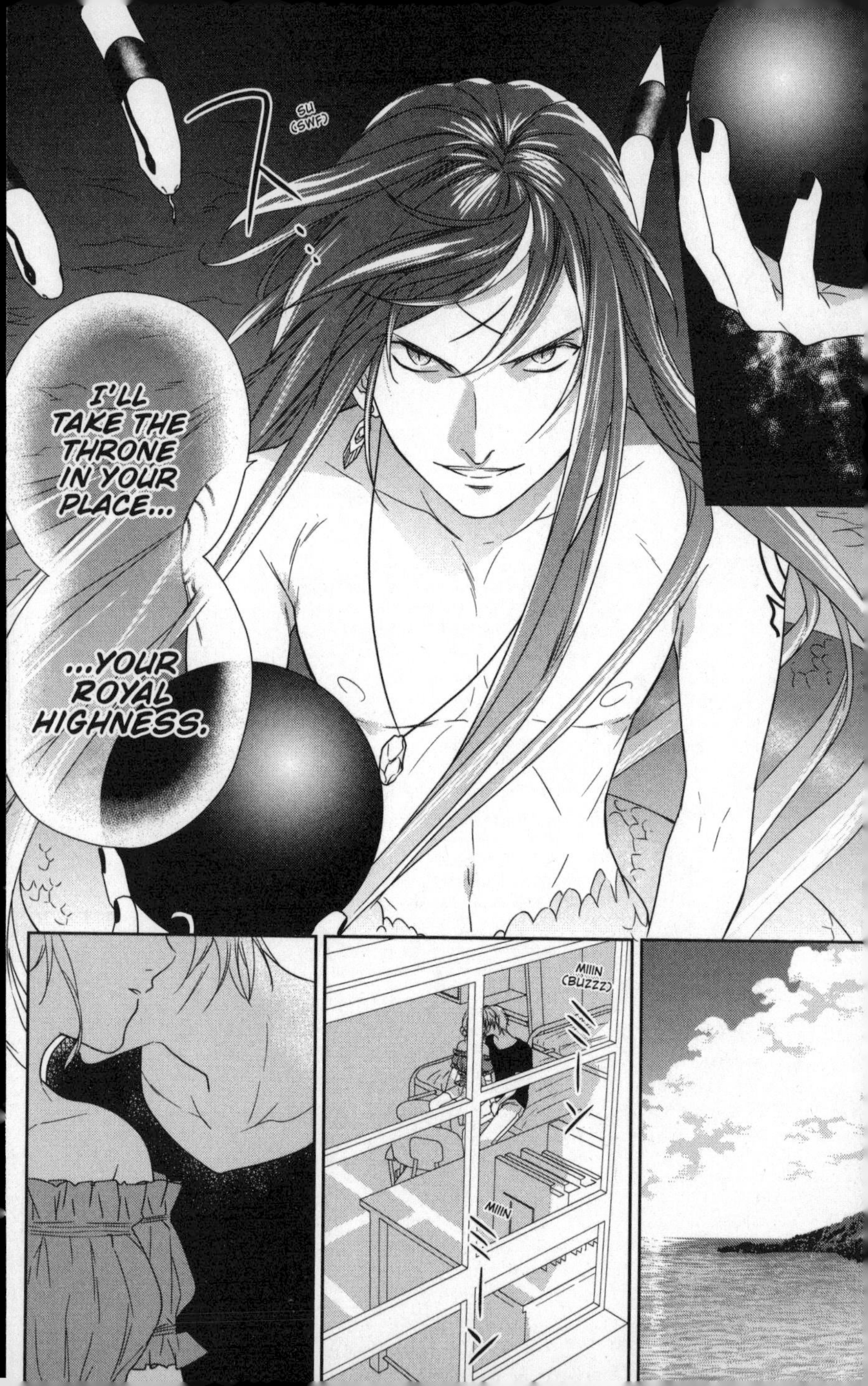
SU (SWF)
I'LL TAKE THE THRONE IN YOUR PLACE...
...YOUR ROYAL HIGHNESS.
MIIIN (BUZZZ)
MIIIN

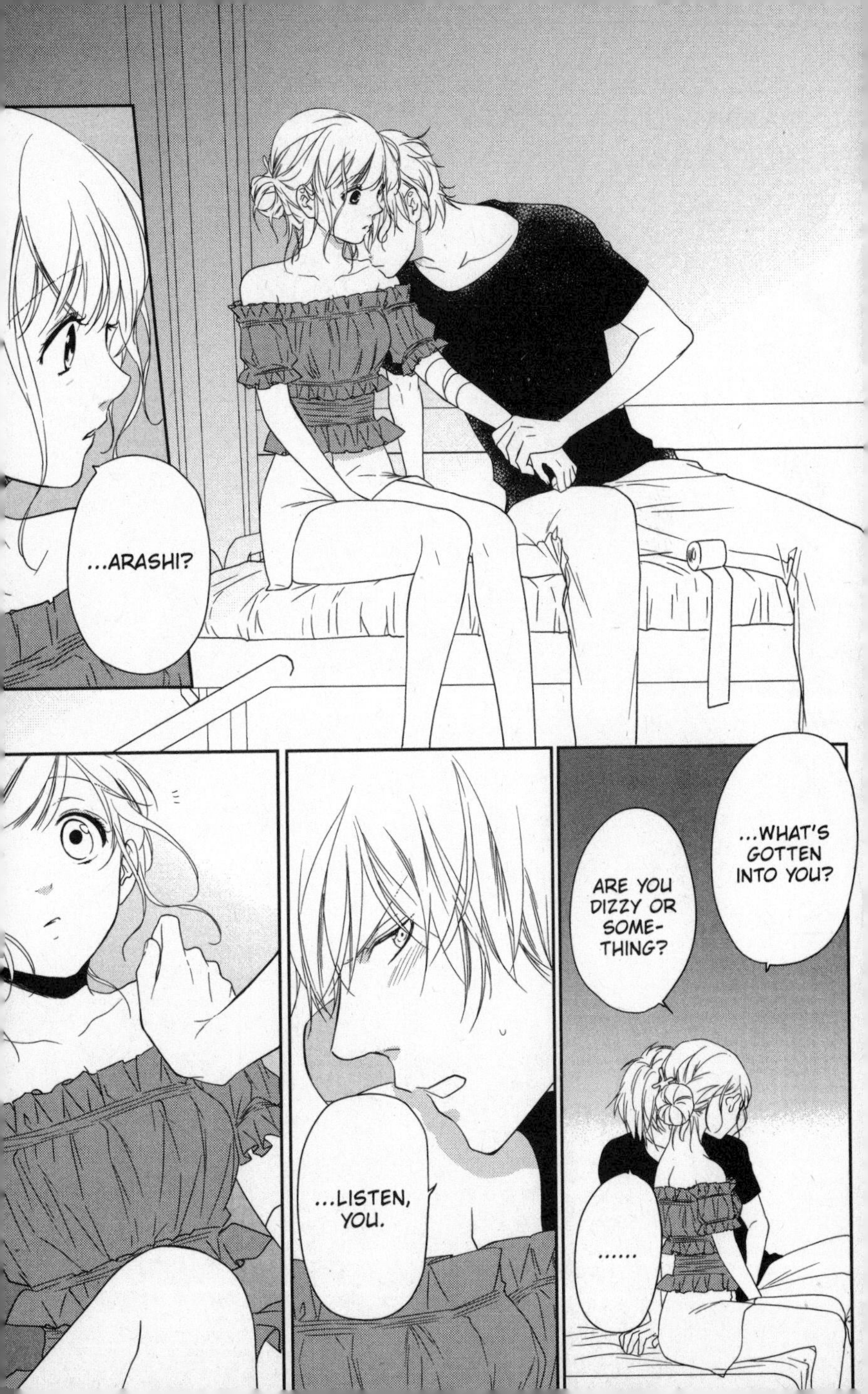
...ARASHI?
...WHAT'S GOTTEN INTO YOU?
ARE YOU DIZZY OR SOME-THING?
......
...LISTEN, YOU.

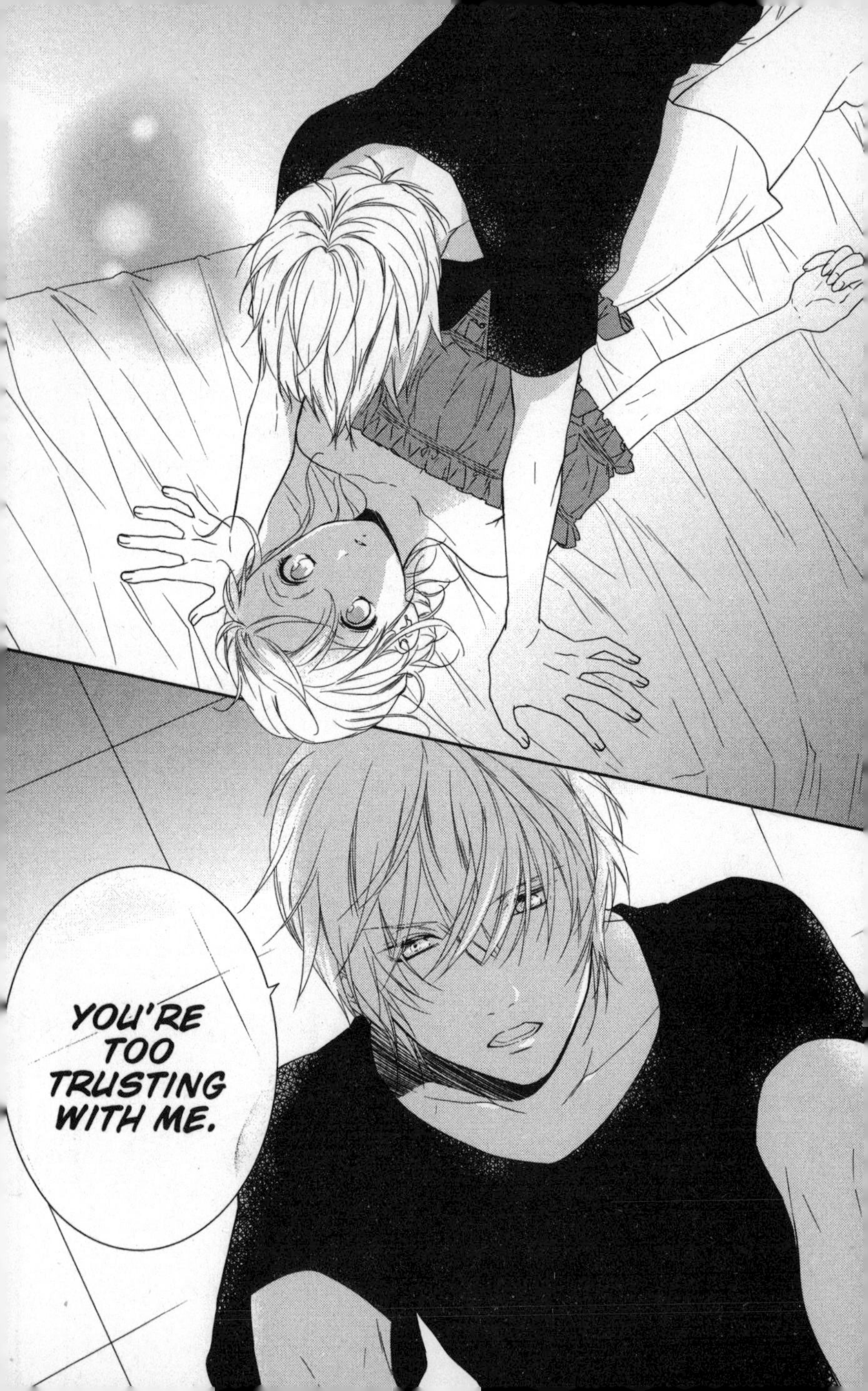
YOU'RE TOO TRUSTING WITH ME.

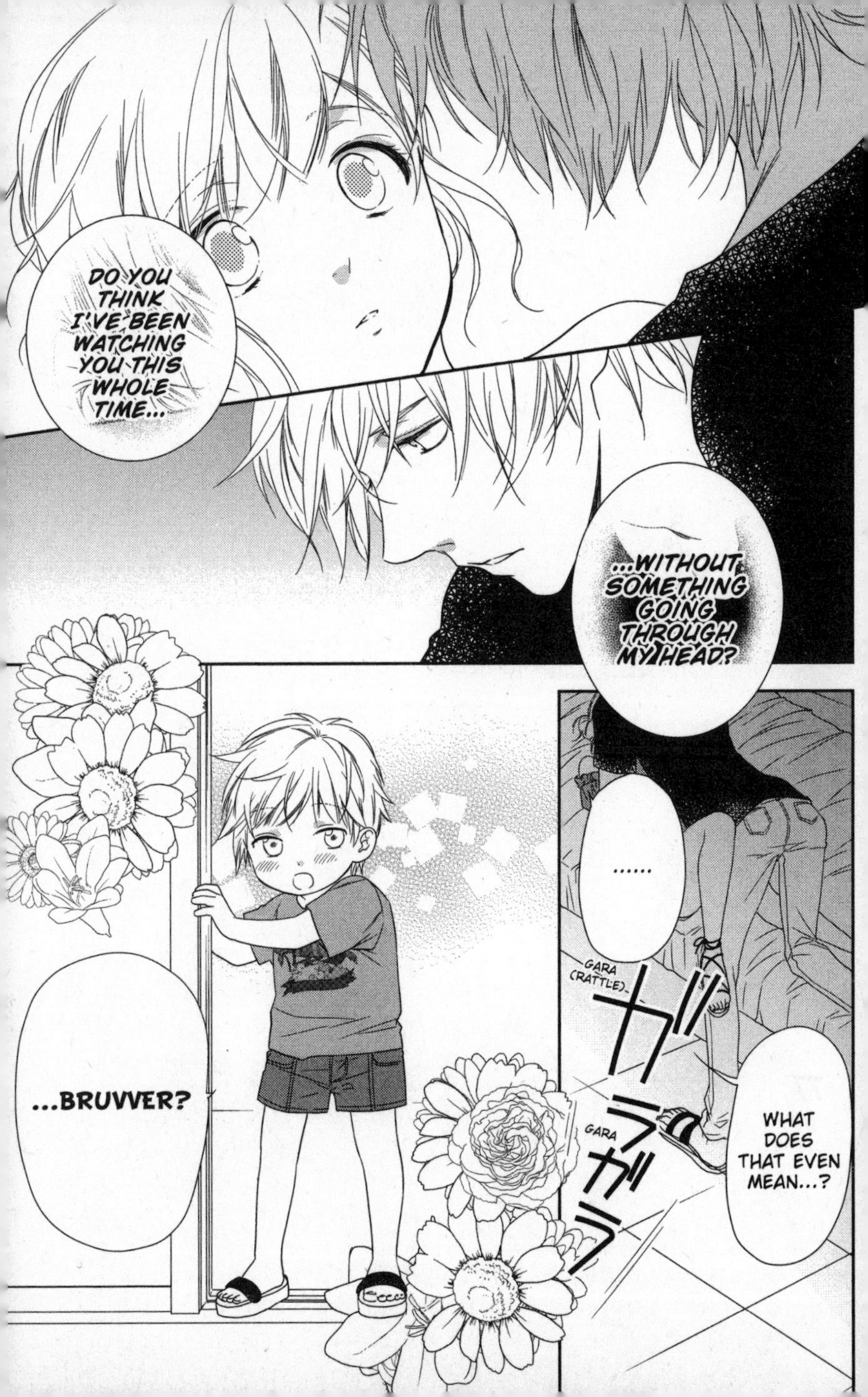
DO YOU THINK I'VE BEEN WATCHING YOU THIS WHOLE TIME...
...WITHOUT SOMETHING GOING THROUGH MY HEAD?
......
GARA (RATTLE)
GARA
WHAT DOES THAT EVEN MEAN...?
...BRUVVER?

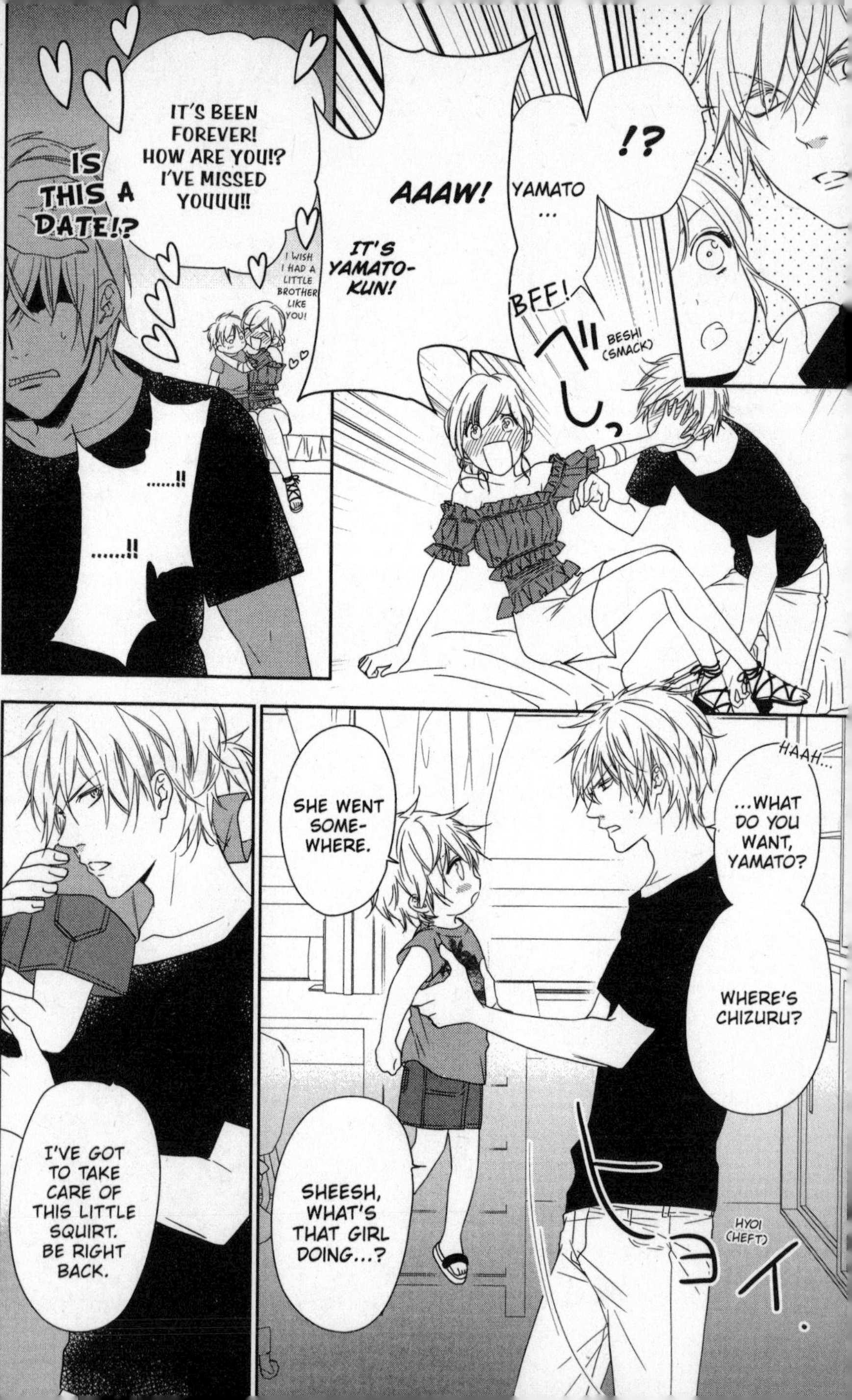
!?
YAMATO ...
AAAW!
IT'S YAMATO-KUN!
BFF!
BESHI (SMACK)
IT'S BEEN FOREVER! HOW ARE YOU!? I'VE MISSED YOUUU!!
I WISH I HAD A LITTLE BROTHER LIKE YOU!
IS THIS A DATE!?
......!!
......!!
HAAAH...
...WHAT DO YOU WANT, YAMATO?
WHERE'S CHIZURU?
SHE WENT SOME-WHERE.
HYOI (HEFT)
SHEESH, WHAT'S THAT GIRL DOING...?
I'VE GOT TO TAKE CARE OF THIS LITTLE SQUIRT. BE RIGHT BACK.

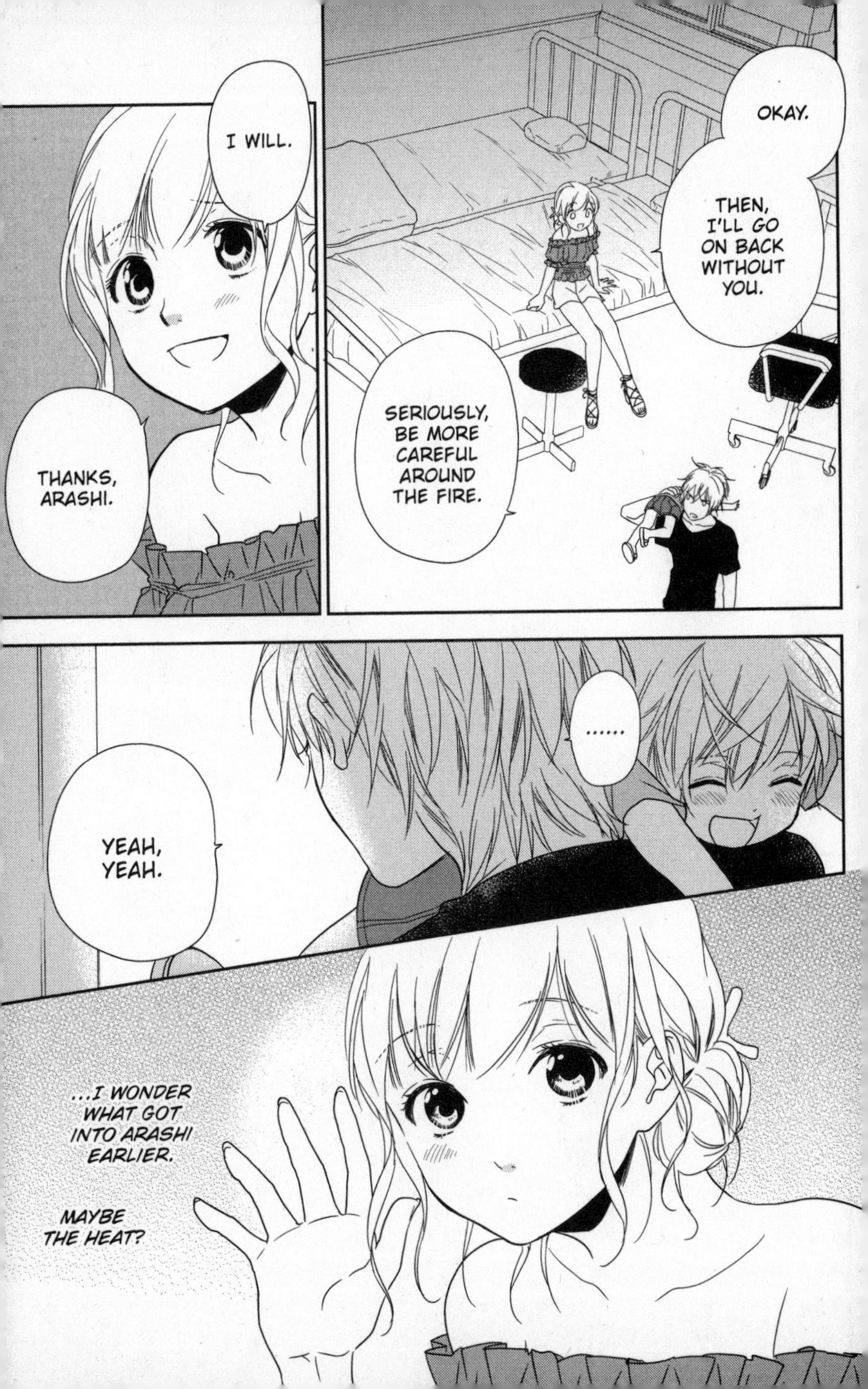
OKAY.
THEN, I'LL GO ON BACK WITHOUT YOU.
SERIOUSLY, BE MORE CAREFUL AROUND THE FIRE.
I WILL.
THANKS, ARASHI.
......
YEAH, YEAH.
...I WONDER WHAT GOT INTO ARASHI EARLIER.
MAYBE THE HEAT?

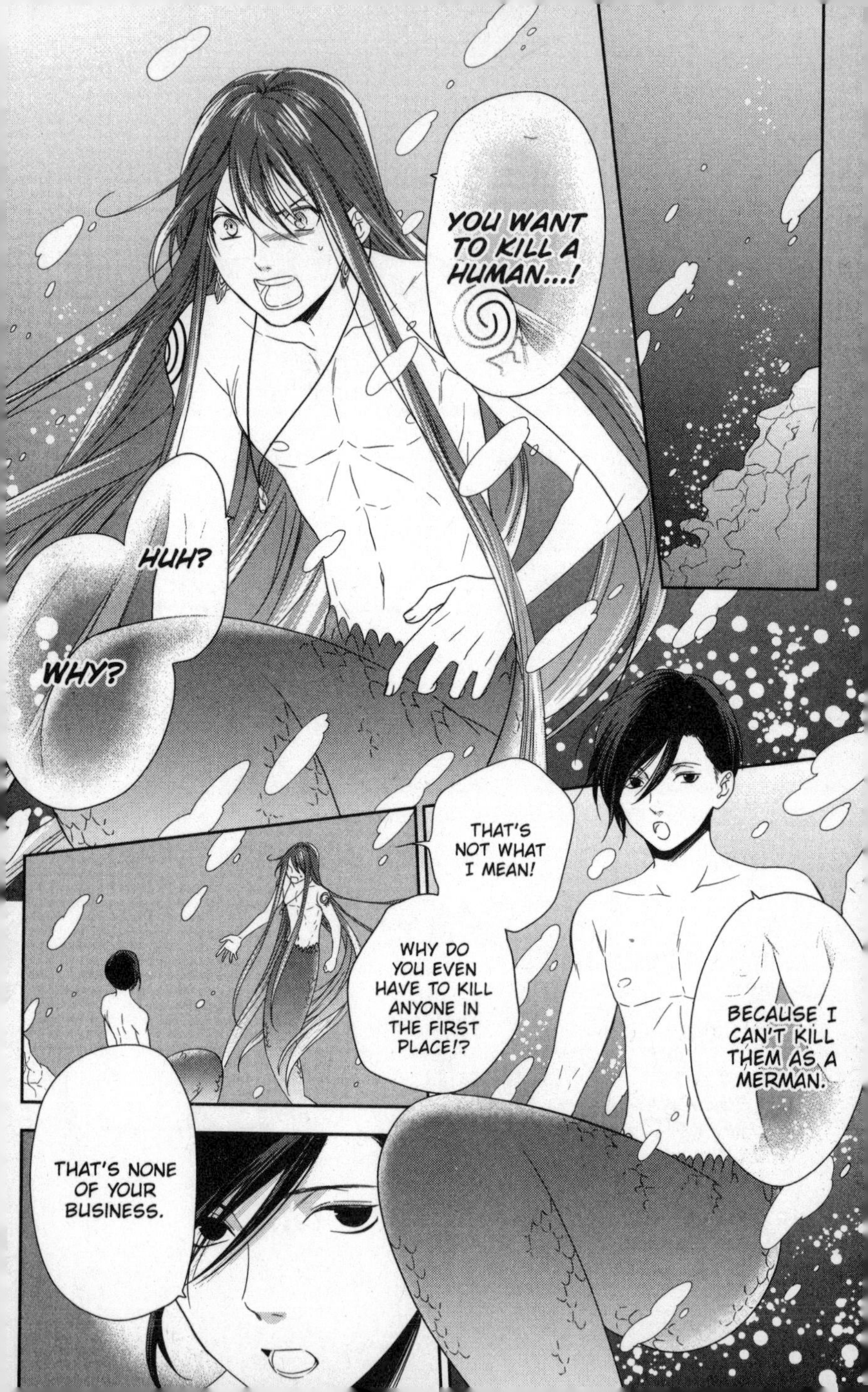
YOU WANT TO KILL A HUMAN...!
HUH?
WHY?
THAT'S NOT WHAT I MEAN!
WHY DO YOU EVEN HAVE TO KILL ANYONE IN THE FIRST PLACE!?
BECAUSE I CAN'T KILL THEM AS A MERMAN.
THAT'S NONE OF YOUR BUSINESS.

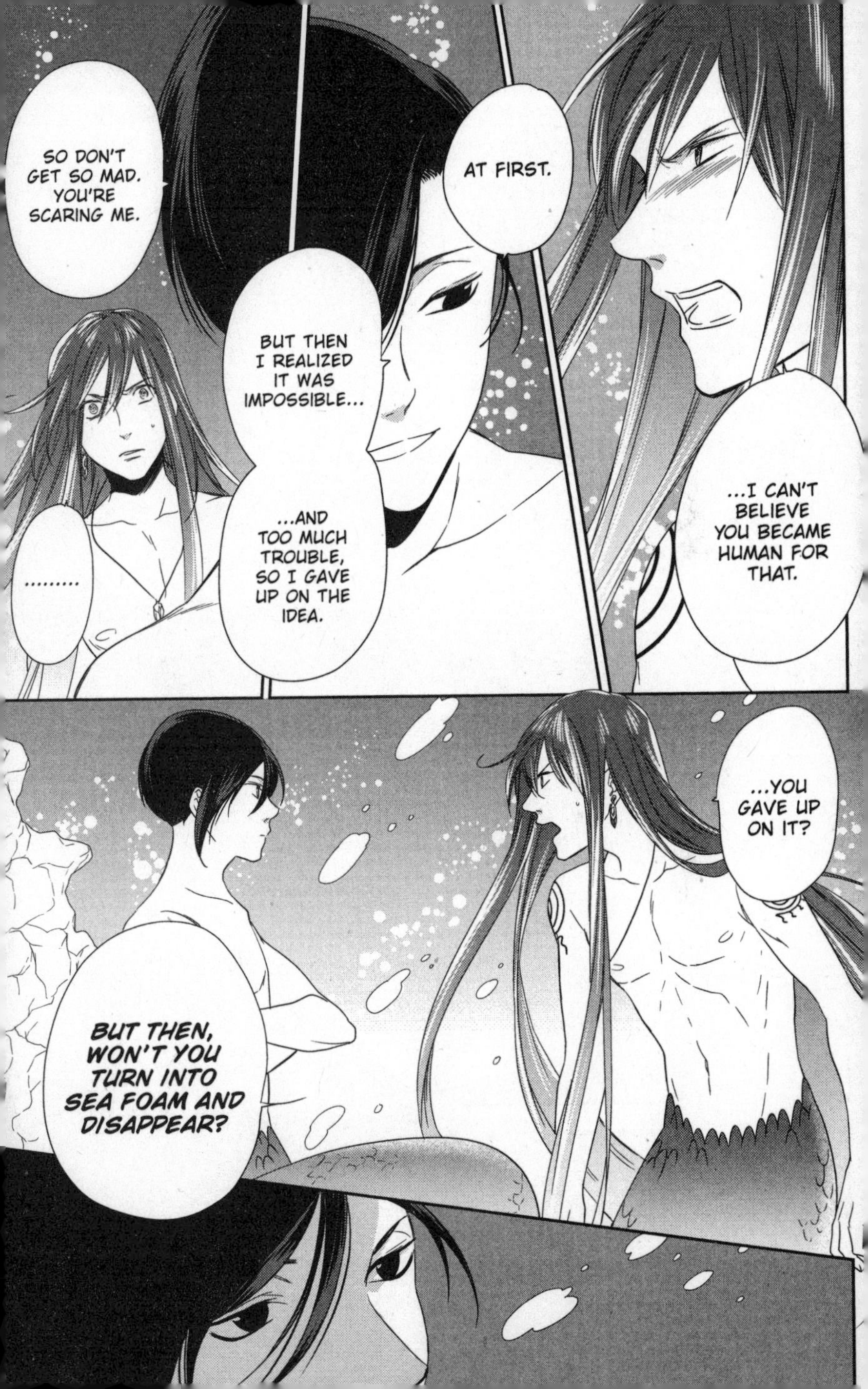
...I CAN'T BELIEVE YOU BECAME HUMAN FOR THAT.
AT FIRST.
BUT THEN I REALIZED IT WAS IMPOSSIBLE...
...AND TOO MUCH TROUBLE, SO I GAVE UP ON THE IDEA.
SO DON'T GET SO MAD. YOU'RE SCARING ME.
....
...YOU GAVE UP ON IT?
BUT THEN, WON'T YOU TURN INTO SEA FOAM AND DISAPPEAR?

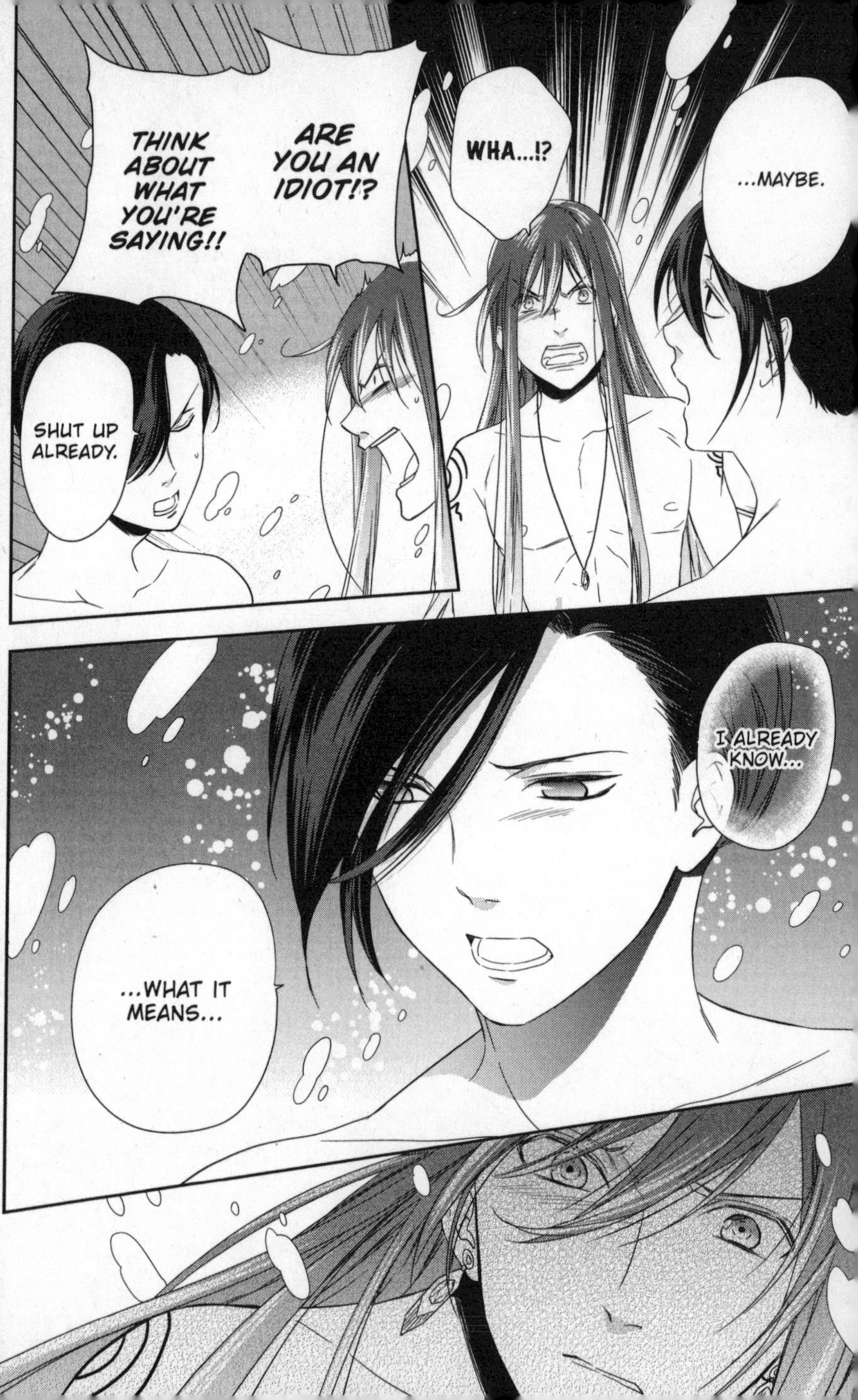
...MAYBE.
WHA...!?
ARE YOU AN IDIOT!?
THINK ABOUT WHAT YOU'RE SAYING!!
SHUT UP ALREADY.
I ALREADY KNOW...
...WHAT IT MEANS...

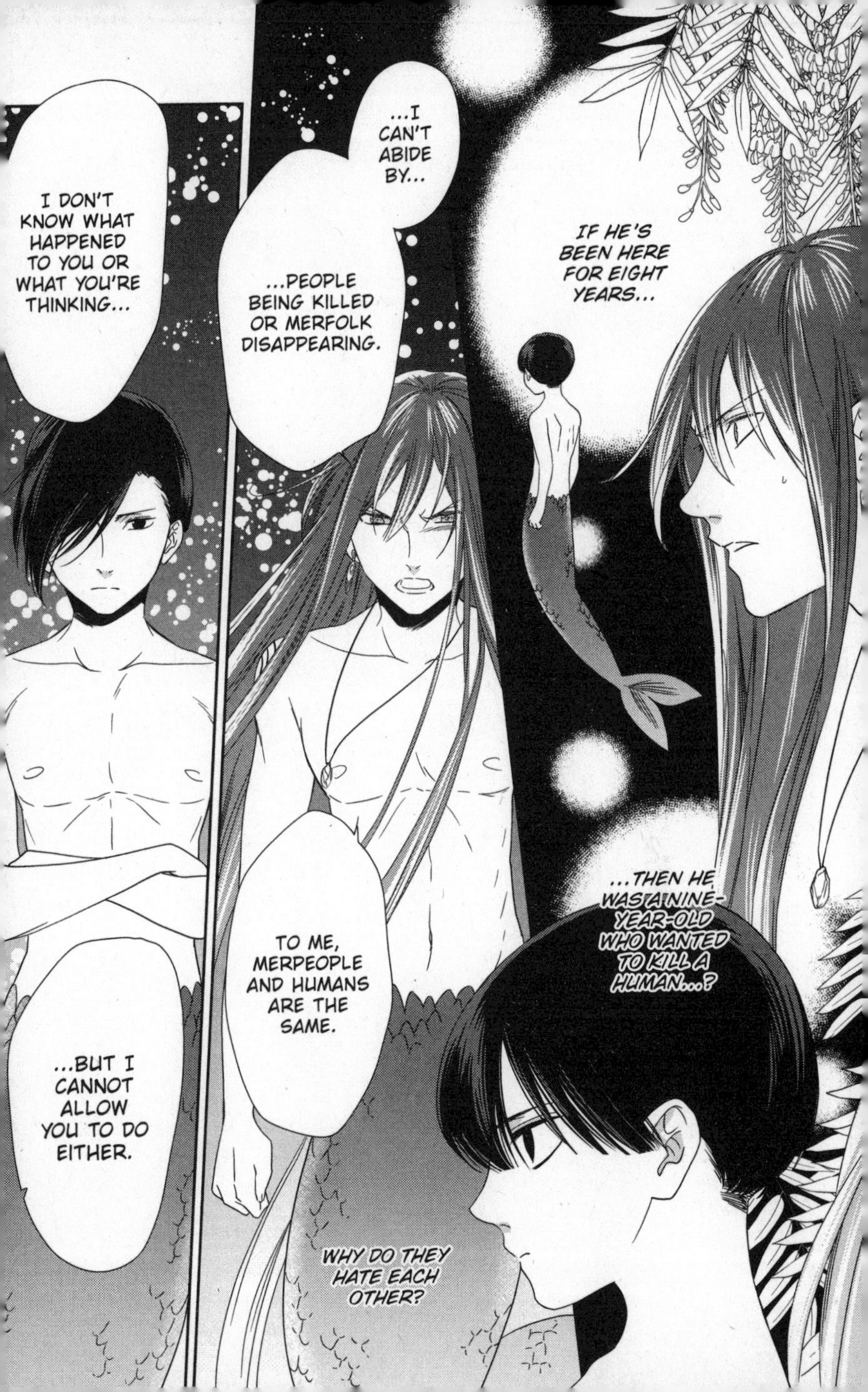
IF HE'S BEEN HERE FOR EIGHT YEARS...
...THEN HE WAS A NINE-YEAR-OLD WHO WANTED TO KILL A HUMAN...?
WHY DO THEY HATE EACH OTHER?
...I CAN'T ABIDE BY...
...PEOPLE BEING KILLED OR MERFOLK DISAPPEARING.
TO ME, MERPEOPLE AND HUMANS ARE THE SAME.
I DON'T KNOW WHAT HAPPENED TO YOU OR WHAT YOU'RE THINKING...
...BUT I CANNOT ALLOW YOU TO DO EITHER.

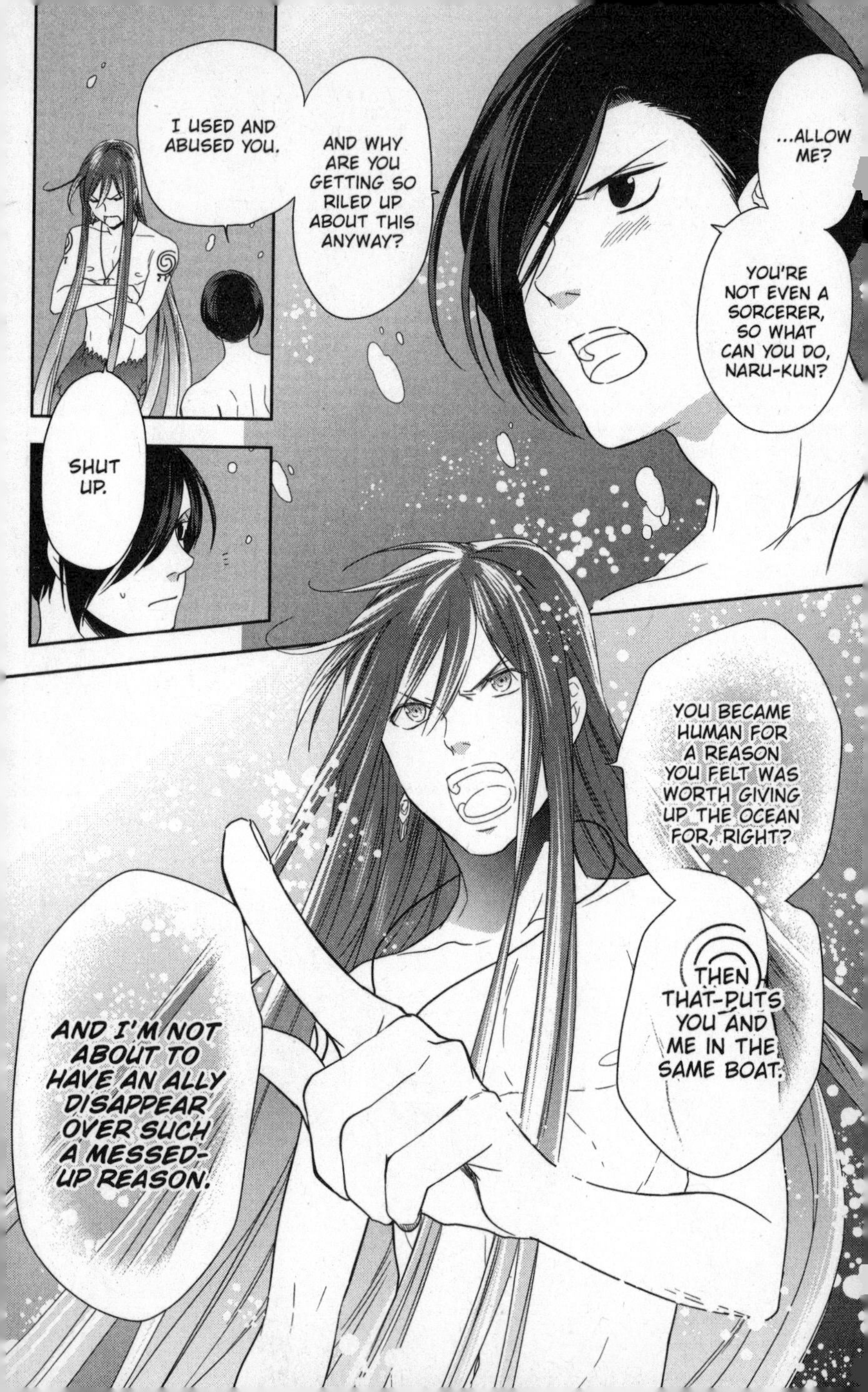

...ALLOW ME?
YOU'RE NOT EVEN A SORCERER, SO WHAT CAN YOU DO, NARU-KUN?
I USED AND ABUSED YOU.
AND WHY ARE YOU GETTING SO RILED UP ABOUT THIS ANYWAY?
SHUT UP.
YOU BECAME HUMAN FOR A REASON YOU FELT WAS WORTH GIVING UP THE OCEAN FOR, RIGHT?
THEN THAT PUTS YOU AND ME IN THE SAME BOAT.
AND I'M NOT ABOUT TO HAVE AN ALLY DISAPPEAR OVER SUCH A MESSED-UP REASON.

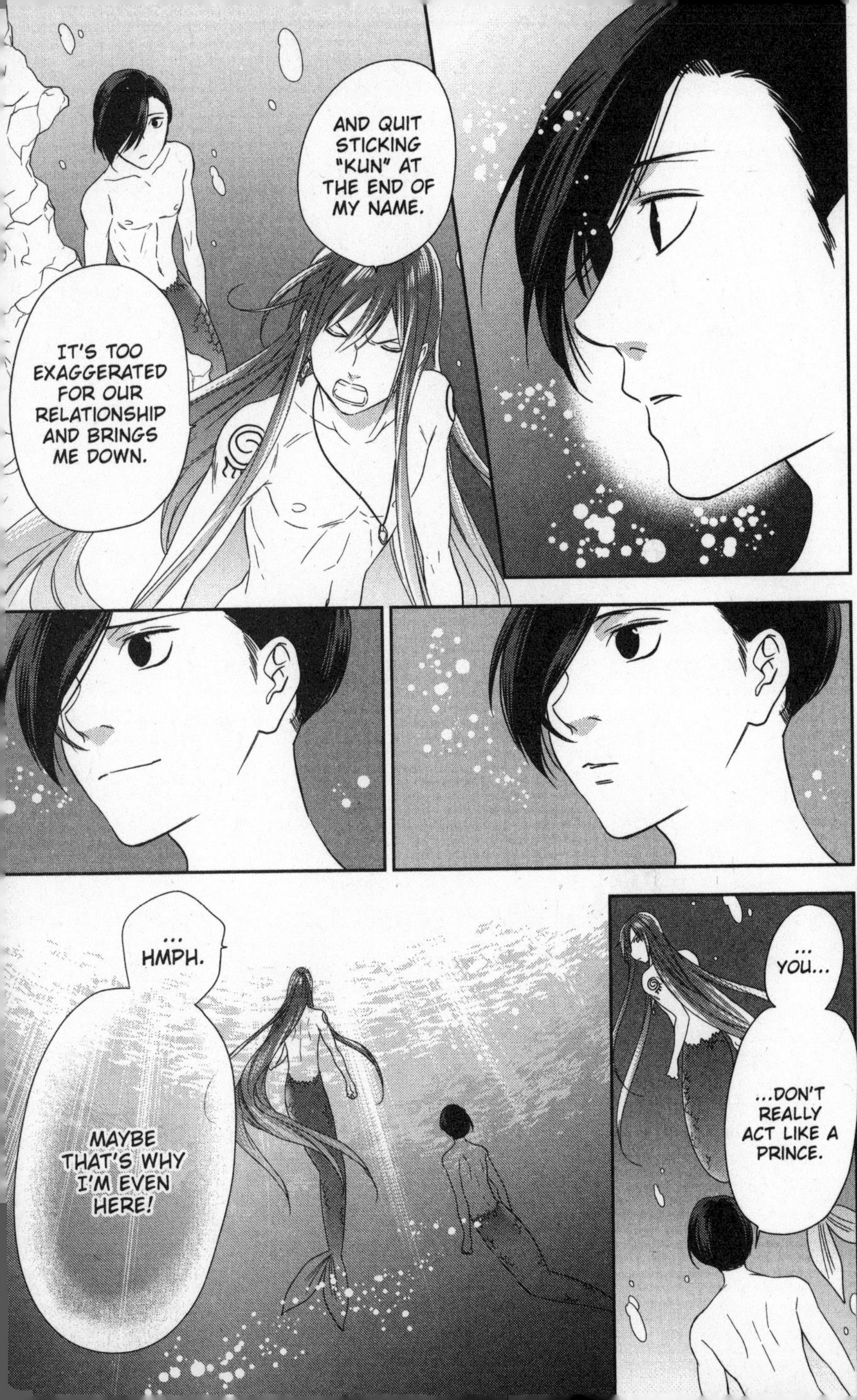
AND QUIT STICKING "KUN" AT THE END OF MY NAME.
IT'S TOO EXAGGERATED FOR OUR RELATIONSHIP AND BRINGS ME DOWN.
... YOU...
...DON'T REALLY ACT LIKE A PRINCE.
... HMPH.
MAYBE THAT'S WHY I'M EVEN HERE!

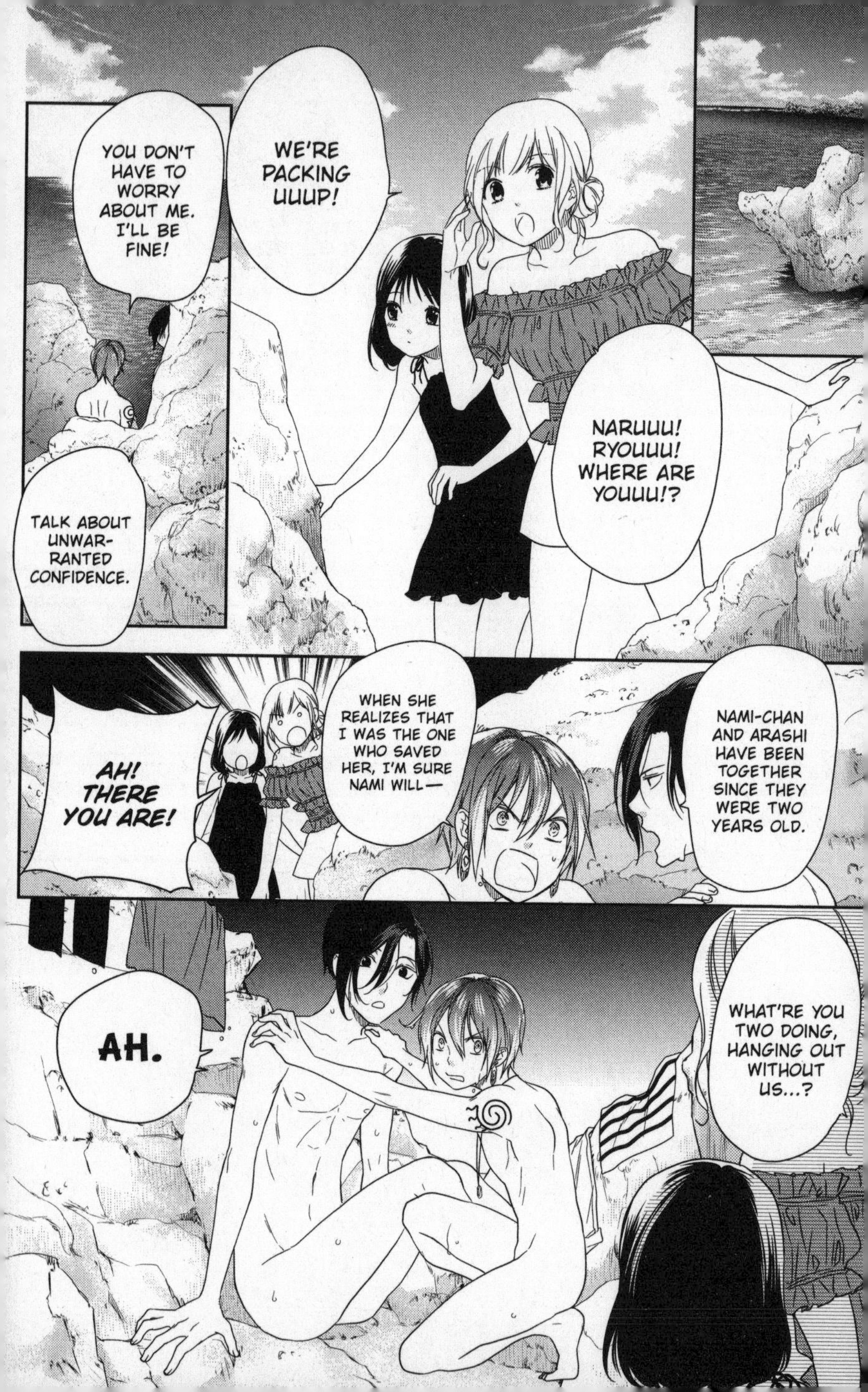
WE'RE PACKING UUUP!
NARUUU! RYOUUU! WHERE ARE YOUUU!?
YOU DON'T HAVE TO WORRY ABOUT ME. I'LL BE FINE!
TALK ABOUT UNWAR-RANTED CONFIDENCE.
NAMI-CHAN AND ARASHI HAVE BEEN TOGETHER SINCE THEY WERE TWO YEARS OLD.
WHEN SHE REALIZES THAT I WAS THE ONE WHO SAVED HER, I'M SURE NAMI WILL—
AH! THERE YOU ARE!
WHAT'RE YOU TWO DOING, HANGING OUT WITHOUT US...?
AH.

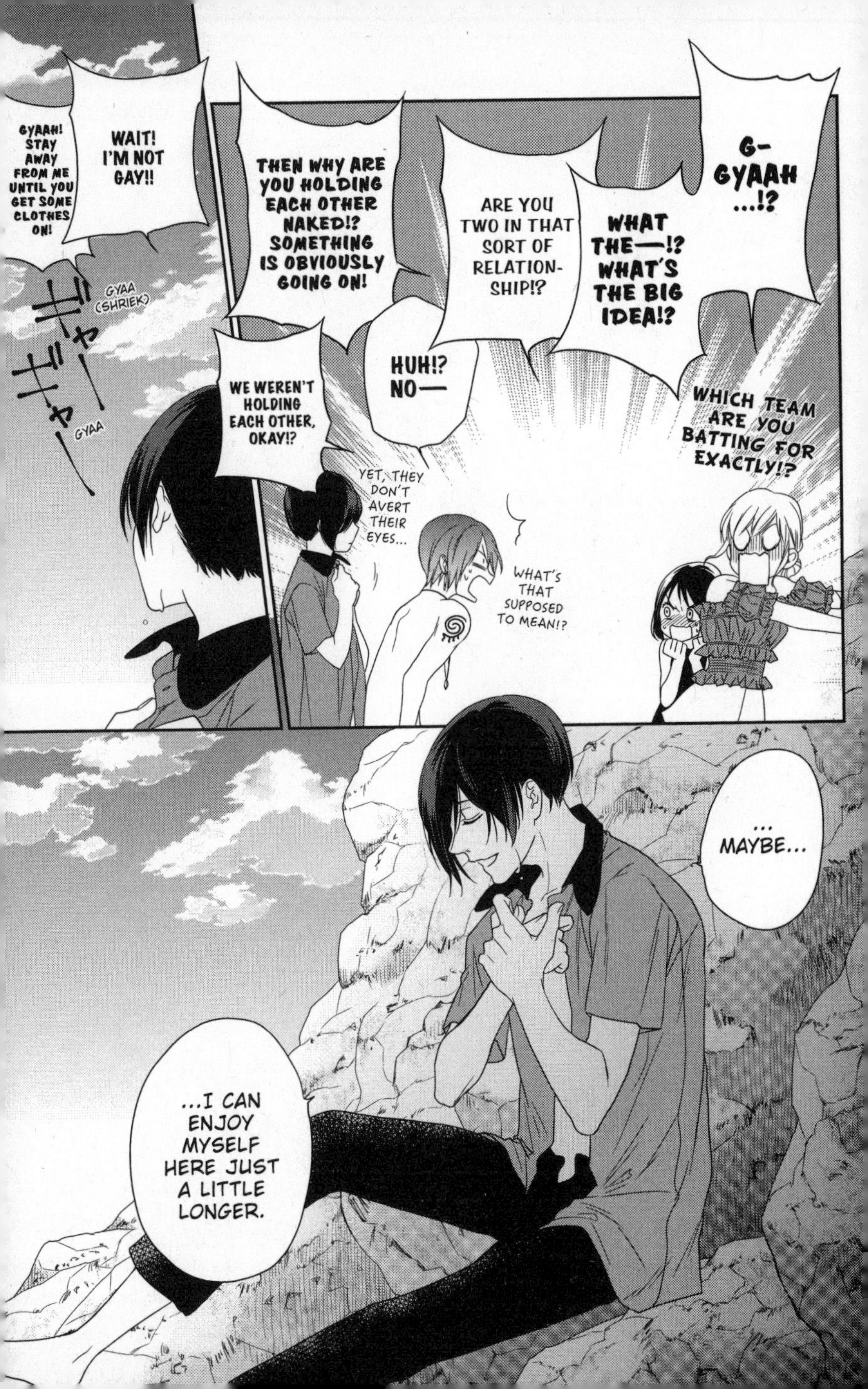
G-GYAAH ...!?
WHAT THE—!? WHAT'S THE BIG IDEA!?
ARE YOU TWO IN THAT SORT OF RELATION-SHIP!?
THEN WHY ARE YOU HOLDING EACH OTHER NAKED!? SOMETHING IS OBVIOUSLY GOING ON!
HUH!? NO—
WHICH TEAM ARE YOU BATTING FOR EXACTLY!?
WE WEREN'T HOLDING EACH OTHER, OKAY!?
YET, THEY DON'T AVERT THEIR EYES...
WHAT'S THAT SUPPOSED TO MEAN!?
WAIT! I'M NOT GAY!!
GYAAH! STAY AWAY FROM ME UNTIL YOU GET SOME CLOTHES ON!
ギャー
GYAA (SHRIEK)
ギャー
GYAA
... MAYBE...
...I CAN ENJOY MYSELF HERE JUST A LITTLE LONGER.

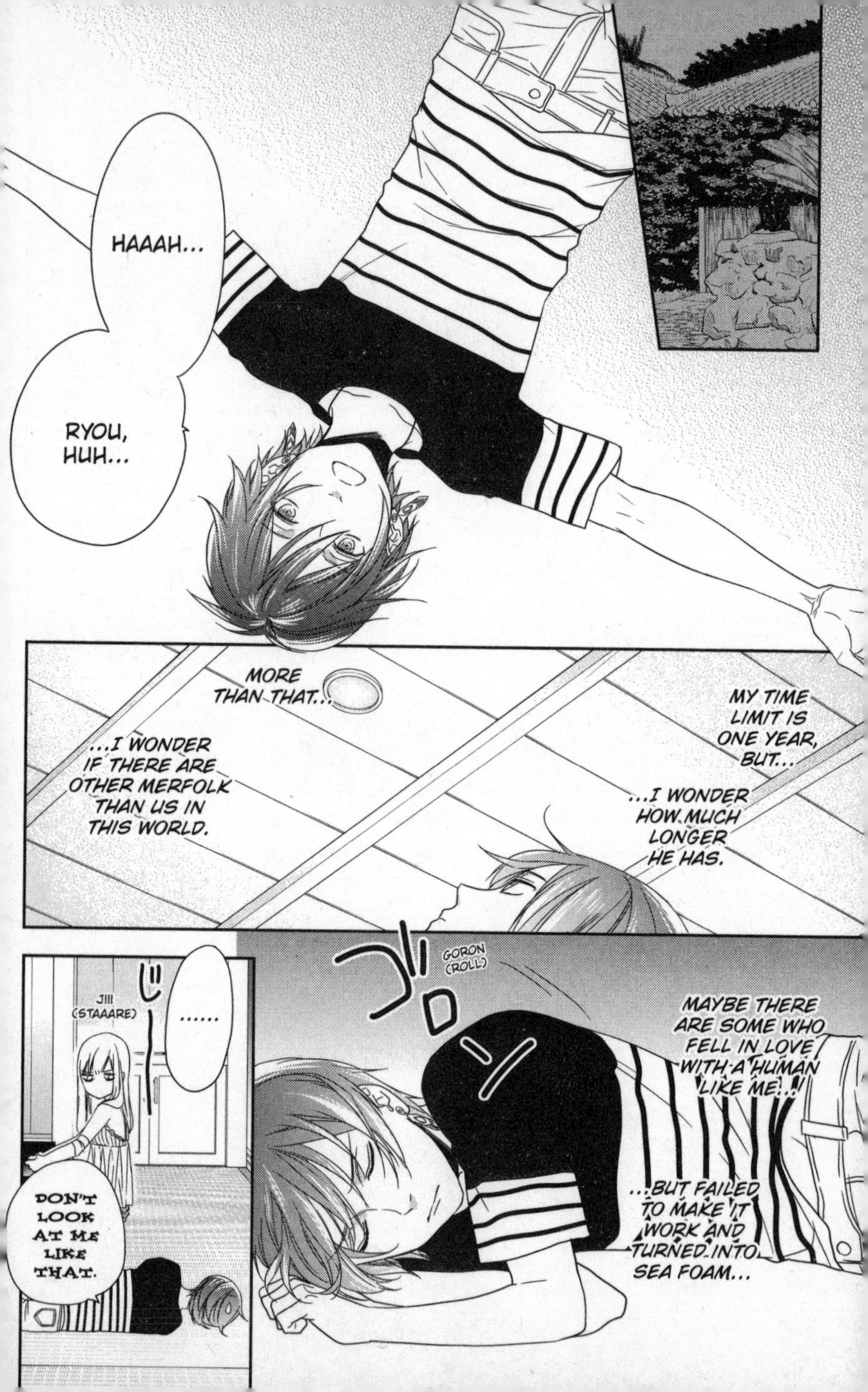
HAAAH...
RYOU, HUH...
MY TIME LIMIT IS ONE YEAR, BUT...
...I WONDER HOW MUCH LONGER HE HAS.
MORE THAN THAT...
...I WONDER IF THERE ARE OTHER MERFOLK THAN US IN THIS WORLD.
GORON (ROLL)
MAYBE THERE ARE SOME WHO FELL IN LOVE WITH A HUMAN LIKE ME...
...BUT FAILED TO MAKE IT WORK AND TURNED INTO SEA FOAM...
JIII (STAAARE)
......
DON'T LOOK AT ME LIKE THAT.

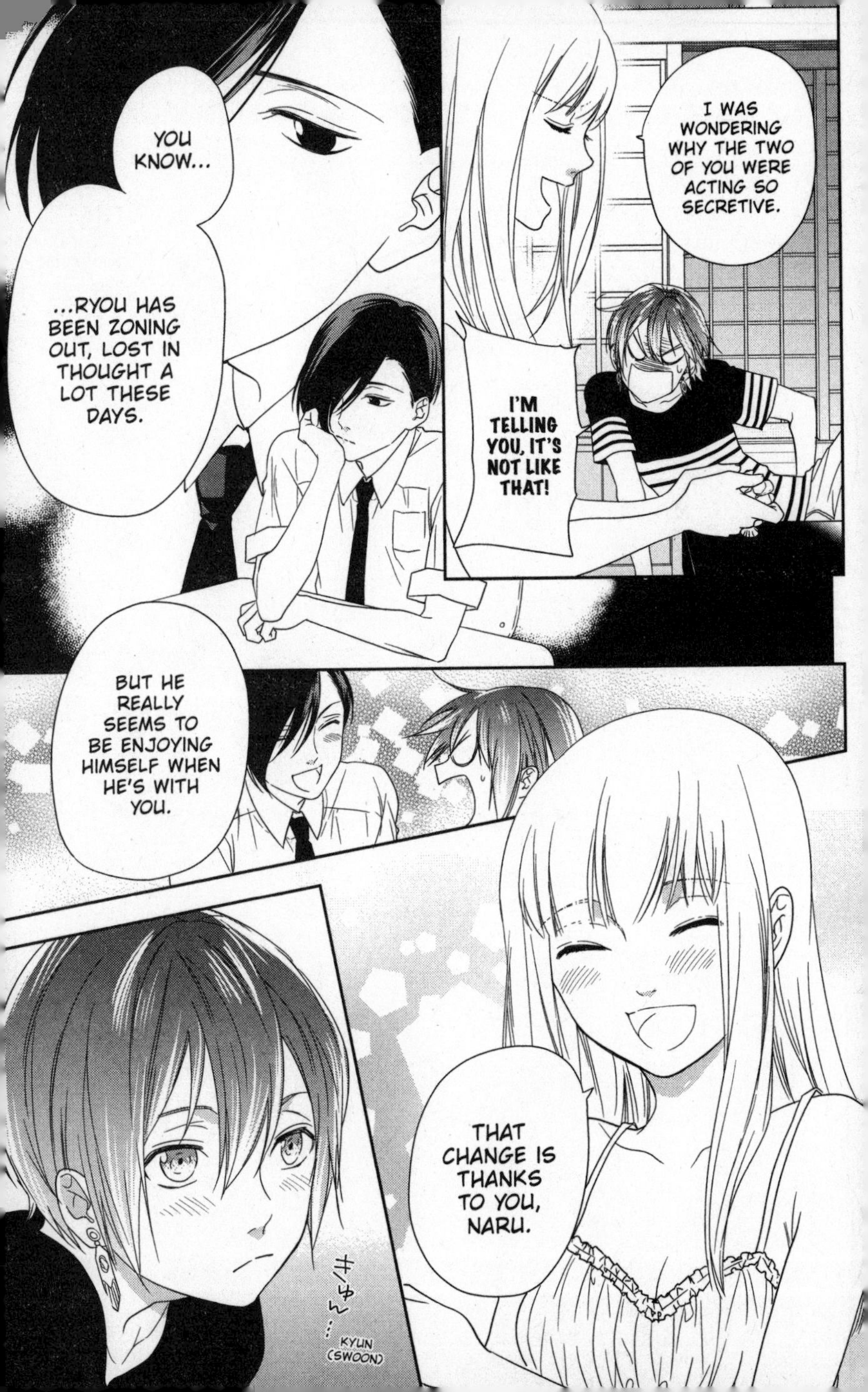
I WAS WONDERING WHY THE TWO OF YOU WERE ACTING SO SECRETIVE.
I'M TELLING YOU, IT'S NOT LIKE THAT!
YOU KNOW...
...RYOU HAS BEEN ZONING OUT, LOST IN THOUGHT A LOT THESE DAYS.
BUT HE REALLY SEEMS TO BE ENJOYING HIMSELF WHEN HE'S WITH YOU.
THAT CHANGE IS THANKS TO YOU, NARU.
キゅん…
KYUN (SWOON)

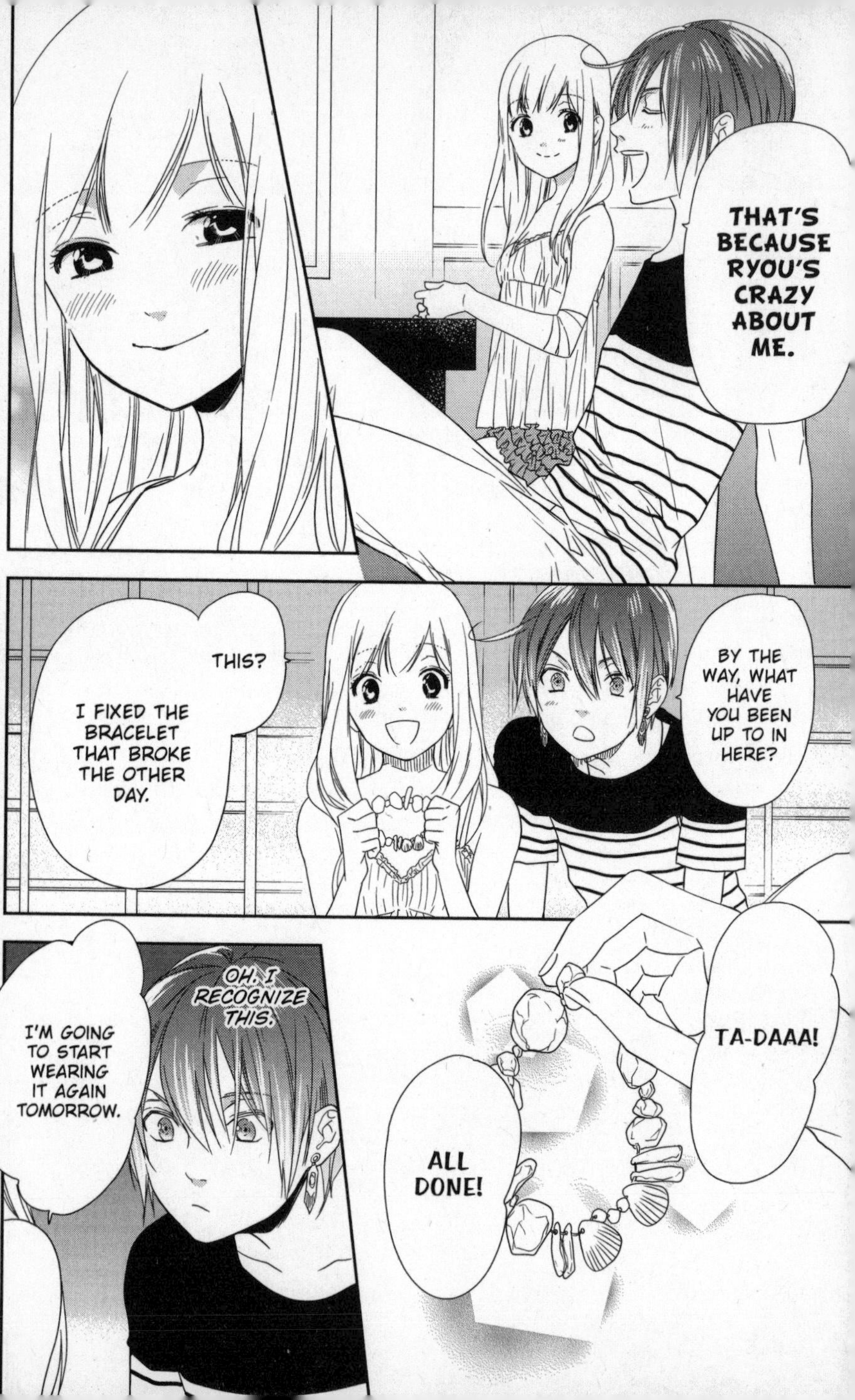
THAT'S BECAUSE RYOU'S CRAZY ABOUT ME.
BY THE WAY, WHAT HAVE YOU BEEN UP TO IN HERE?
THIS?
I FIXED THE BRACELET THAT BROKE THE OTHER DAY.
TA-DAAA!
ALL DONE!
OH. I RECOGNIZE THIS.
I'M GOING TO START WEARING IT AGAIN TOMORROW.

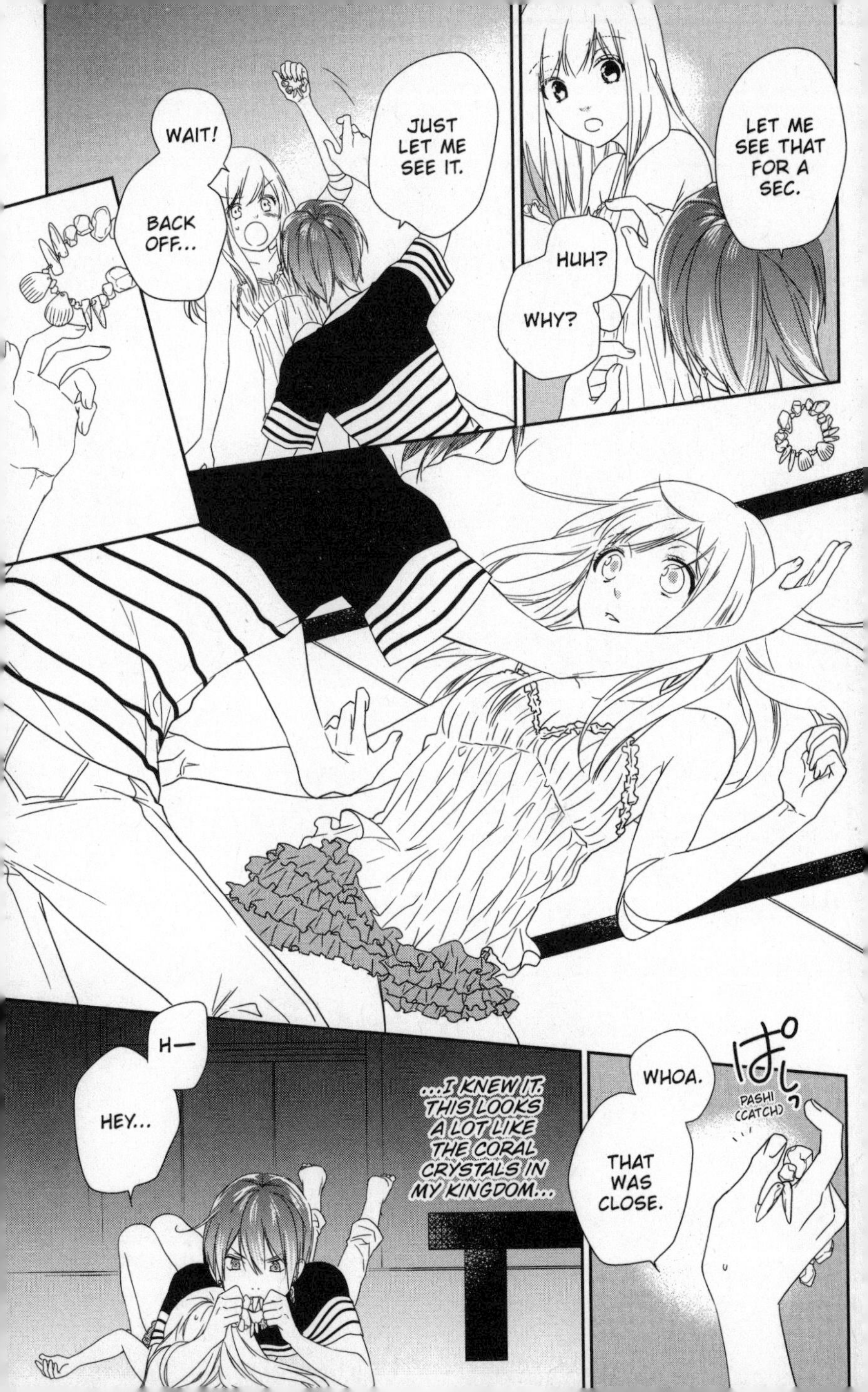
LET ME SEE THAT FOR A SEC.
HUH? WHY?
JUST LET ME SEE IT.
WAIT! BACK OFF...
ぱし
PASHI (CATCH)
WHOA. THAT WAS CLOSE.
...I KNEW IT. THIS LOOKS A LOT LIKE THE CORAL CRYSTALS IN MY KINGDOM...
H— HEY...

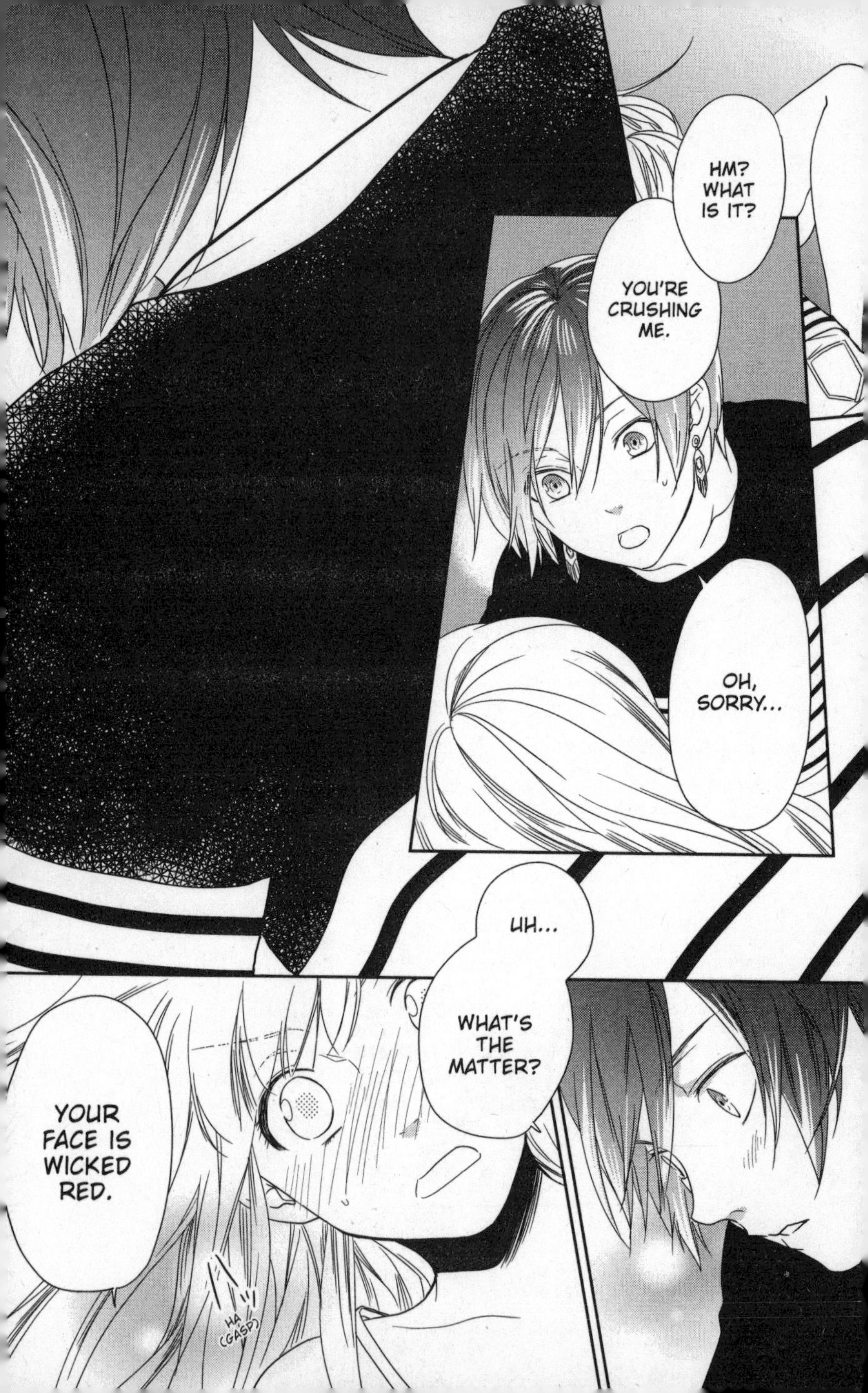
HM? WHAT IS IT?
YOU'RE CRUSHING ME.
OH, SORRY...
UH...
WHAT'S THE MATTER?
YOUR FACE IS WICKED RED.
HA (GASP)

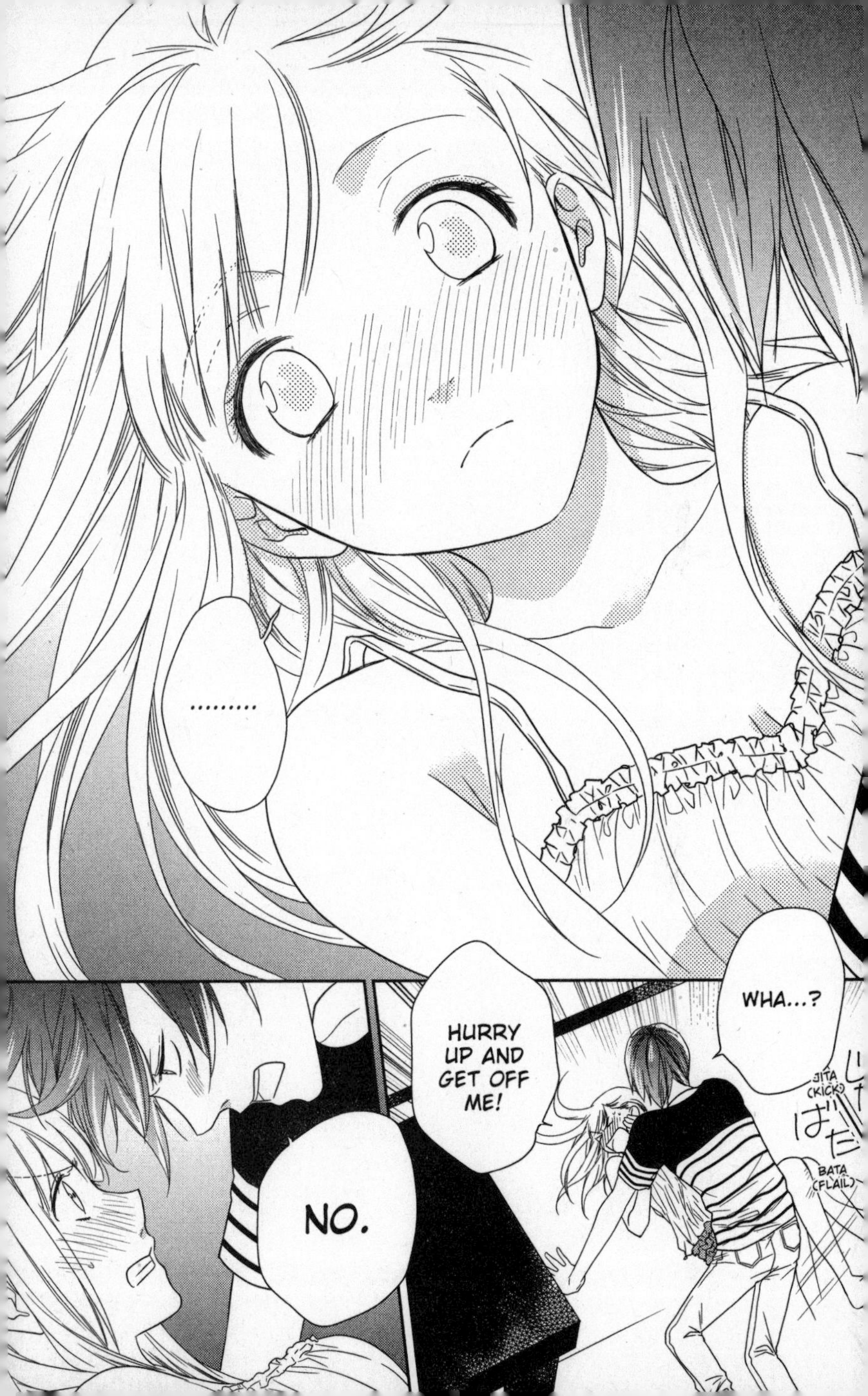
....
WHA...?
じた
JITA (KICK)
ばた
BATA (FLAIL)
HURRY UP AND GET OFF ME!
NO.

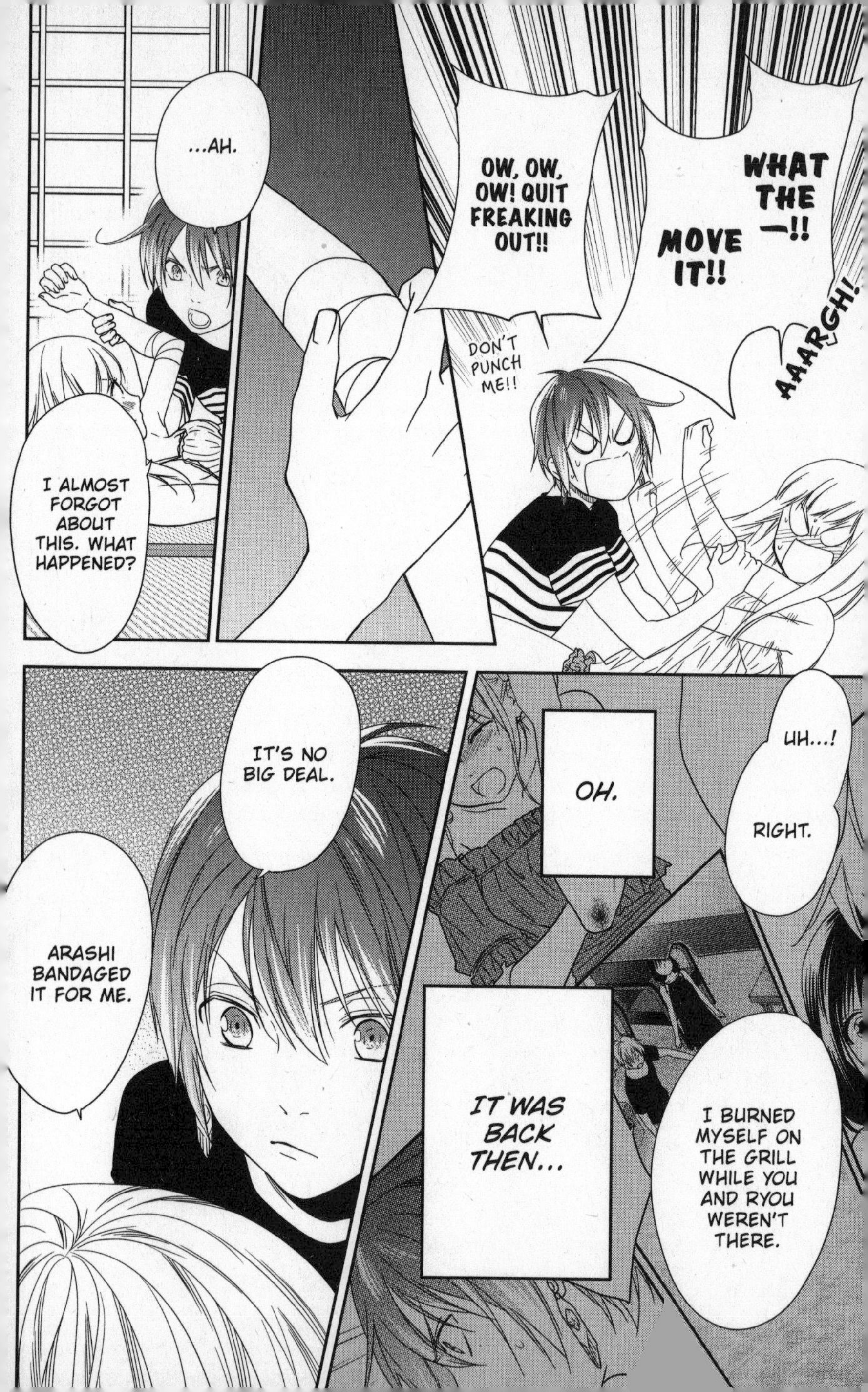
WHAT THE—!!
MOVE IT!!
OW, OW, OW! QUIT FREAKING OUT!!
AAARGH!
DON'T PUNCH ME!!
...AH.
I ALMOST FORGOT ABOUT THIS. WHAT HAPPENED?
UH...! RIGHT.
OH.
I BURNED MYSELF ON THE GRILL WHILE YOU AND RYOU WEREN'T THERE.
IT WAS BACK THEN...
IT'S NO BIG DEAL.
ARASHI BANDAGED IT FOR ME.

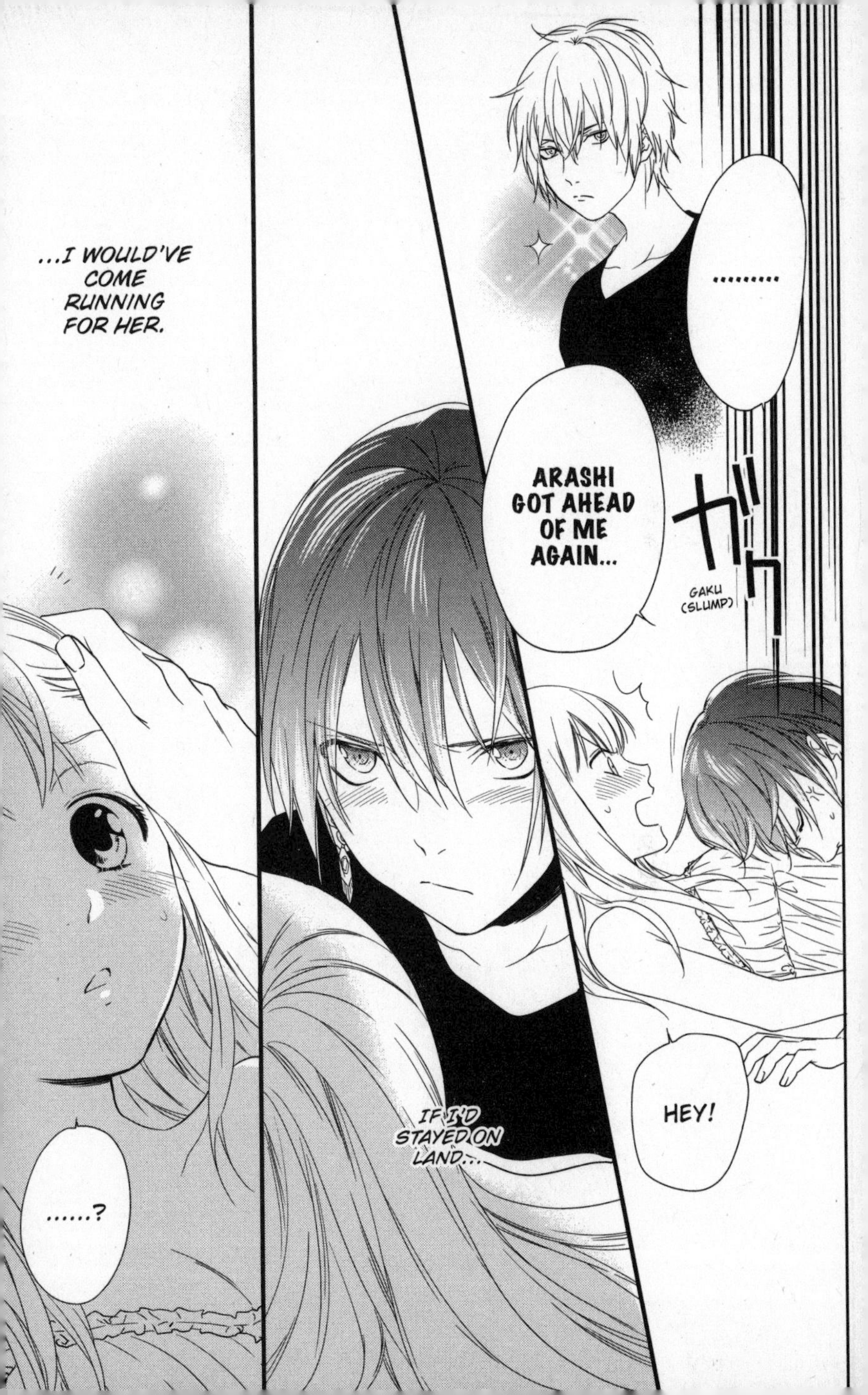
....
ARASHI GOT AHEAD OF ME AGAIN...
GAKU (SLUMP)
HEY!
IF I'D STAYED ON LAND...
...I WOULD'VE COME RUNNING FOR HER.
......?

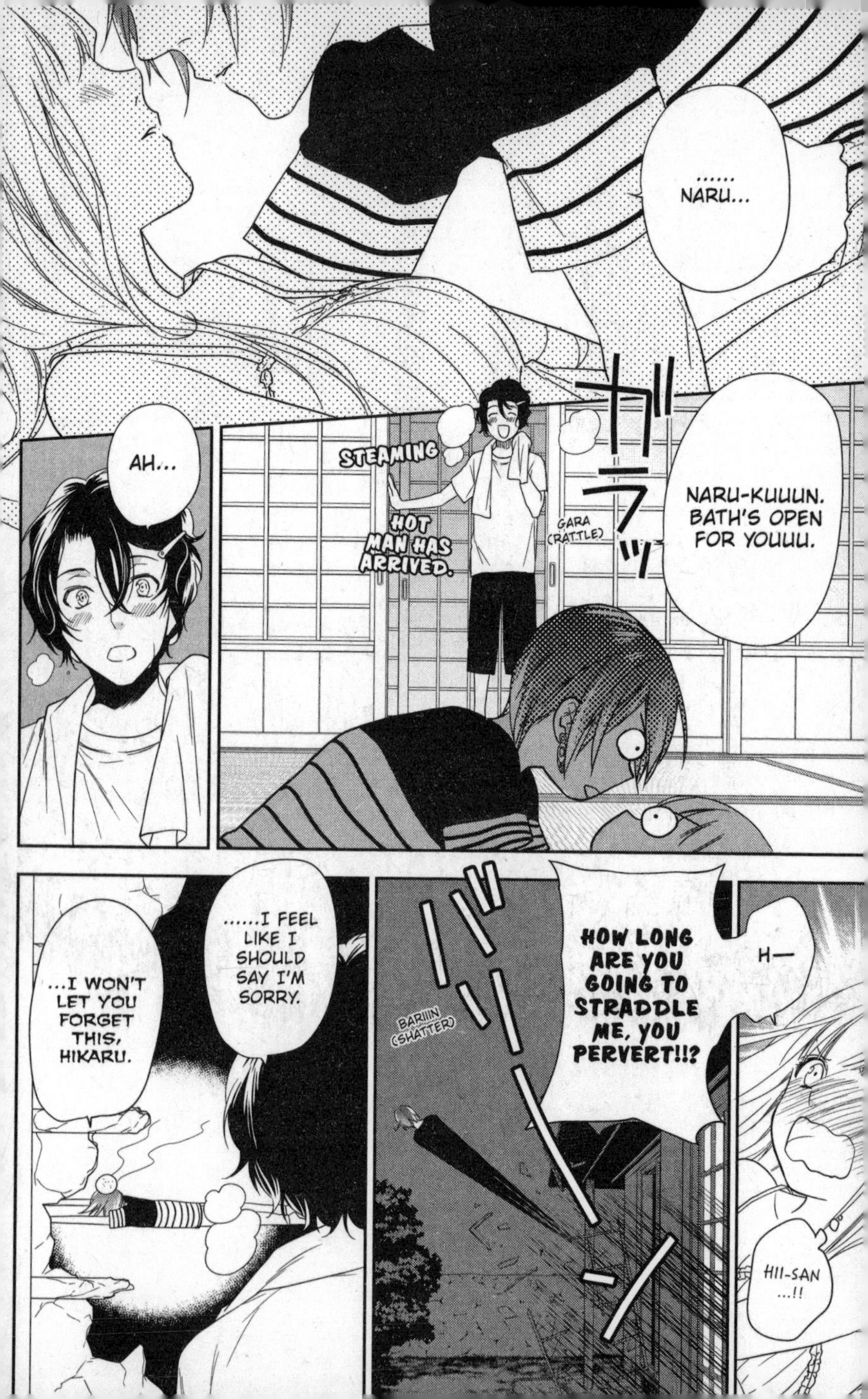
......
NARU...
NARU-KUUUN. BATH'S OPEN FOR YOUUU.
GARA (RATTLE)
STEAMING
HOT MAN HAS ARRIVED.
AH...
H—
HII-SAN ...!!
HOW LONG ARE YOU GOING TO STRADDLE ME, YOU PERVERT!!?
BARIIIN (SHATTER)
......I FEEL LIKE I SHOULD SAY I'M SORRY.
...I WON'T LET YOU FORGET THIS, HIKARU.

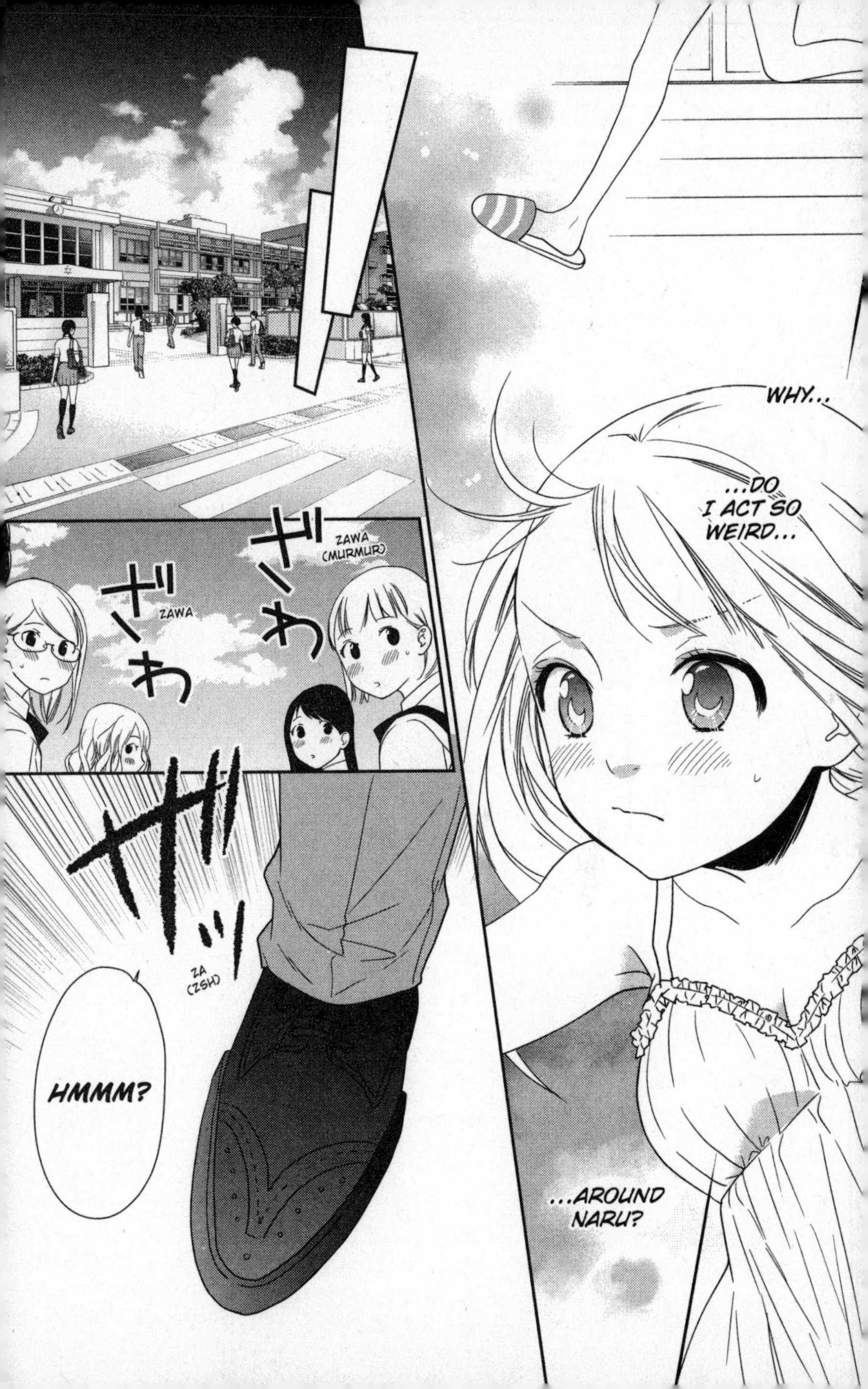
WHY...
...DO I ACT SO WEIRD...
...AROUND NARU?
ざわ
ZAWA (MURMUR)
ざわ
ZAWA
ザッ
ZA (ZSH)
HMMM?

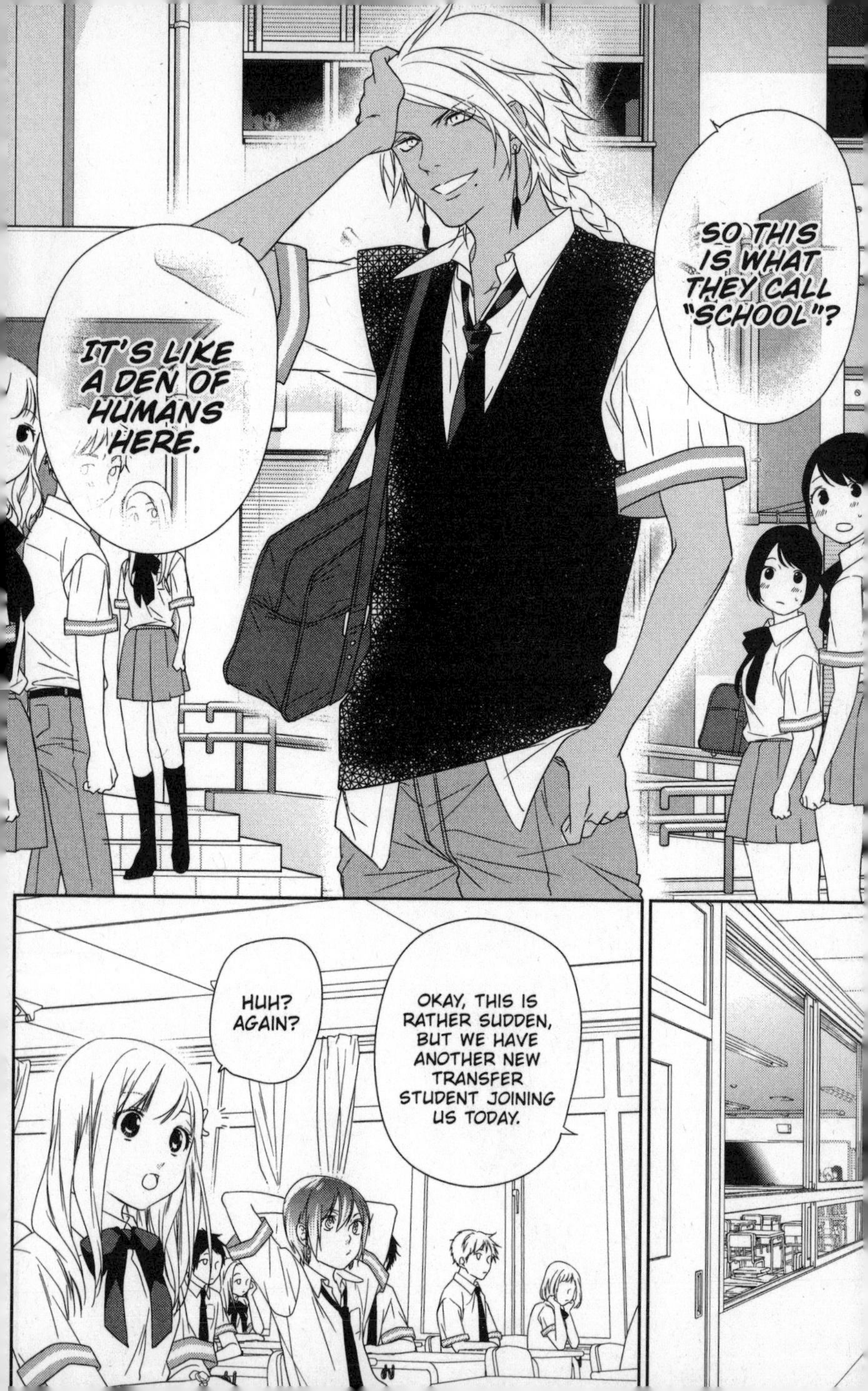
SO THIS IS WHAT THEY CALL "SCHOOL"?
IT'S LIKE A DEN OF HUMANS HERE.
OKAY, THIS IS RATHER SUDDEN, BUT WE HAVE ANOTHER NEW TRANSFER STUDENT JOINING US TODAY.
HUH? AGAIN?

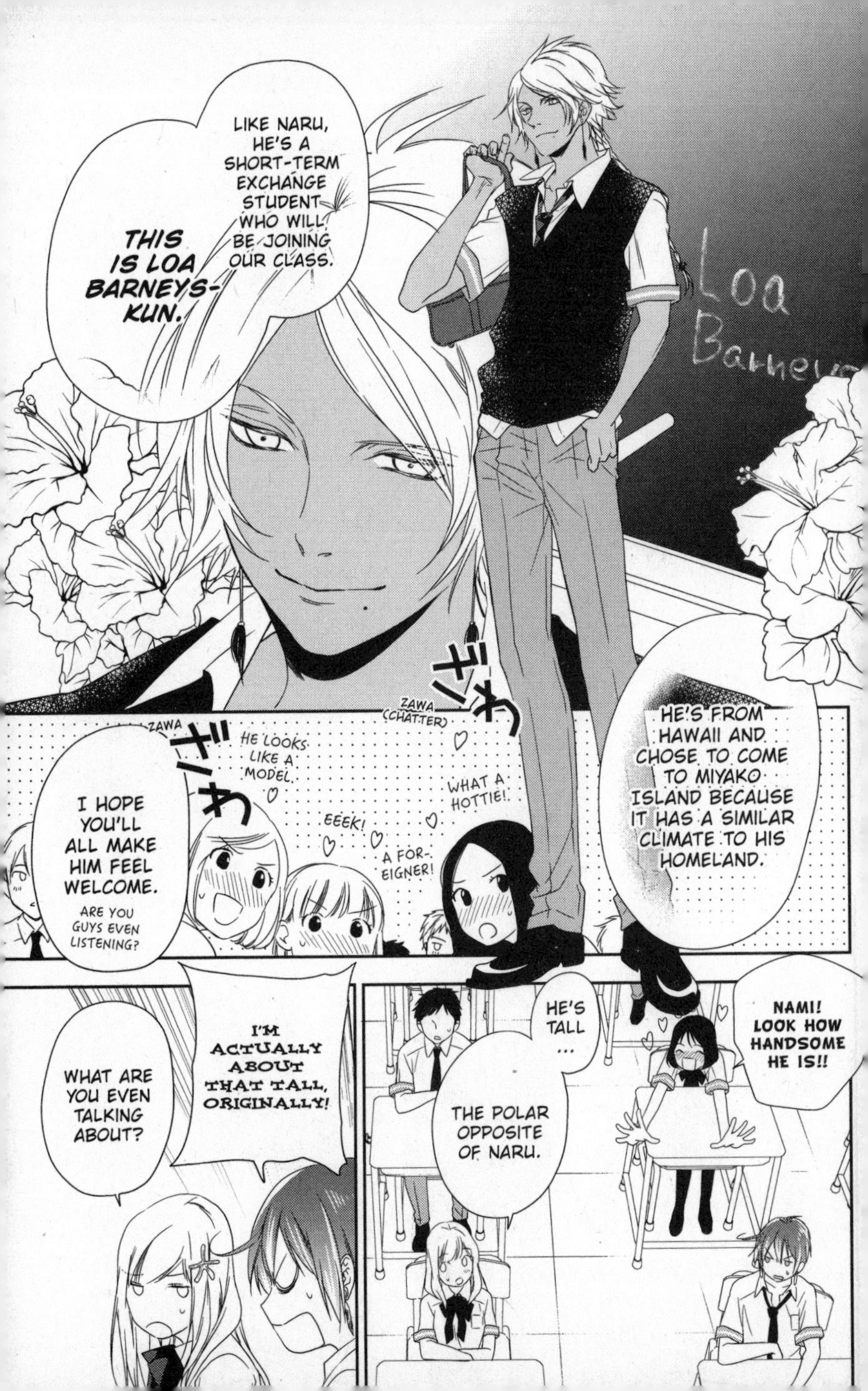
THIS IS LOA BARNEYS-KUN.
LIKE NARU, HE'S A SHORT-TERM EXCHANGE STUDENT WHO WILL BE JOINING OUR CLASS.
Loa Barneys
ZAWA (CHATTER)
HE'S FROM HAWAII AND CHOSE TO COME TO MIYAKO ISLAND BECAUSE IT HAS A SIMILAR CLIMATE TO HIS HOMELAND.
WHAT A HOTTIE!
A FOR-EIGNER!
EEEK!
HE LOOKS LIKE A MODEL.
ZAWA
I HOPE YOU'LL ALL MAKE HIM FEEL WELCOME.
ARE YOU GUYS EVEN LISTENING?
NAMI! LOOK HOW HANDSOME HE IS!!
HE'S TALL ...
THE POLAR OPPOSITE OF NARU.
I'M ACTUALLY ABOUT THAT TALL, ORIGINALLY!
WHAT ARE YOU EVEN TALKING ABOUT?

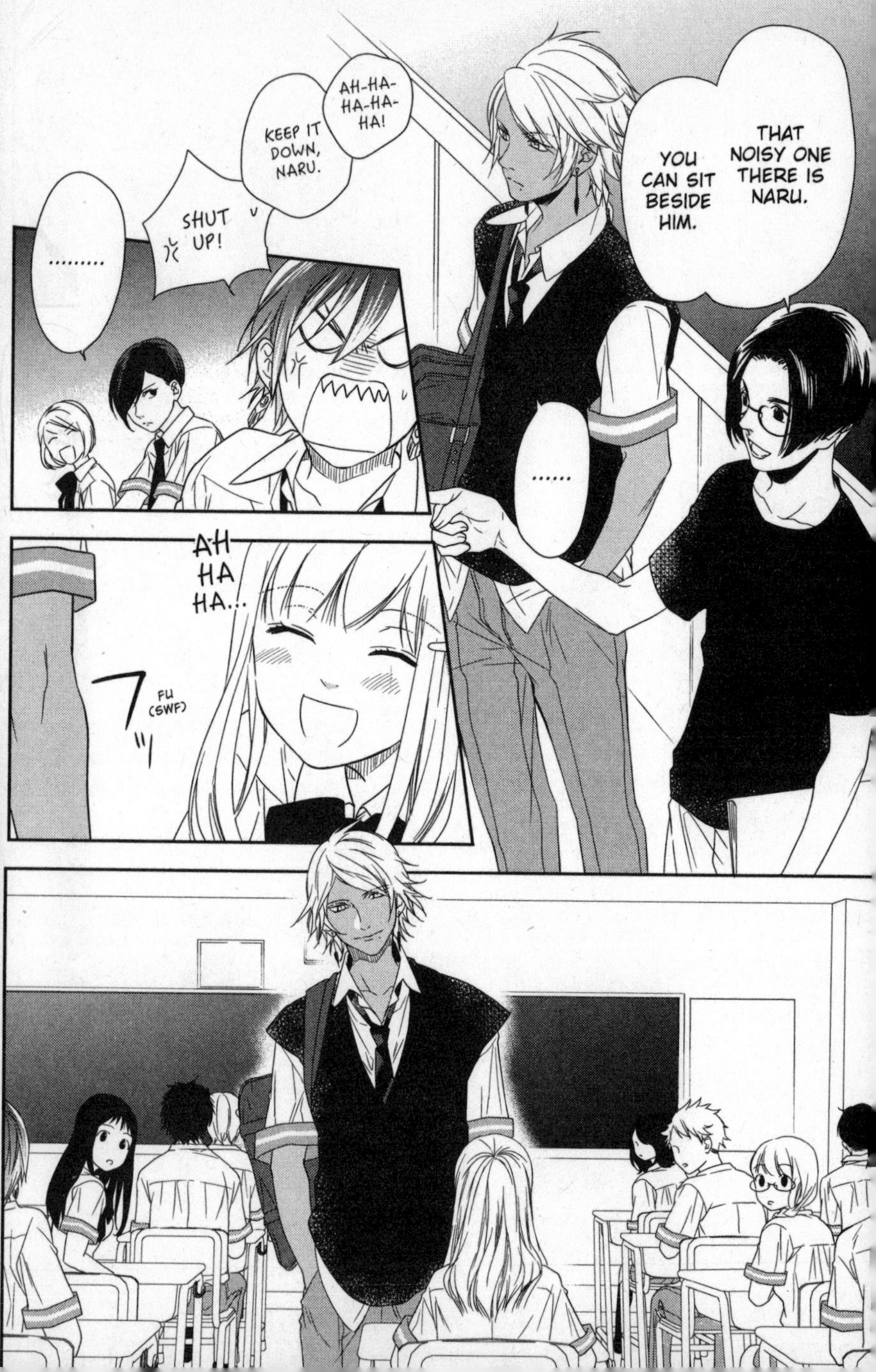
THAT NOISY ONE THERE IS NARU.
YOU CAN SIT BESIDE HIM.
......
AH-HA-HA-HA-HA!
KEEP IT DOWN, NARU.
SHUT UP!
....
AH HA HA...
FU (SWF)

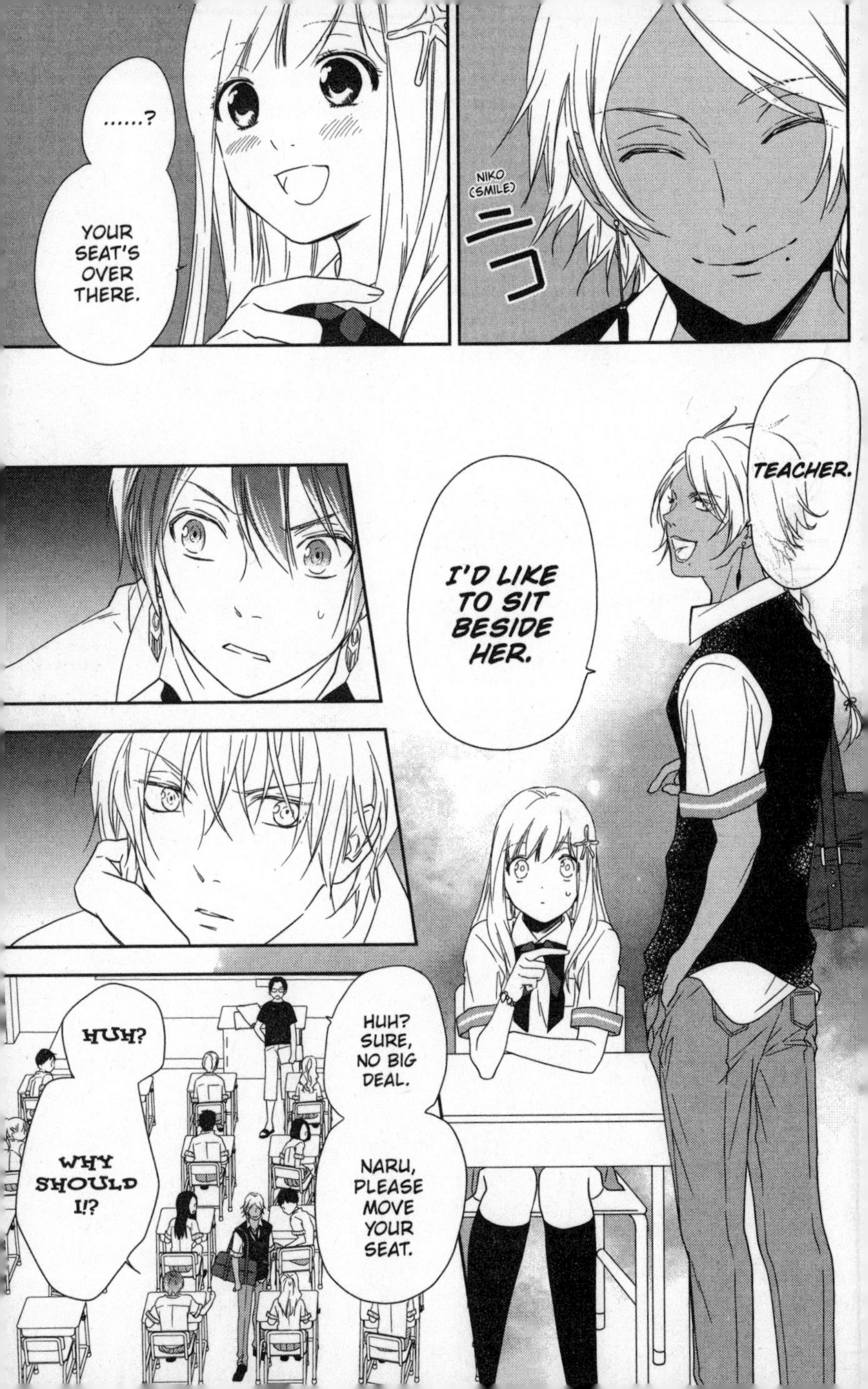
ニコ
NIKO (SMILE)
......?
YOUR SEAT'S OVER THERE.
TEACHER.
I'D LIKE TO SIT BESIDE HER.
HUH? SURE, NO BIG DEAL.
NARU, PLEASE MOVE YOUR SEAT.
HUH?
WHY SHOULD I!?

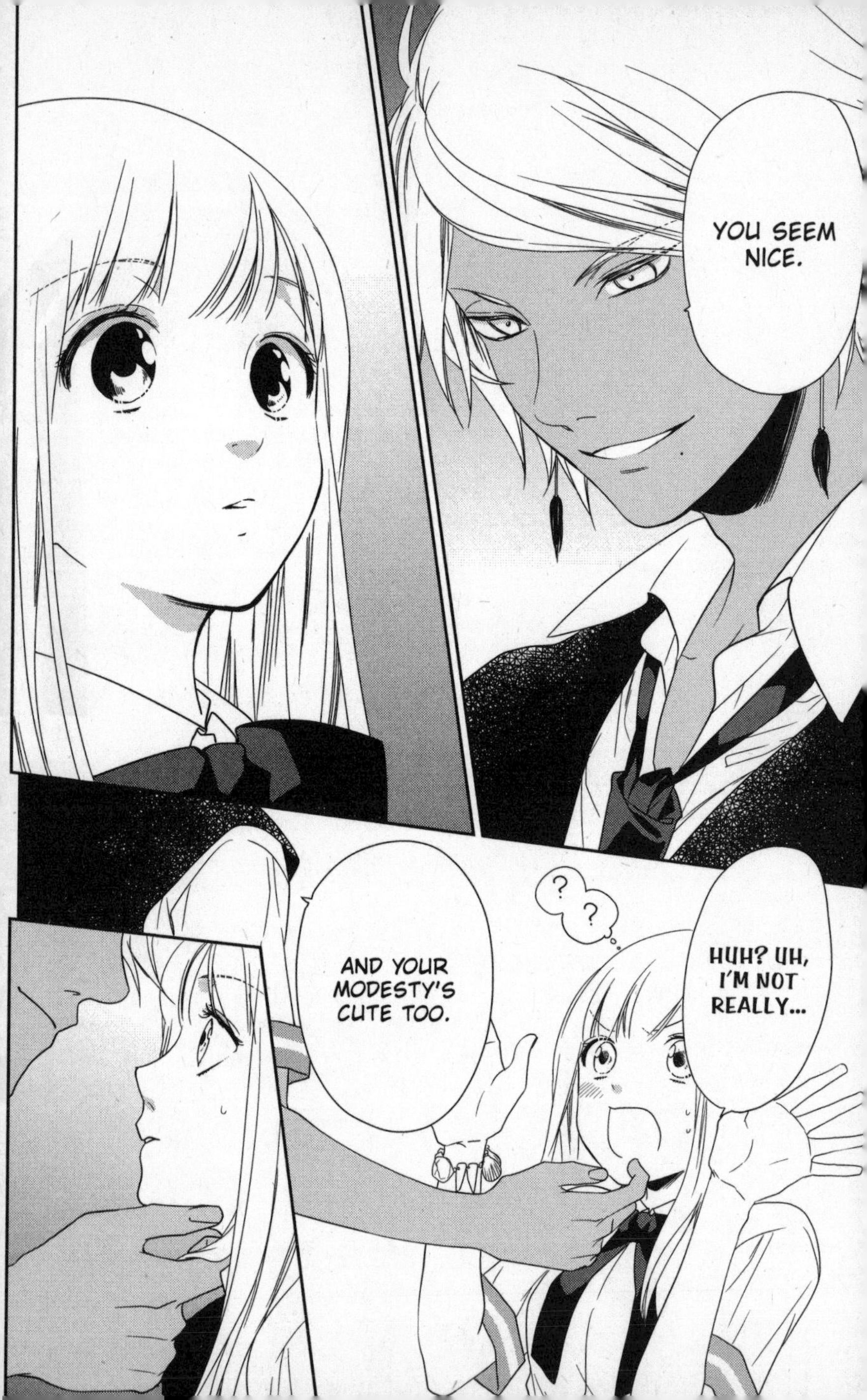
YOU SEEM NICE.
HUH? UH, I'M NOT REALLY...
? ?
AND YOUR MODESTY'S CUTE TOO.

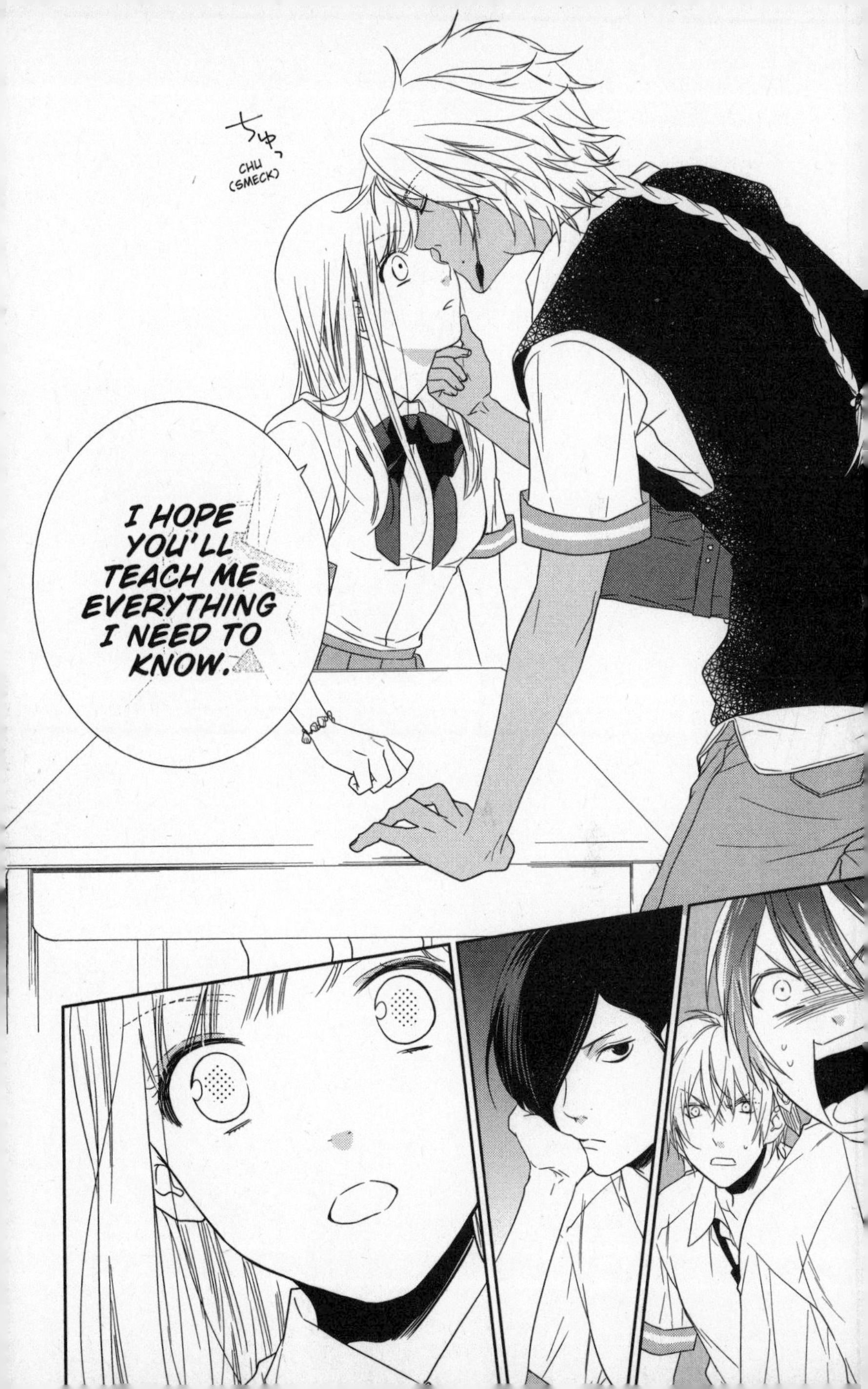
ちゅっ
CHU (SMECK)
I HOPE YOU'LL TEACH ME EVERYTHING I NEED TO KNOW.

MERMAID BOYS

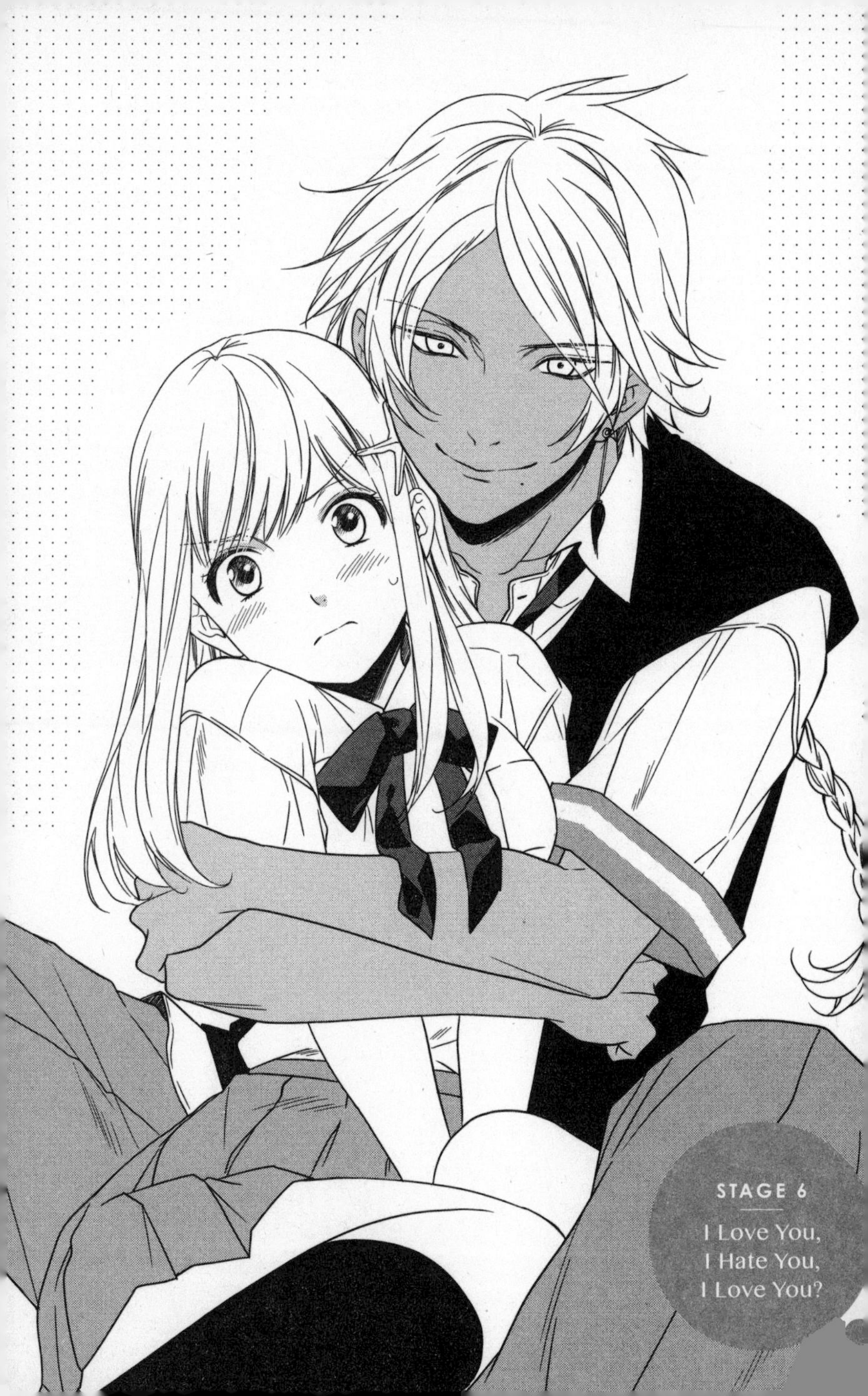
STAGE 6
I Love You,
I Hate You,
I Love You?

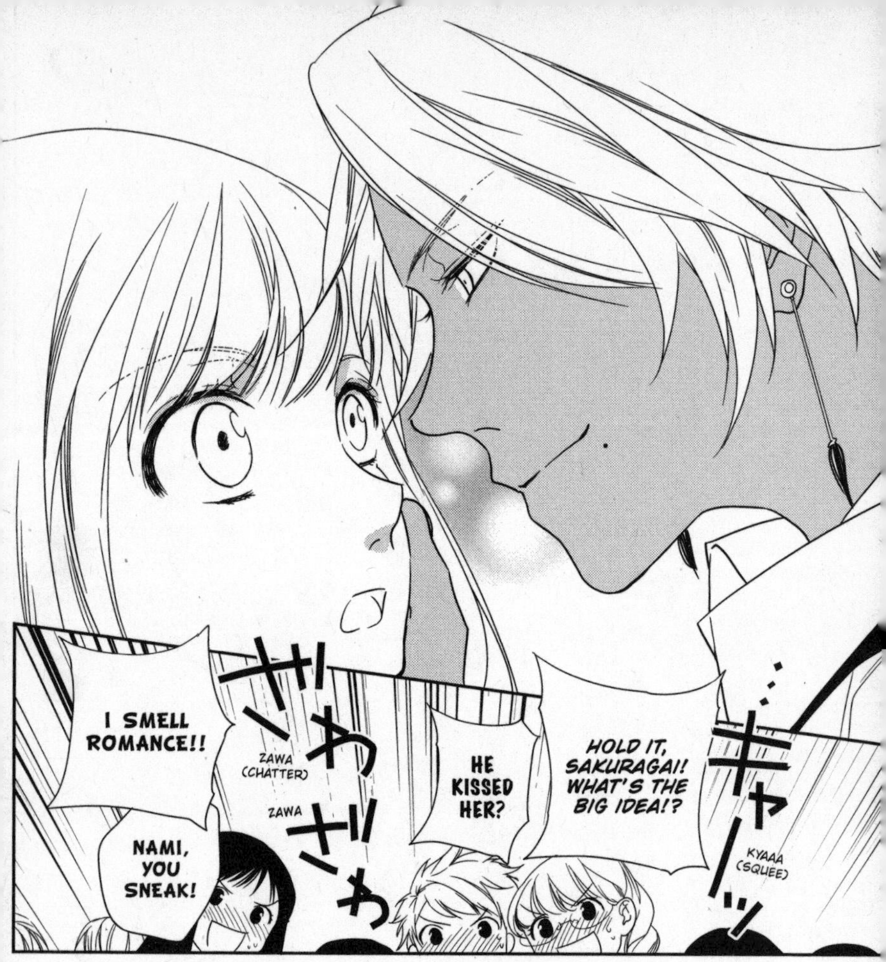

…
ギャーッ
KYAAA (SQUEE)
HOLD IT, SAKURAGAI! WHAT'S THE BIG IDEA!?
HE KISSED HER?
ざわざわ
ZAWA (CHATTER)
ZAWA
I SMELL ROMANCE!!
NAMI, YOU SNEAK!

MERMAID BOYS

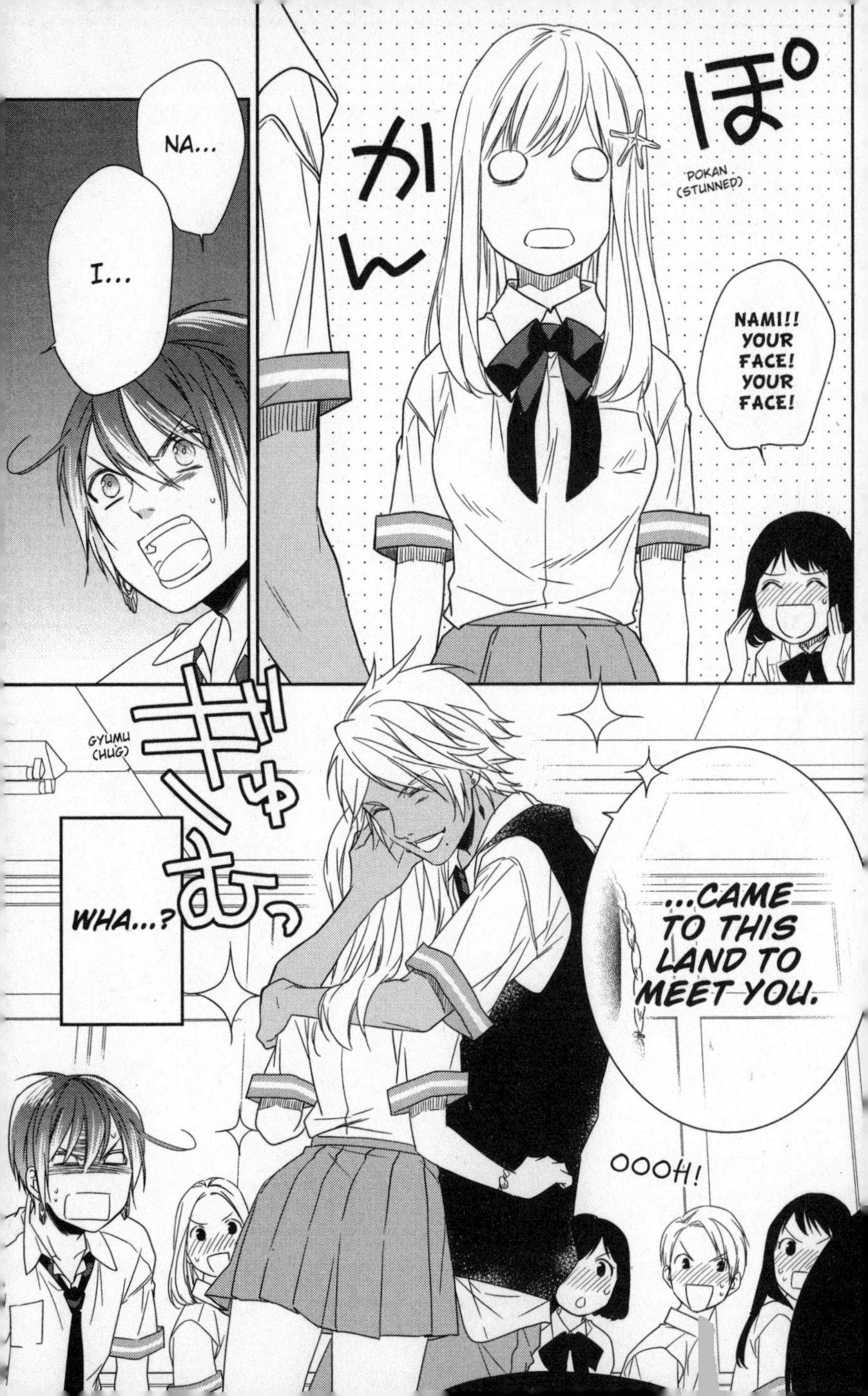
ぽかん
POKAN (STUNNED)
NAMI!! YOUR FACE! YOUR FACE!
NA...
I...
...CAME TO THIS LAND TO MEET YOU.
OOOH!
ぎゅむっ
GYUMU (HUG)
WHA...?

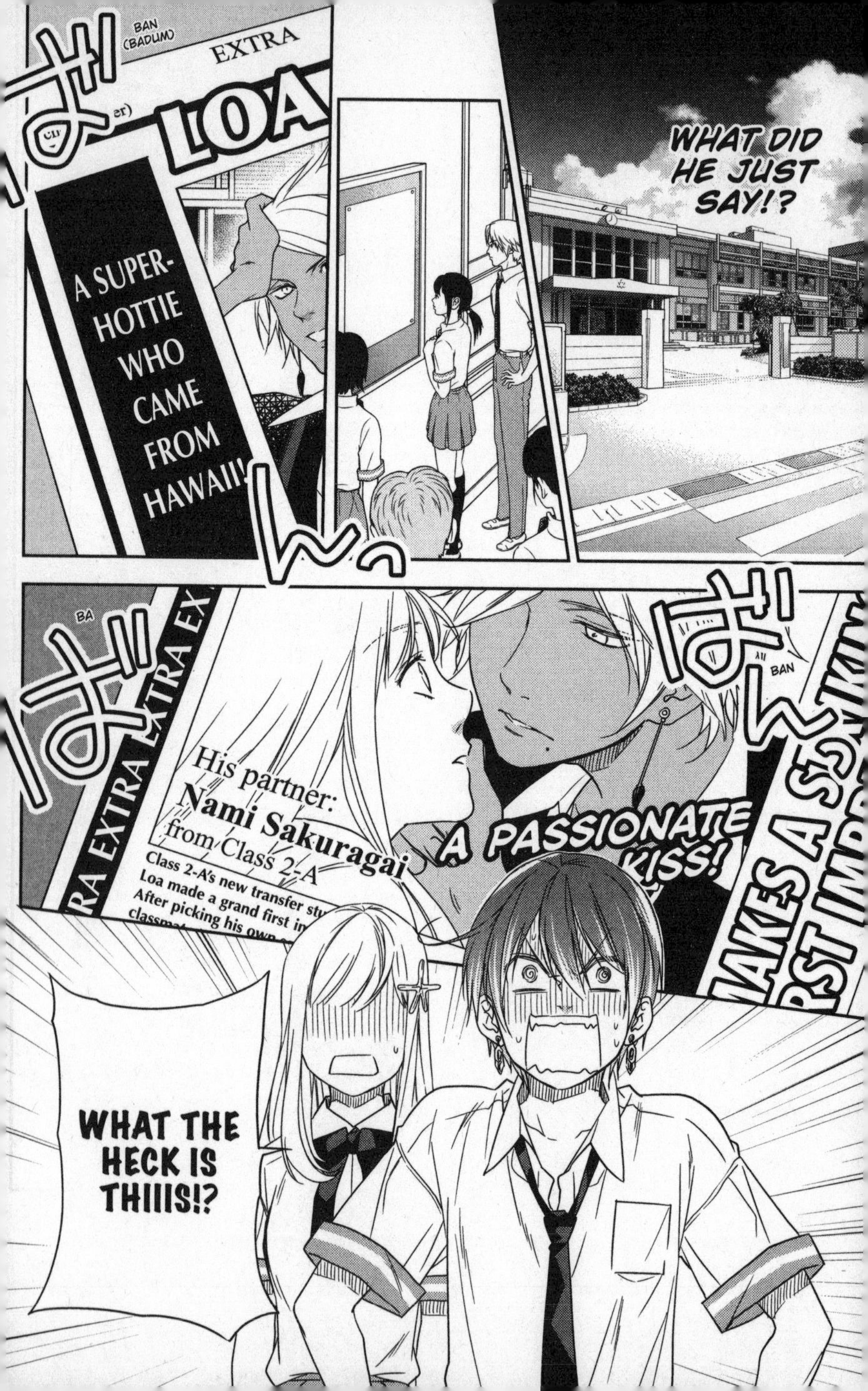

WHAT DID HE JUST SAY!?
BAN (BADUM)
EXTRA
LOA
A SUPER-HOTTIE WHO CAME FROM HAWAII!
BAN
A PASSIONATE KISS!
BA
EXTRA EXTRA EXTRA
His partner: Nami Sakuragai from Class 2-A
Class 2-A's new transfer stu
Loa made a grand first in
After picking his own
WHAT THE HECK IS THIIIS!?

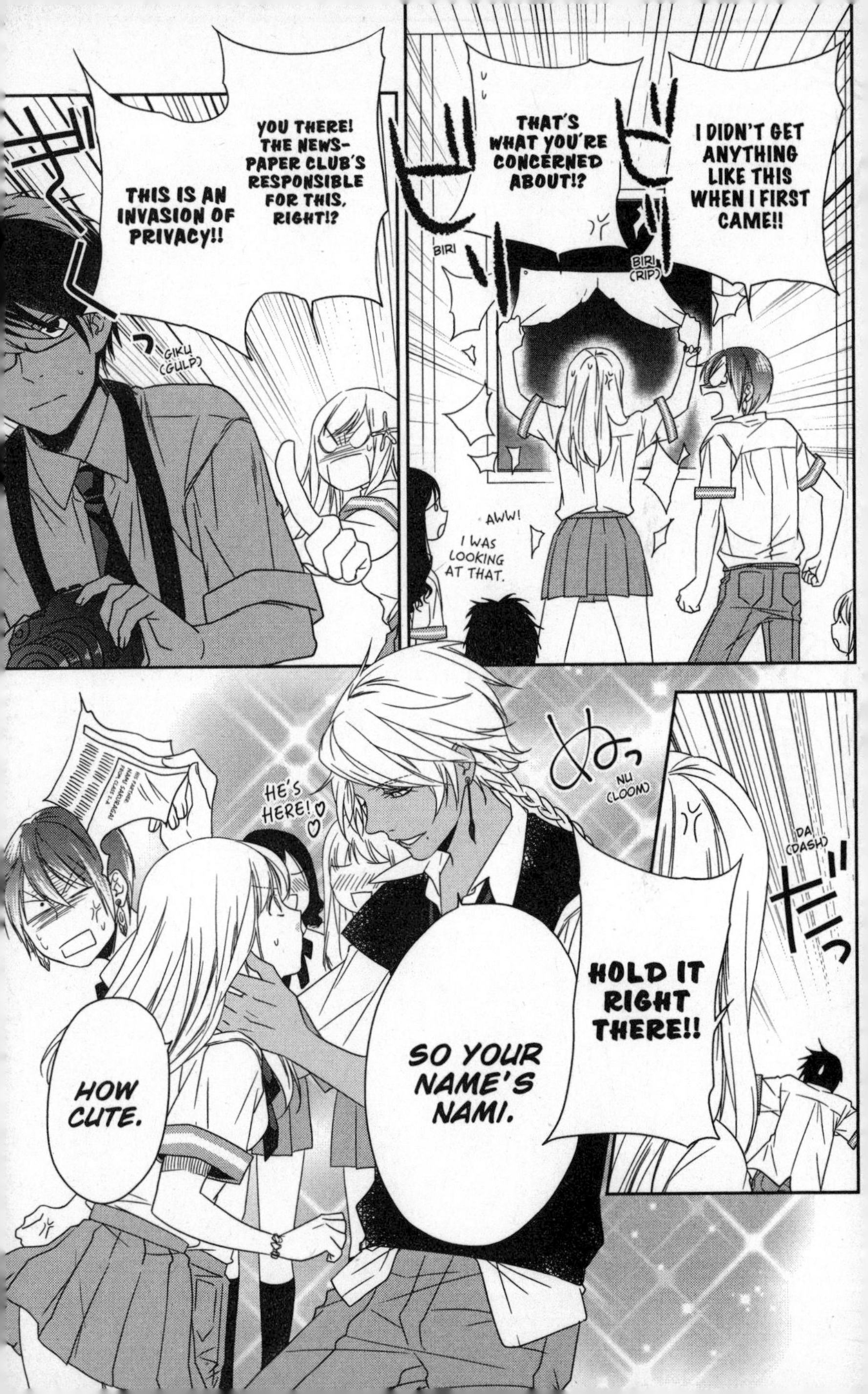
I DIDN'T GET ANYTHING LIKE THIS WHEN I FIRST CAME!!
THAT'S WHAT YOU'RE CONCERNED ABOUT!?
BIRI
BIRI (RIP)
AWW! I WAS LOOKING AT THAT.
YOU THERE! THE NEWS-PAPER CLUB'S RESPONSIBLE FOR THIS, RIGHT!?
THIS IS AN INVASION OF PRIVACY!!
GIKU (GULP)
ぬっ
NU (LOOM)
DA (DASH)
HOLD IT RIGHT THERE!!
HE'S HERE!
SO YOUR NAME'S NAMI.
HOW CUTE.

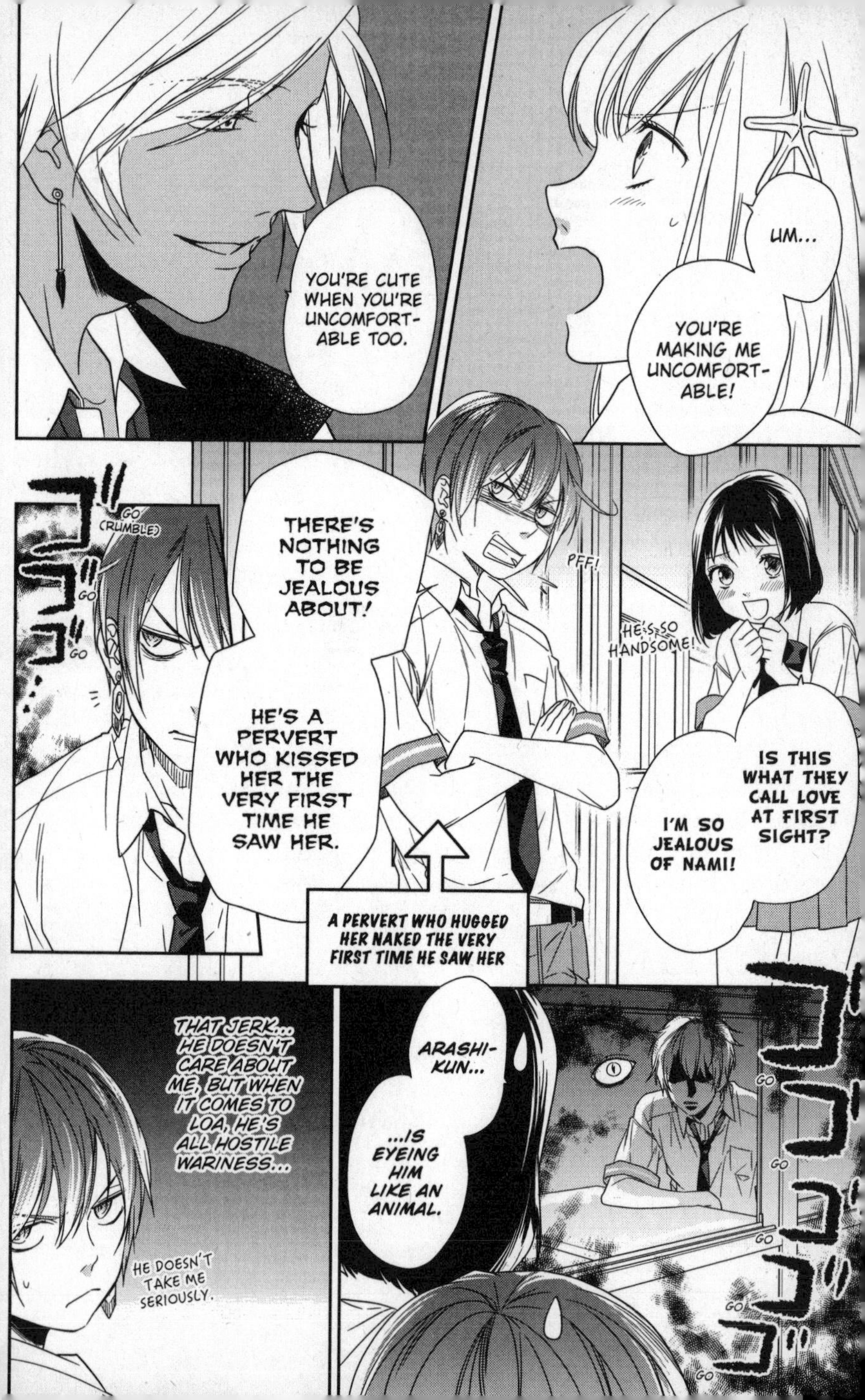
UM...
YOU'RE MAKING ME UNCOMFORT-ABLE!
YOU'RE CUTE WHEN YOU'RE UNCOMFORT-ABLE TOO.
HE'S SO HANDSOME!
IS THIS WHAT THEY CALL LOVE AT FIRST SIGHT?
I'M SO JEALOUS OF NAMI!
PFF!
THERE'S NOTHING TO BE JEALOUS ABOUT!
HE'S A PERVERT WHO KISSED HER THE VERY FIRST TIME HE SAW HER.
A PERVERT WHO HUGGED HER NAKED THE VERY FIRST TIME HE SAW HER
GO (RUMBLE)
GO
GO
GO
GO
GO
GO
ARASHI-KUN...
...IS EYEING HIM LIKE AN ANIMAL.
THAT JERK... HE DOESN'T CARE ABOUT ME, BUT WHEN IT COMES TO LOA, HE'S ALL HOSTILE WARINESS...
HE DOESN'T TAKE ME SERIOUSLY.

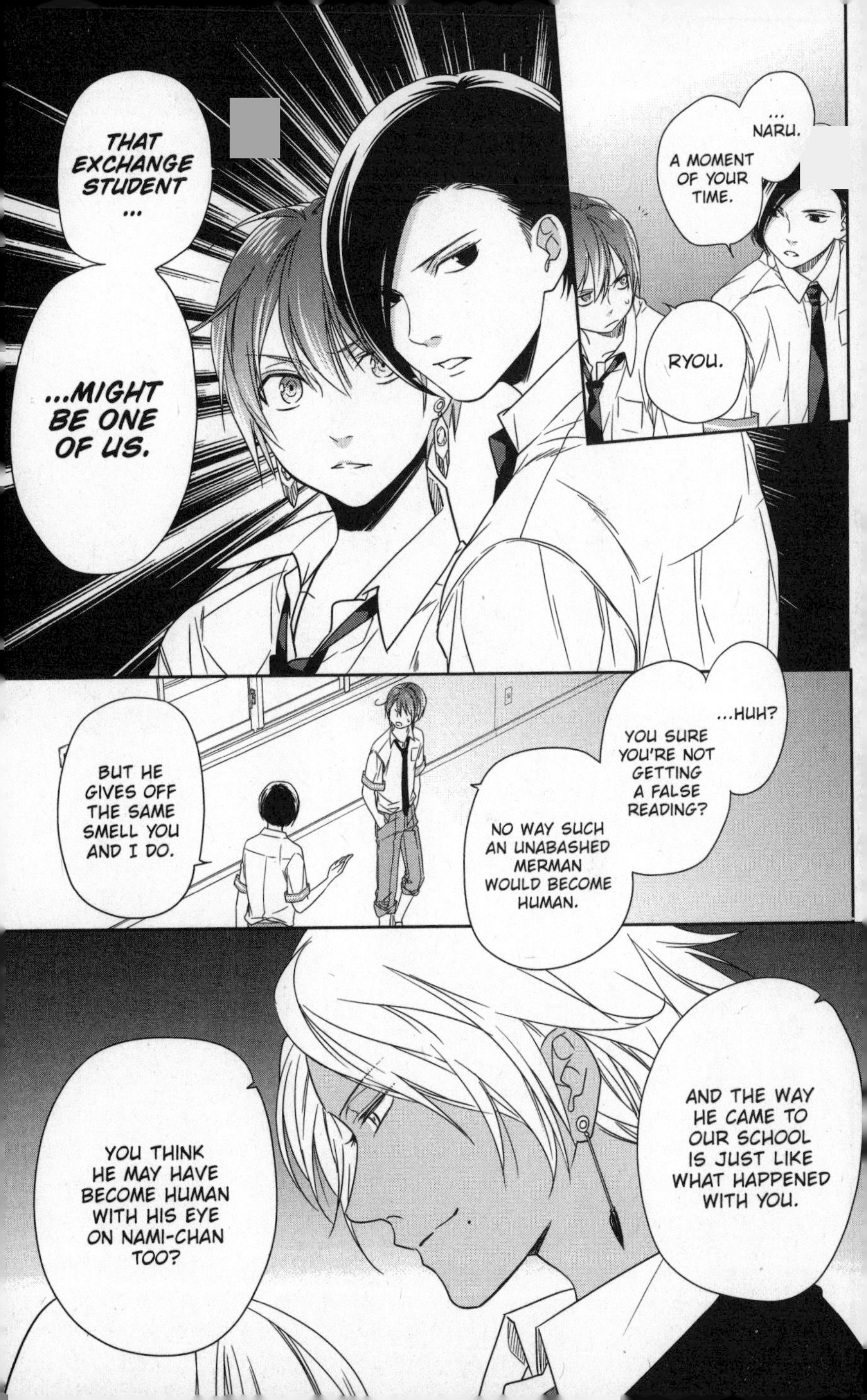
... NARU. A MOMENT OF YOUR TIME.
RYOU.
THAT EXCHANGE STUDENT ...
...MIGHT BE ONE OF US.
...HUH?
YOU SURE YOU'RE NOT GETTING A FALSE READING?
NO WAY SUCH AN UNABASHED MERMAN WOULD BECOME HUMAN.
BUT HE GIVES OFF THE SAME SMELL YOU AND I DO.
AND THE WAY HE CAME TO OUR SCHOOL IS JUST LIKE WHAT HAPPENED WITH YOU.
YOU THINK HE MAY HAVE BECOME HUMAN WITH HIS EYE ON NAMI-CHAN TOO?

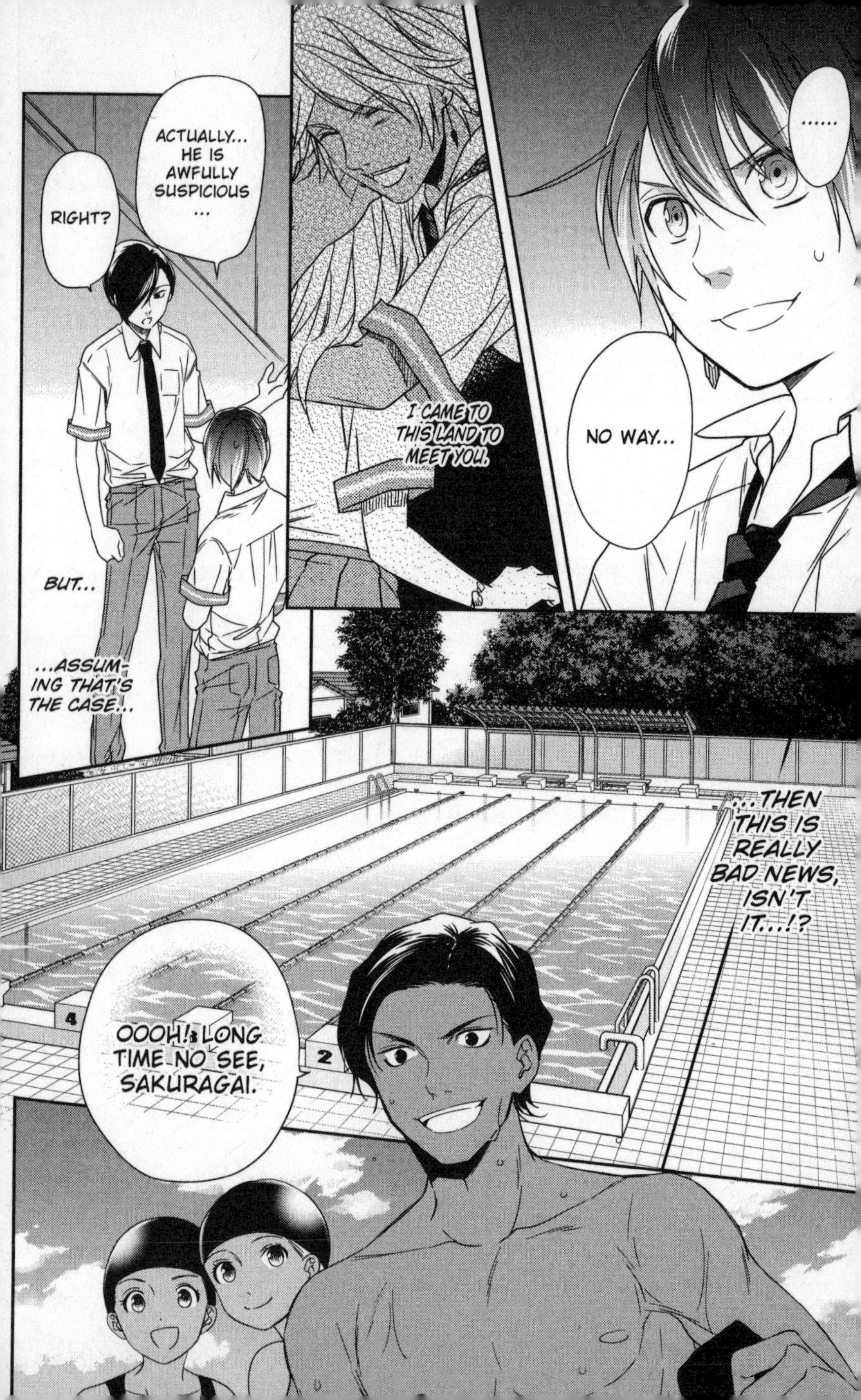
......
NO WAY...
I CAME TO THIS LAND TO MEET YOU.
ACTUALLY... HE IS AWFULLY SUSPICIOUS ...
RIGHT?
BUT...
...ASSUMING THAT'S THE CASE...
...THEN THIS IS REALLY BAD NEWS, ISN'T IT...!?
OOOH! LONG TIME NO SEE, SAKURAGAI.

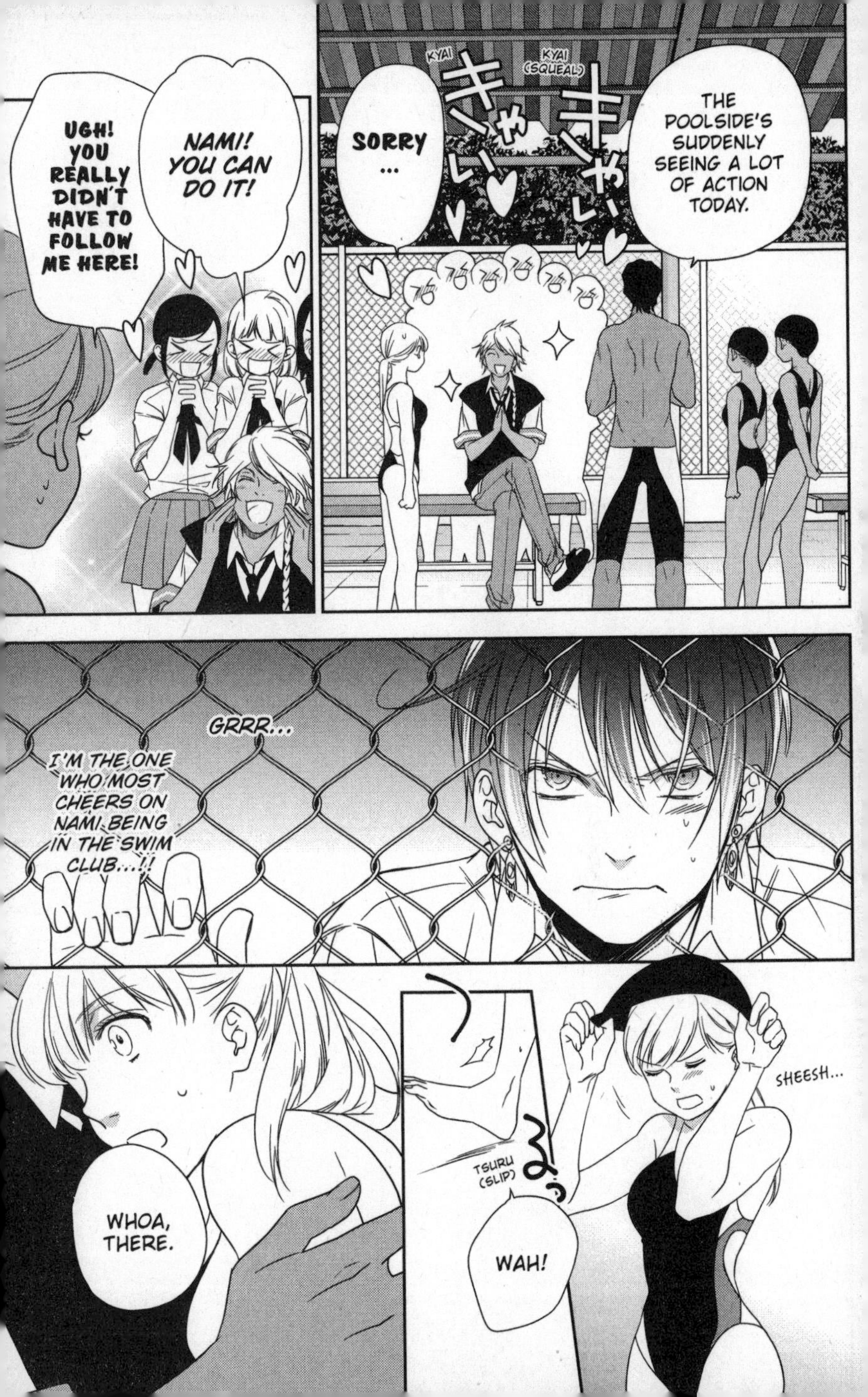
THE POOLSIDE'S SUDDENLY SEEING A LOT OF ACTION TODAY.
KYAI (SQUEAL)
KYAI
SORRY...
NAMI! YOU CAN DO IT!
UGH! YOU REALLY DIDN'T HAVE TO FOLLOW ME HERE!
GRRR...
I'M THE ONE WHO MOST CHEERS ON NAMI BEING IN THE SWIM CLUB...!!
SHEESH...
TSURU (SLIP)
WAH!
WHOA, THERE.

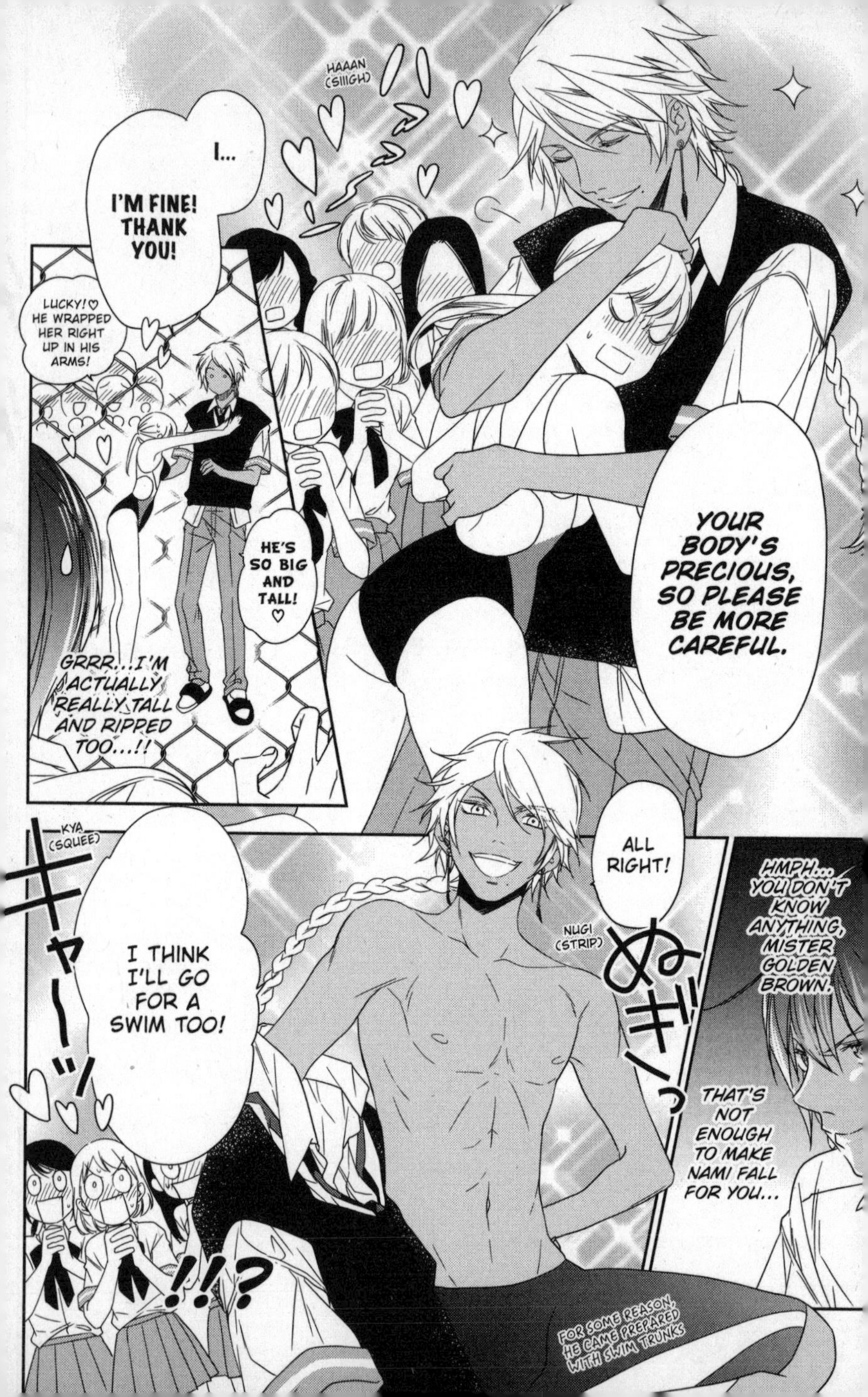
HAAAN (SIIIGH)
I...
I'M FINE! THANK YOU!
YOUR BODY'S PRECIOUS, SO PLEASE BE MORE CAREFUL.
LUCKY! ♡ HE WRAPPED HER RIGHT UP IN HIS ARMS!
HE'S SO BIG AND TALL! ♡
GRRR...I'M ACTUALLY REALLY TALL AND RIPPED TOO...!!
HMPH... YOU DON'T KNOW ANYTHING, MISTER GOLDEN BROWN.
THAT'S NOT ENOUGH TO MAKE NAMI FALL FOR YOU...
ALL RIGHT!
NUGI (STRIP)
I THINK I'LL GO FOR A SWIM TOO!
KYA (SQUEE)
!!?
FOR SOME REASON, HE CAME PREPARED WITH SWIM TRUNKS

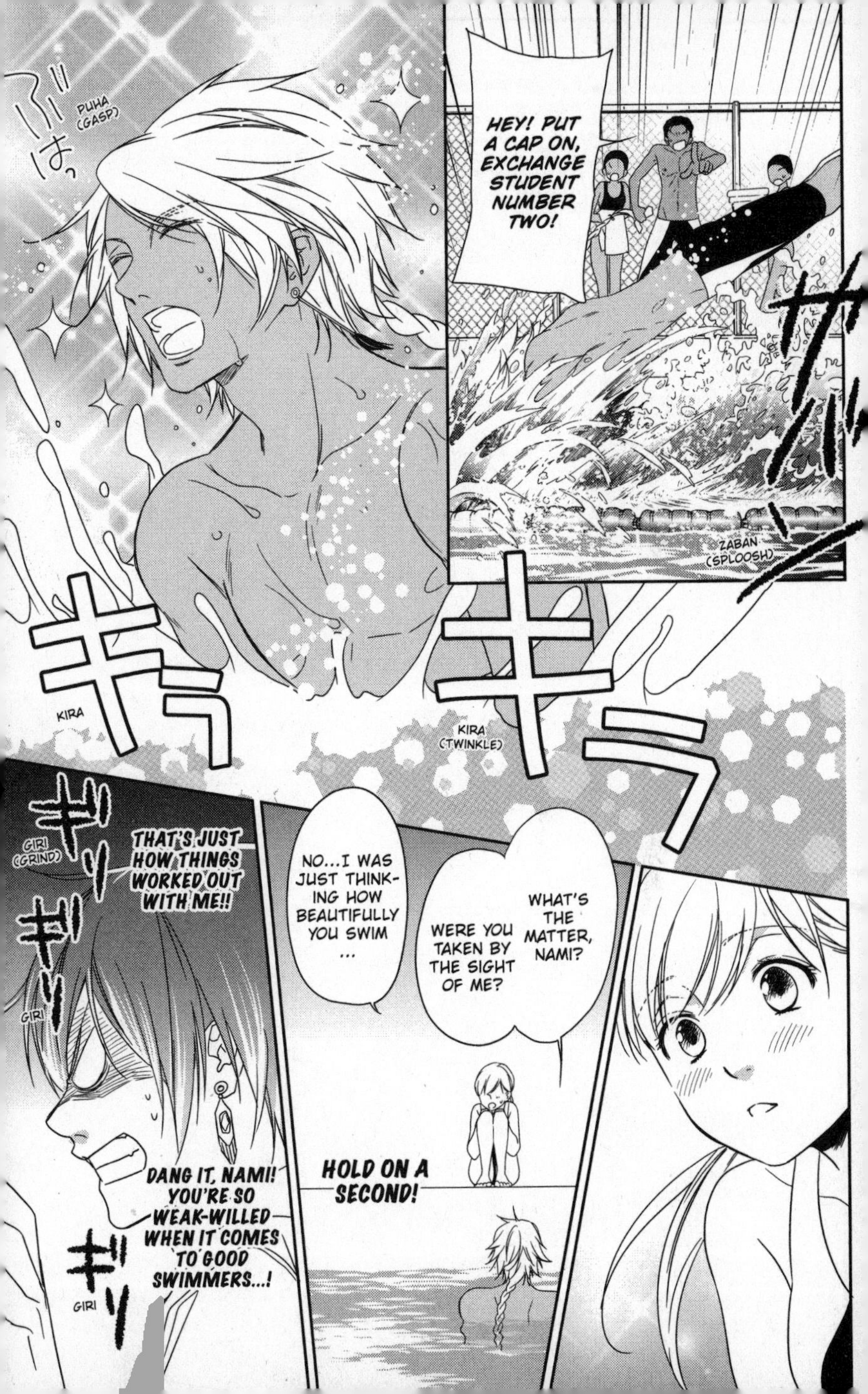
HEY! PUT A CAP ON, EXCHANGE STUDENT NUMBER TWO!
ZABAN (SPLOOSH)
PUHA (GASP)
KIRA
KIRA (TWINKLE)
WHAT'S THE MATTER, NAMI?
WERE YOU TAKEN BY THE SIGHT OF ME?
NO...I WAS JUST THINKING HOW BEAUTIFULLY YOU SWIM ...
HOLD ON A SECOND!
GIRI (GRIND)
THAT'S JUST HOW THINGS WORKED OUT WITH ME!!
GIRI
DANG IT, NAMI! YOU'RE SO WEAK-WILLED WHEN IT COMES TO GOOD SWIMMERS...!
GIRI

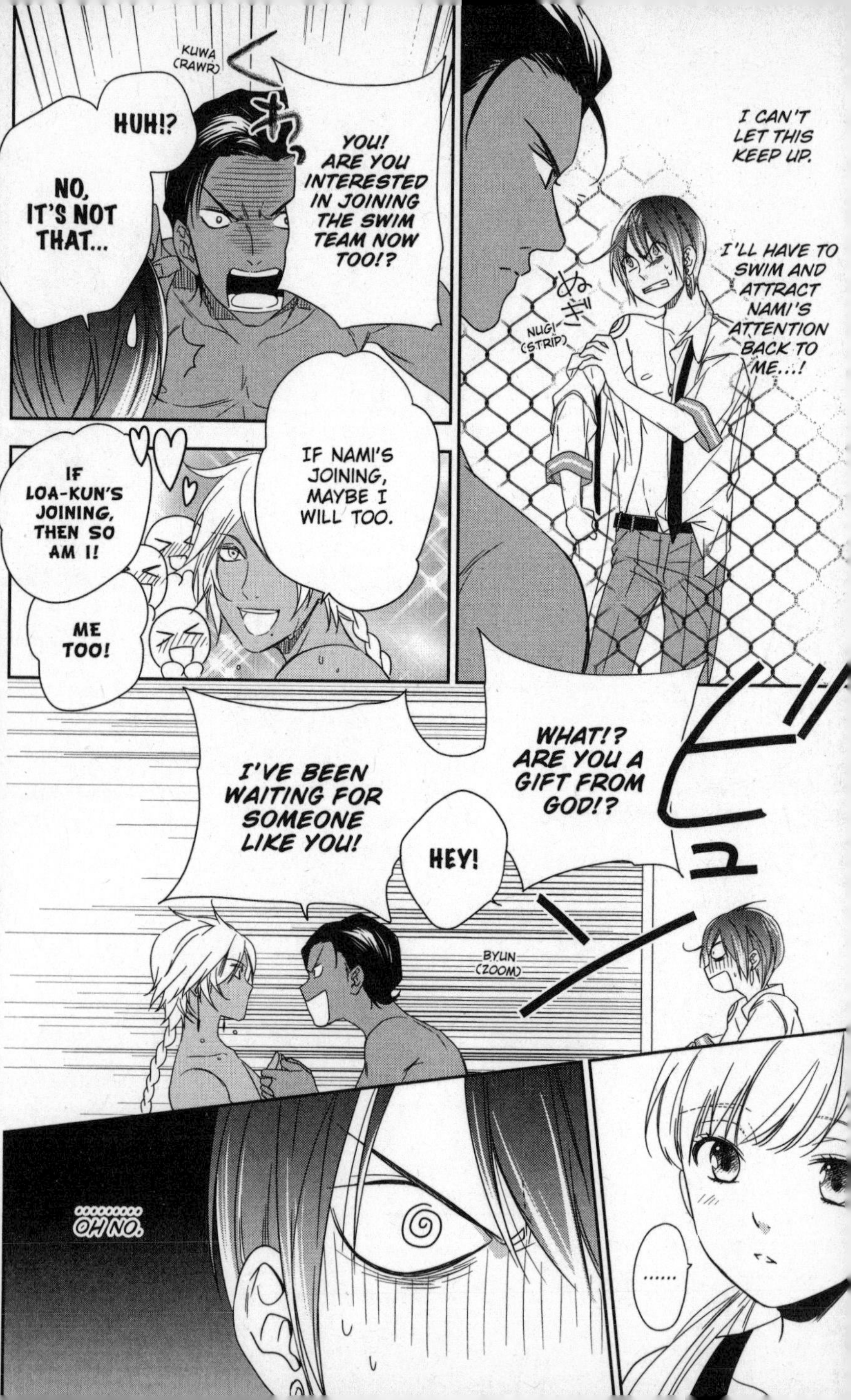
I CAN'T LET THIS KEEP UP.
I'LL HAVE TO SWIM AND ATTRACT NAMI'S ATTENTION BACK TO ME...!
ぬぎ
NUGI (STRIP)
KUWA (RAWR)
YOU! ARE YOU INTERESTED IN JOINING THE SWIM TEAM NOW TOO!?
HUH!?
NO, IT'S NOT THAT...
IF NAMI'S JOINING, MAYBE I WILL TOO.
IF LOA-KUN'S JOINING, THEN SO AM I!
ME TOO!
WHAT!? ARE YOU A GIFT FROM GOD!?
BYUN (ZOOM)
I'VE BEEN WAITING FOR SOMEONE LIKE YOU!
HEY!
......
OH NO.

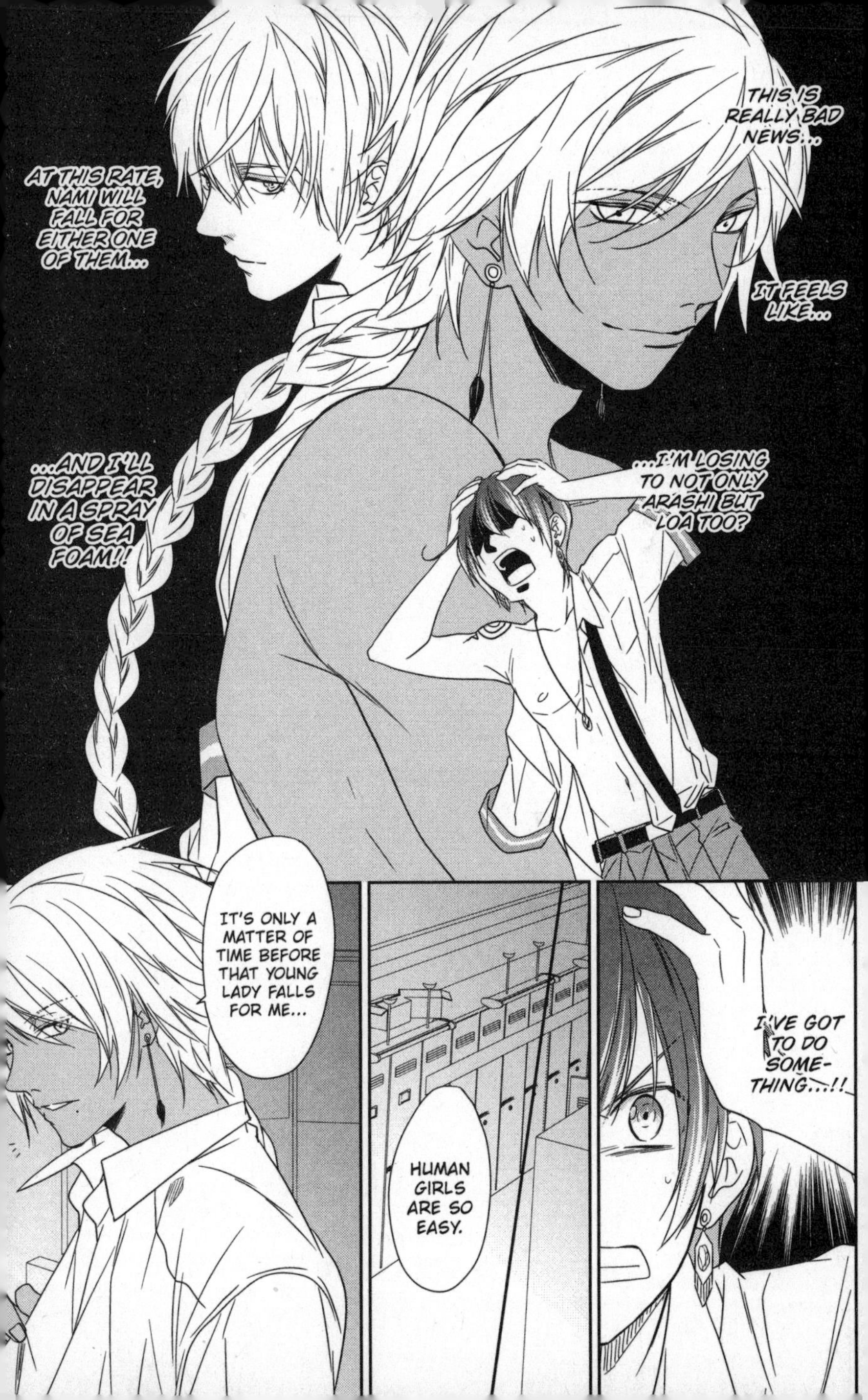
THIS IS REALLY BAD NEWS...
IT FEELS LIKE...
...I'M LOSING TO NOT ONLY ARASHI BUT LOA TOO?
AT THIS RATE, NAMI WILL FALL FOR EITHER ONE OF THEM...
...AND I'LL DISAPPEAR IN A SPRAY OF SEA FOAM!!
I'VE GOT TO DO SOME-THING...!!
HUMAN GIRLS ARE SO EASY.
IT'S ONLY A MATTER OF TIME BEFORE THAT YOUNG LADY FALLS FOR ME...

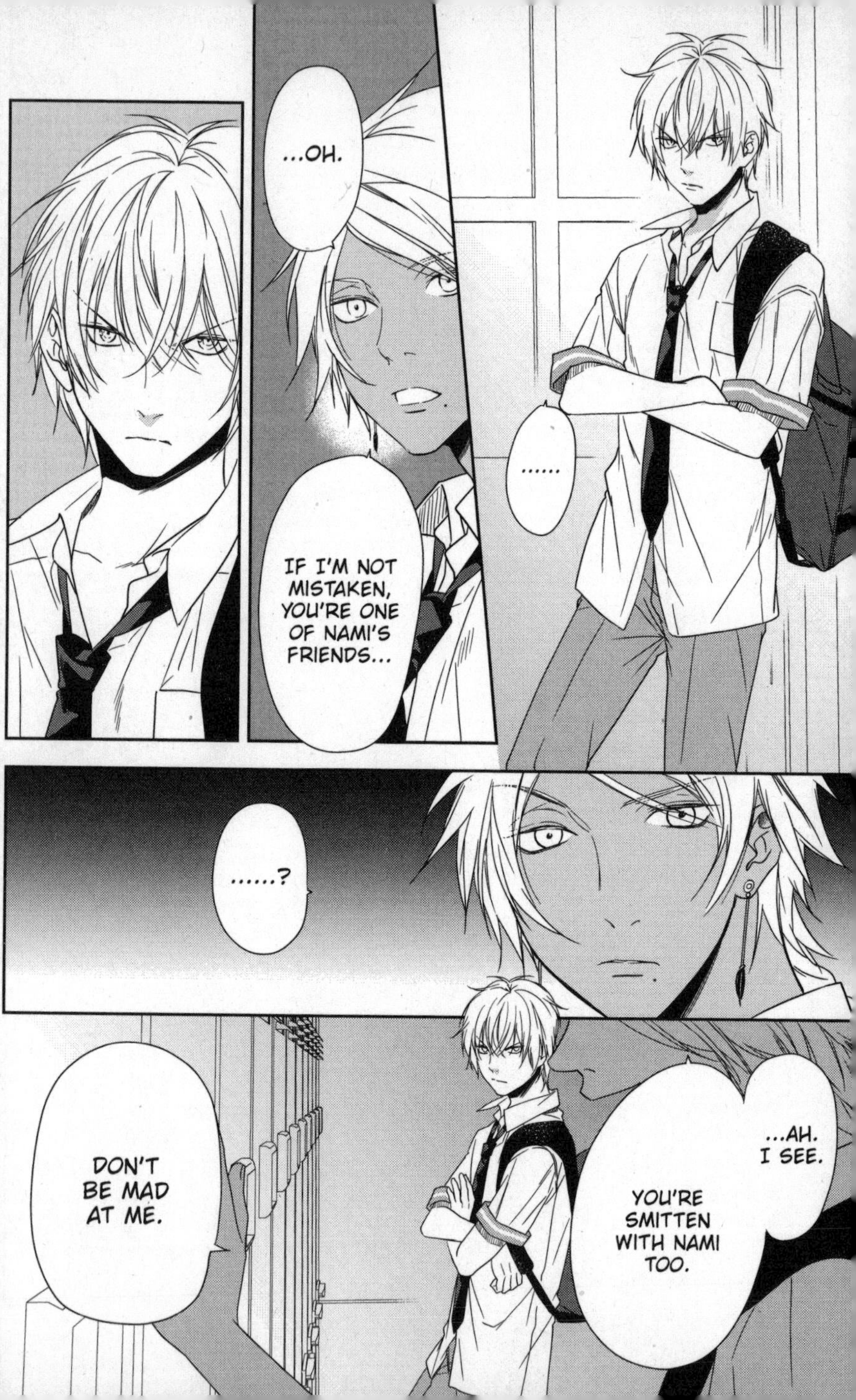
......
...OH.
IF I'M NOT MISTAKEN, YOU'RE ONE OF NAMI'S FRIENDS...
......?
...AH. I SEE.
YOU'RE SMITTEN WITH NAMI TOO.
DON'T BE MAD AT ME.

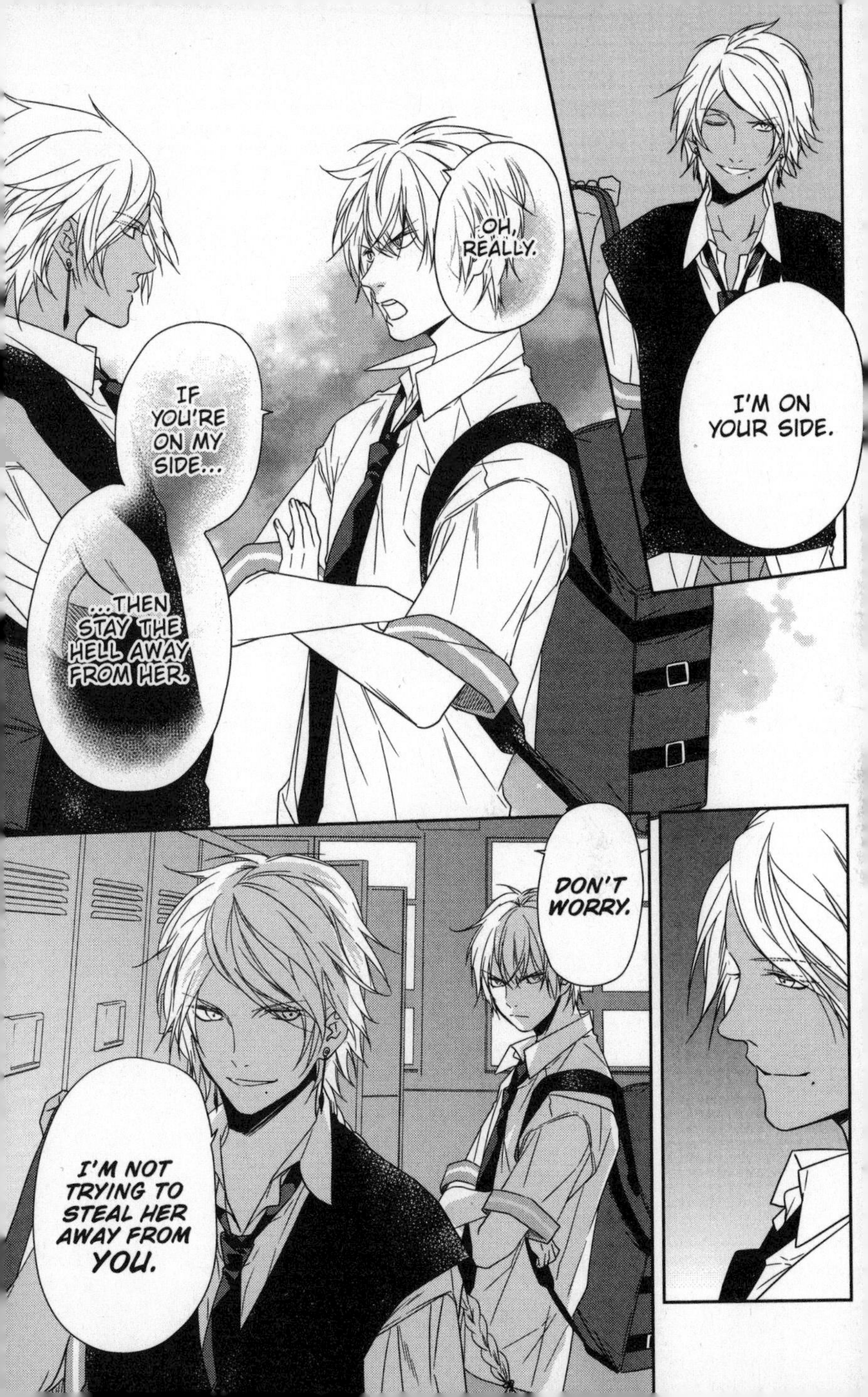
I'M ON YOUR SIDE.
OH, REALLY.
IF YOU'RE ON MY SIDE...
...THEN STAY THE HELL AWAY FROM HER.
DON'T WORRY.
I'M NOT TRYING TO STEAL HER AWAY FROM YOU.

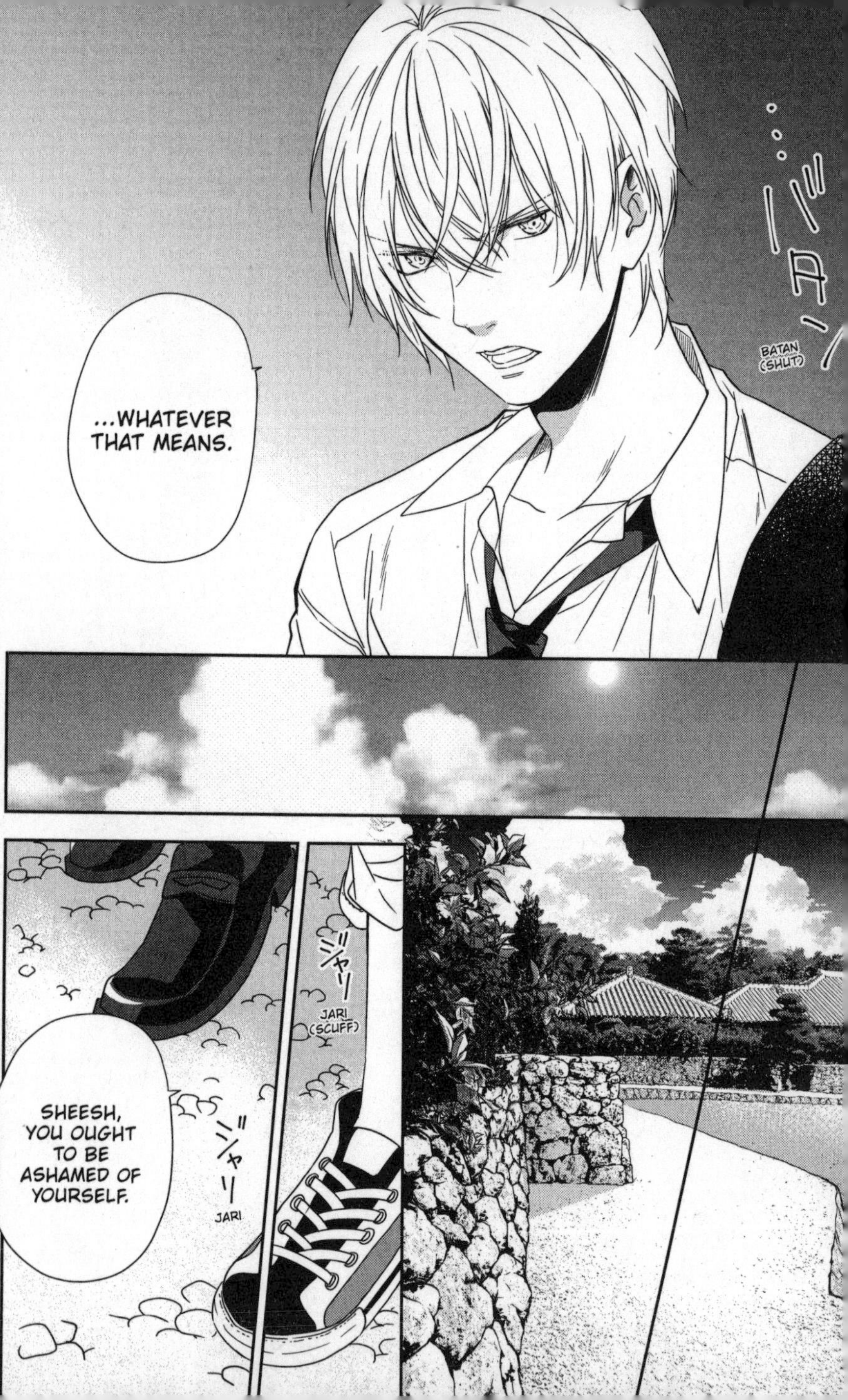
…バターン
BATAN (SHUT)
...WHATEVER THAT MEANS.
ジャリ
JARI (SCUFF)
ジャリ
JARI
SHEESH, YOU OUGHT TO BE ASHAMED OF YOURSELF.

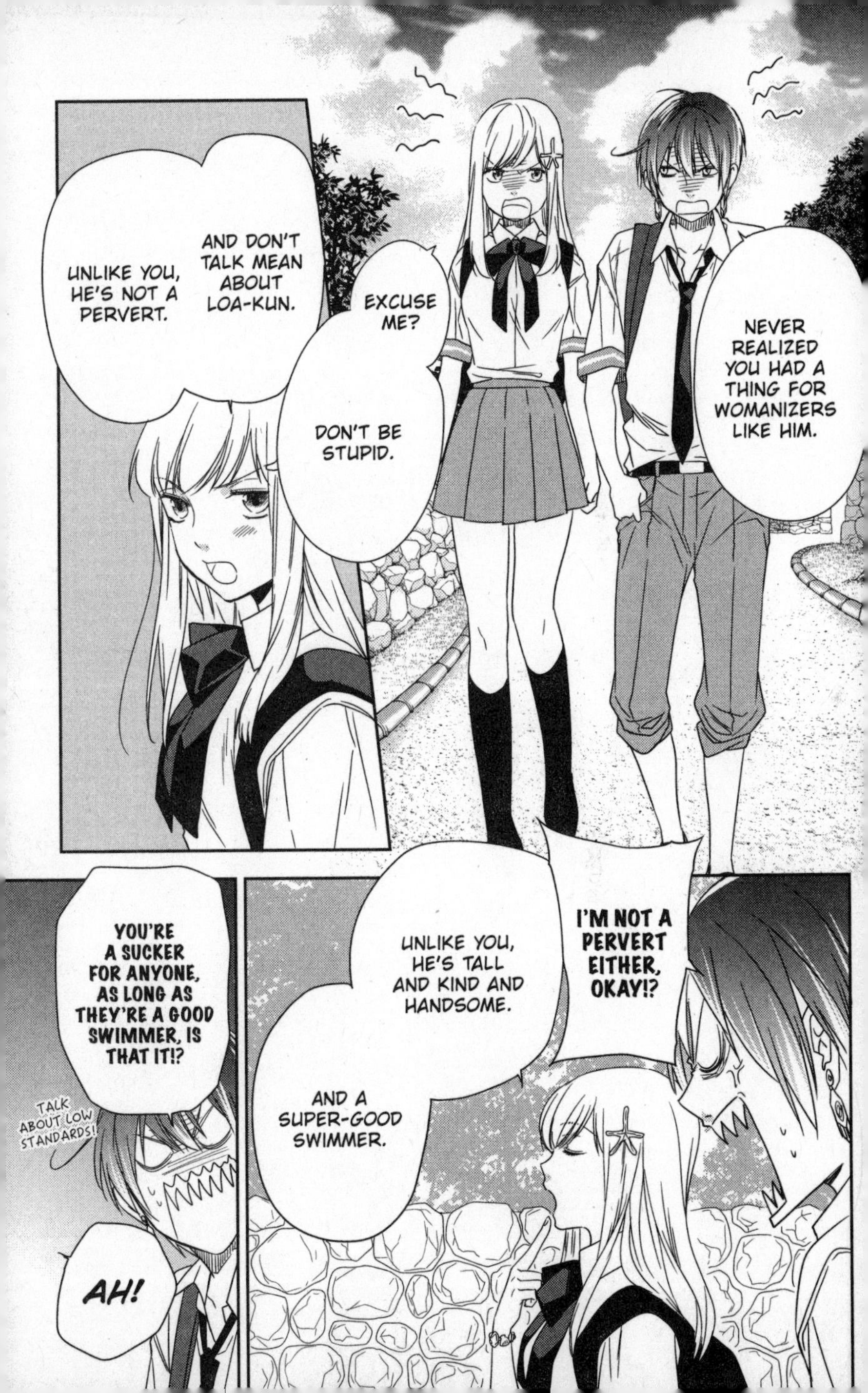
NEVER REALIZED YOU HAD A THING FOR WOMANIZERS LIKE HIM.
EXCUSE ME?
DON'T BE STUPID.
AND DON'T TALK MEAN ABOUT LOA-KUN.
UNLIKE YOU, HE'S NOT A PERVERT.
I'M NOT A PERVERT EITHER, OKAY!?
UNLIKE YOU, HE'S TALL AND KIND AND HANDSOME.
AND A SUPER-GOOD SWIMMER.
YOU'RE A SUCKER FOR ANYONE, AS LONG AS THEY'RE A GOOD SWIMMER, IS THAT IT!?
TALK ABOUT LOW STANDARDS!
AH!

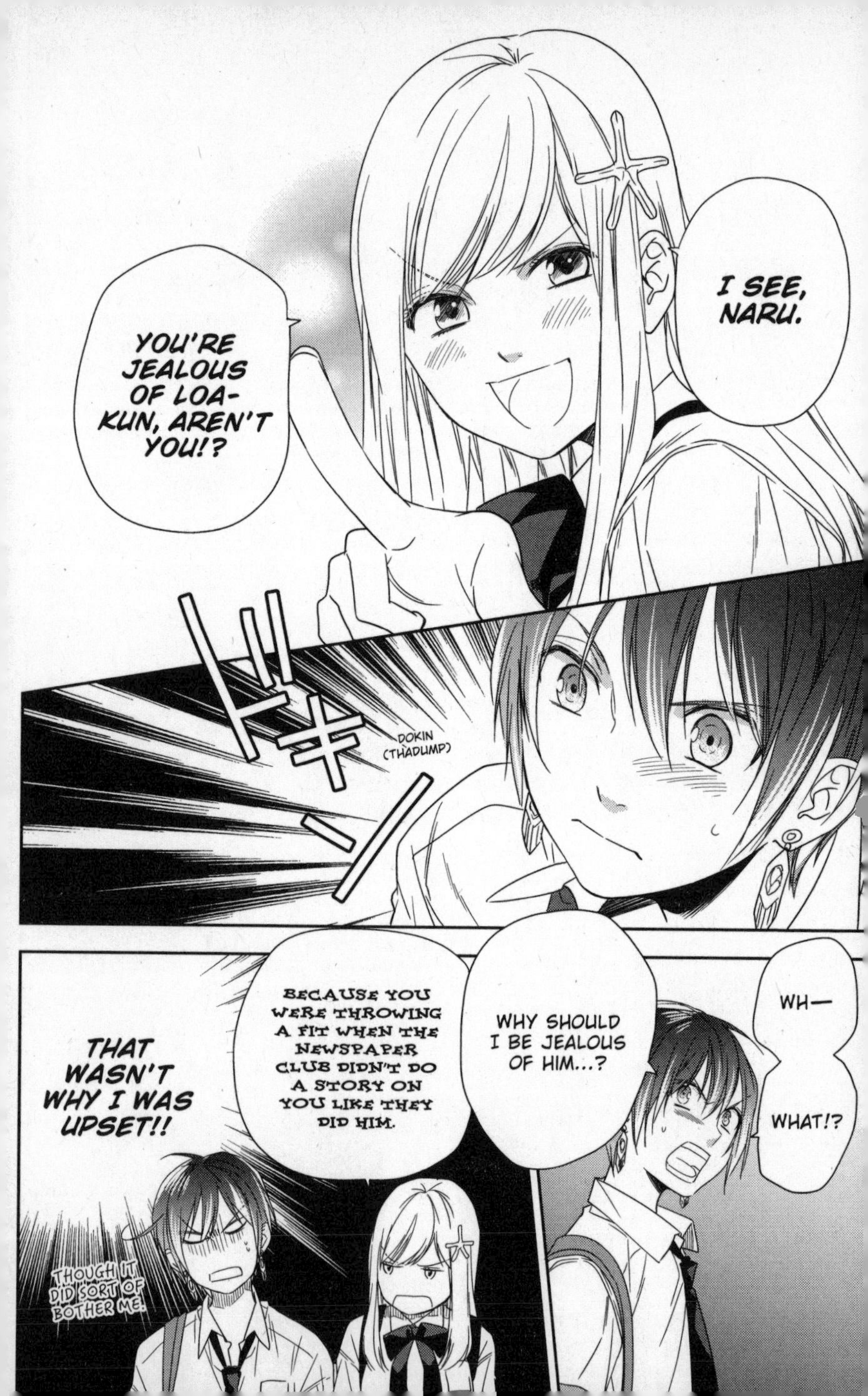

I SEE, NARU.
YOU'RE JEALOUS OF LOA-KUN, AREN'T YOU!?
DOKIN (THADUMP)
WH—
WHAT!?
WHY SHOULD I BE JEALOUS OF HIM...?
BECAUSE YOU WERE THROWING A FIT WHEN THE NEWSPAPER CLUB DIDN'T DO A STORY ON YOU LIKE THEY DID HIM.
THAT WASN'T WHY I WAS UPSET!!
THOUGH IT DID SORT OF BOTHER ME.

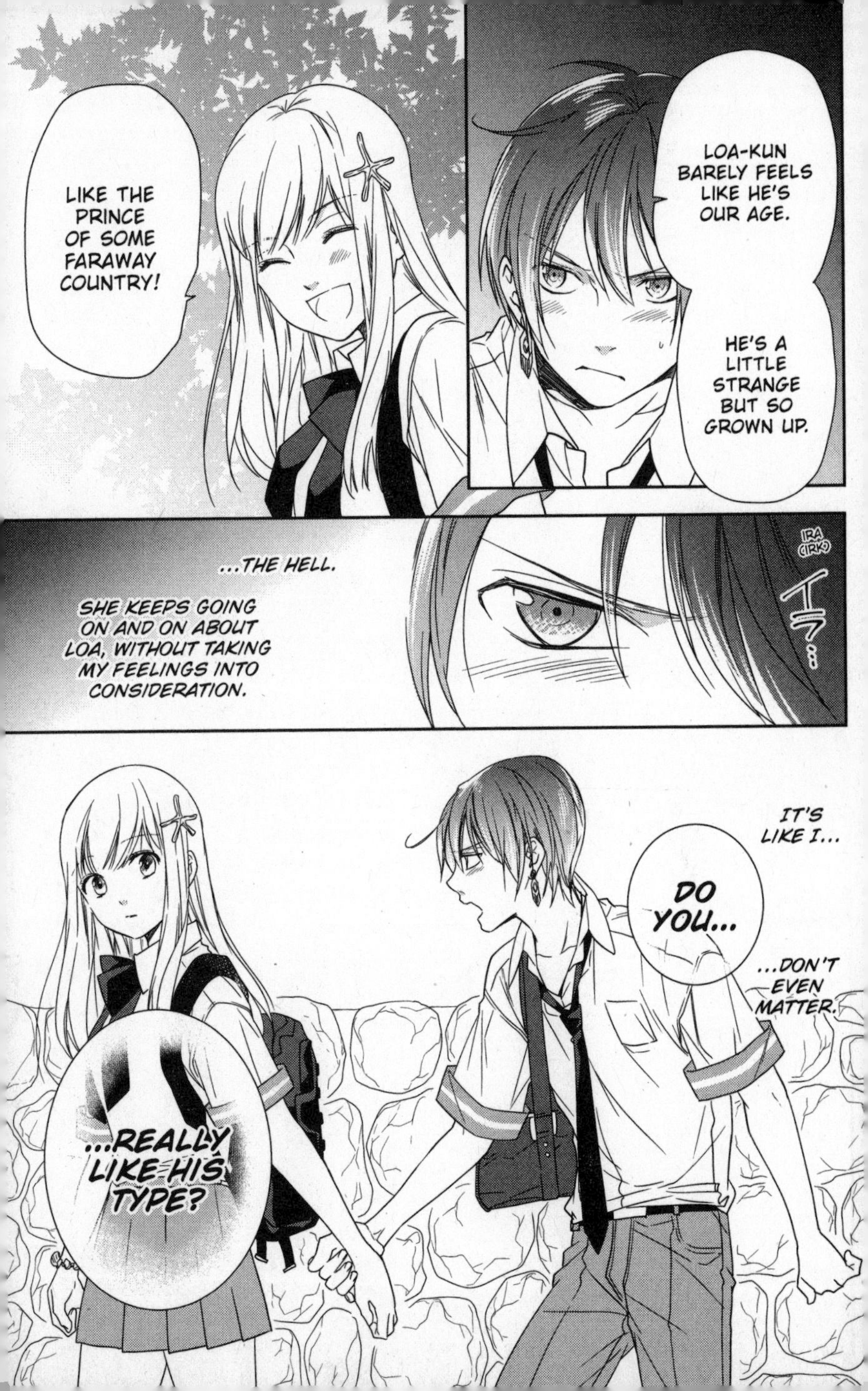
LOA-KUN BARELY FEELS LIKE HE'S OUR AGE.
HE'S A LITTLE STRANGE BUT SO GROWN UP.
LIKE THE PRINCE OF SOME FARAWAY COUNTRY!
イラ…
IRA (IRK)
...THE HELL.
SHE KEEPS GOING ON AND ON ABOUT LOA, WITHOUT TAKING MY FEELINGS INTO CONSIDERATION.
IT'S LIKE I...
DO YOU...
...DON'T EVEN MATTER.
...REALLY LIKE HIS TYPE?

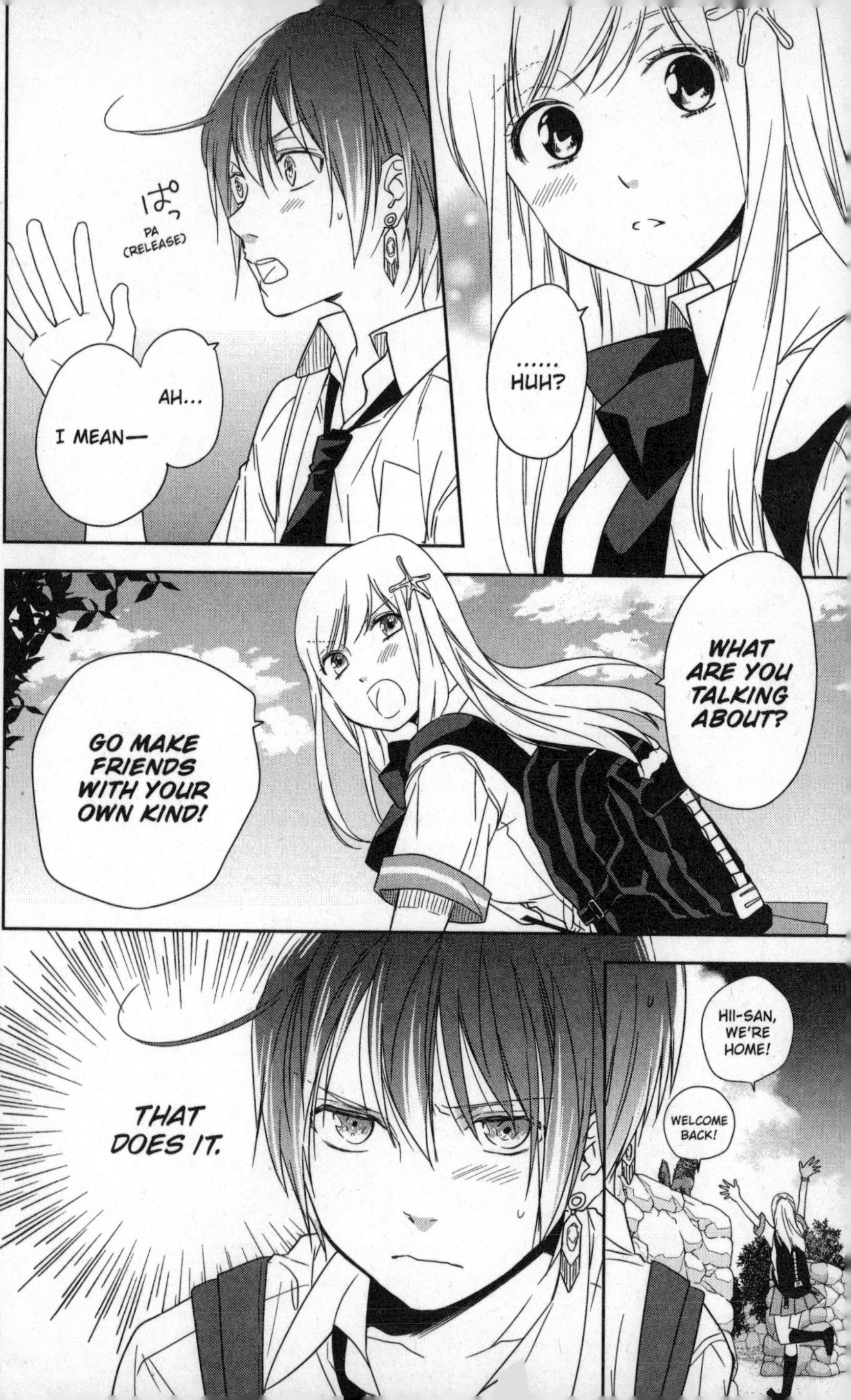
......
HUH?
ぱっ
PA (RELEASE)
AH...
I MEAN—
WHAT ARE YOU TALKING ABOUT?
GO MAKE FRIENDS WITH YOUR OWN KIND!
HII-SAN, WE'RE HOME!
WELCOME BACK!
THAT DOES IT.

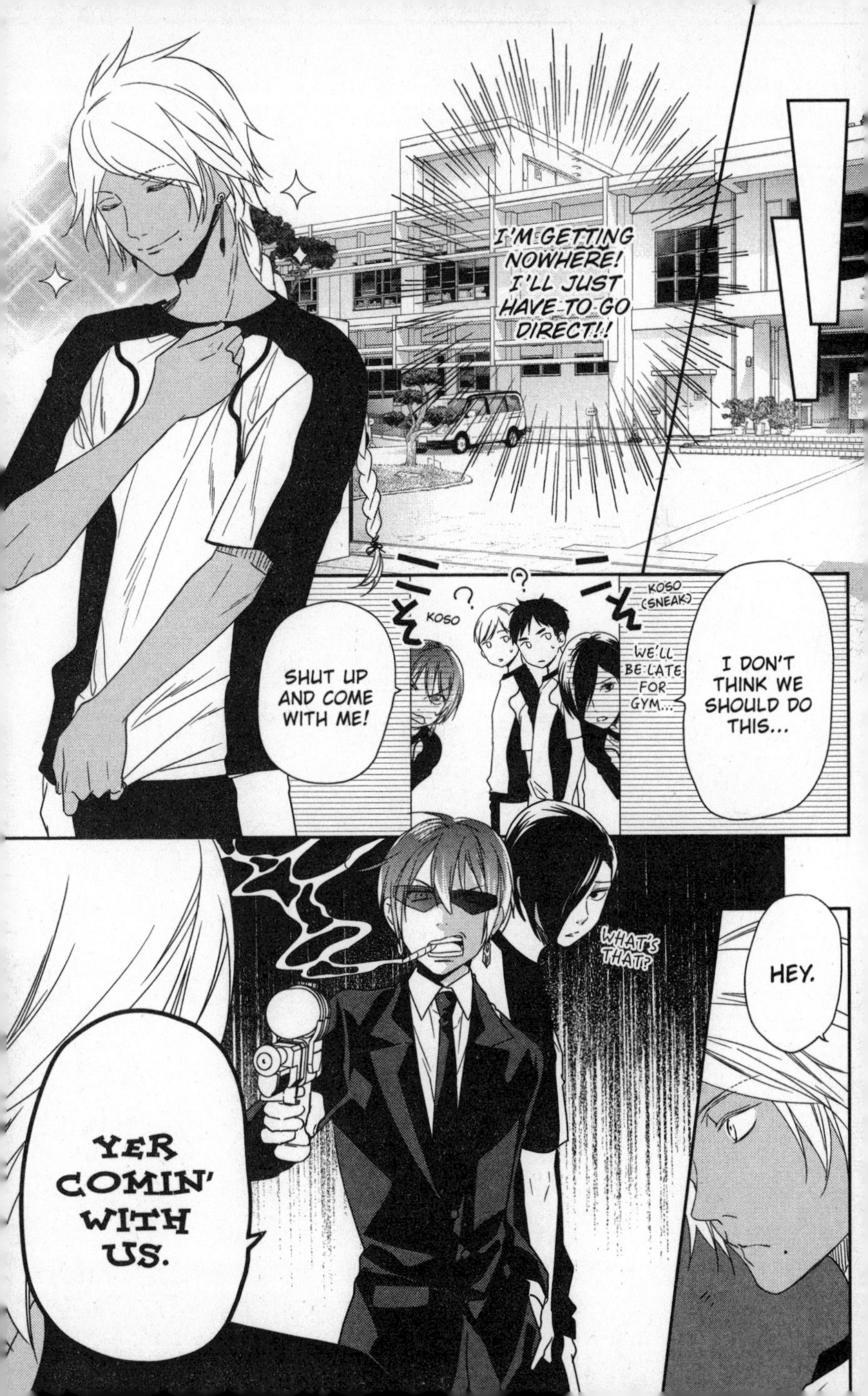
I'M GETTING NOWHERE! I'LL JUST HAVE TO GO DIRECT!!
KOSO (SNEAK)
I DON'T THINK WE SHOULD DO THIS...
WE'LL BE LATE FOR GYM...
KOSO
SHUT UP AND COME WITH ME!
HEY.
WHAT'S THAT?
YER COMIN' WITH US.

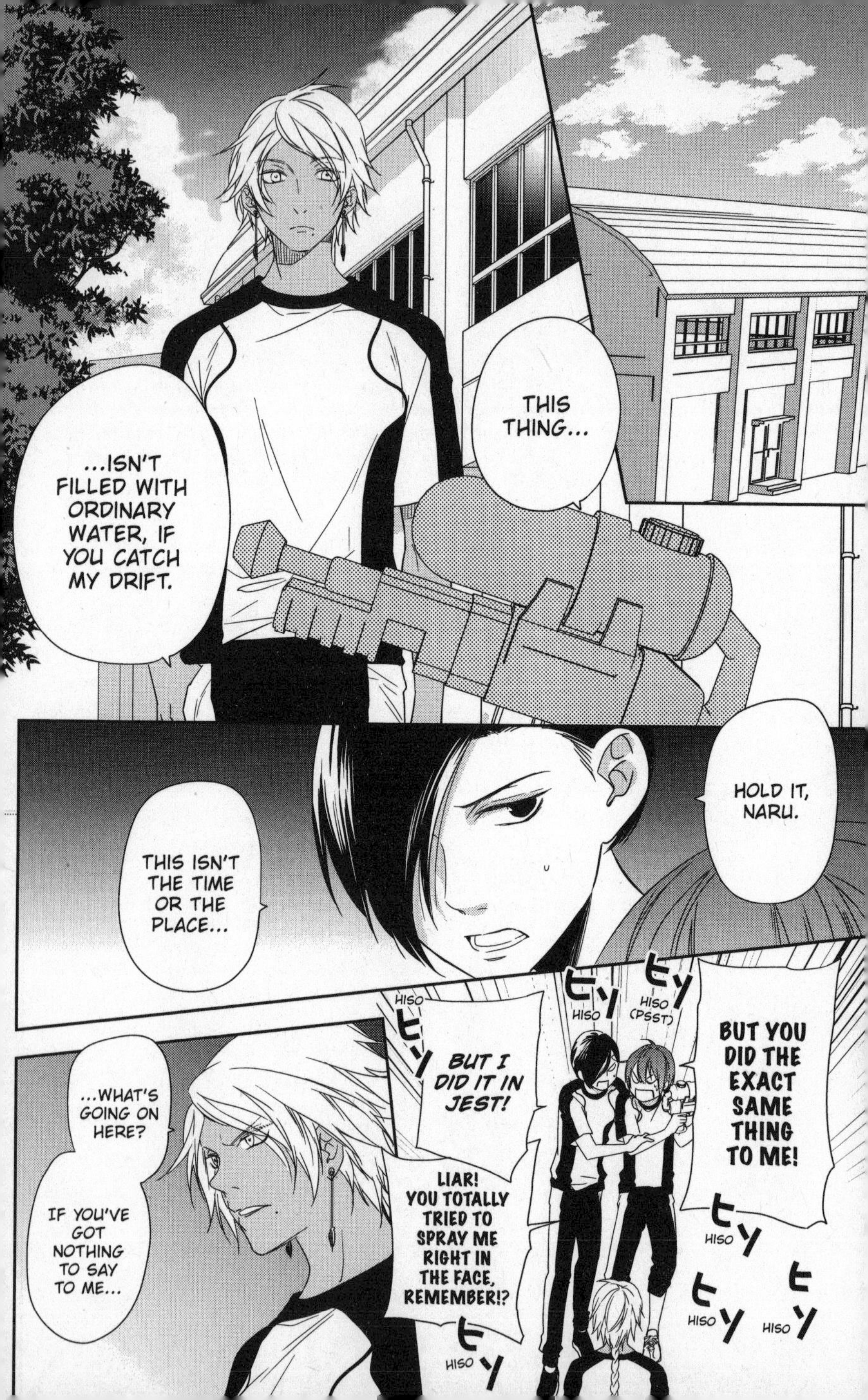
THIS THING...
...ISN'T FILLED WITH ORDINARY WATER, IF YOU CATCH MY DRIFT.
HOLD IT, NARU.
THIS ISN'T THE TIME OR THE PLACE...
ヒソ HISO
ヒソ HISO (PSST)
BUT YOU DID THE EXACT SAME THING TO ME!
ヒソ HISO
BUT I DID IT IN JEST!
LIAR! YOU TOTALLY TRIED TO SPRAY ME RIGHT IN THE FACE, REMEMBER!?
ヒソ HISO
ヒソ HISO
ヒソ HISO
ヒソ HISO
...WHAT'S GOING ON HERE?
IF YOU'VE GOT NOTHING TO SAY TO ME...

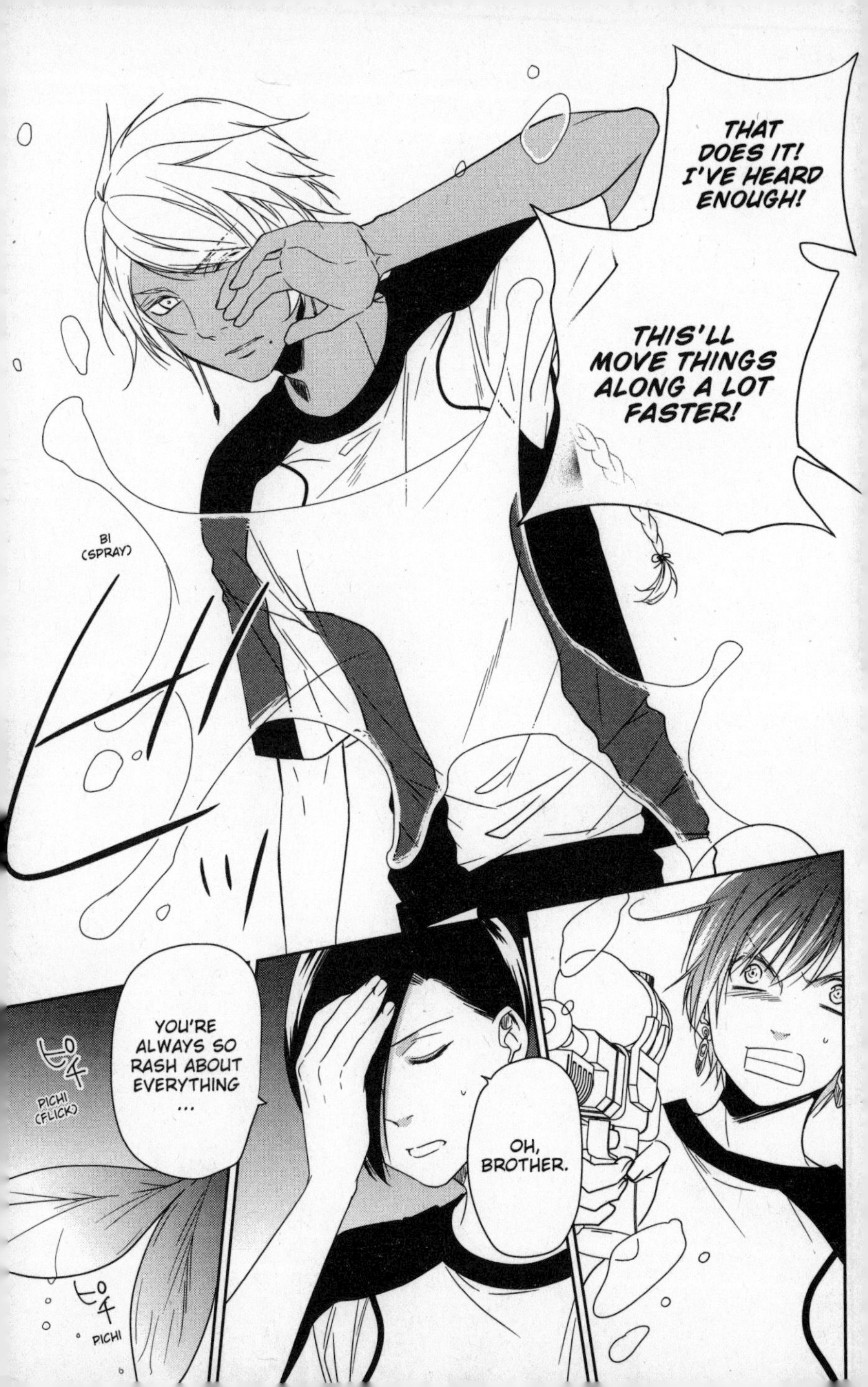
THAT DOES IT! I'VE HEARD ENOUGH!
THIS'LL MOVE THINGS ALONG A LOT FASTER!
BI (SPRAY)
OH, BROTHER.
YOU'RE ALWAYS SO RASH ABOUT EVERYTHING ...
PICHI (FLICK)
PICHI

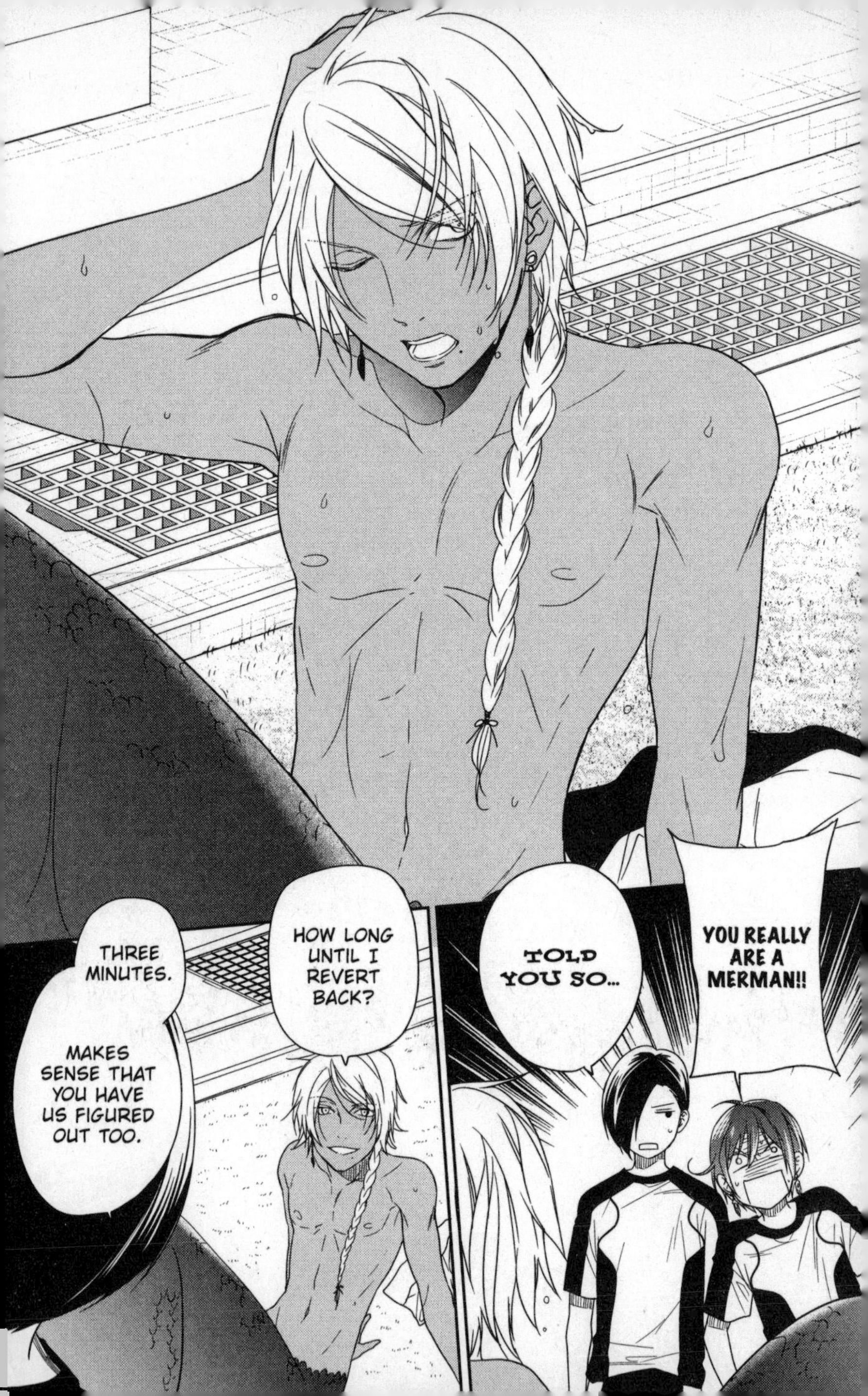
YOU REALLY ARE A MERMAN!!
TOLD YOU SO...
HOW LONG UNTIL I REVERT BACK?
THREE MINUTES.
MAKES SENSE THAT YOU HAVE US FIGURED OUT TOO.

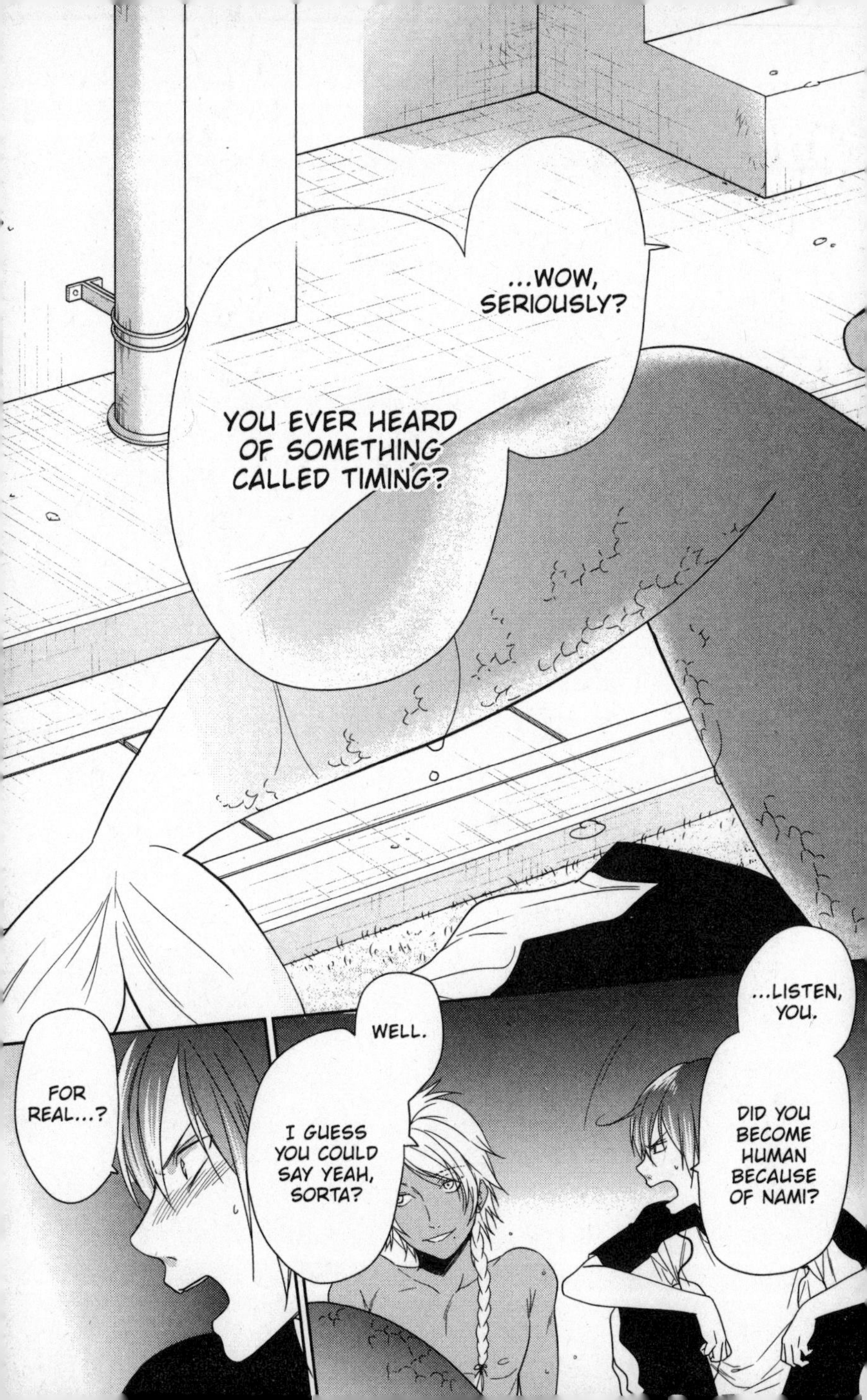
...WOW, SERIOUSLY?
YOU EVER HEARD OF SOMETHING CALLED TIMING?
...LISTEN, YOU.
DID YOU BECOME HUMAN BECAUSE OF NAMI?
WELL.
I GUESS YOU COULD SAY YEAH, SORTA?
FOR REAL...?

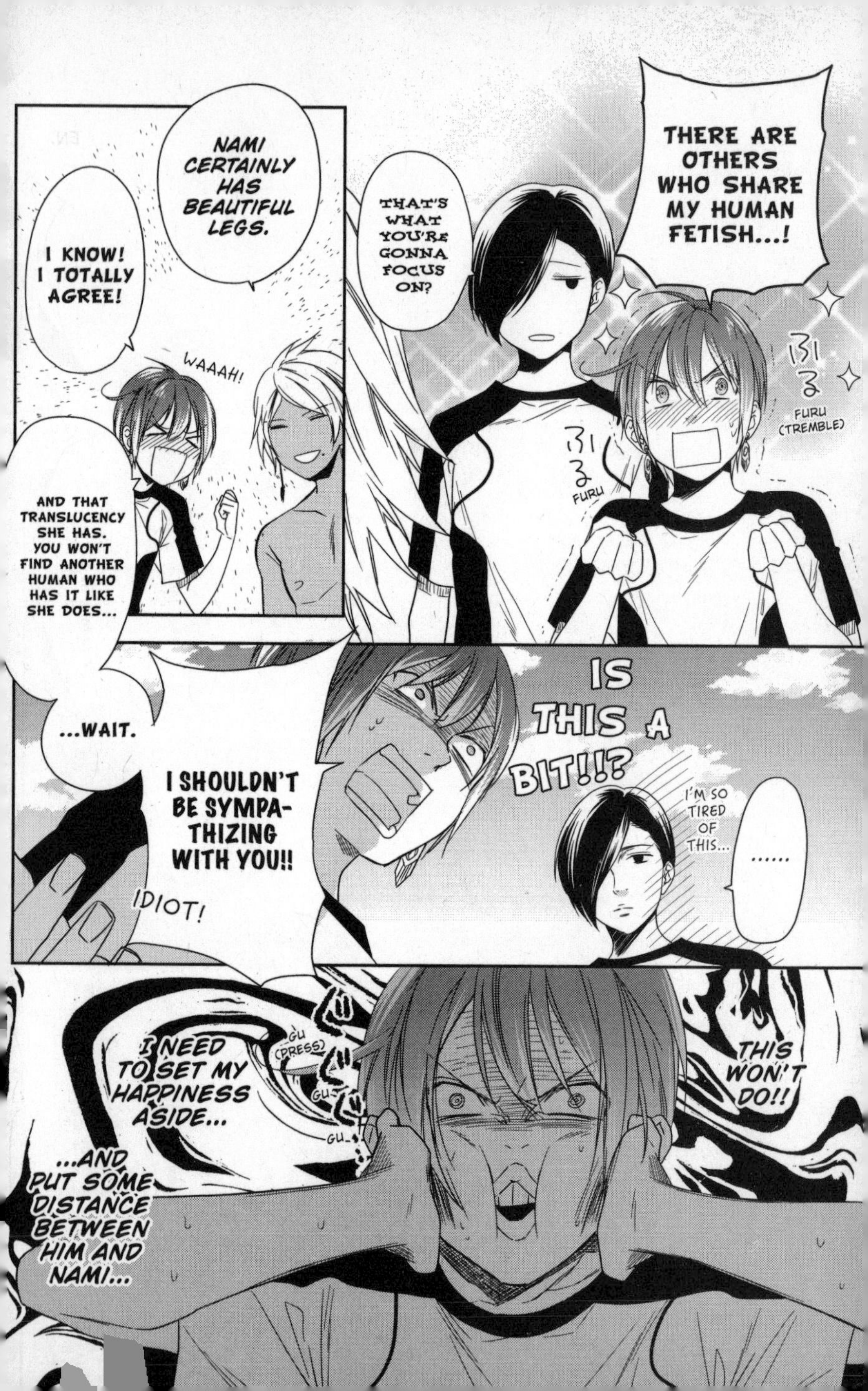
THERE ARE OTHERS WHO SHARE MY HUMAN FETISH...!
ふる
FURU (TREMBLE)
ふる
FURU
THAT'S WHAT YOU'RE GONNA FOCUS ON?
NAMI CERTAINLY HAS BEAUTIFUL LEGS.
I KNOW! I TOTALLY AGREE!
WAAAH!
AND THAT TRANSLUCENCY SHE HAS. YOU WON'T FIND ANOTHER HUMAN WHO HAS IT LIKE SHE DOES...
IS THIS A BIT!!?
I'M SO TIRED OF THIS...
......
...WAIT.
I SHOULDN'T BE SYMPA-THIZING WITH YOU!!
IDIOT!
THIS WON'T DO!!
I NEED TO SET MY HAPPINESS ASIDE...
GU (PRESS)
GU-
GU-
...AND PUT SOME DISTANCE BETWEEN HIM AND NAMI...

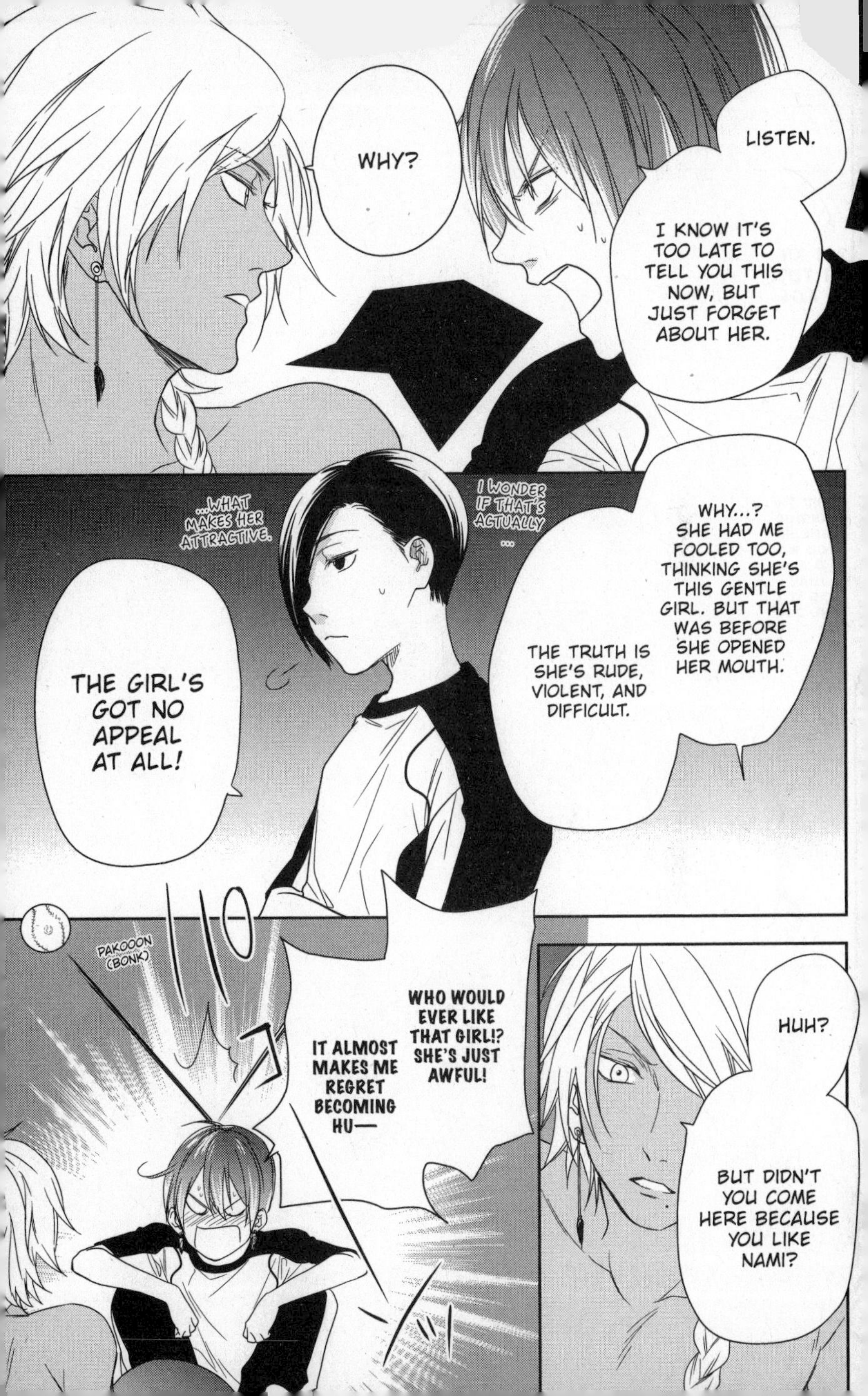
LISTEN.
I KNOW IT'S TOO LATE TO TELL YOU THIS NOW, BUT JUST FORGET ABOUT HER.
WHY?
WHY...? SHE HAD ME FOOLED TOO, THINKING SHE'S THIS GENTLE GIRL. BUT THAT WAS BEFORE SHE OPENED HER MOUTH.
THE TRUTH IS SHE'S RUDE, VIOLENT, AND DIFFICULT.
I WONDER IF THAT'S ACTUALLY...
...WHAT MAKES HER ATTRACTIVE.
THE GIRL'S GOT NO APPEAL AT ALL!
HUH?
BUT DIDN'T YOU COME HERE BECAUSE YOU LIKE NAMI?
WHO WOULD EVER LIKE THAT GIRL!? SHE'S JUST AWFUL!
IT ALMOST MAKES ME REGRET BECOMING HU—
PAKOOON (BONK)

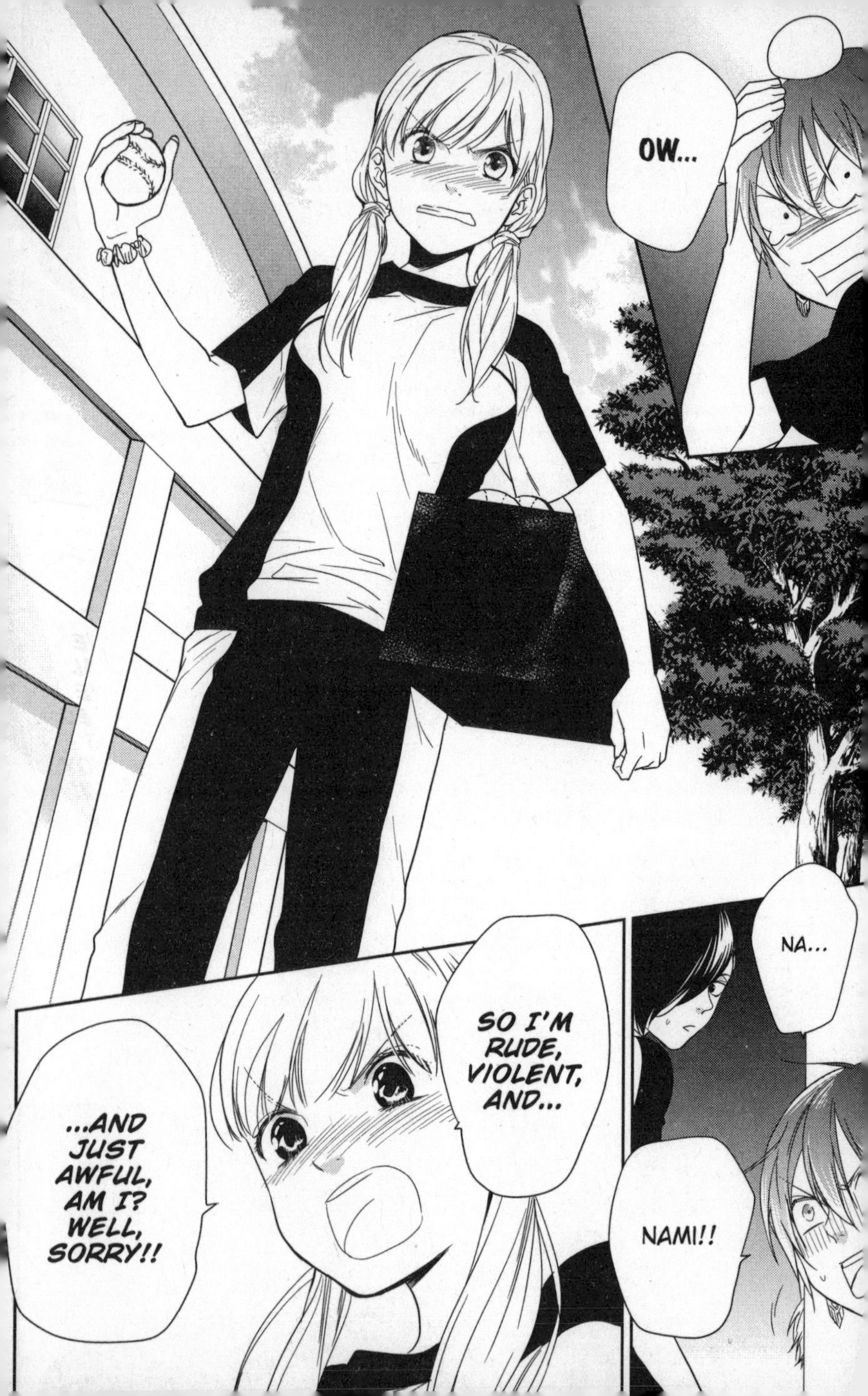
OW...
NA...
NAMI!!
SO I'M RUDE, VIOLENT, AND...
...AND JUST AWFUL, AM I? WELL, SORRY!!

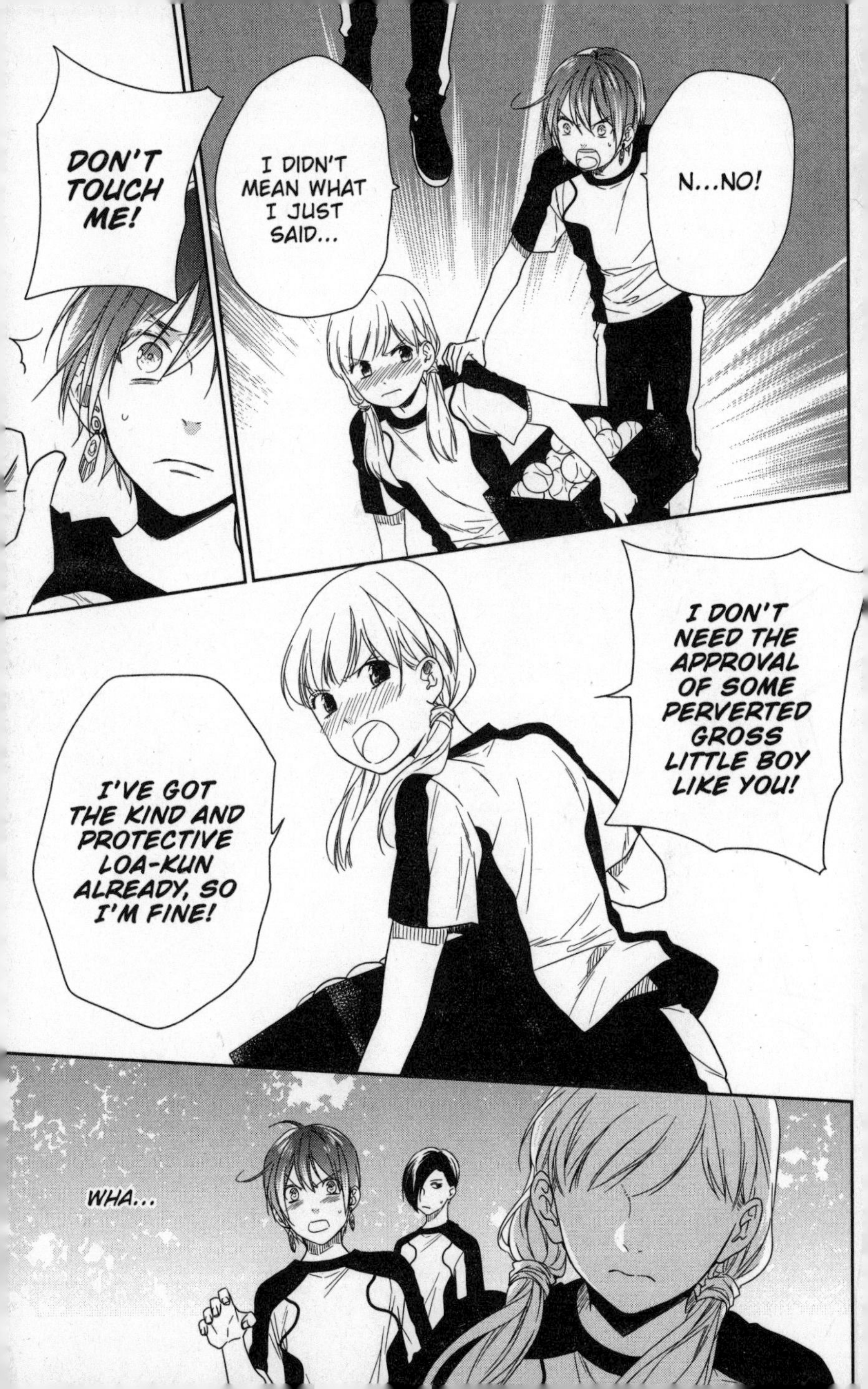
N...NO!
I DIDN'T MEAN WHAT I JUST SAID...
DON'T TOUCH ME!
I DON'T NEED THE APPROVAL OF SOME PERVERTED GROSS LITTLE BOY LIKE YOU!
I'VE GOT THE KIND AND PROTECTIVE LOA-KUN ALREADY, SO I'M FINE!
WHA...

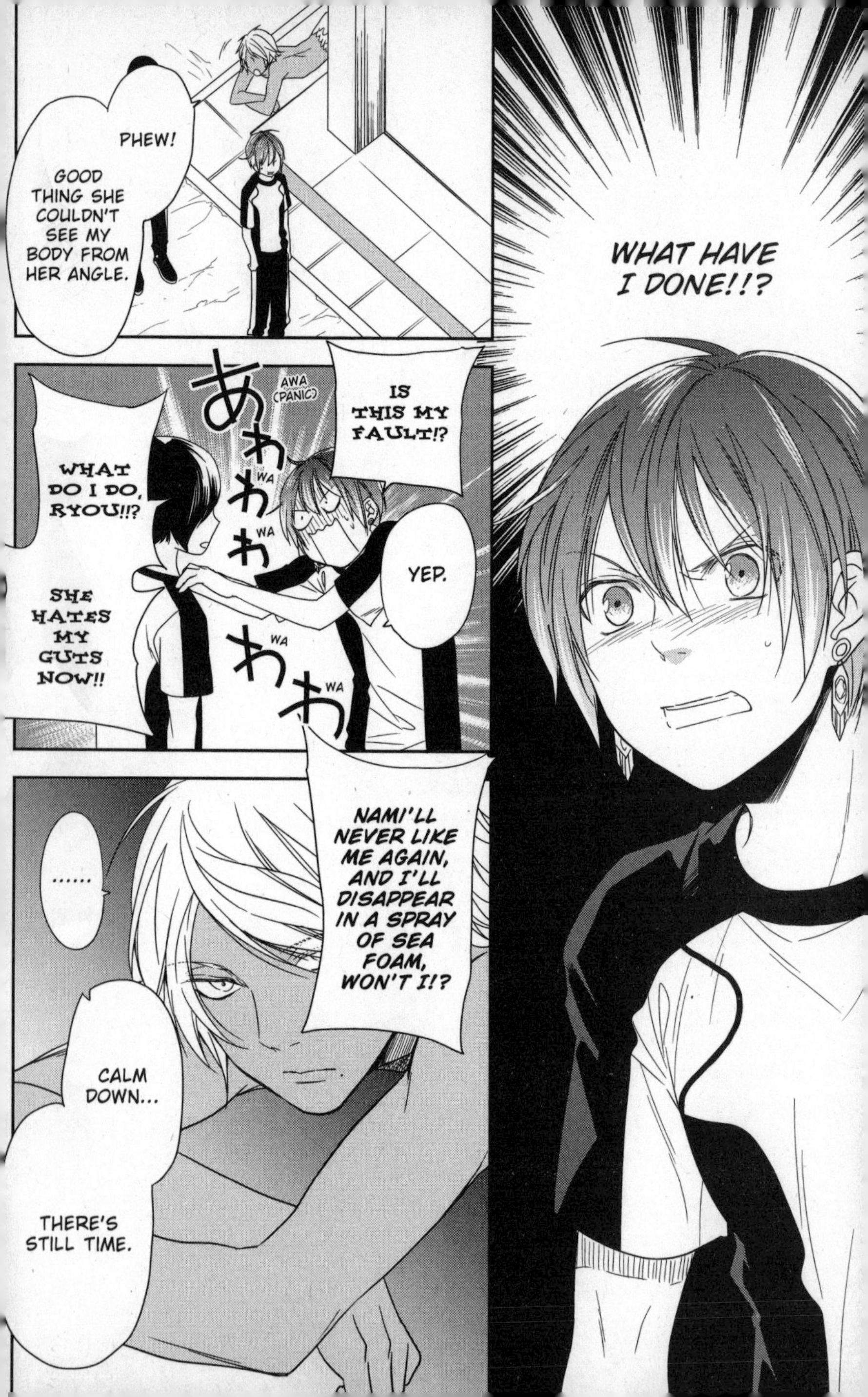
WHAT HAVE I DONE!!?
PHEW!
GOOD THING SHE COULDN'T SEE MY BODY FROM HER ANGLE.
IS THIS MY FAULT!?
あわわわわ
AWA (PANIC)
WA
WA
WA
WA
WHAT DO I DO, RYOU!!?
YEP.
SHE HATES MY GUTS NOW!!
NAMI'LL NEVER LIKE ME AGAIN, AND I'LL DISAPPEAR IN A SPRAY OF SEA FOAM, WON'T I!?
......
CALM DOWN...
THERE'S STILL TIME.

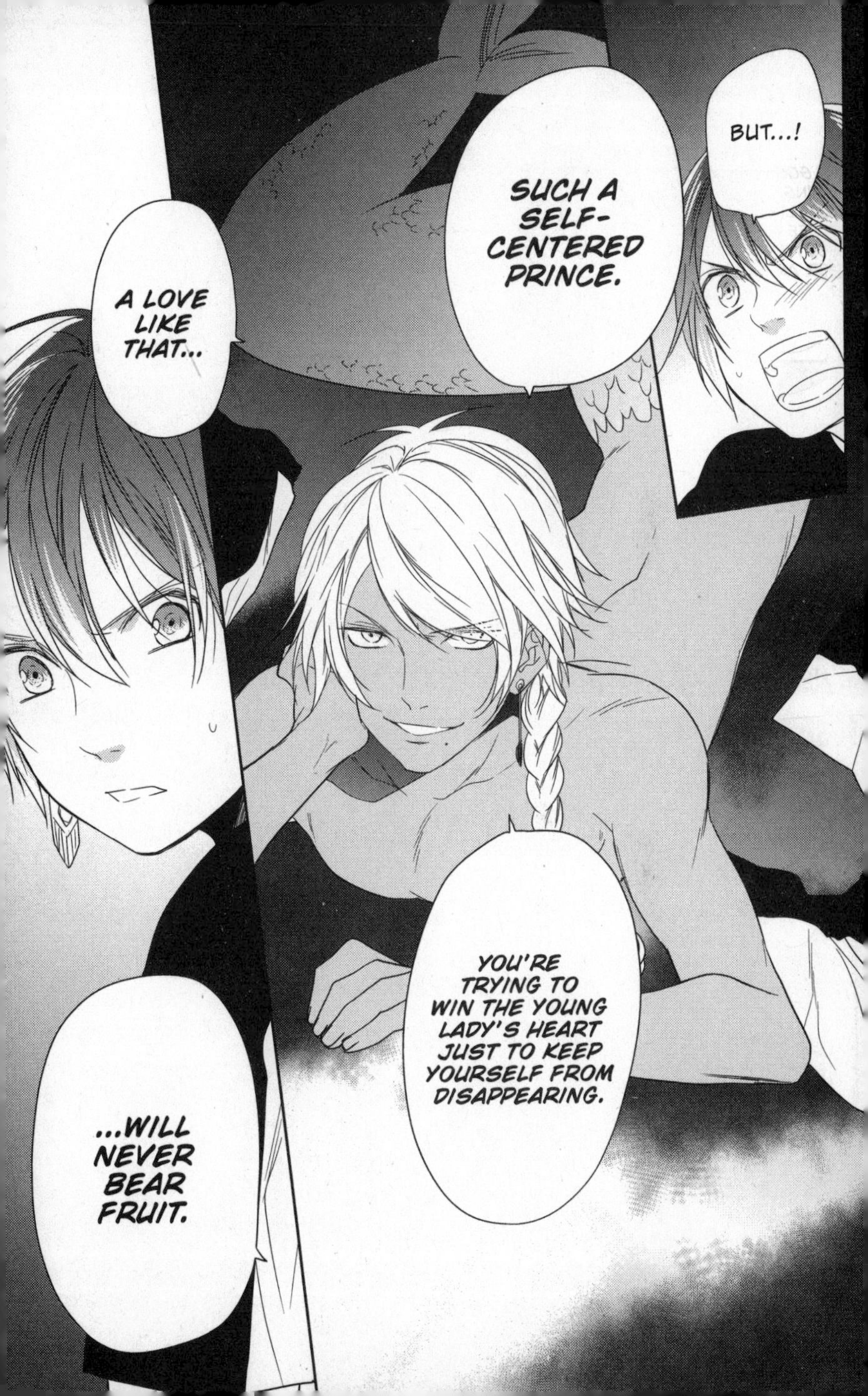
BUT...!
SUCH A SELF-CENTERED PRINCE.
A LOVE LIKE THAT...
YOU'RE TRYING TO WIN THE YOUNG LADY'S HEART JUST TO KEEP YOURSELF FROM DISAPPEARING.
...WILL NEVER BEAR FRUIT.

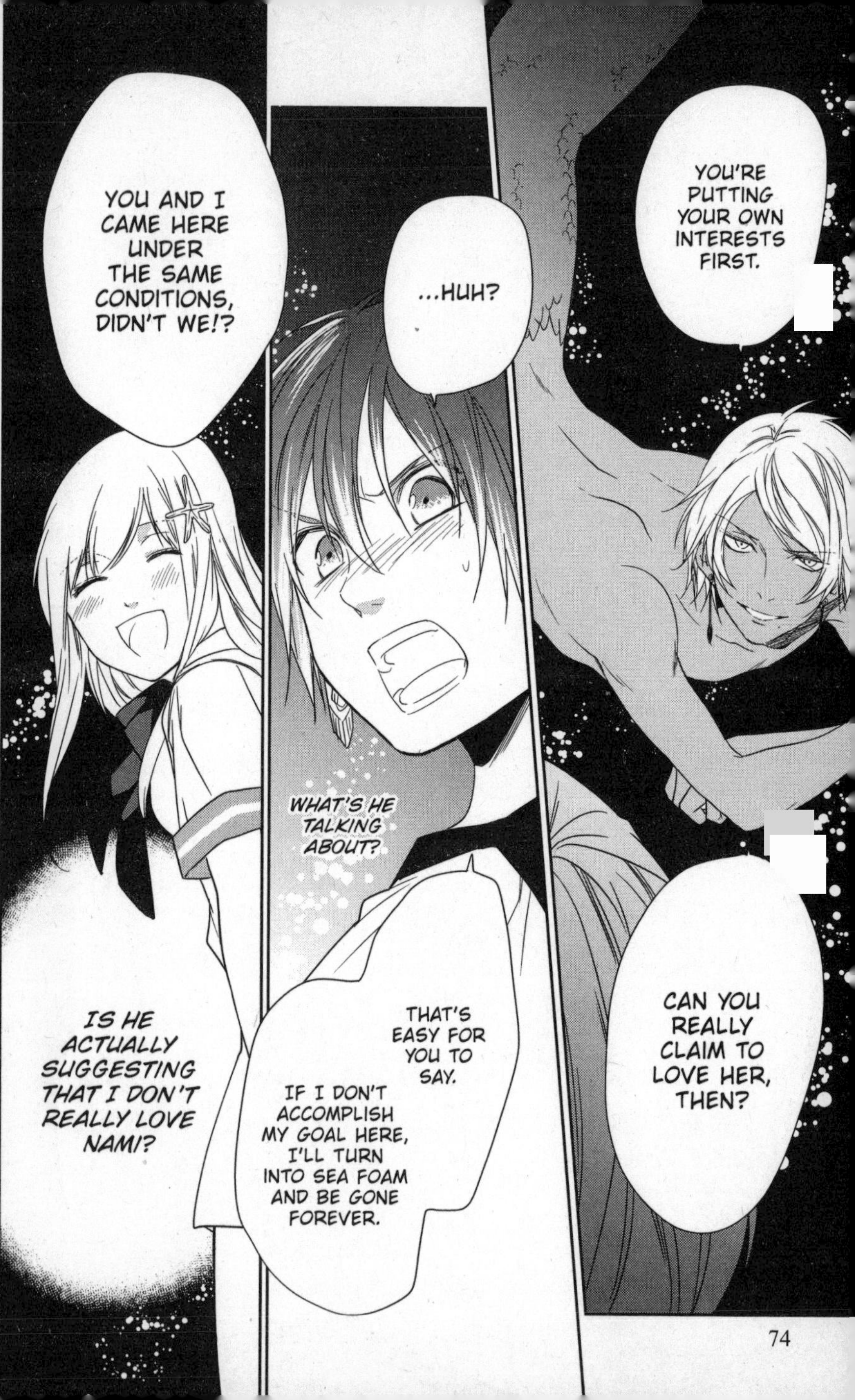
YOU'RE PUTTING YOUR OWN INTERESTS FIRST.
CAN YOU REALLY CLAIM TO LOVE HER, THEN?
...HUH?
WHAT'S HE TALKING ABOUT?
THAT'S EASY FOR YOU TO SAY.
IF I DON'T ACCOMPLISH MY GOAL HERE, I'LL TURN INTO SEA FOAM AND BE GONE FOREVER.
YOU AND I CAME HERE UNDER THE SAME CONDITIONS, DIDN'T WE!?
IS HE ACTUALLY SUGGESTING THAT I DON'T REALLY LOVE NAMI?

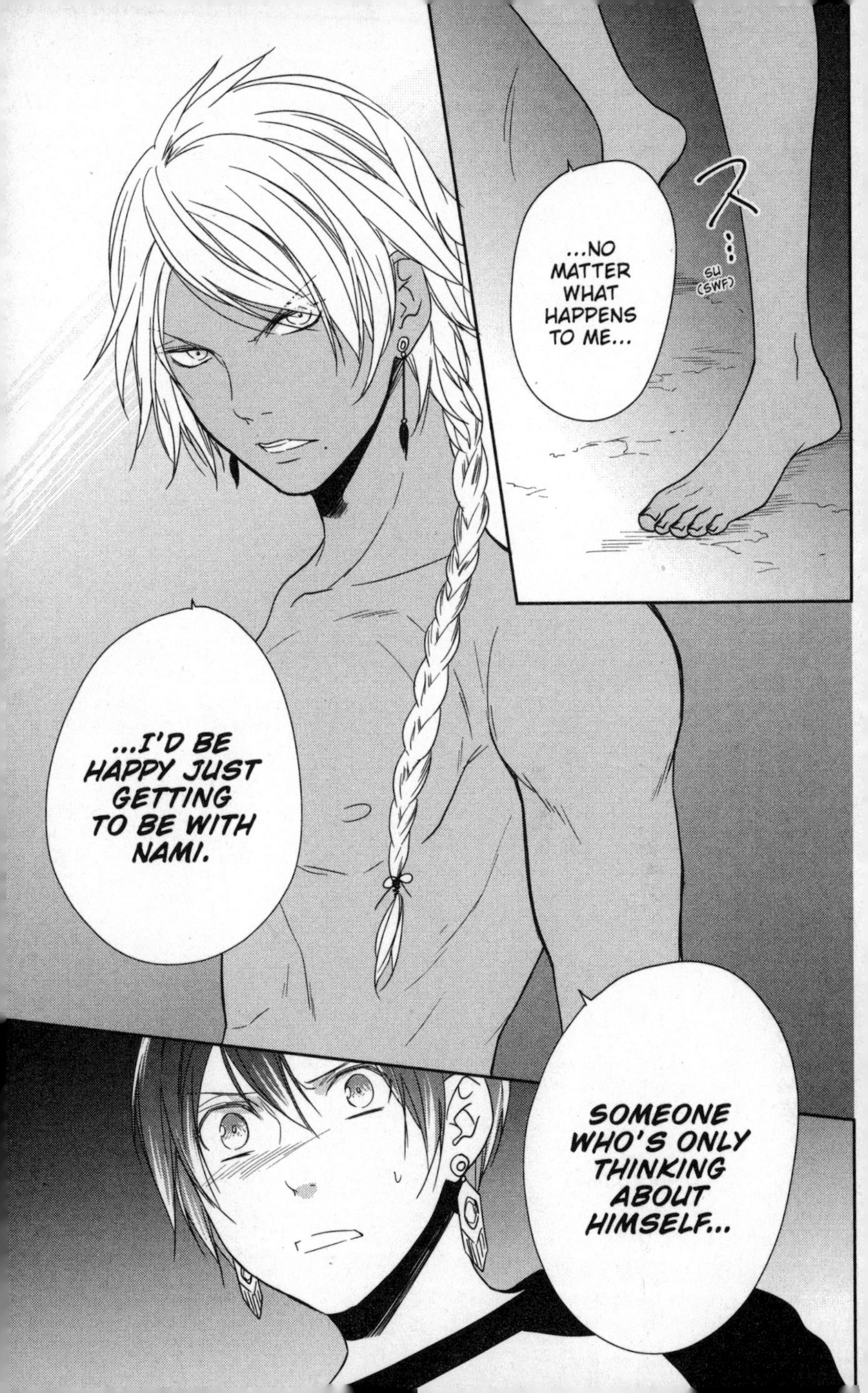

ス…
SU (SWF)
...NO MATTER WHAT HAPPENS TO ME...
...I'D BE HAPPY JUST GETTING TO BE WITH NAMI.
SOMEONE WHO'S ONLY THINKING ABOUT HIMSELF...

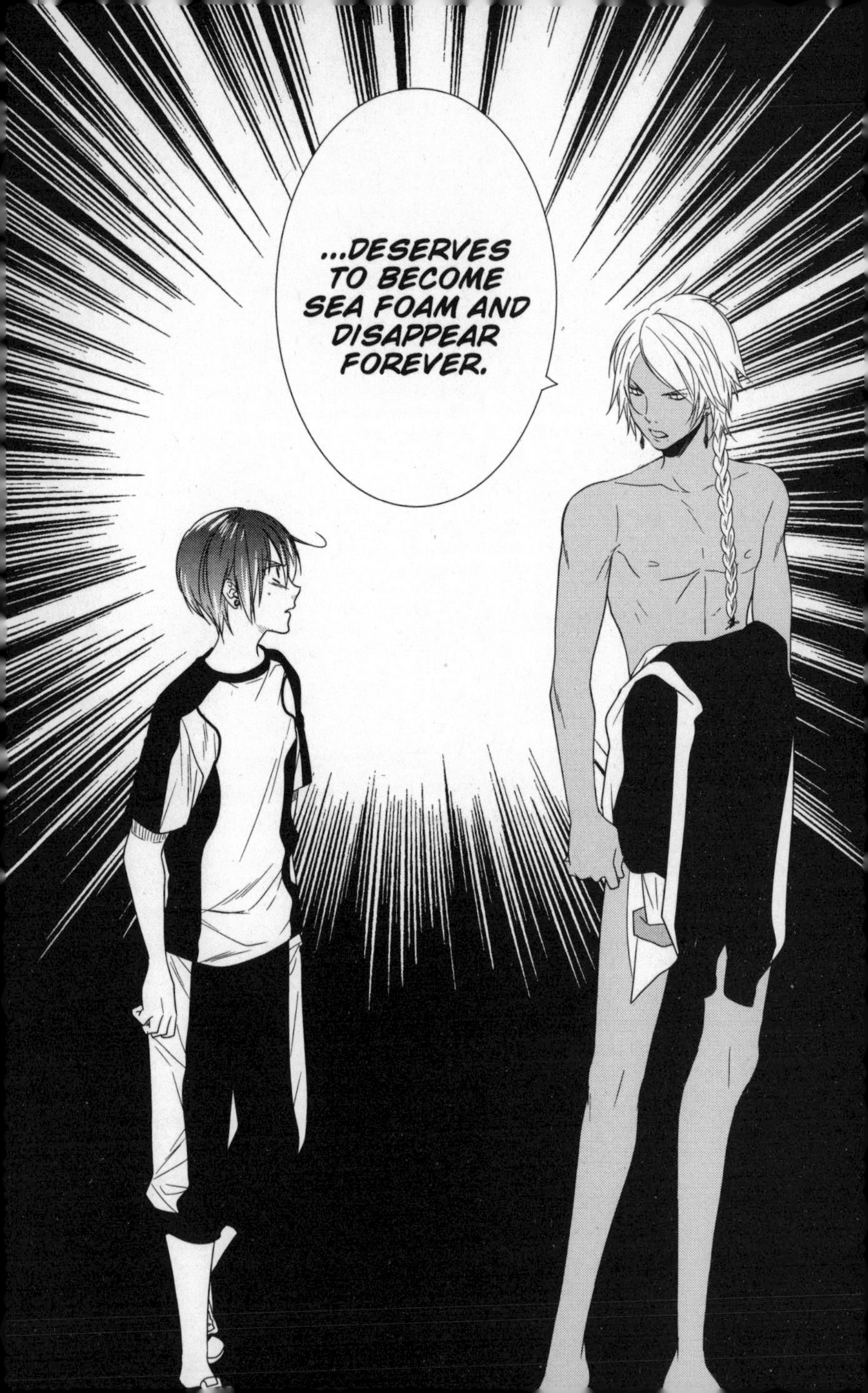
...DESERVES TO BECOME SEA FOAM AND DISAPPEAR FOREVER.

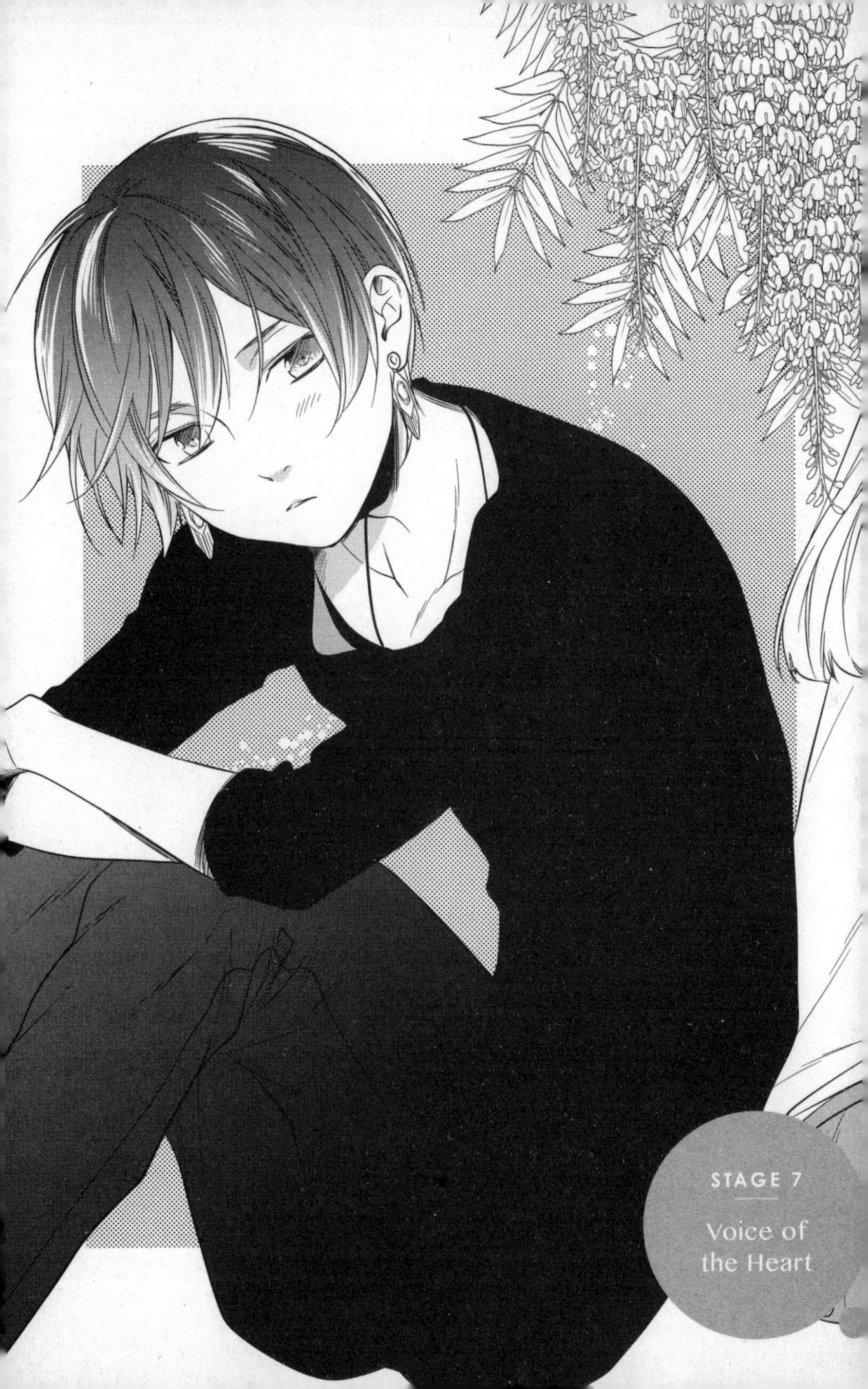
STAGE 7
Voice of the Heart

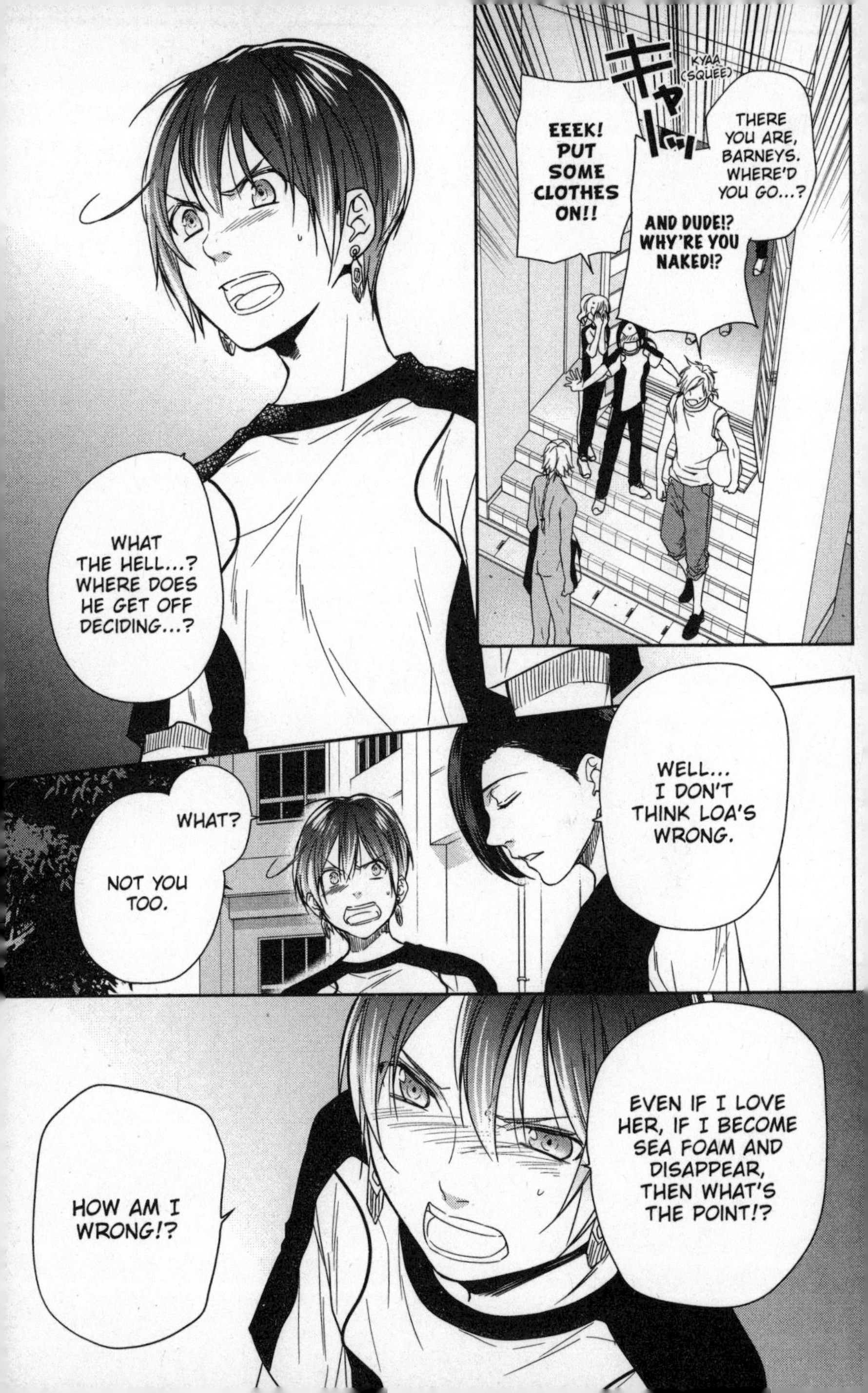
キャーッ
KYAA (SQUEE)
THERE YOU ARE, BARNEYS. WHERE'D YOU GO...?
AND DUDE!? WHY'RE YOU NAKED!?
EEEK! PUT SOME CLOTHES ON!!
WHAT THE HELL...? WHERE DOES HE GET OFF DECIDING...?
WELL... I DON'T THINK LOA'S WRONG.
WHAT?
NOT YOU TOO.
EVEN IF I LOVE HER, IF I BECOME SEA FOAM AND DISAPPEAR, THEN WHAT'S THE POINT!?
HOW AM I WRONG!?

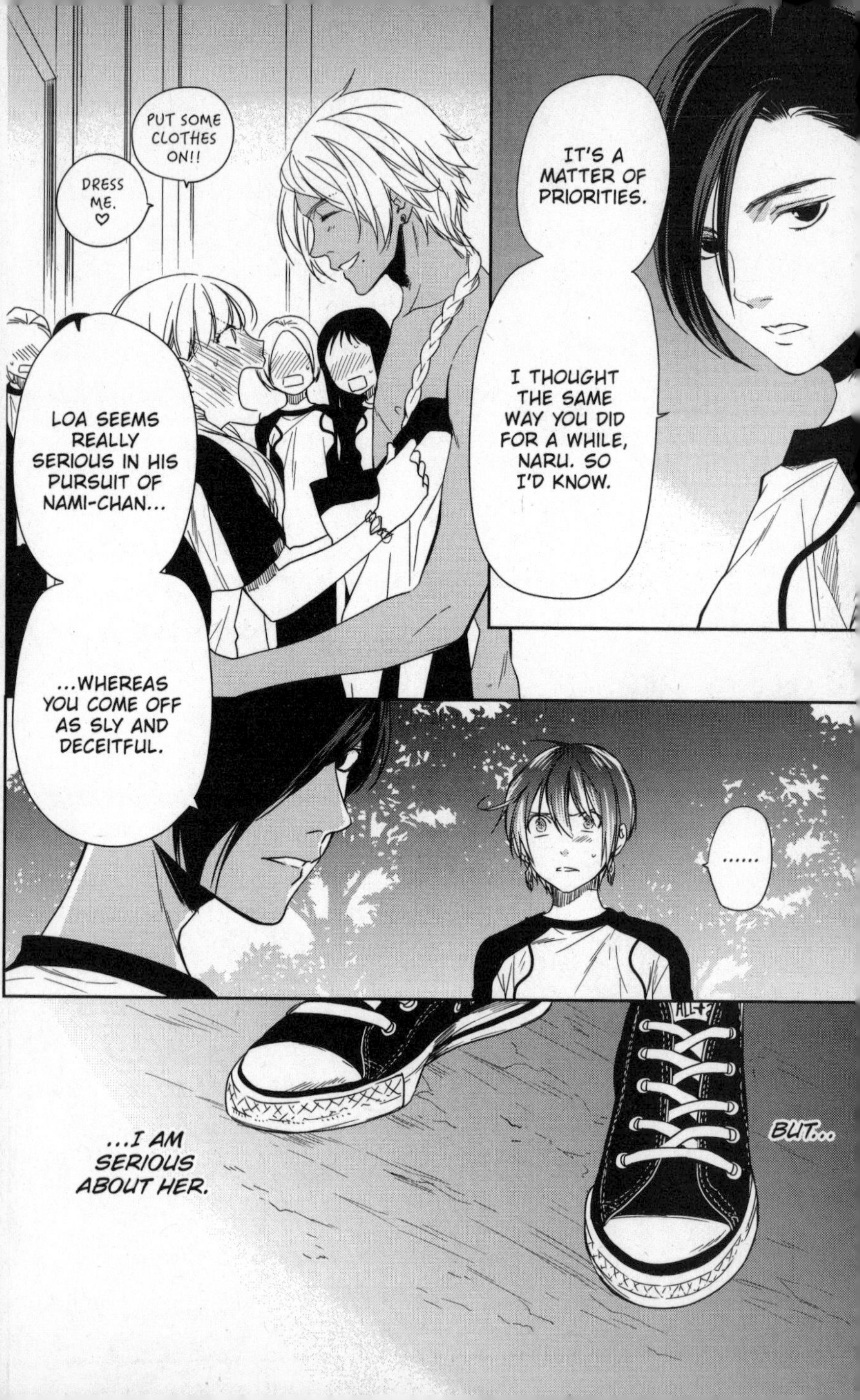
IT'S A MATTER OF PRIORITIES.
I THOUGHT THE SAME WAY YOU DID FOR A WHILE, NARU. SO I'D KNOW.
PUT SOME CLOTHES ON!!
DRESS ME. ♡
LOA SEEMS REALLY SERIOUS IN HIS PURSUIT OF NAMI-CHAN...
...WHEREAS YOU COME OFF AS SLY AND DECEITFUL.
......
BUT...
...I AM SERIOUS ABOUT HER.

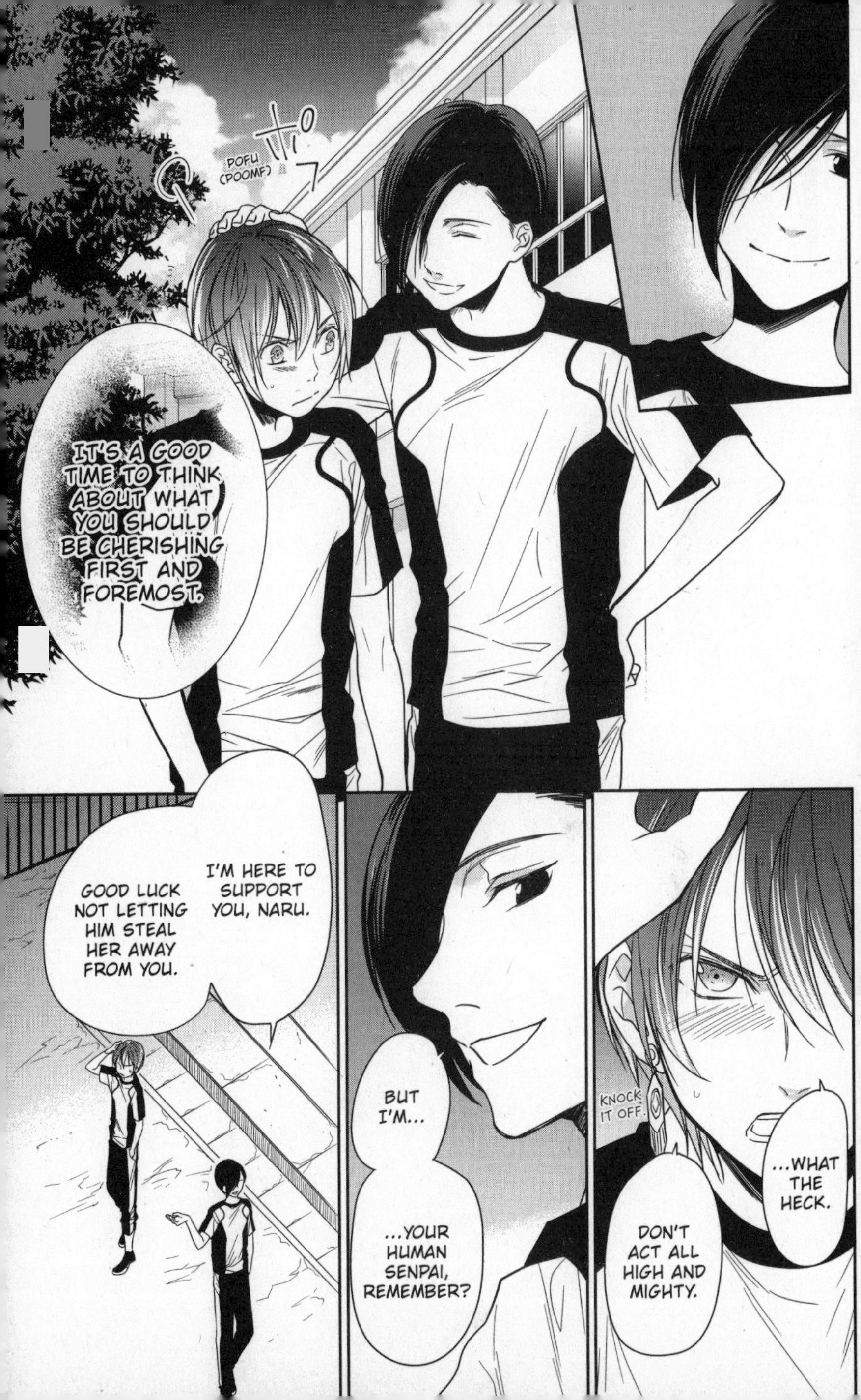
POFU (POOMF)
IT'S A GOOD TIME TO THINK ABOUT WHAT YOU SHOULD BE CHERISHING FIRST AND FOREMOST.
...WHAT THE HECK.
DON'T ACT ALL HIGH AND MIGHTY.
KNOCK IT OFF.
BUT I'M...
...YOUR HUMAN SENPAI, REMEMBER?
I'M HERE TO SUPPORT YOU, NARU.
GOOD LUCK NOT LETTING HIM STEAL HER AWAY FROM YOU.

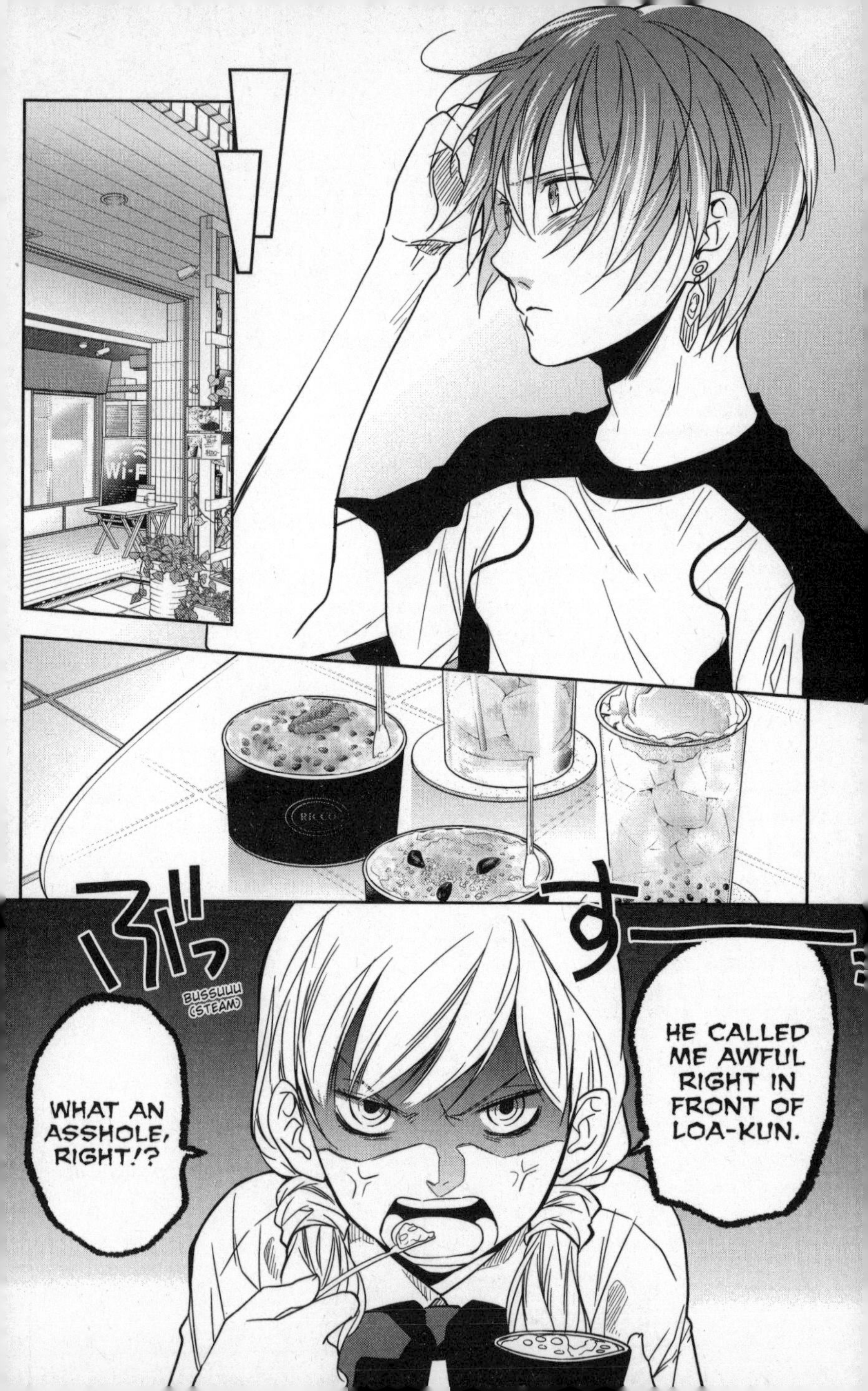

BUSSUUU (STEAM)
HE CALLED ME AWFUL RIGHT IN FRONT OF LOA-KUN.
WHAT AN ASSHOLE, RIGHT!?

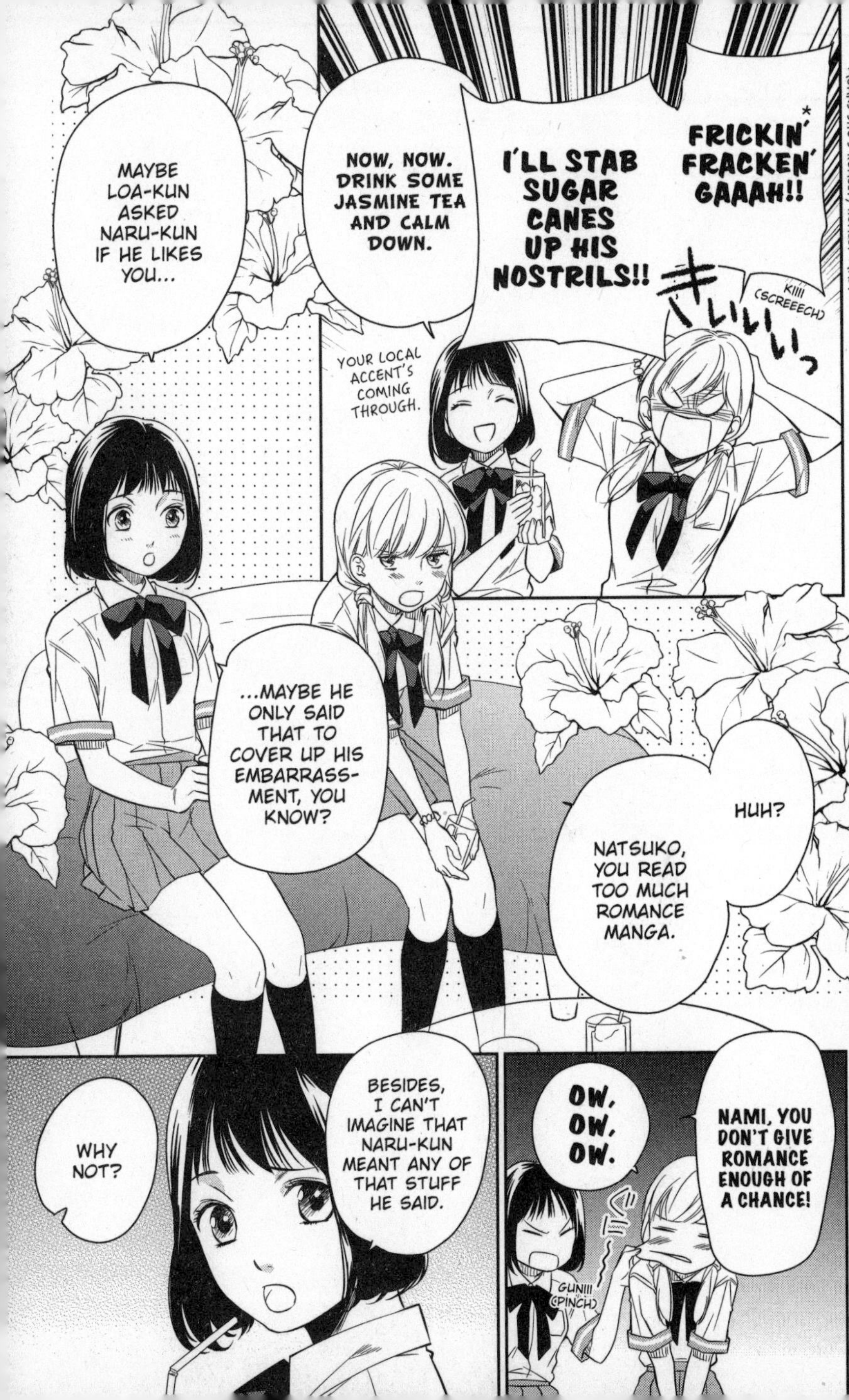
FRICKIN' FRACKEN' GAAAH!!*
I'LL STAB SUGAR CANES UP HIS NOSTRILS!!
NOW, NOW. DRINK SOME JASMINE TEA AND CALM DOWN.
KIIII (SCREEECH)
YOUR LOCAL ACCENT'S COMING THROUGH.
MAYBE LOA-KUN ASKED NARU-KUN IF HE LIKES YOU...
...MAYBE HE ONLY SAID THAT TO COVER UP HIS EMBARRASS-MENT, YOU KNOW?
HUH?
NATSUKO, YOU READ TOO MUCH ROMANCE MANGA.
NAMI, YOU DON'T GIVE ROMANCE ENOUGH OF A CHANCE!
OW, OW, OW.
GUNIII (PINCH)
BESIDES, I CAN'T IMAGINE THAT NARU-KUN MEANT ANY OF THAT STUFF HE SAID.
WHY NOT?

*MEANS SHE'S REALLY, REALLY MAD.

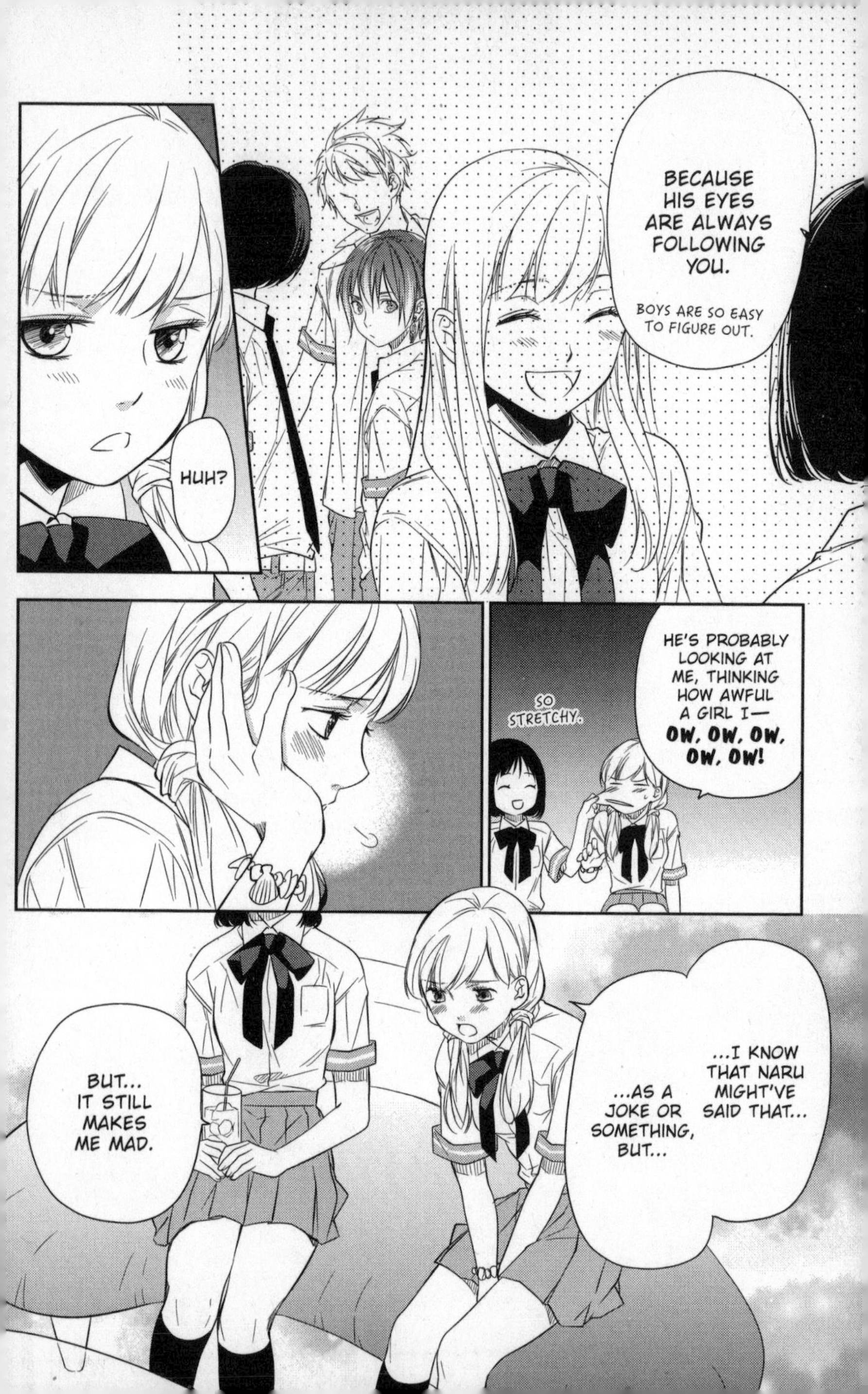
BECAUSE HIS EYES ARE ALWAYS FOLLOWING YOU.
BOYS ARE SO EASY TO FIGURE OUT.
HUH?
HE'S PROBABLY LOOKING AT ME, THINKING HOW AWFUL A GIRL I— OW, OW, OW, OW, OW!
SO STRETCHY.
...I KNOW THAT NARU MIGHT'VE SAID THAT...
...AS A JOKE OR SOMETHING, BUT...
BUT... IT STILL MAKES ME MAD.

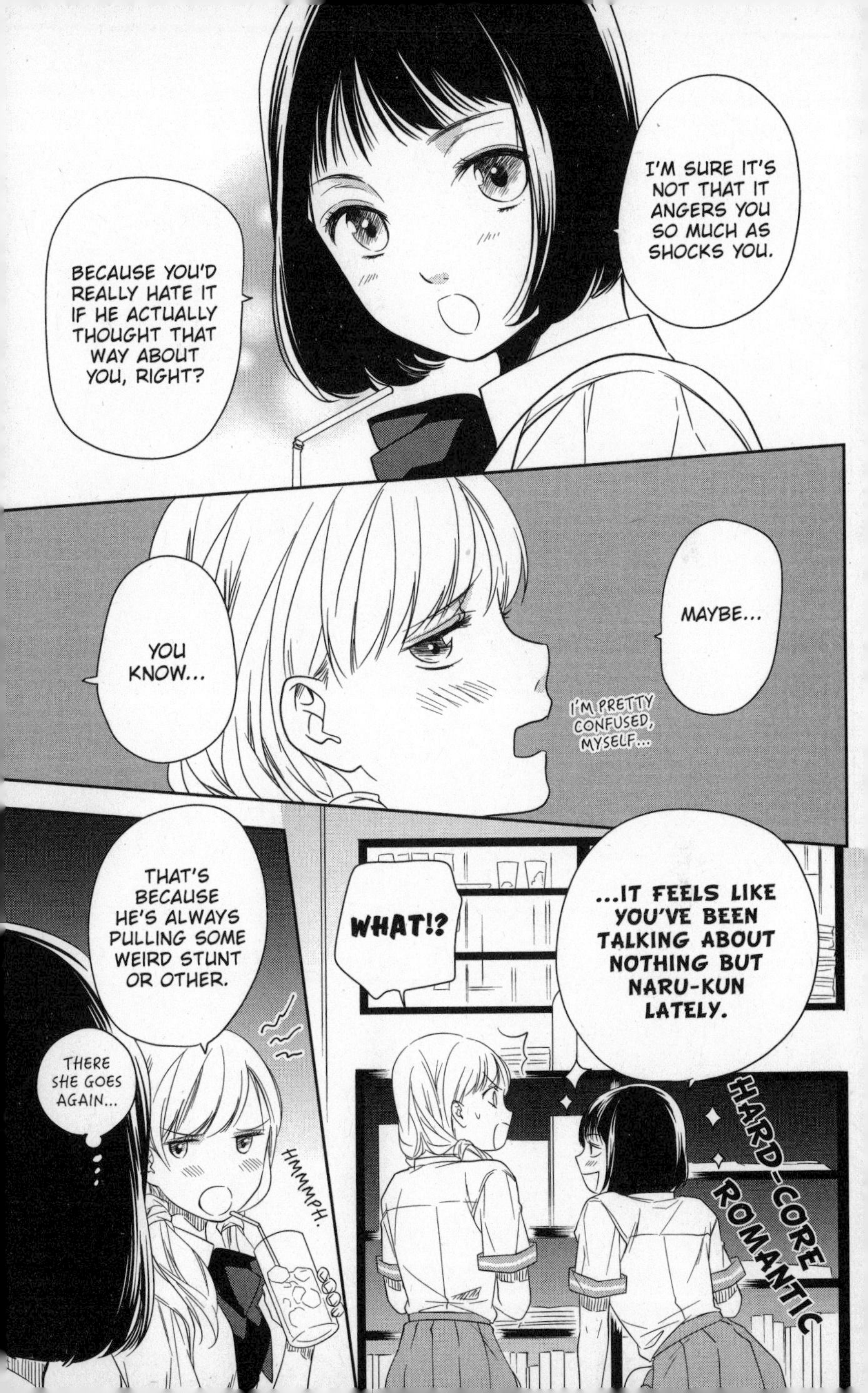
I'M SURE IT'S NOT THAT IT ANGERS YOU SO MUCH AS SHOCKS YOU.
BECAUSE YOU'D REALLY HATE IT IF HE ACTUALLY THOUGHT THAT WAY ABOUT YOU, RIGHT?
MAYBE...
I'M PRETTY CONFUSED, MYSELF...
YOU KNOW...
...IT FEELS LIKE YOU'VE BEEN TALKING ABOUT NOTHING BUT NARU-KUN LATELY.
WHAT!?
HARD-CORE ROMANTIC
THAT'S BECAUSE HE'S ALWAYS PULLING SOME WEIRD STUNT OR OTHER.
HMMMPH.
THERE SHE GOES AGAIN...

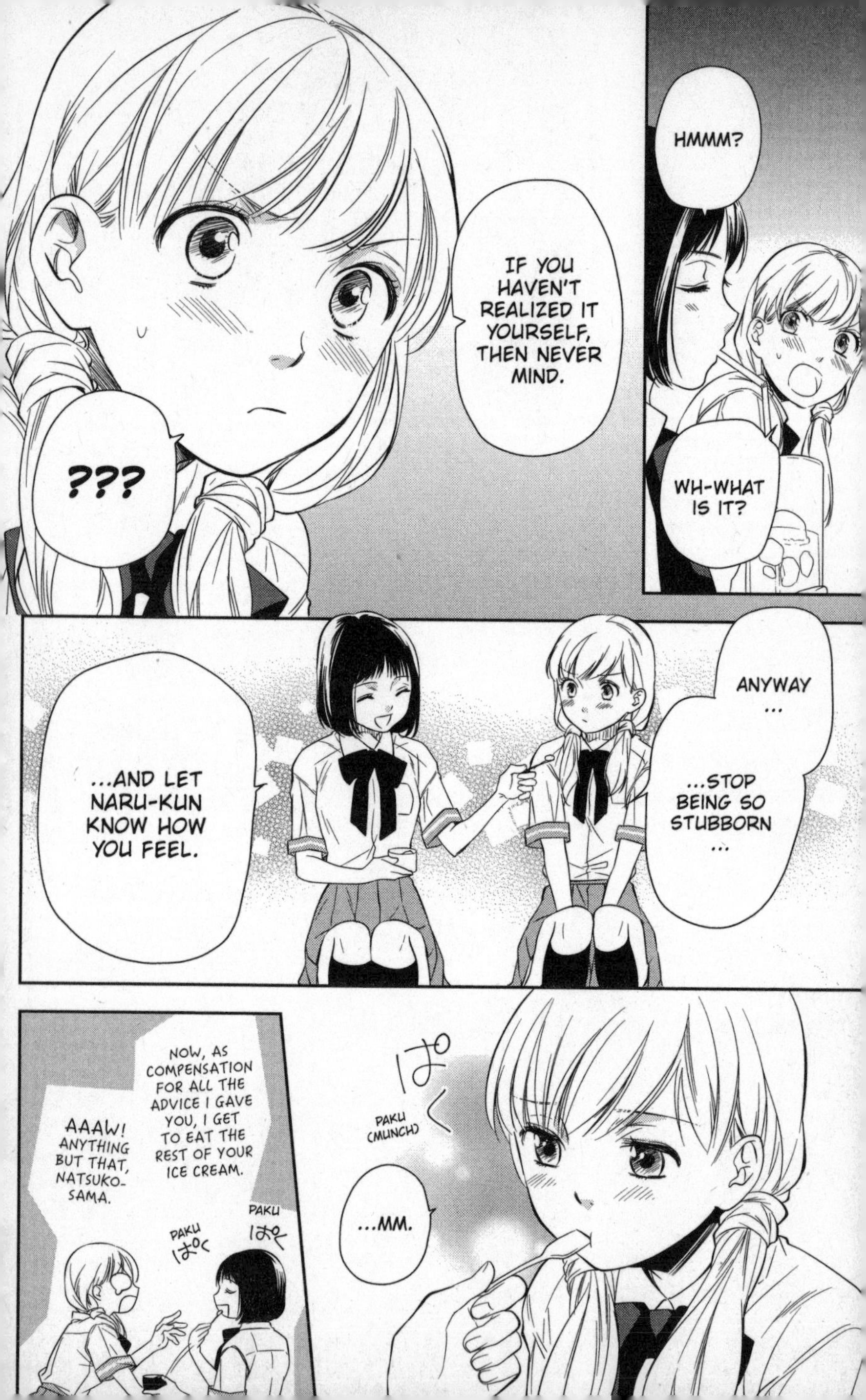
HMMM?
WH-WHAT IS IT?
IF YOU HAVEN'T REALIZED IT YOURSELF, THEN NEVER MIND.
???
ANYWAY ...
...STOP BEING SO STUBBORN ...
...AND LET NARU-KUN KNOW HOW YOU FEEL.
ぱく
PAKU (MUNCH)
...MM.
NOW, AS COMPENSATION FOR ALL THE ADVICE I GAVE YOU, I GET TO EAT THE REST OF YOUR ICE CREAM.
AAAW! ANYTHING BUT THAT, NATSUKO-SAMA.
PAKU ぱく
PAKU ぱく

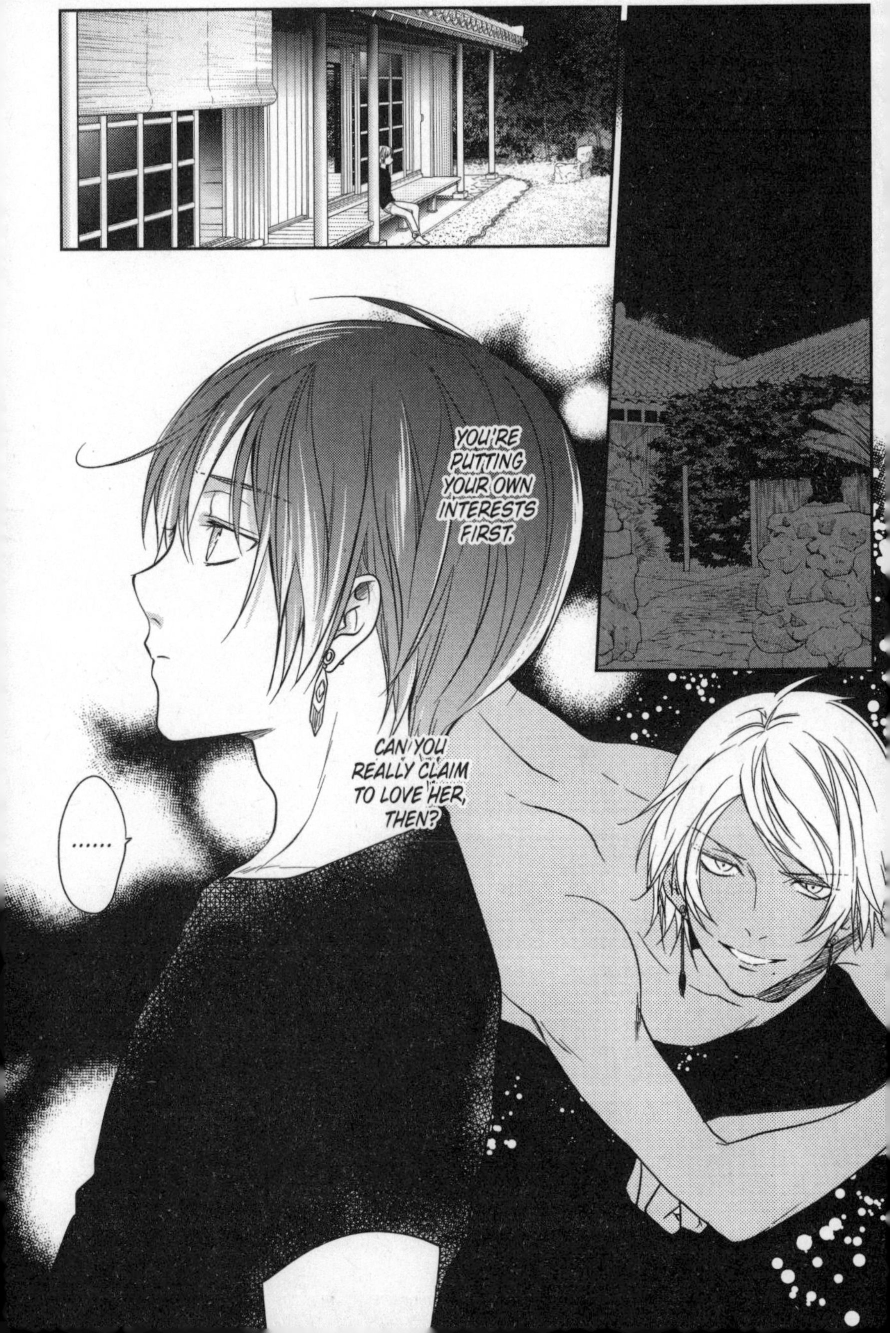
YOU'RE PUTTING YOUR OWN INTERESTS FIRST.
CAN YOU REALLY CLAIM TO LOVE HER, THEN?
......

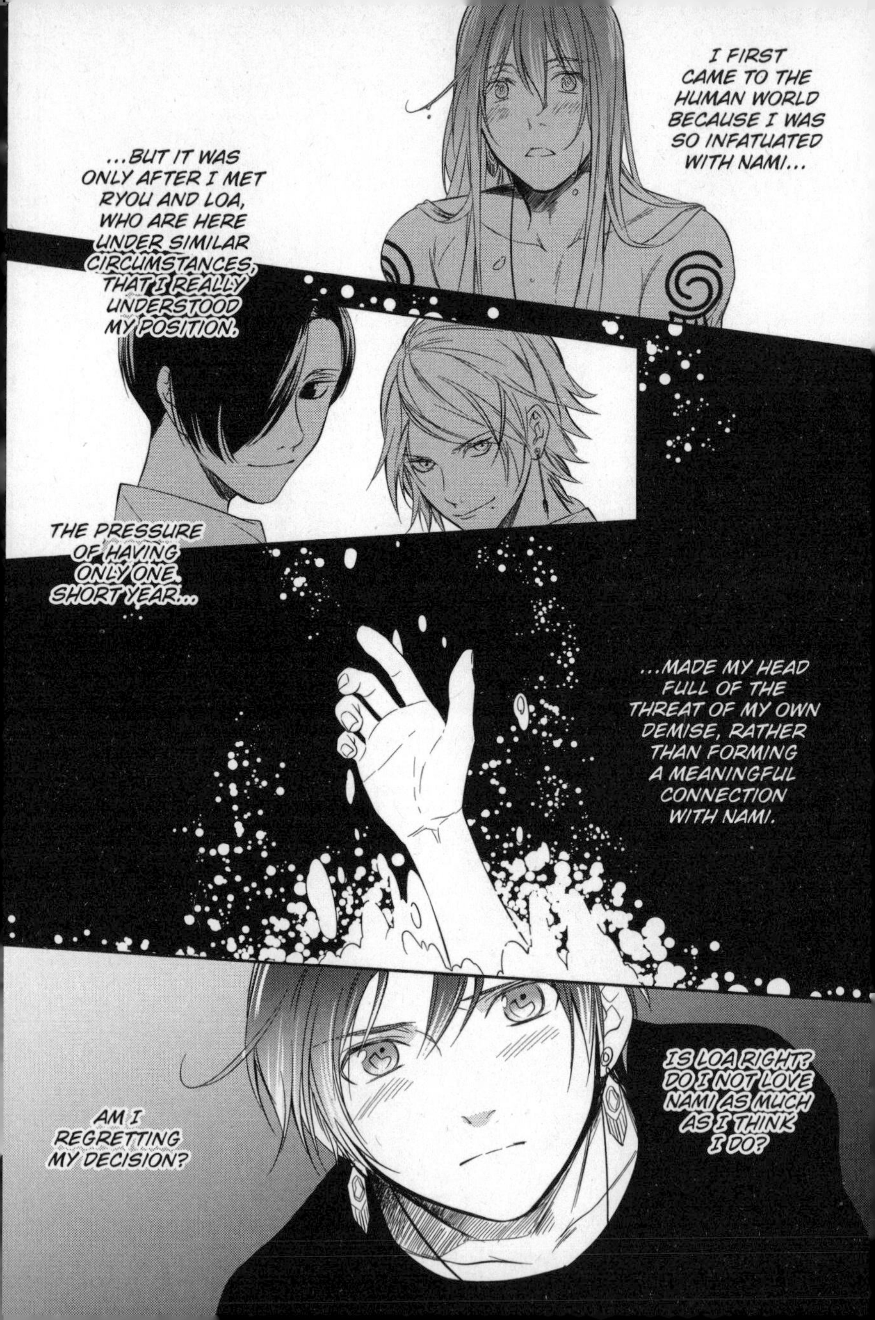
I FIRST CAME TO THE HUMAN WORLD BECAUSE I WAS SO INFATUATED WITH NAMI...
...BUT IT WAS ONLY AFTER I MET RYOU AND LOA, WHO ARE HERE UNDER SIMILAR CIRCUMSTANCES, THAT I REALLY UNDERSTOOD MY POSITION.
THE PRESSURE OF HAVING ONLY ONE SHORT YEAR...
...MADE MY HEAD FULL OF THE THREAT OF MY OWN DEMISE, RATHER THAN FORMING A MEANINGFUL CONNECTION WITH NAMI.
IS LOA RIGHT? DO I NOT LOVE NAMI AS MUCH AS I THINK I DO?
AM I REGRETTING MY DECISION?

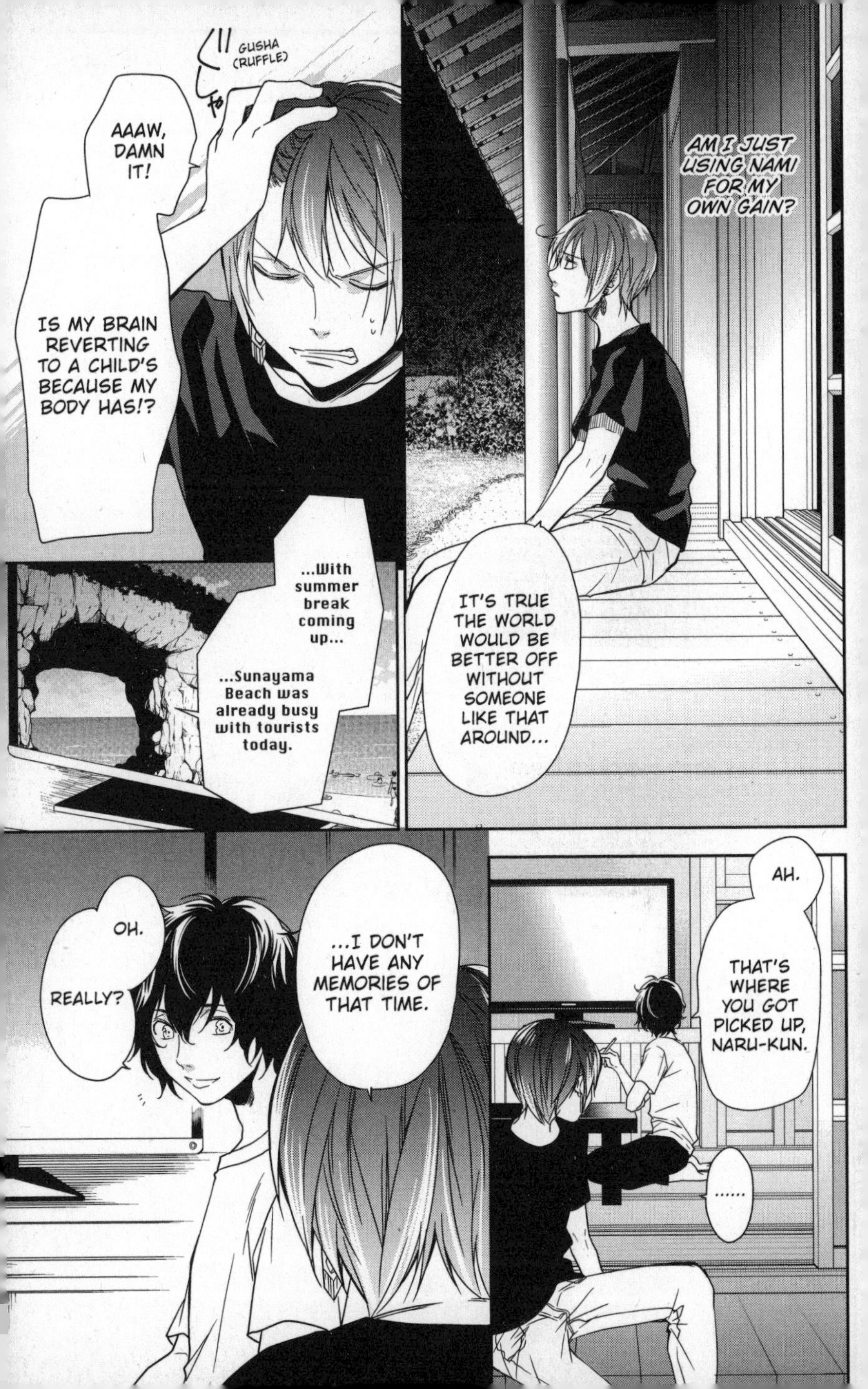
AM I JUST USING NAMI FOR MY OWN GAIN?
IT'S TRUE THE WORLD WOULD BE BETTER OFF WITHOUT SOMEONE LIKE THAT AROUND...
GUSHA (RUFFLE)
AAAW, DAMN IT!
IS MY BRAIN REVERTING TO A CHILD'S BECAUSE MY BODY HAS!?
...With summer break coming up...
...Sunayama Beach was already busy with tourists today.
AH.
THAT'S WHERE YOU GOT PICKED UP, NARU-KUN.
......
...I DON'T HAVE ANY MEMORIES OF THAT TIME.
OH.
REALLY?

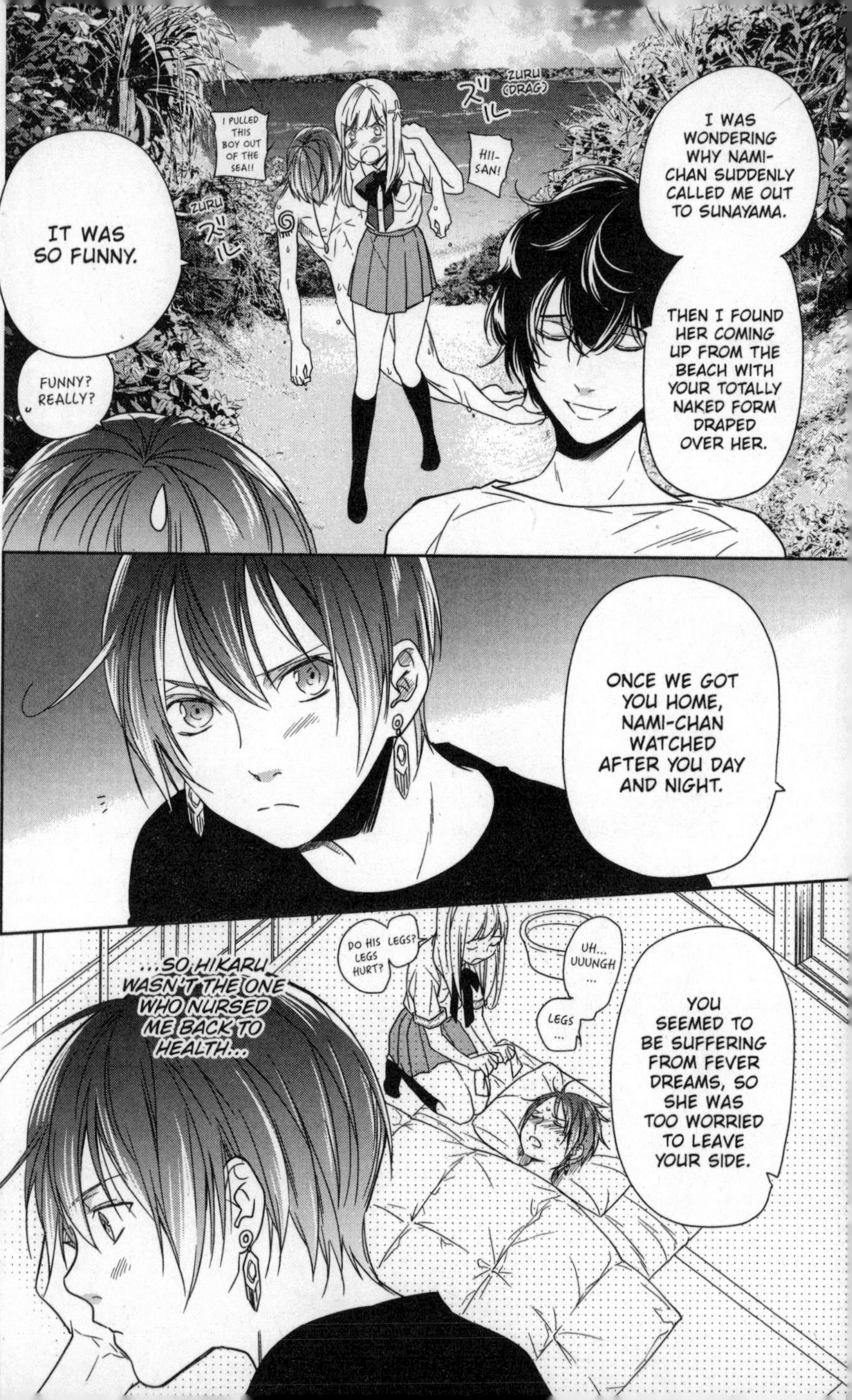
I WAS WONDERING WHY NAMI-CHAN SUDDENLY CALLED ME OUT TO SUNAYAMA.
ZURU (DRAG)
HII-SAN!
I PULLED THIS BOY OUT OF THE SEA!!
ZURU
THEN I FOUND HER COMING UP FROM THE BEACH WITH YOUR TOTALLY NAKED FORM DRAPED OVER HER.
IT WAS SO FUNNY.
FUNNY? REALLY?
ONCE WE GOT YOU HOME, NAMI-CHAN WATCHED AFTER YOU DAY AND NIGHT.
YOU SEEMED TO BE SUFFERING FROM FEVER DREAMS, SO SHE WAS TOO WORRIED TO LEAVE YOUR SIDE.
UH... UUUNGH ...
LEGS ...
LEGS?
DO HIS LEGS HURT?
...SO HIKARU WASN'T THE ONE WHO NURSED ME BACK TO HEALTH...

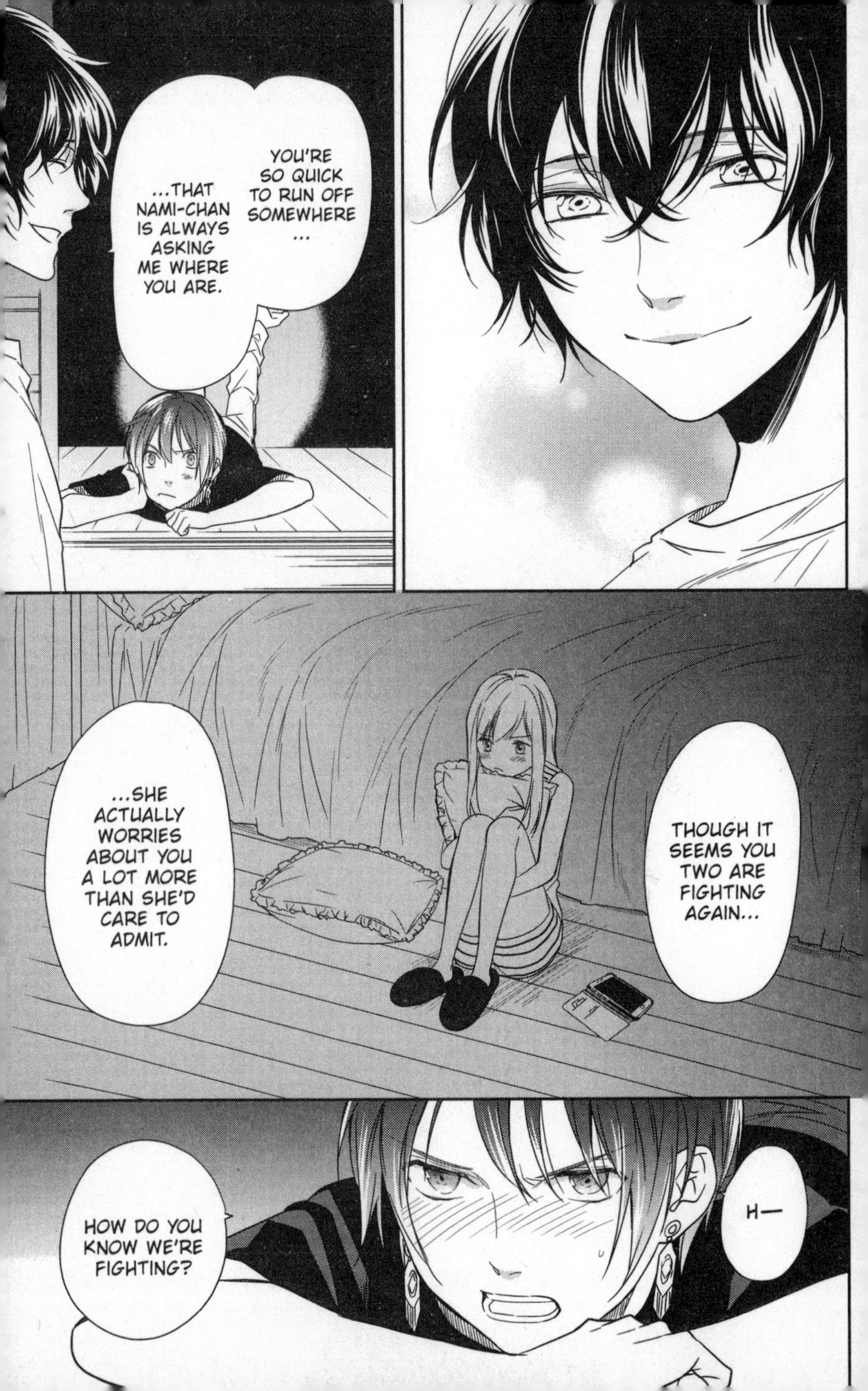
YOU'RE SO QUICK TO RUN OFF SOMEWHERE ...
...THAT NAMI-CHAN IS ALWAYS ASKING ME WHERE YOU ARE.
THOUGH IT SEEMS YOU TWO ARE FIGHTING AGAIN...
...SHE ACTUALLY WORRIES ABOUT YOU A LOT MORE THAN SHE'D CARE TO ADMIT.
H—
HOW DO YOU KNOW WE'RE FIGHTING?

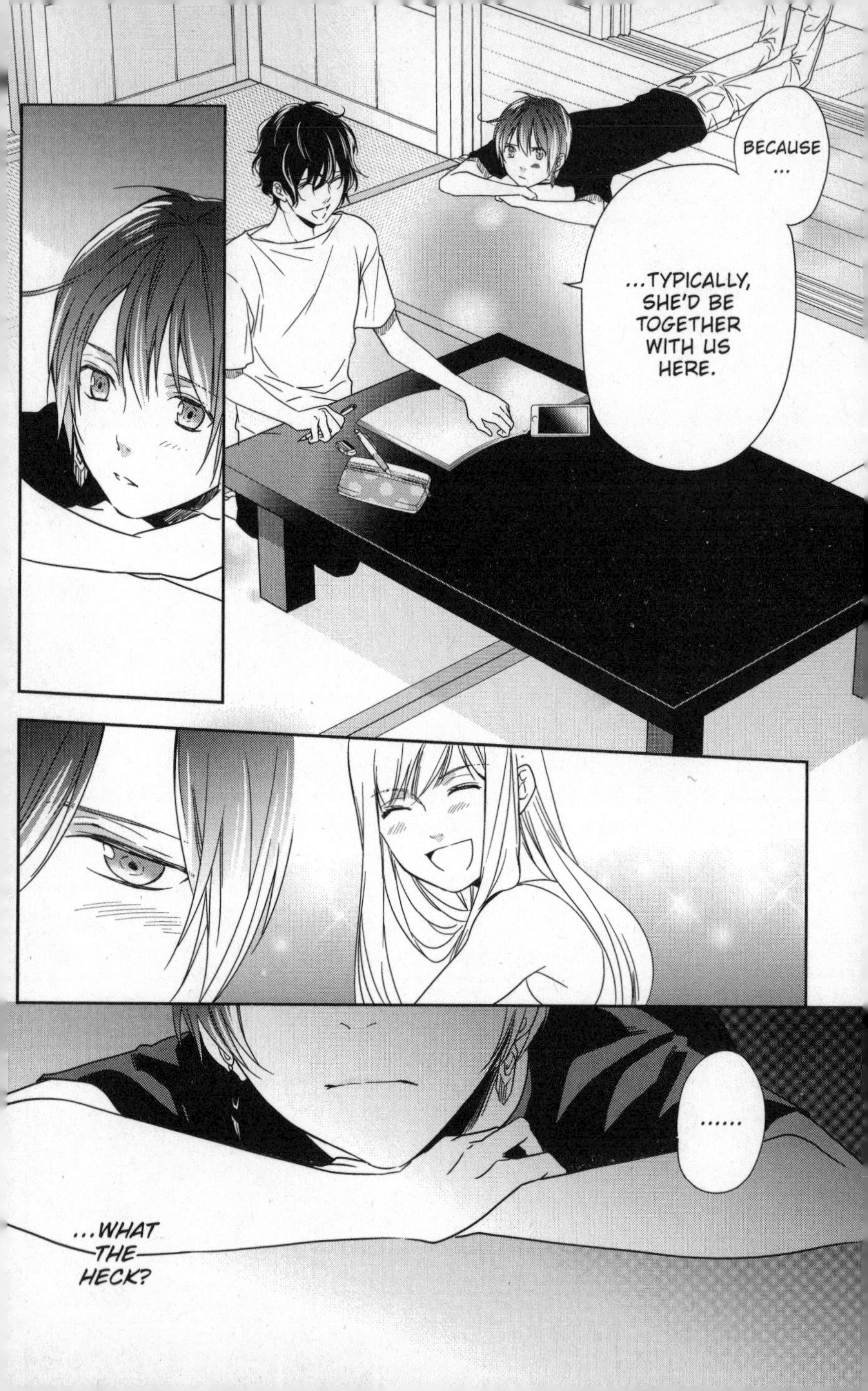
BECAUSE ...
...TYPICALLY, SHE'D BE TOGETHER WITH US HERE.
......
...WHAT THE HECK?

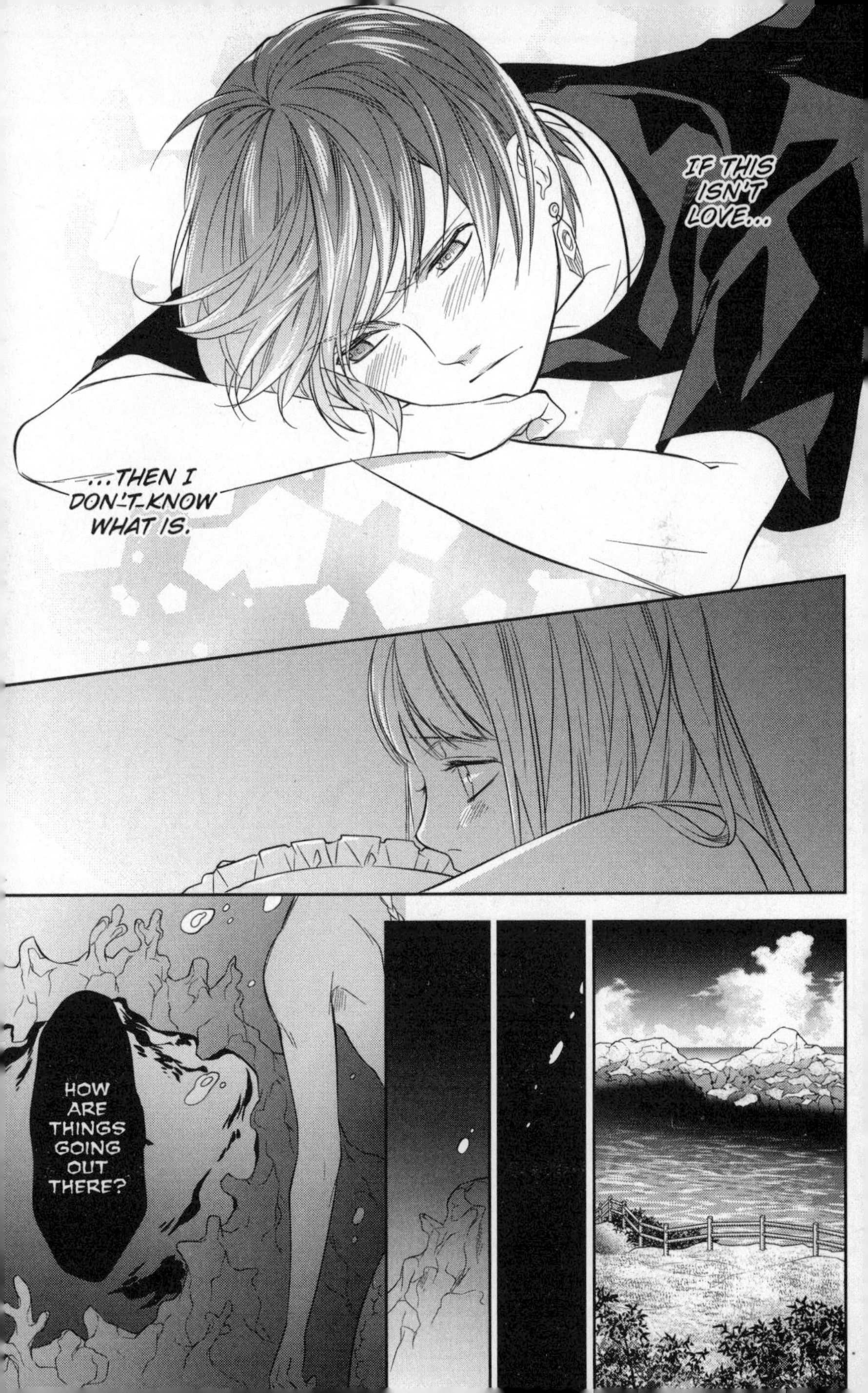
IF THIS ISN'T LOVE...
...THEN I DON'T KNOW WHAT IS.
HOW ARE THINGS GOING OUT THERE?

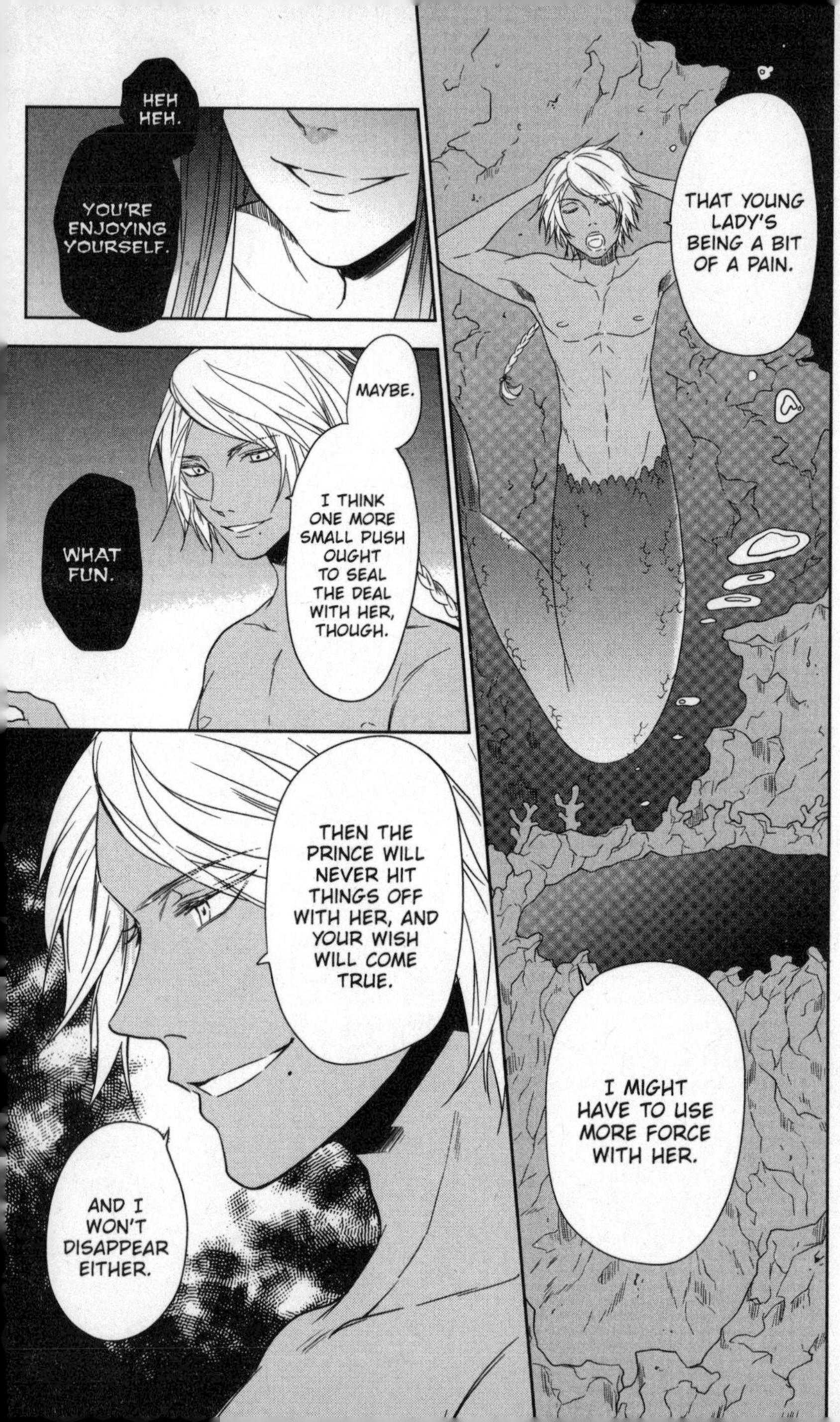
THAT YOUNG LADY'S BEING A BIT OF A PAIN.
I MIGHT HAVE TO USE MORE FORCE WITH HER.
HEH HEH.
YOU'RE ENJOYING YOURSELF.
MAYBE.
I THINK ONE MORE SMALL PUSH OUGHT TO SEAL THE DEAL WITH HER, THOUGH.
WHAT FUN.
THEN THE PRINCE WILL NEVER HIT THINGS OFF WITH HER, AND YOUR WISH WILL COME TRUE.
AND I WON'T DISAPPEAR EITHER.

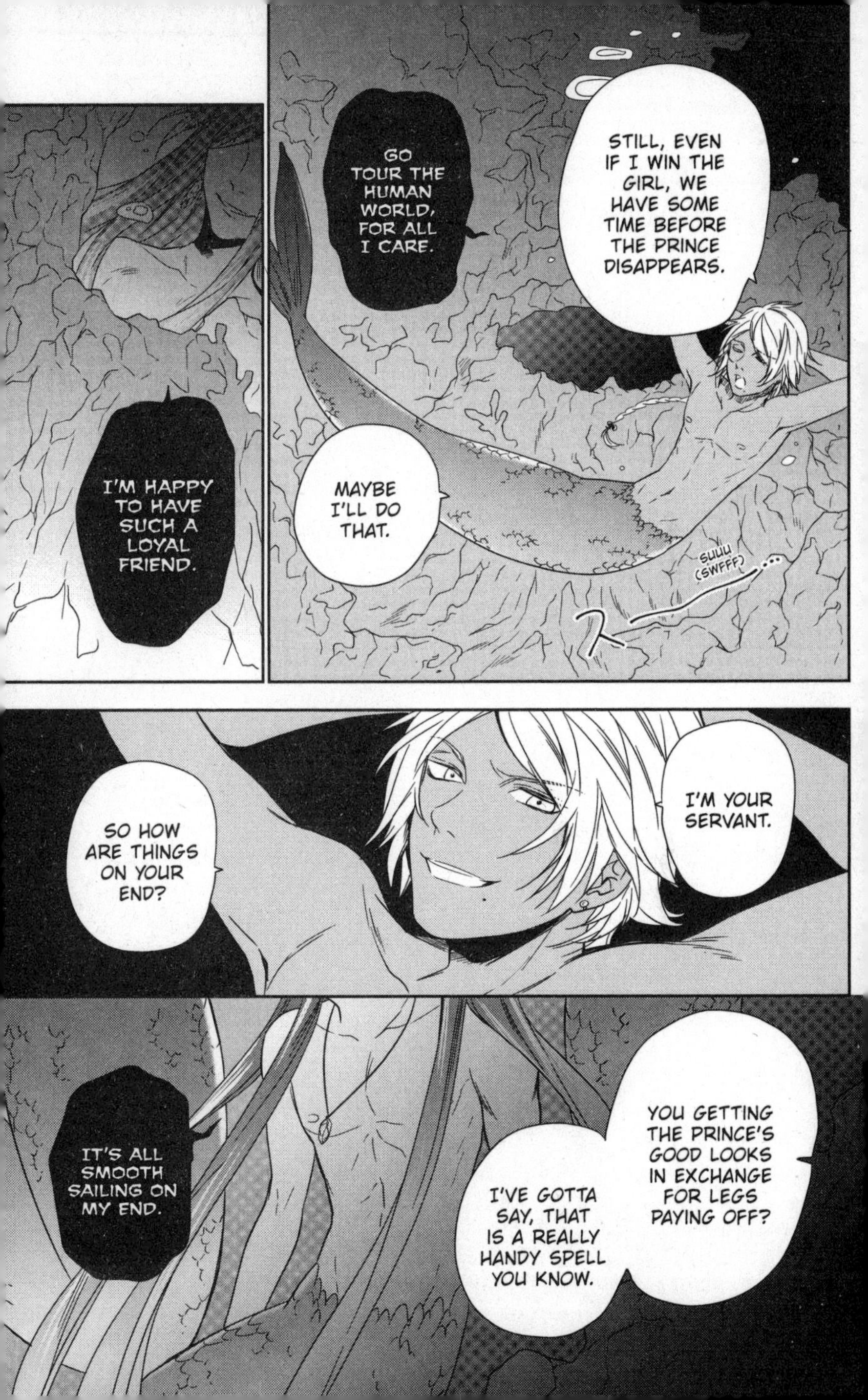
STILL, EVEN IF I WIN THE GIRL, WE HAVE SOME TIME BEFORE THE PRINCE DISAPPEARS.
GO TOUR THE HUMAN WORLD, FOR ALL I CARE.
MAYBE I'LL DO THAT.
suuu (SWFFF)...
I'M HAPPY TO HAVE SUCH A LOYAL FRIEND.
I'M YOUR SERVANT.
SO HOW ARE THINGS ON YOUR END?
YOU GETTING THE PRINCE'S GOOD LOOKS IN EXCHANGE FOR LEGS PAYING OFF?
I'VE GOTTA SAY, THAT IS A REALLY HANDY SPELL YOU KNOW.
IT'S ALL SMOOTH SAILING ON MY END.

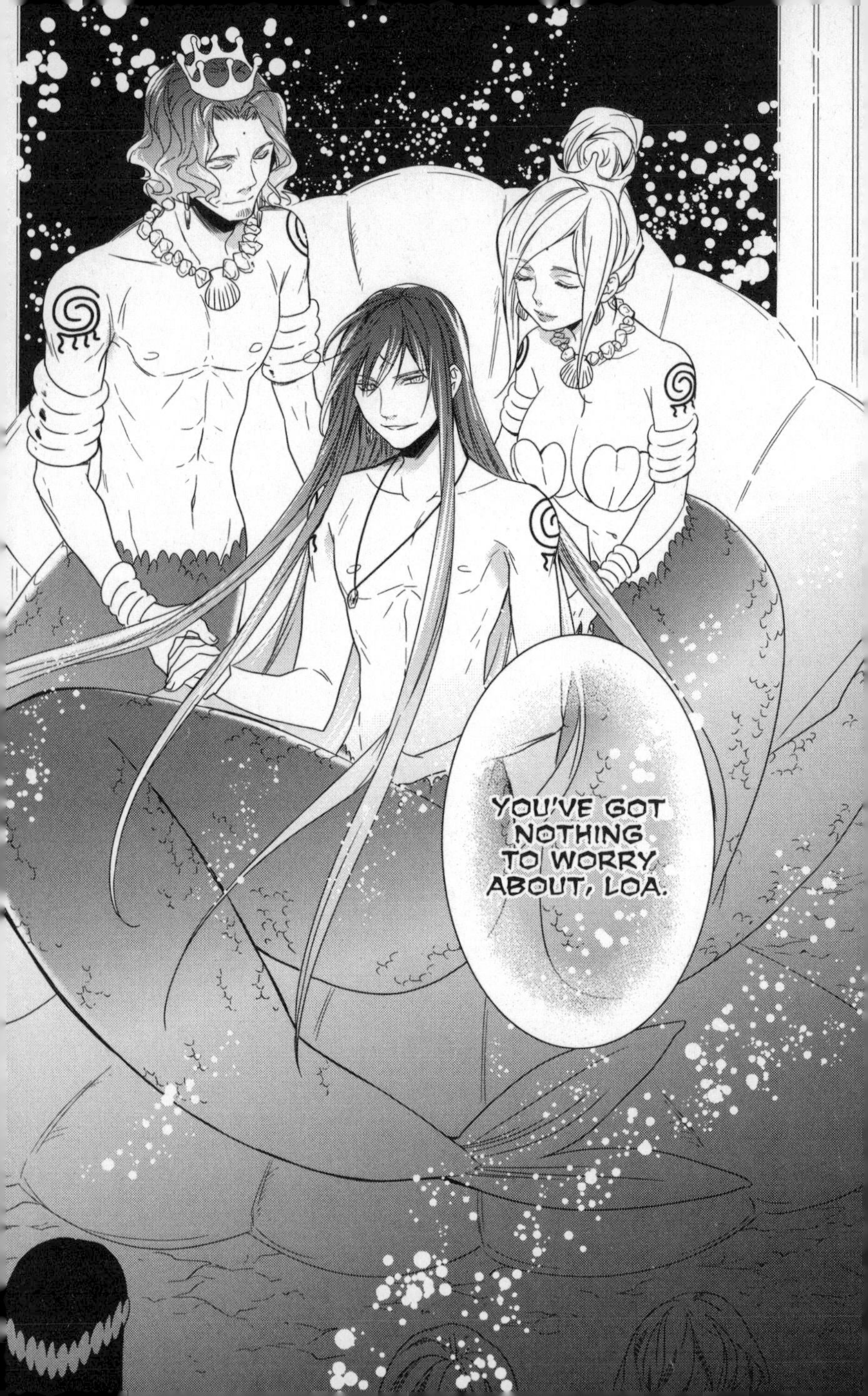
YOU'VE GOT NOTHING TO WORRY ABOUT, LOA.

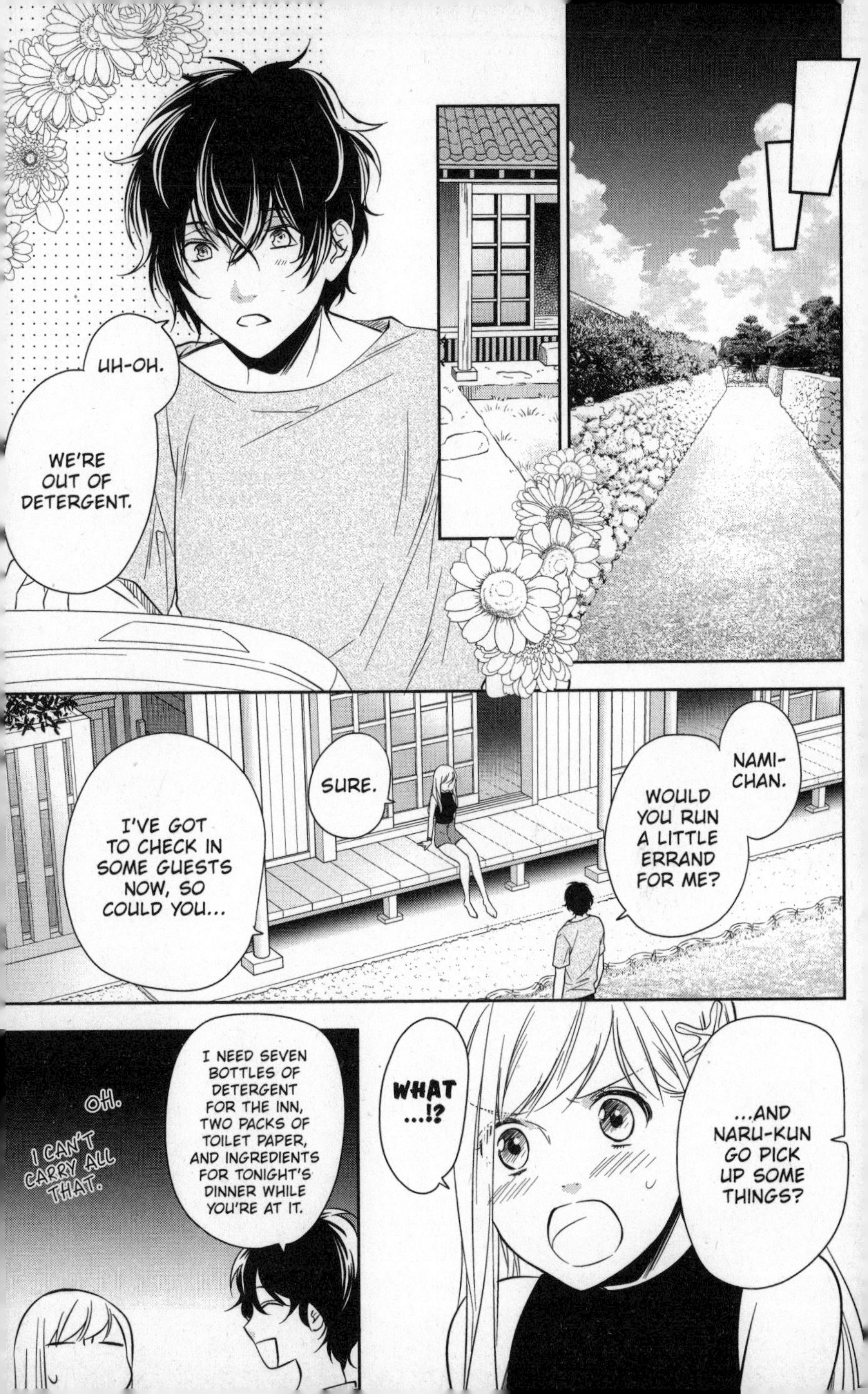
UH-OH.
WE'RE OUT OF DETERGENT.
NAMI-CHAN.
WOULD YOU RUN A LITTLE ERRAND FOR ME?
SURE.
I'VE GOT TO CHECK IN SOME GUESTS NOW, SO COULD YOU...
...AND NARU-KUN GO PICK UP SOME THINGS?
WHAT...!?
I NEED SEVEN BOTTLES OF DETERGENT FOR THE INN, TWO PACKS OF TOILET PAPER, AND INGREDIENTS FOR TONIGHT'S DINNER WHILE YOU'RE AT IT.
OH.
I CAN'T CARRY ALL THAT.

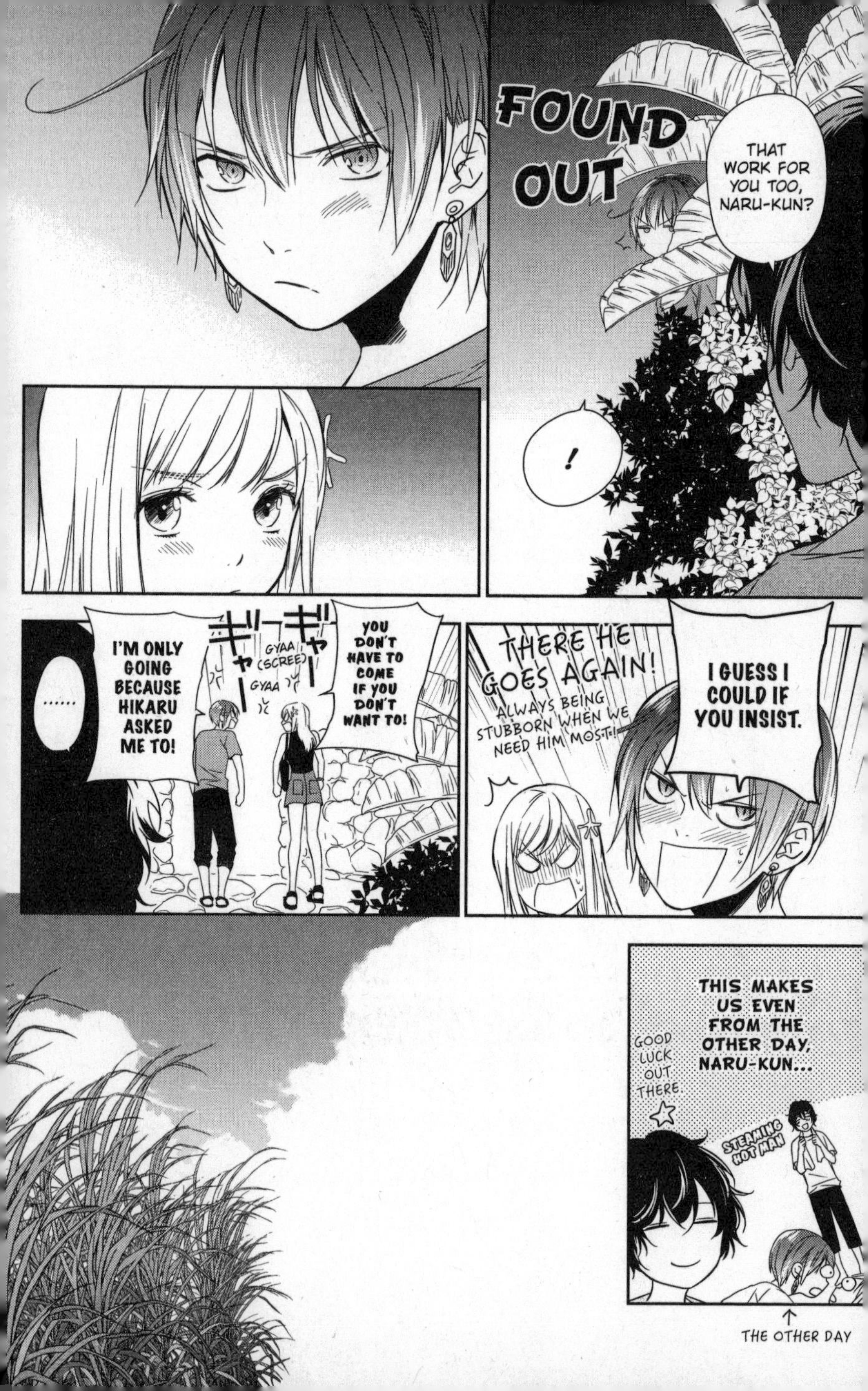
FOUND OUT
THAT WORK FOR YOU TOO, NARU-KUN?
!
I GUESS I COULD IF YOU INSIST.
THERE HE GOES AGAIN!
ALWAYS BEING STUBBORN WHEN WE NEED HIM MOST!
YOU DON'T HAVE TO COME IF YOU DON'T WANT TO!
ギャー ギャー
GYAA (SCREE) GYAA
I'M ONLY GOING BECAUSE HIKARU ASKED ME TO!
......
THIS MAKES US EVEN FROM THE OTHER DAY, NARU-KUN...
GOOD LUCK OUT THERE.
STEAMING HOT MAN
THE OTHER DAY

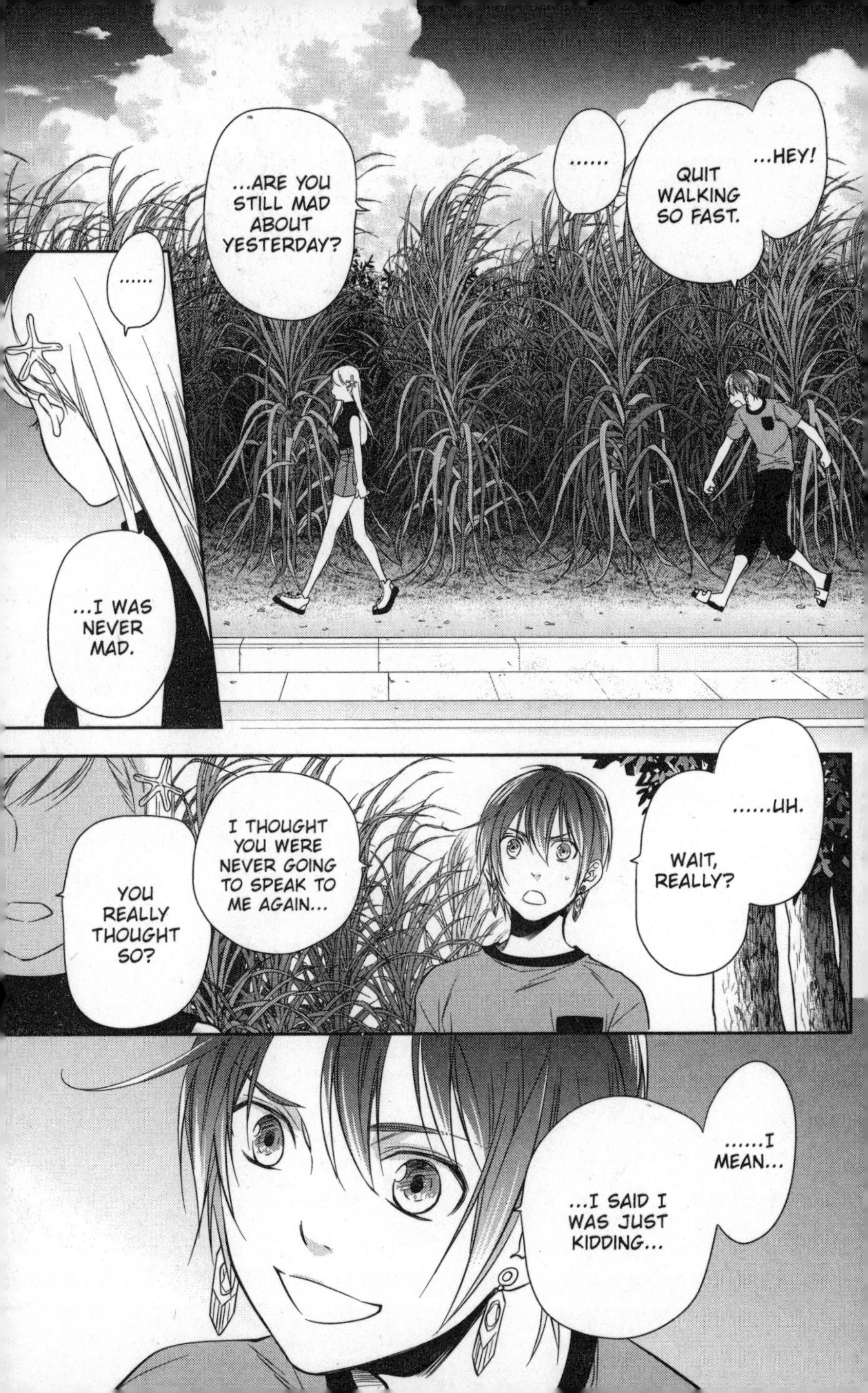
...HEY! QUIT WALKING SO FAST.
......
...ARE YOU STILL MAD ABOUT YESTERDAY?
......
...I WAS NEVER MAD.
......UH. WAIT, REALLY?
I THOUGHT YOU WERE NEVER GOING TO SPEAK TO ME AGAIN...
YOU REALLY THOUGHT SO?
......I MEAN...
...I SAID I WAS JUST KIDDING...

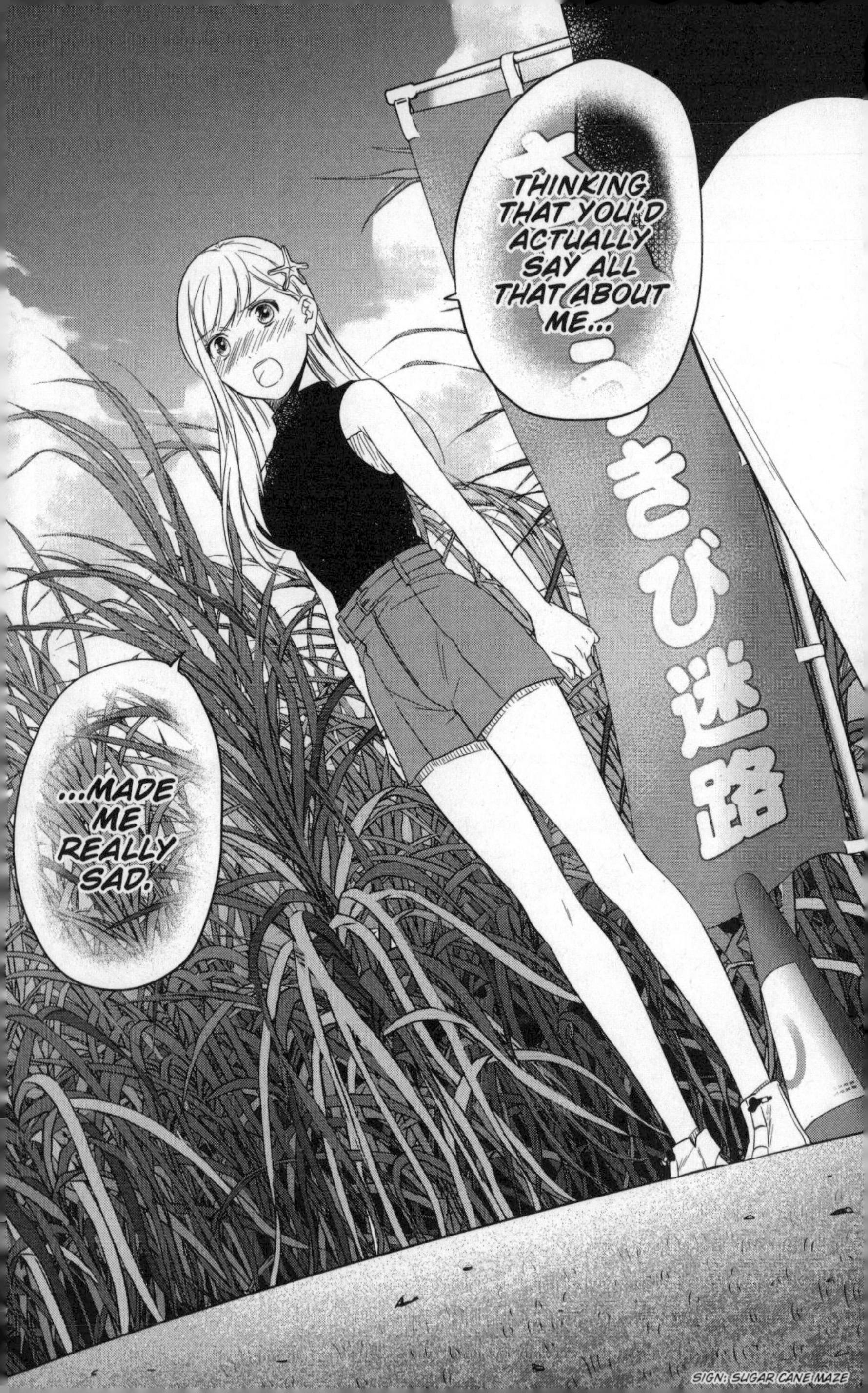
THINKING THAT YOU'D ACTUALLY SAY ALL THAT ABOUT ME...
...MADE ME REALLY SAD.
きび迷路
SIGN: SUGAR CANE MAZE

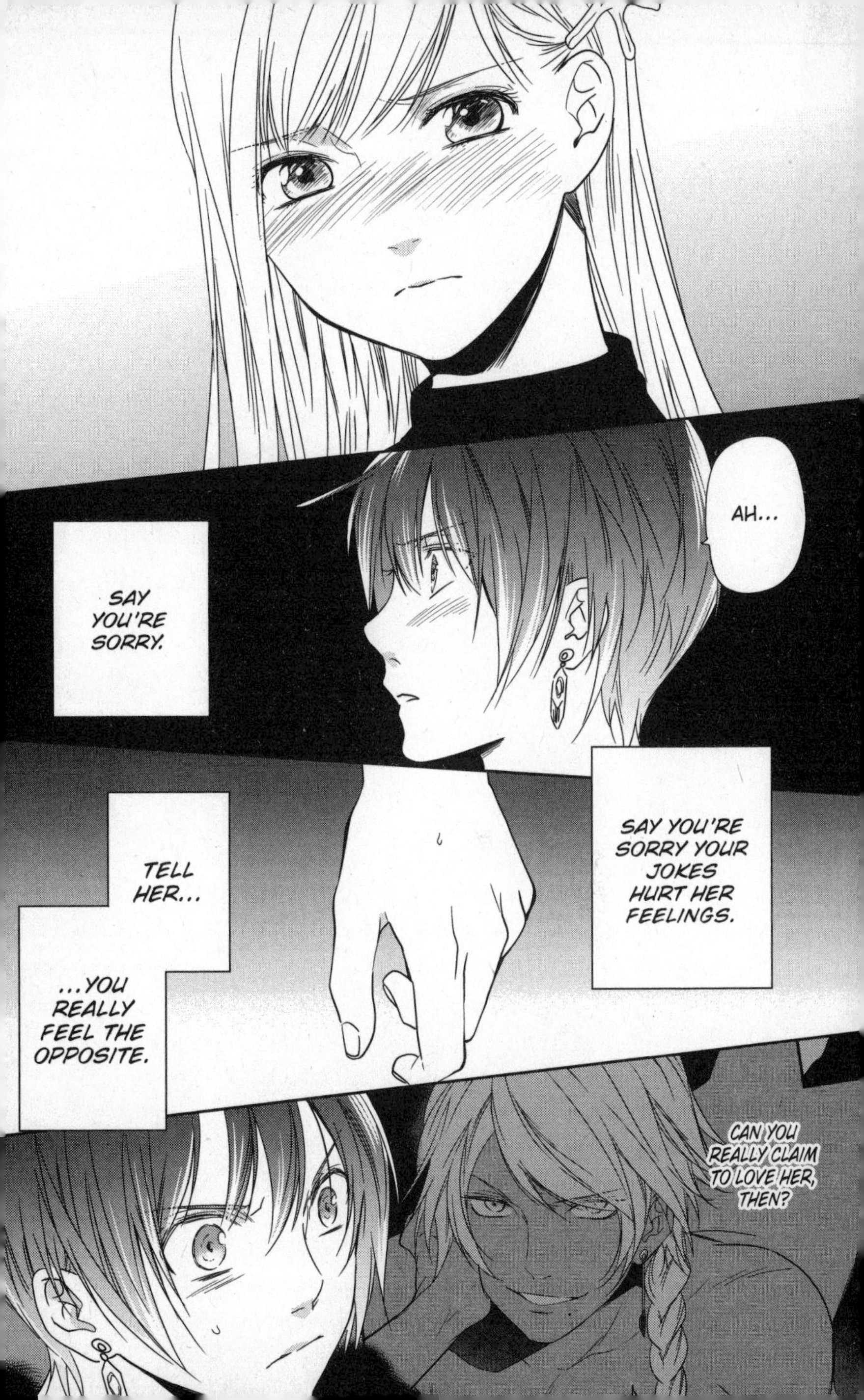
AH...
SAY YOU'RE SORRY.
SAY YOU'RE SORRY YOUR JOKES HURT HER FEELINGS.
TELL HER...
...YOU REALLY FEEL THE OPPOSITE.
CAN YOU REALLY CLAIM TO LOVE HER, THEN?

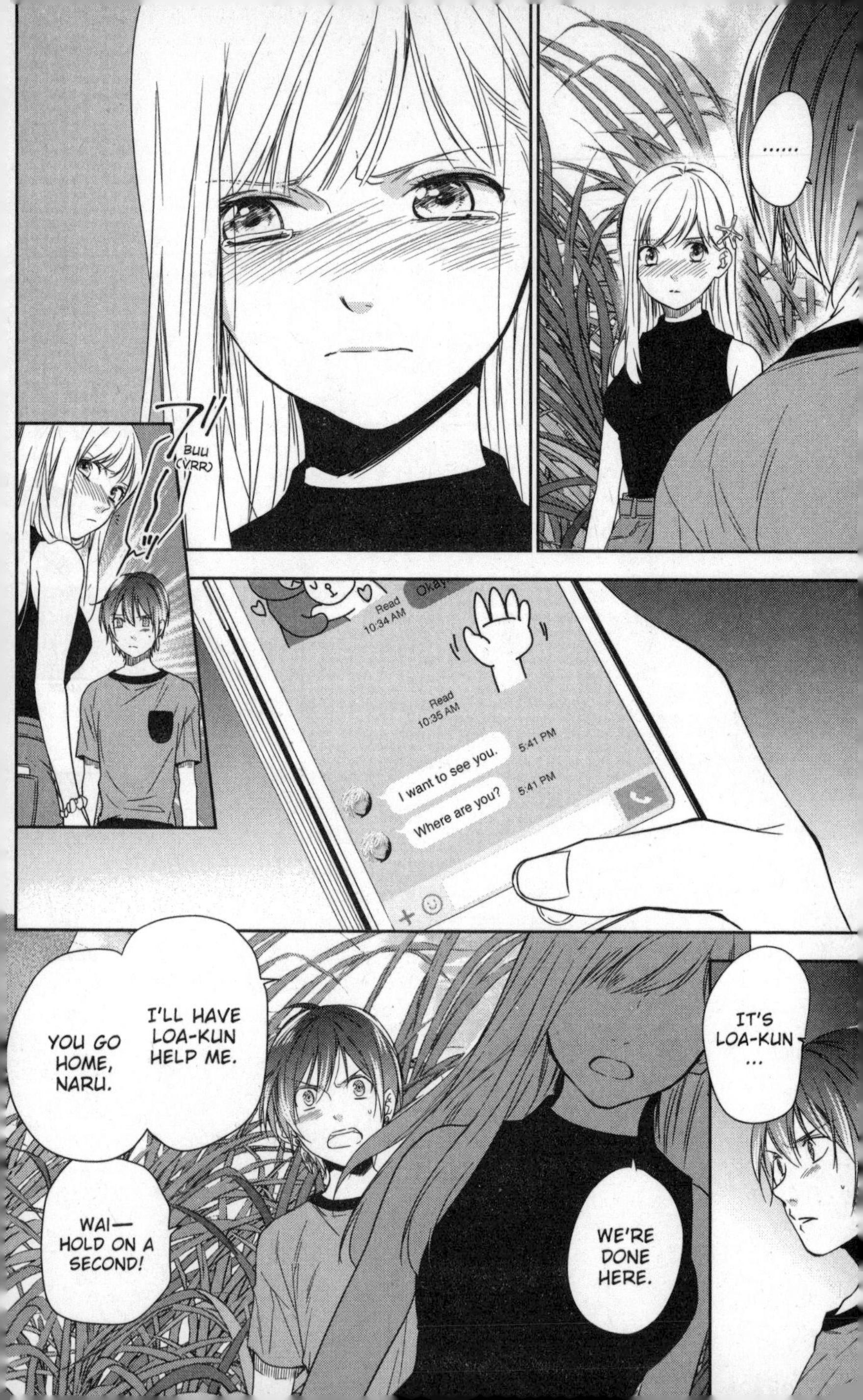

......
BUU (VRR)
Okay
Read 10:34 AM
Read 10:35 AM
I want to see you.
5:41 PM
Where are you?
5:41 PM
IT'S LOA-KUN...
WE'RE DONE HERE.
I'LL HAVE LOA-KUN HELP ME.
YOU GO HOME, NARU.
WAI— HOLD ON A SECOND!

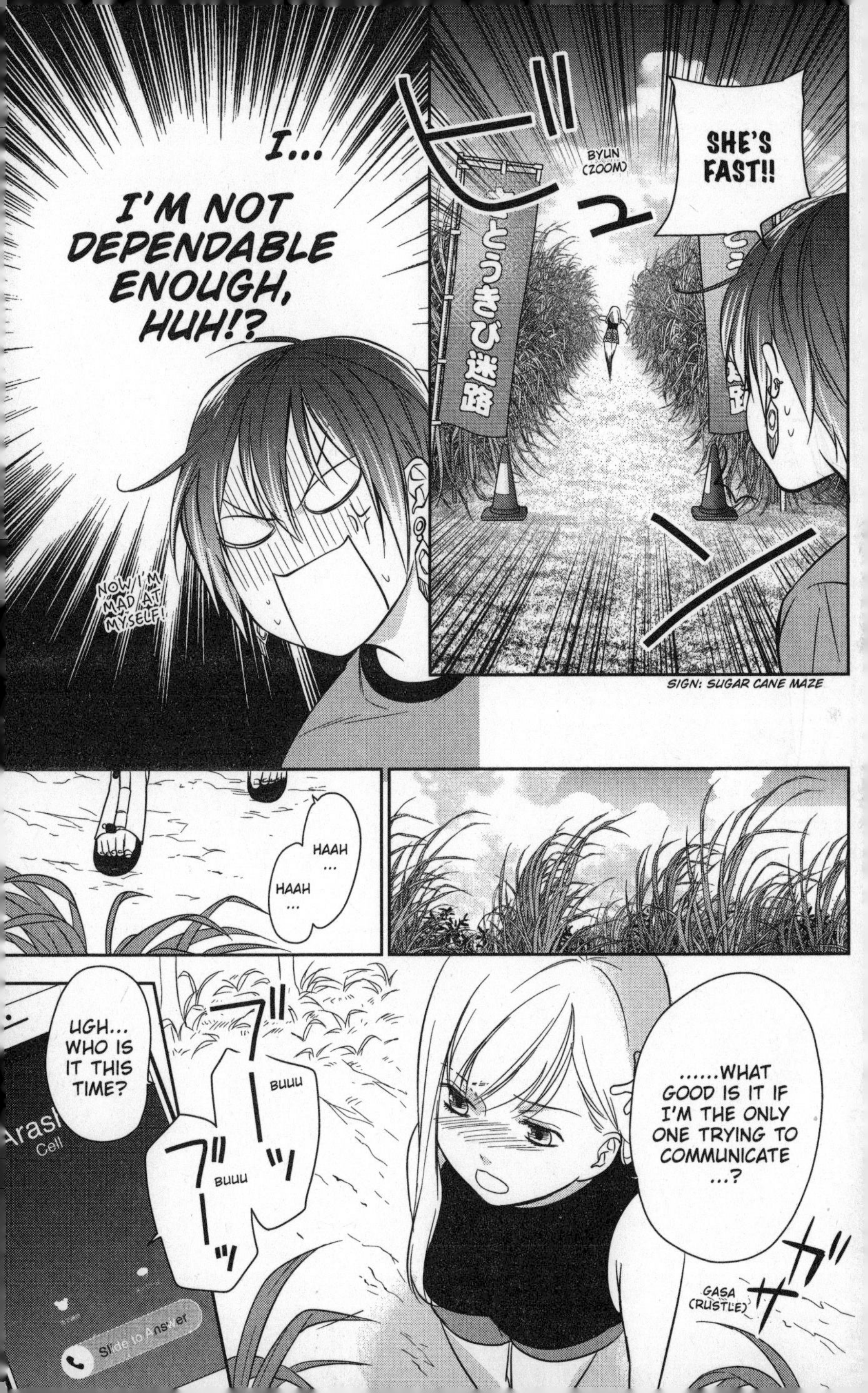
SHE'S FAST!!
BYUN (ZOOM)
とうきび迷路
SIGN: SUGAR CANE MAZE
I...
I'M NOT DEPENDABLE ENOUGH, HUH!?
NOW I'M MAD AT MYSELF!
HAAH... HAAH...
......WHAT GOOD IS IT IF I'M THE ONLY ONE TRYING TO COMMUNICATE...?
GASA (RUSTLE)
UGH... WHO IS IT THIS TIME?
BUUU
BUUU
Cell
Slide to Answer

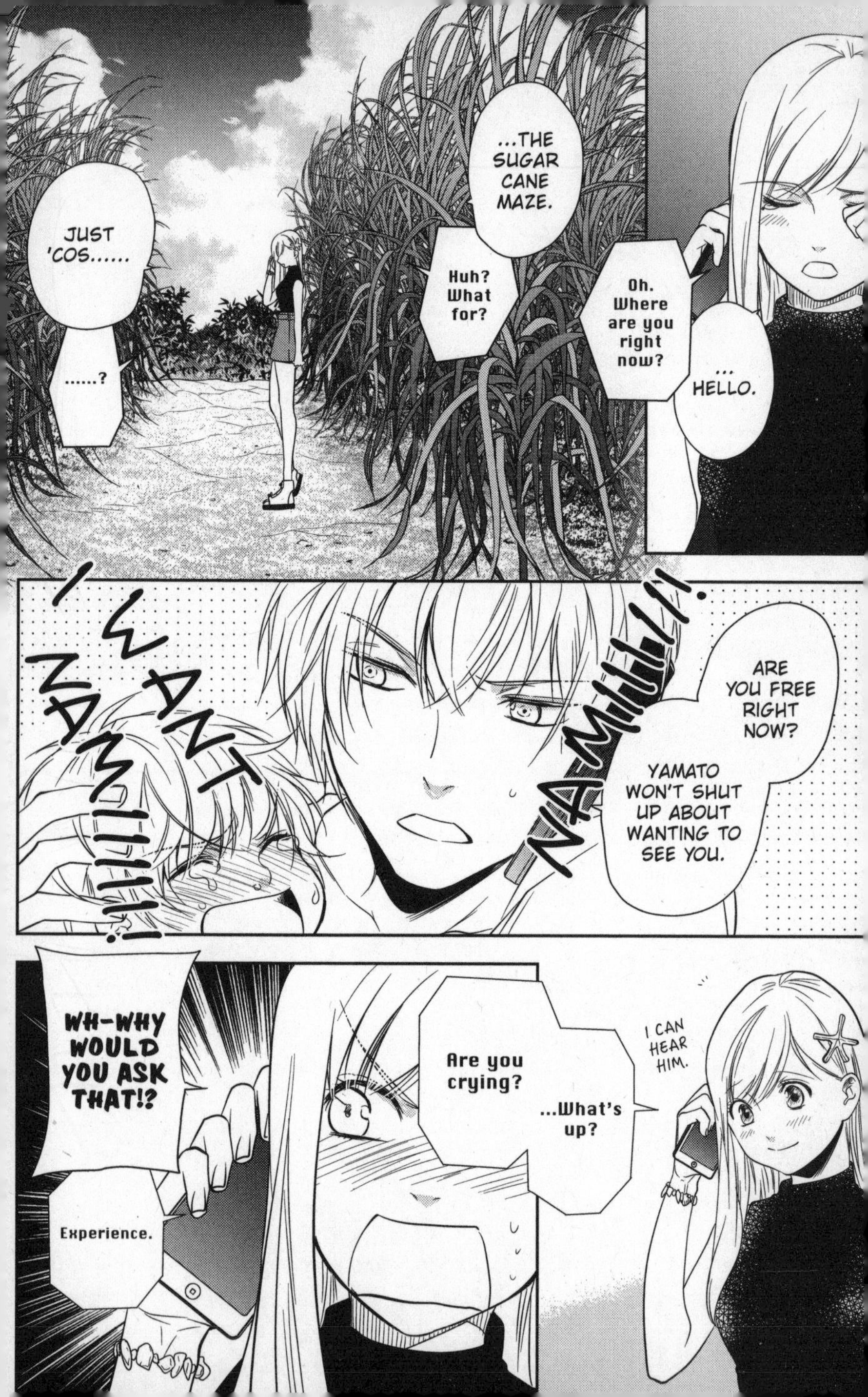
...HELLO.
Oh. Where are you right now?
...THE SUGAR CANE MAZE.
Huh? What for?
JUST 'COS......
......?
ARE YOU FREE RIGHT NOW?
YAMATO WON'T SHUT UP ABOUT WANTING TO SEE YOU.
NAMIIIII!!!
I WANT NAMI!!!!!!!
I CAN HEAR HIM.
Are you crying?
...What's up?
WH-WHY WOULD YOU ASK THAT!?
Experience.

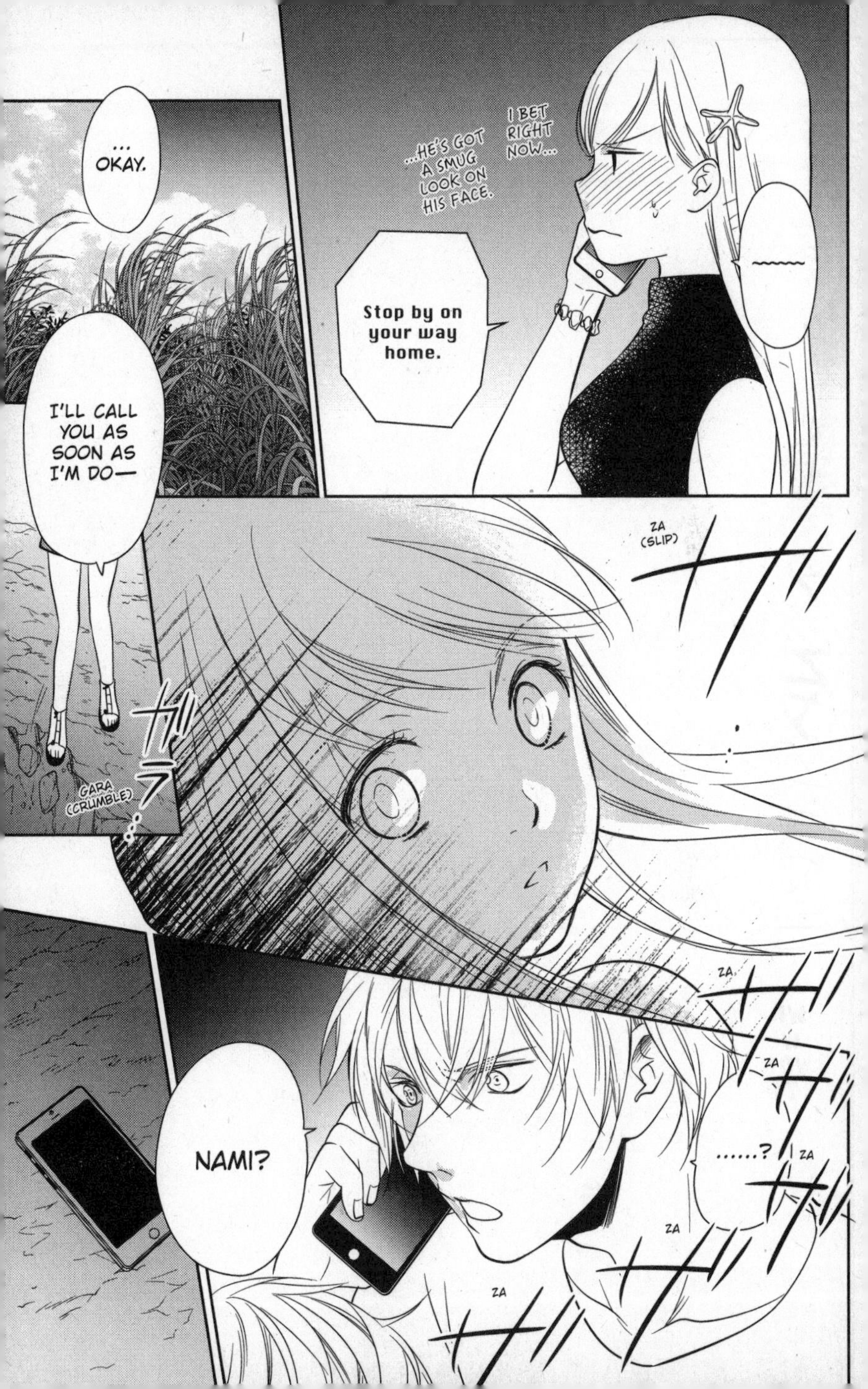

I BET RIGHT NOW...
...HE'S GOT A SMUG LOOK ON HIS FACE.
Stop by on your way home.
...OKAY.
I'LL CALL YOU AS SOON AS I'M DO—
ZA (SLIP)
GARA (CRUMBLE)
ZA
ZA
......?
ZA
ZA
ZA
NAMI?

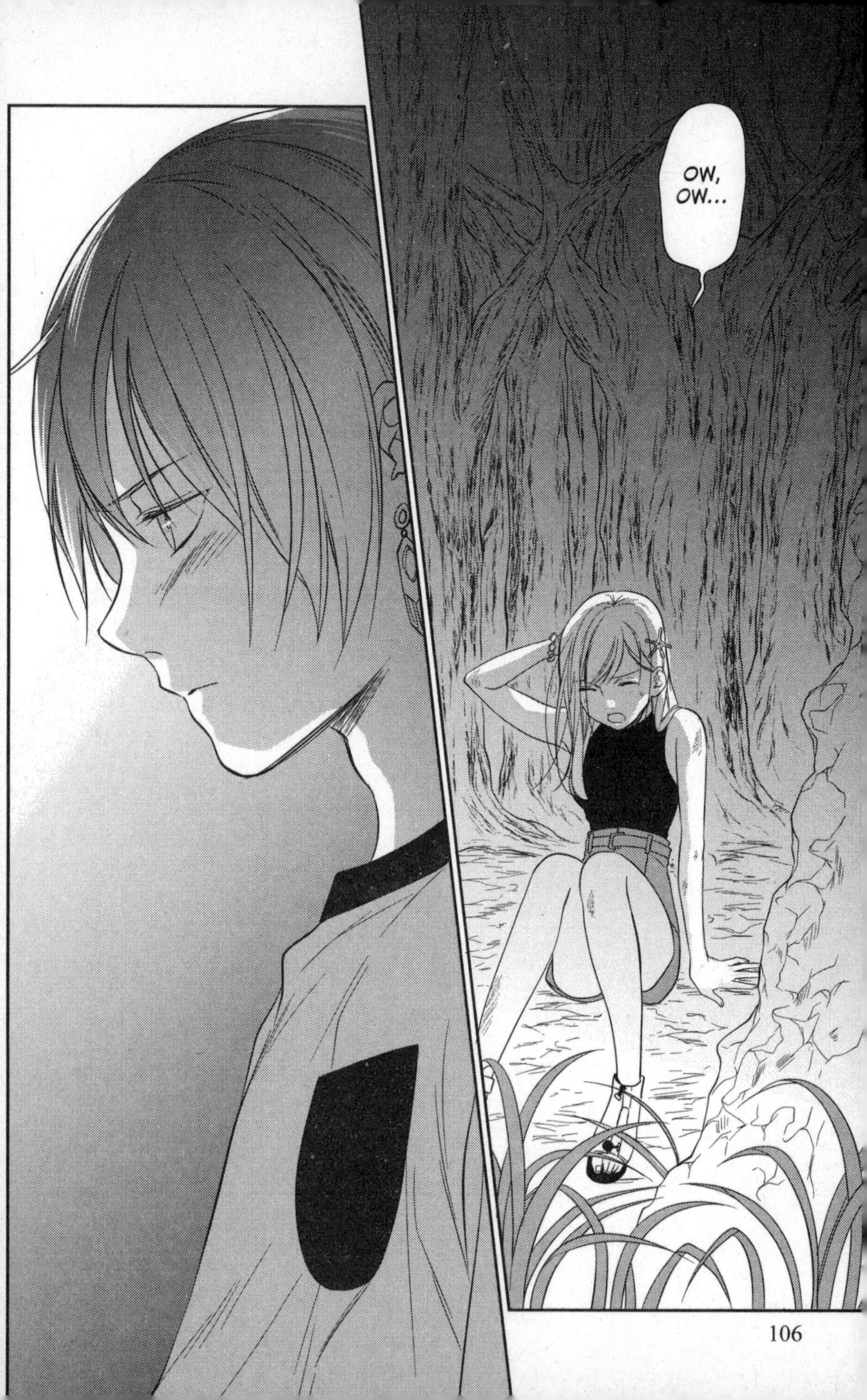
OW, OW...

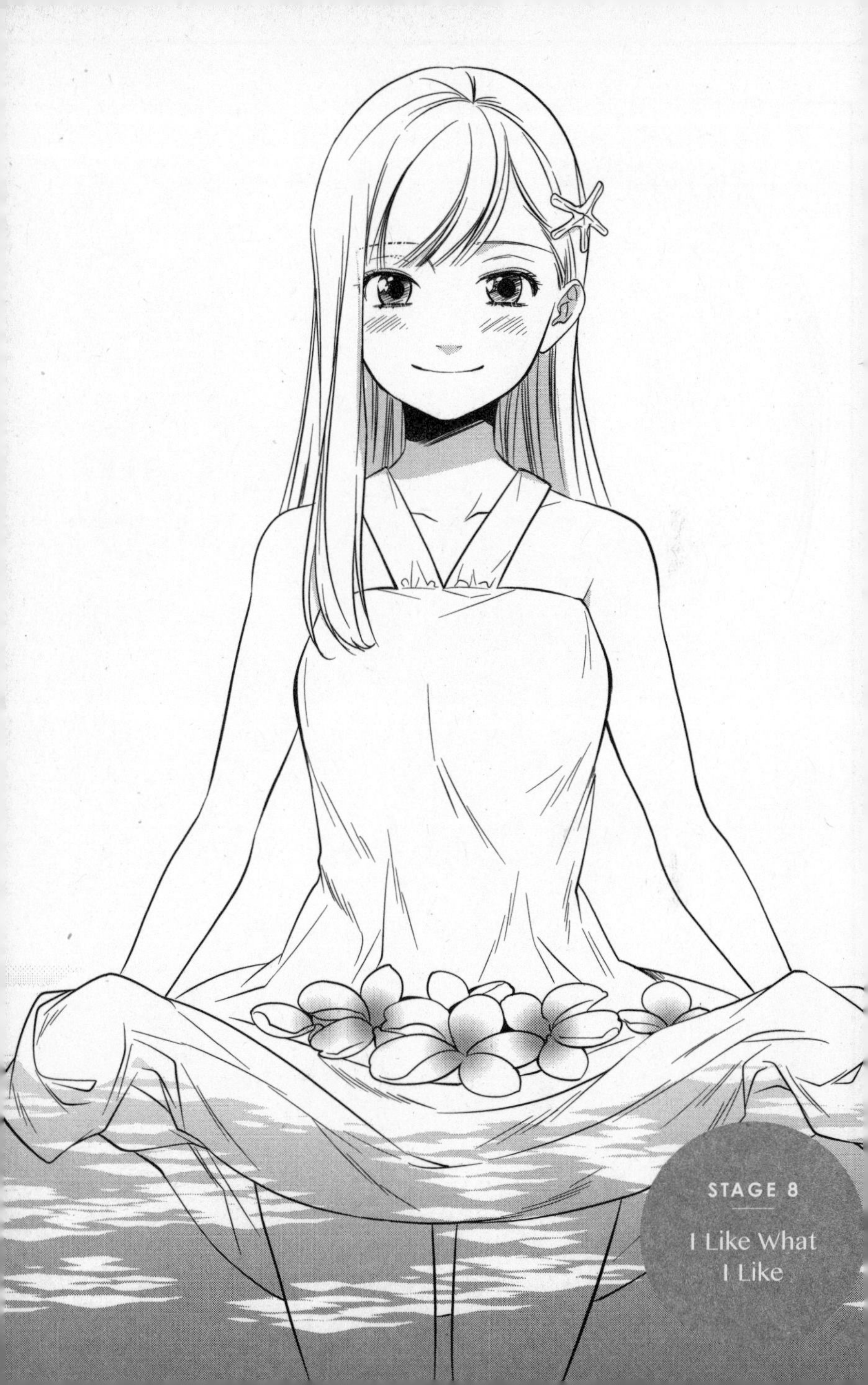
STAGE 8
I Like What I Like

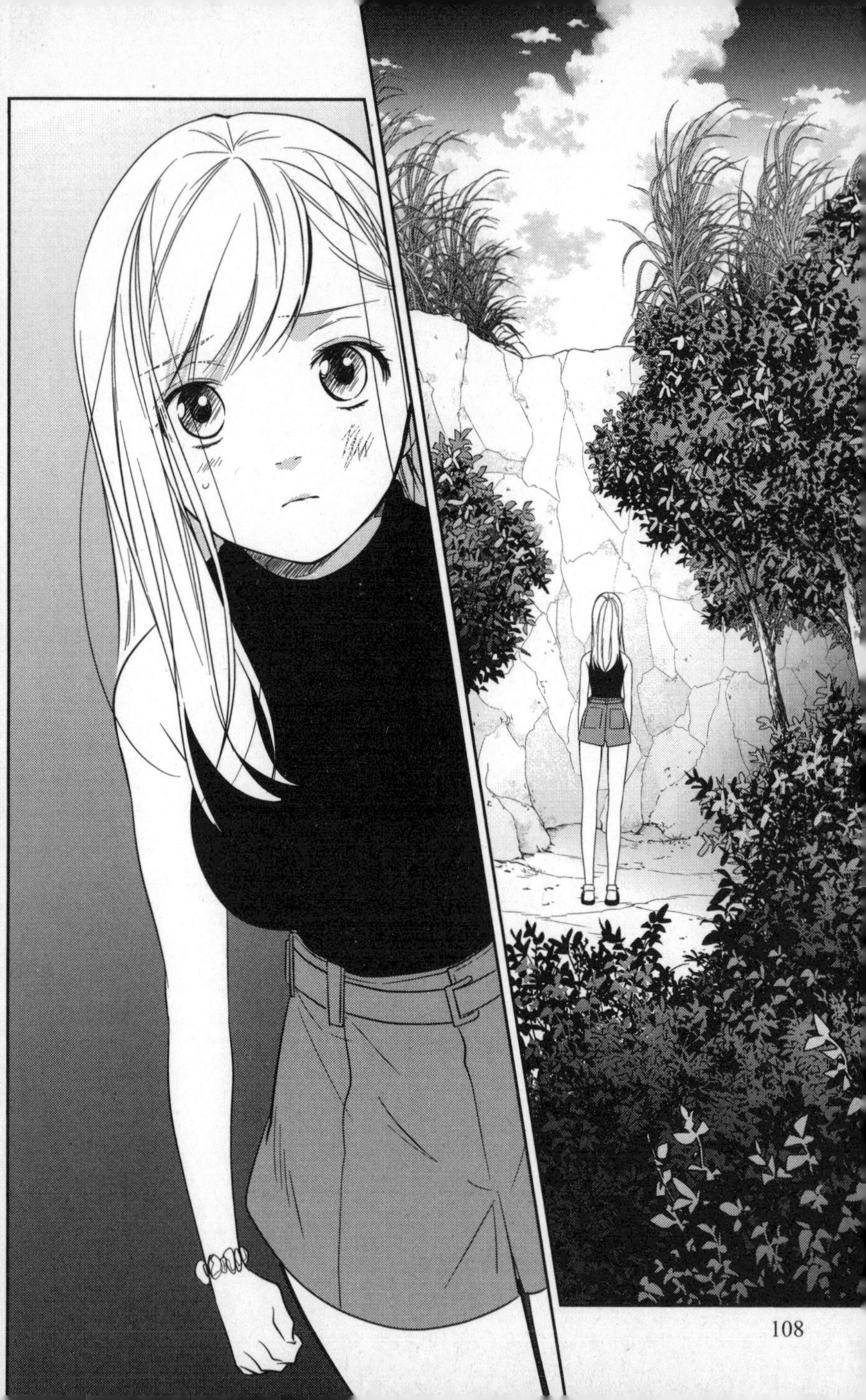

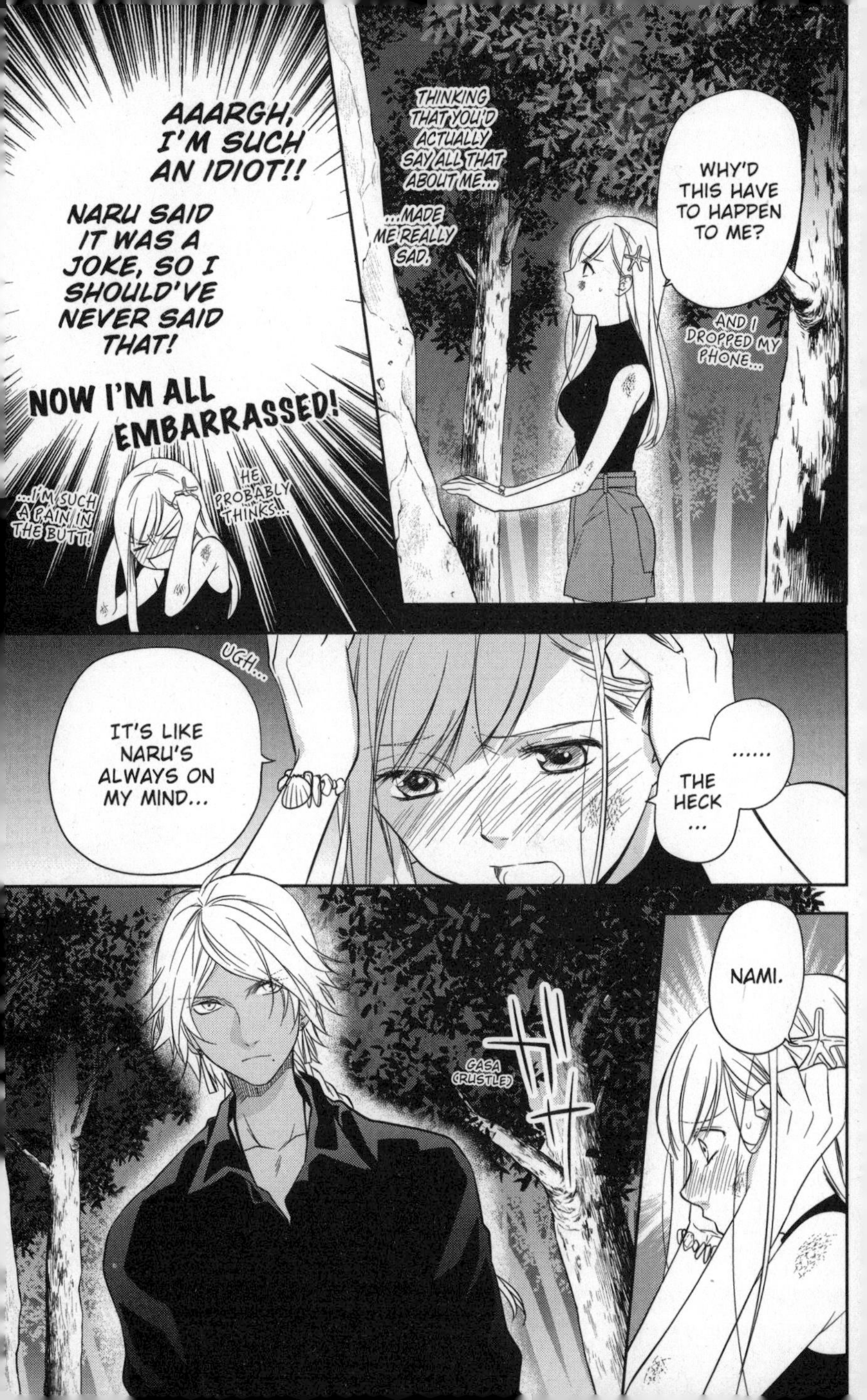
WHY'D THIS HAVE TO HAPPEN TO ME?
AND I DROPPED MY PHONE...
THINKING THAT YOU'D ACTUALLY SAY ALL THAT ABOUT ME...
...MADE ME REALLY SAD.
AAARGH, I'M SUCH AN IDIOT!!
NARU SAID IT WAS A JOKE, SO I SHOULD'VE NEVER SAID THAT!
NOW I'M ALL EMBARRASSED!
HE PROBABLY THINKS...
...I'M SUCH A PAIN IN THE BUTT!
...... THE HECK ...
UGH...
IT'S LIKE NARU'S ALWAYS ON MY MIND...
NAMI.
GASA (RUSTLE)

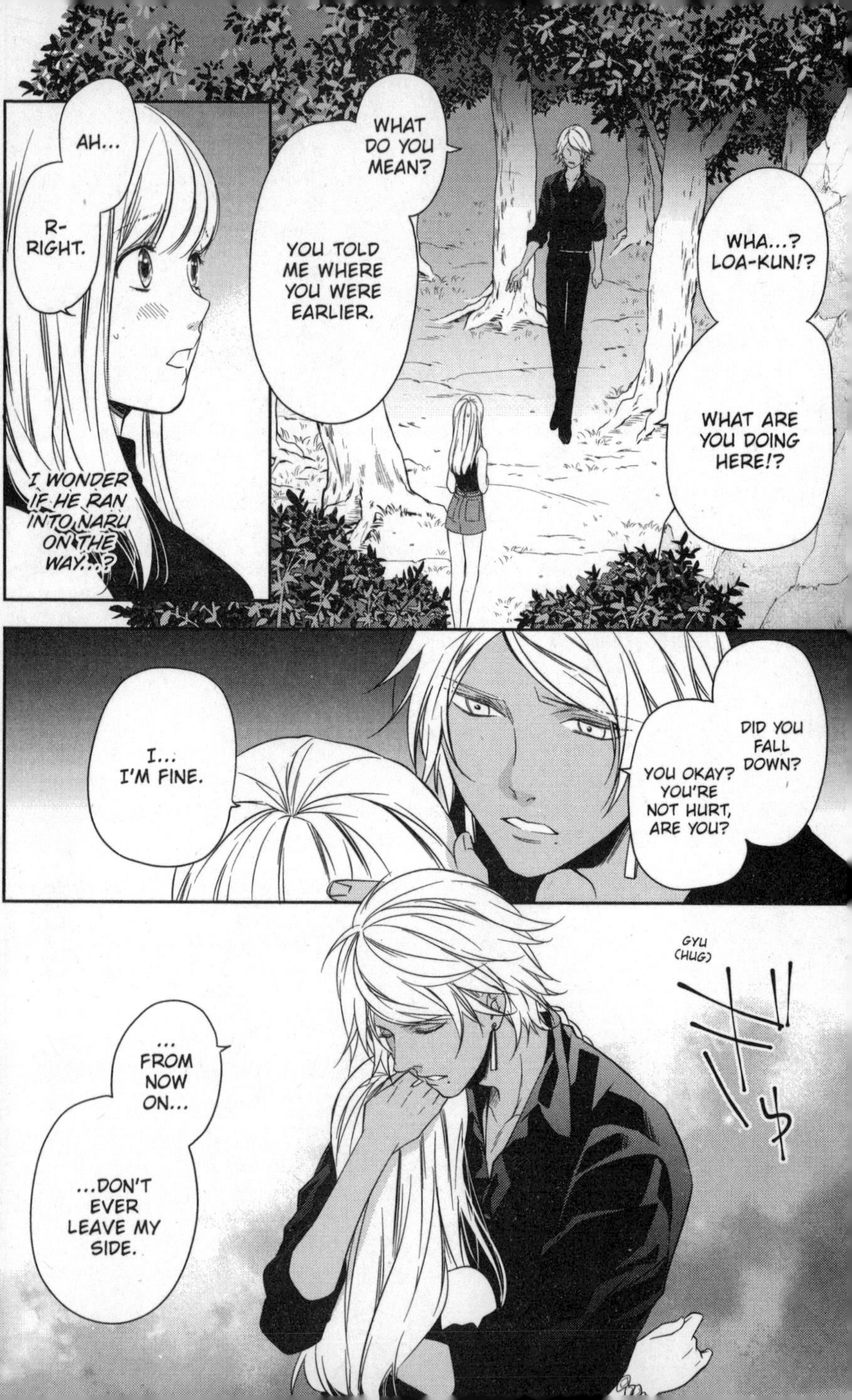
WHA...? LOA-KUN!?
WHAT ARE YOU DOING HERE!?
WHAT DO YOU MEAN?
YOU TOLD ME WHERE YOU WERE EARLIER.
AH...
R-RIGHT.
I WONDER IF HE RAN INTO NARU ON THE WAY...?
DID YOU FALL DOWN?
YOU OKAY? YOU'RE NOT HURT, ARE YOU?
I... I'M FINE.
GYU (HUG)
...FROM NOW ON...
...DON'T EVER LEAVE MY SIDE.

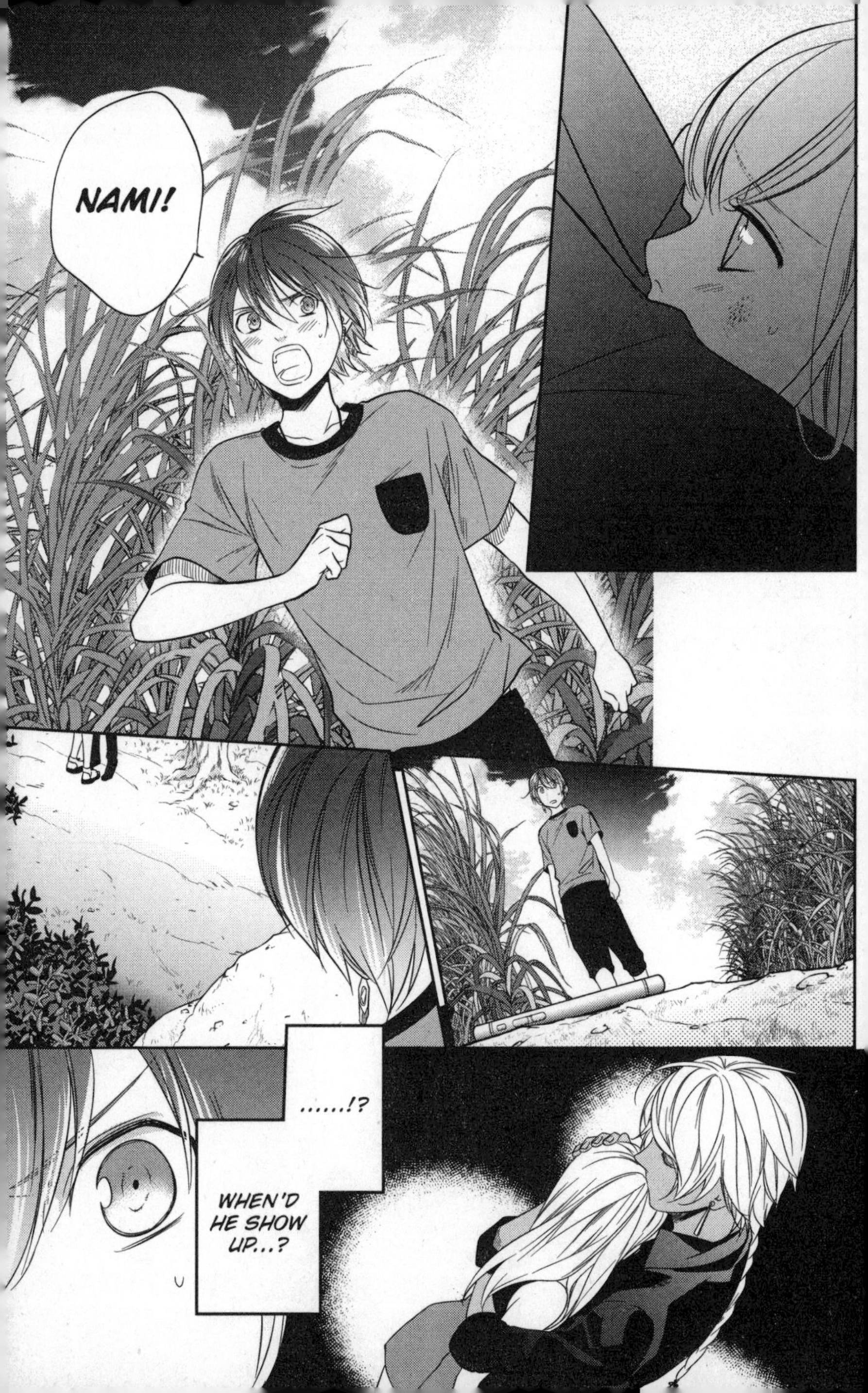
NAMI!
......!?
WHEN'D HE SHOW UP...?

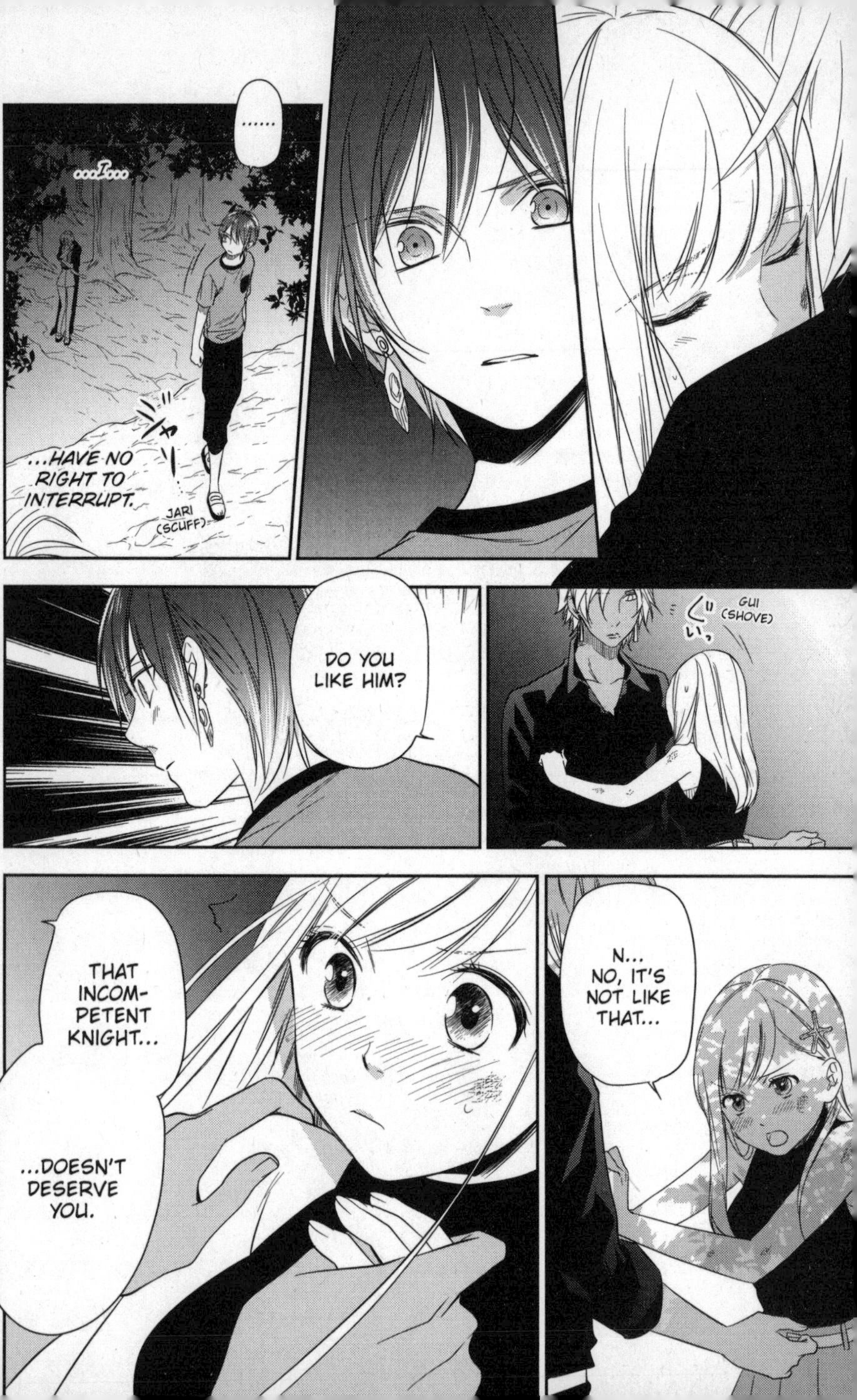
......
...I...
...HAVE NO RIGHT TO INTERRUPT.
JARI (SCUFF)
GUI (SHOVE)
DO YOU LIKE HIM?
N... NO, IT'S NOT LIKE THAT...
THAT INCOMPETENT KNIGHT...
...DOESN'T DESERVE YOU.

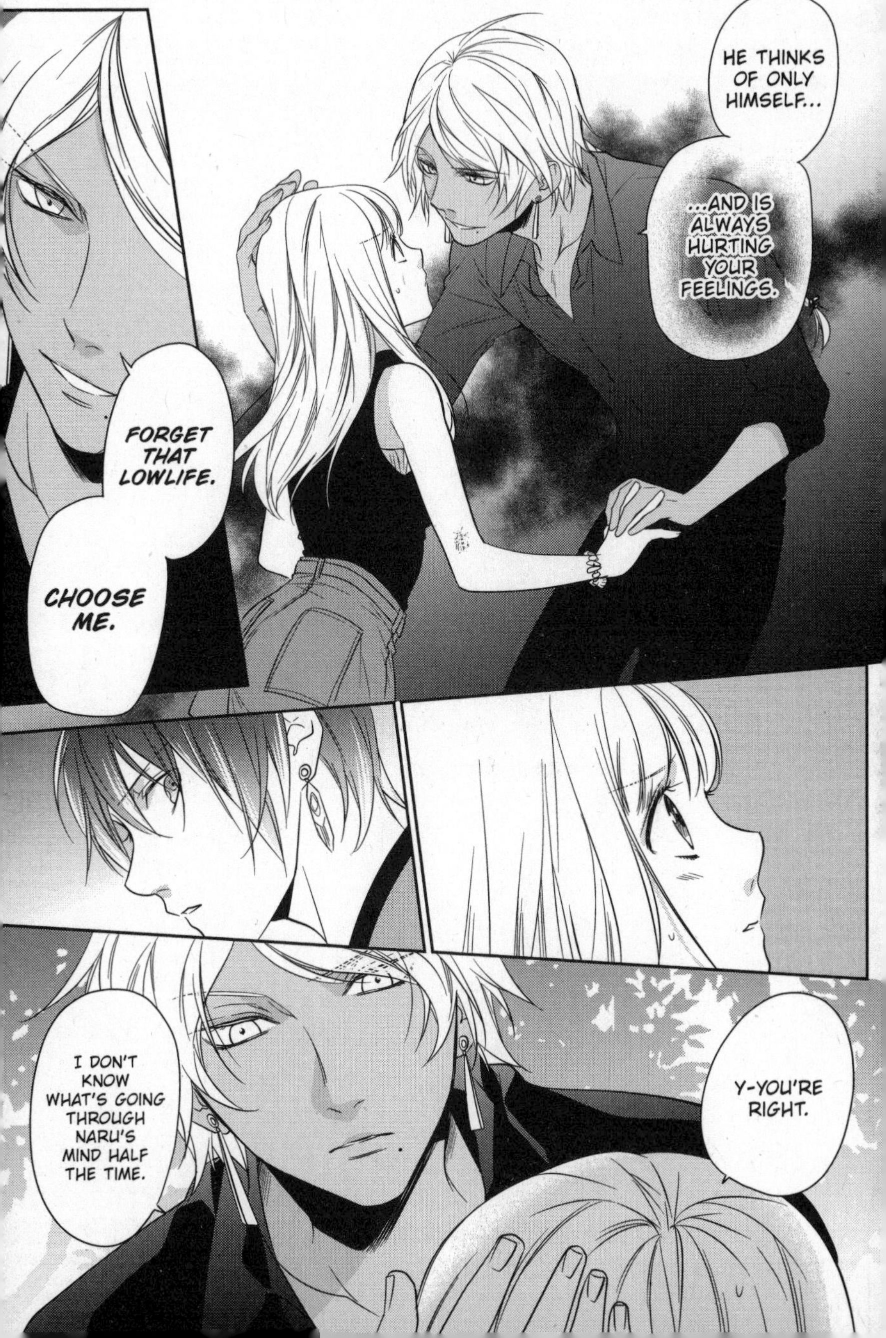
HE THINKS OF ONLY HIMSELF...
...AND IS ALWAYS HURTING YOUR FEELINGS.
FORGET THAT LOWLIFE.
CHOOSE ME.
Y-YOU'RE RIGHT.
I DON'T KNOW WHAT'S GOING THROUGH NARU'S MIND HALF THE TIME.

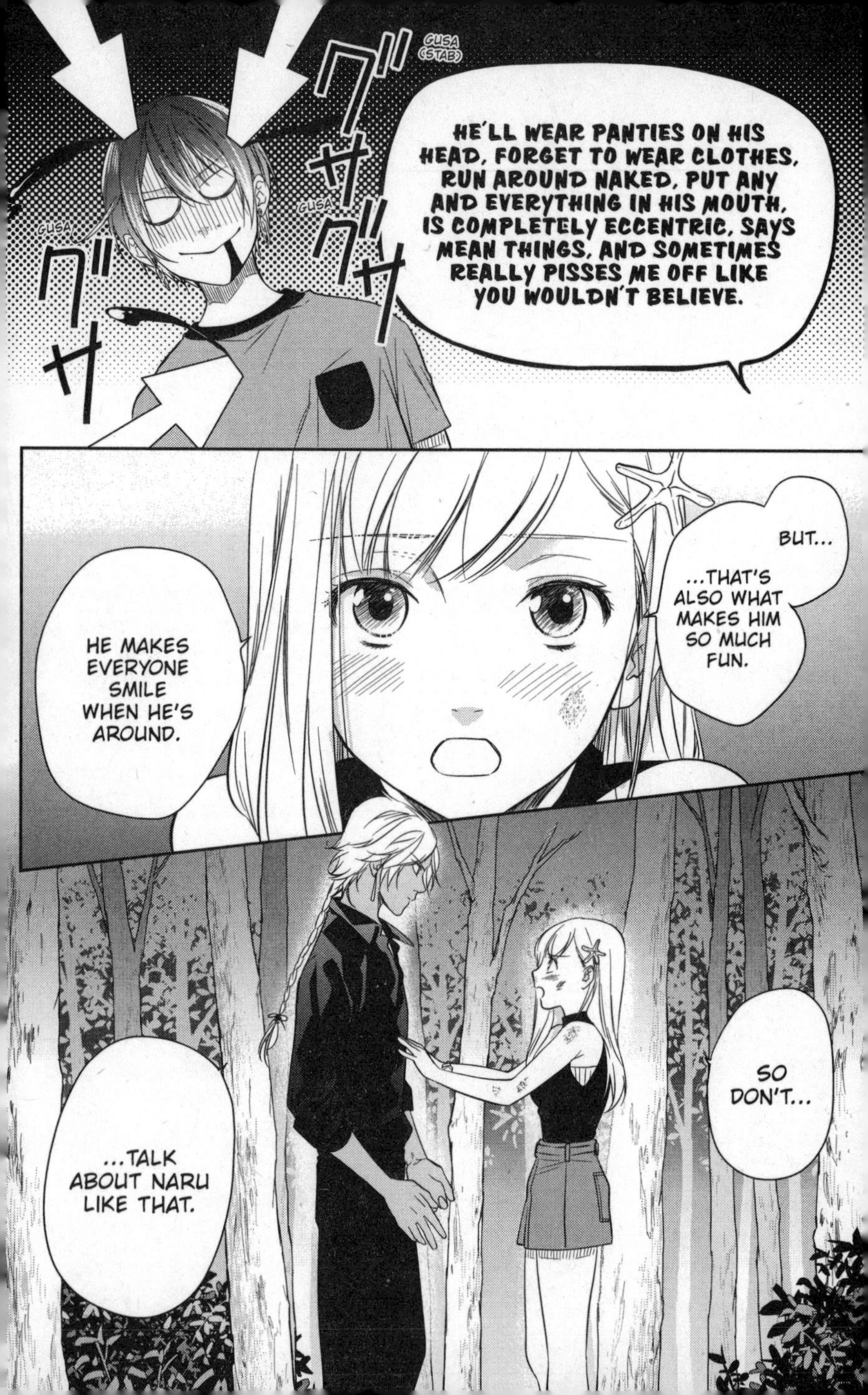
GUSA (STAB)
HE'LL WEAR PANTIES ON HIS HEAD, FORGET TO WEAR CLOTHES, RUN AROUND NAKED, PUT ANY AND EVERYTHING IN HIS MOUTH, IS COMPLETELY ECCENTRIC, SAYS MEAN THINGS, AND SOMETIMES REALLY PISSES ME OFF LIKE YOU WOULDN'T BELIEVE.
GUSA
GUSA
BUT...
...THAT'S ALSO WHAT MAKES HIM SO MUCH FUN.
HE MAKES EVERYONE SMILE WHEN HE'S AROUND.
SO DON'T...
...TALK ABOUT NARU LIKE THAT.

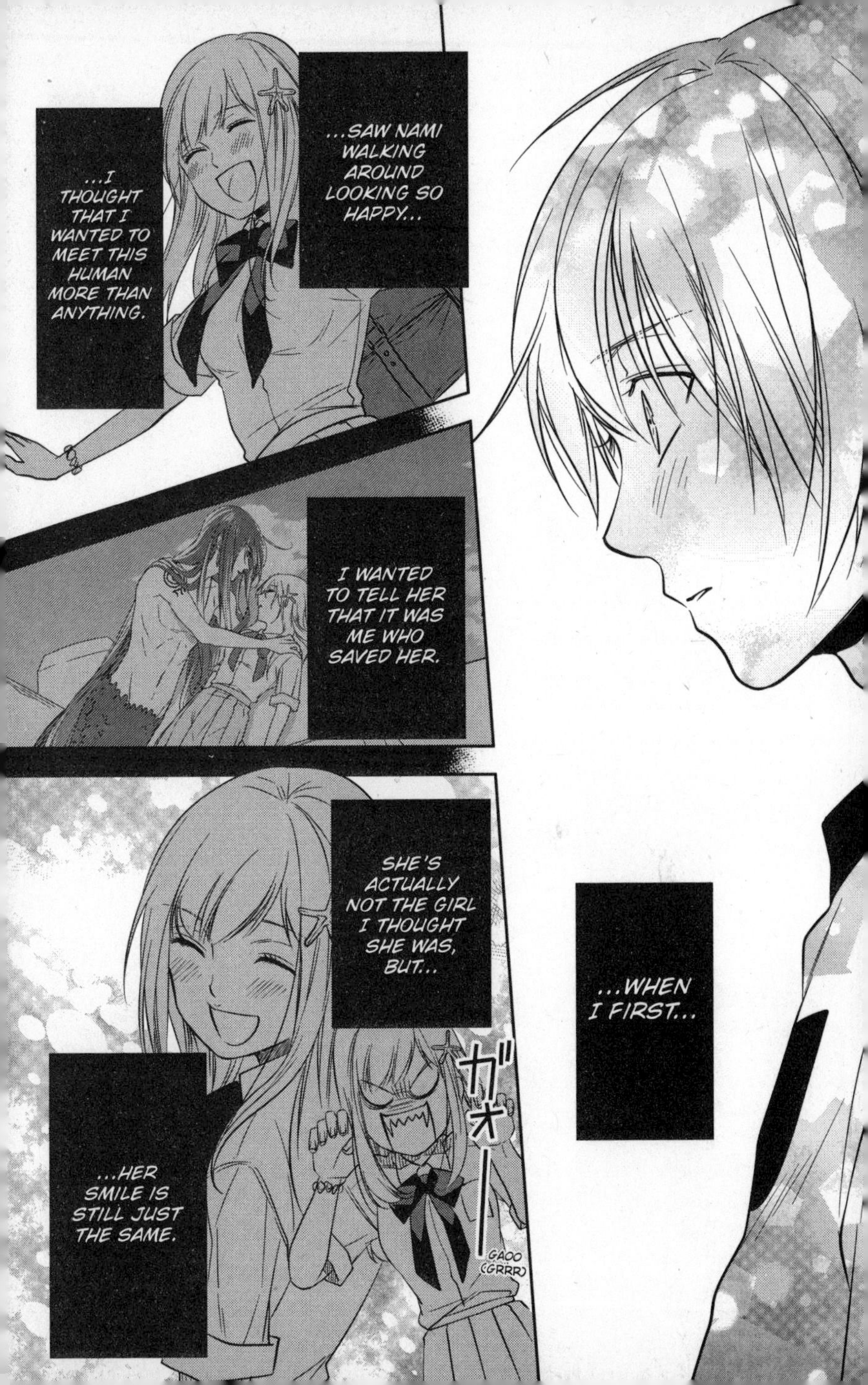

...WHEN I FIRST...
...SAW NAMI WALKING AROUND LOOKING SO HAPPY...
...I THOUGHT THAT I WANTED TO MEET THIS HUMAN MORE THAN ANYTHING.
I WANTED TO TELL HER THAT IT WAS ME WHO SAVED HER.
SHE'S ACTUALLY NOT THE GIRL I THOUGHT SHE WAS, BUT...
ガオー
GAOO (GRRR)
...HER SMILE IS STILL JUST THE SAME.

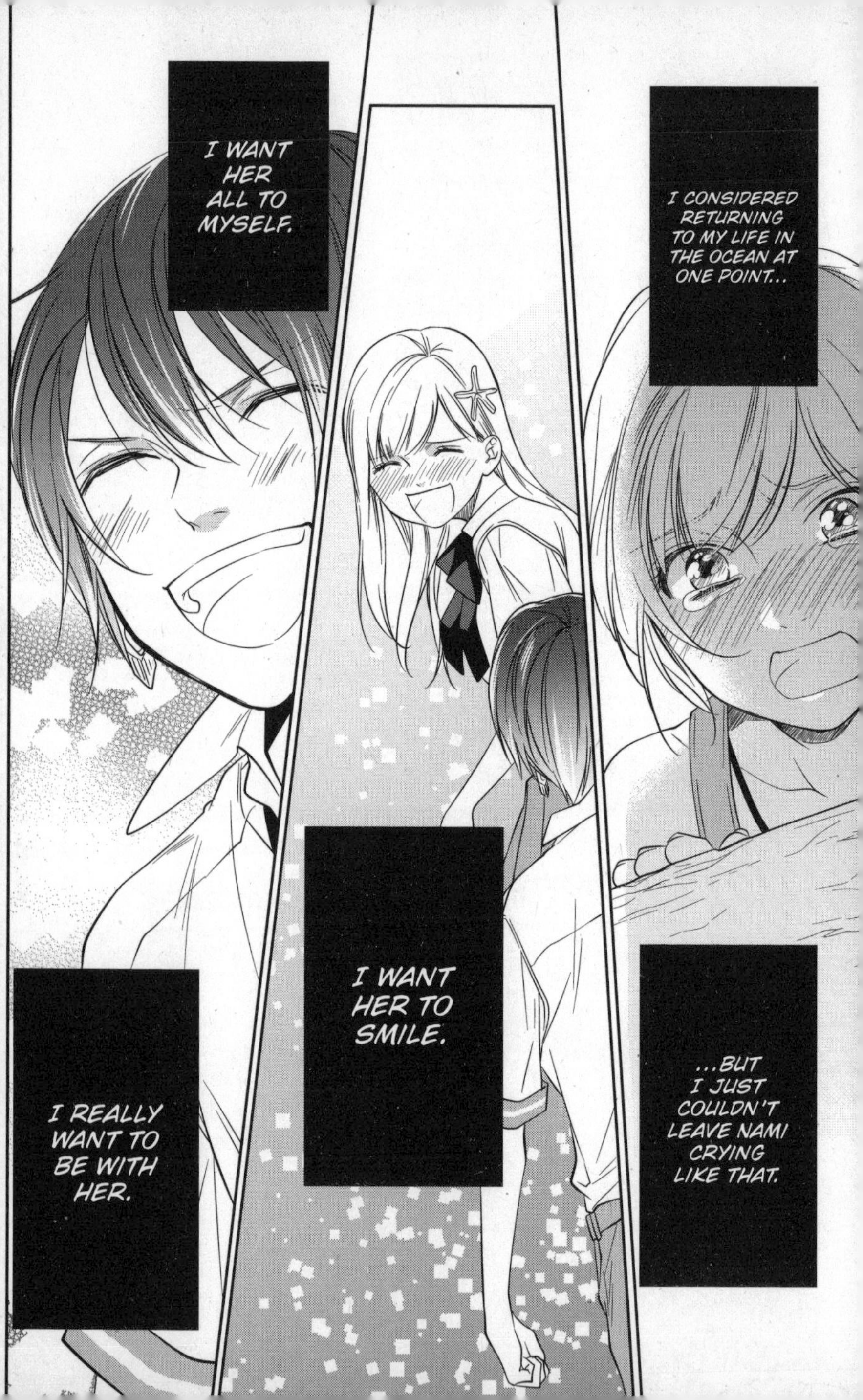
I CONSIDERED RETURNING TO MY LIFE IN THE OCEAN AT ONE POINT...
...BUT I JUST COULDN'T LEAVE NAMI CRYING LIKE THAT.
I WANT HER TO SMILE.
I WANT HER ALL TO MYSELF.
I REALLY WANT TO BE WITH HER.

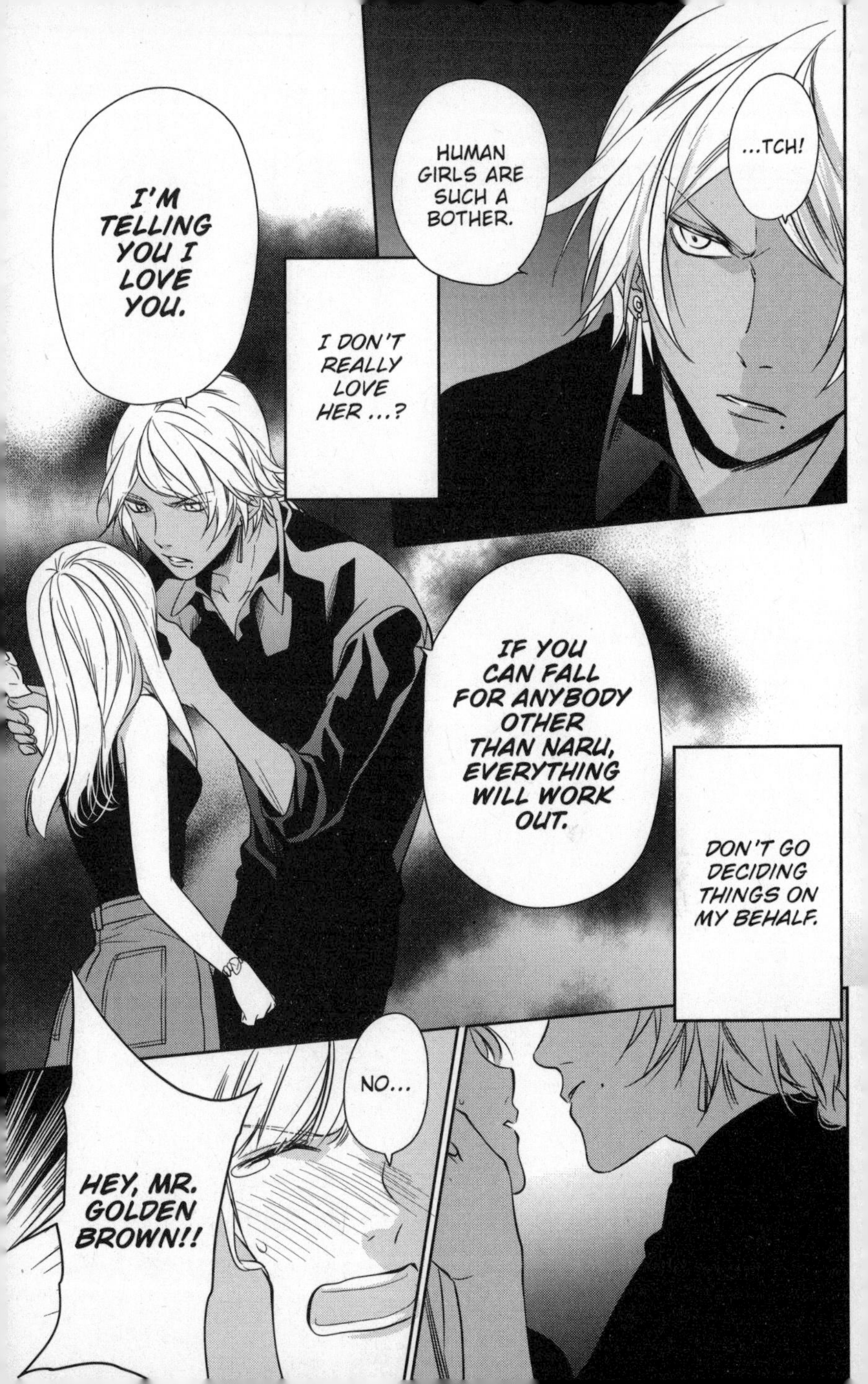
...TCH!
HUMAN GIRLS ARE SUCH A BOTHER.
I DON'T REALLY LOVE HER ...?
I'M TELLING YOU I LOVE YOU.
IF YOU CAN FALL FOR ANYBODY OTHER THAN NARU, EVERYTHING WILL WORK OUT.
DON'T GO DECIDING THINGS ON MY BEHALF.
NO...
HEY, MR. GOLDEN BROWN!!

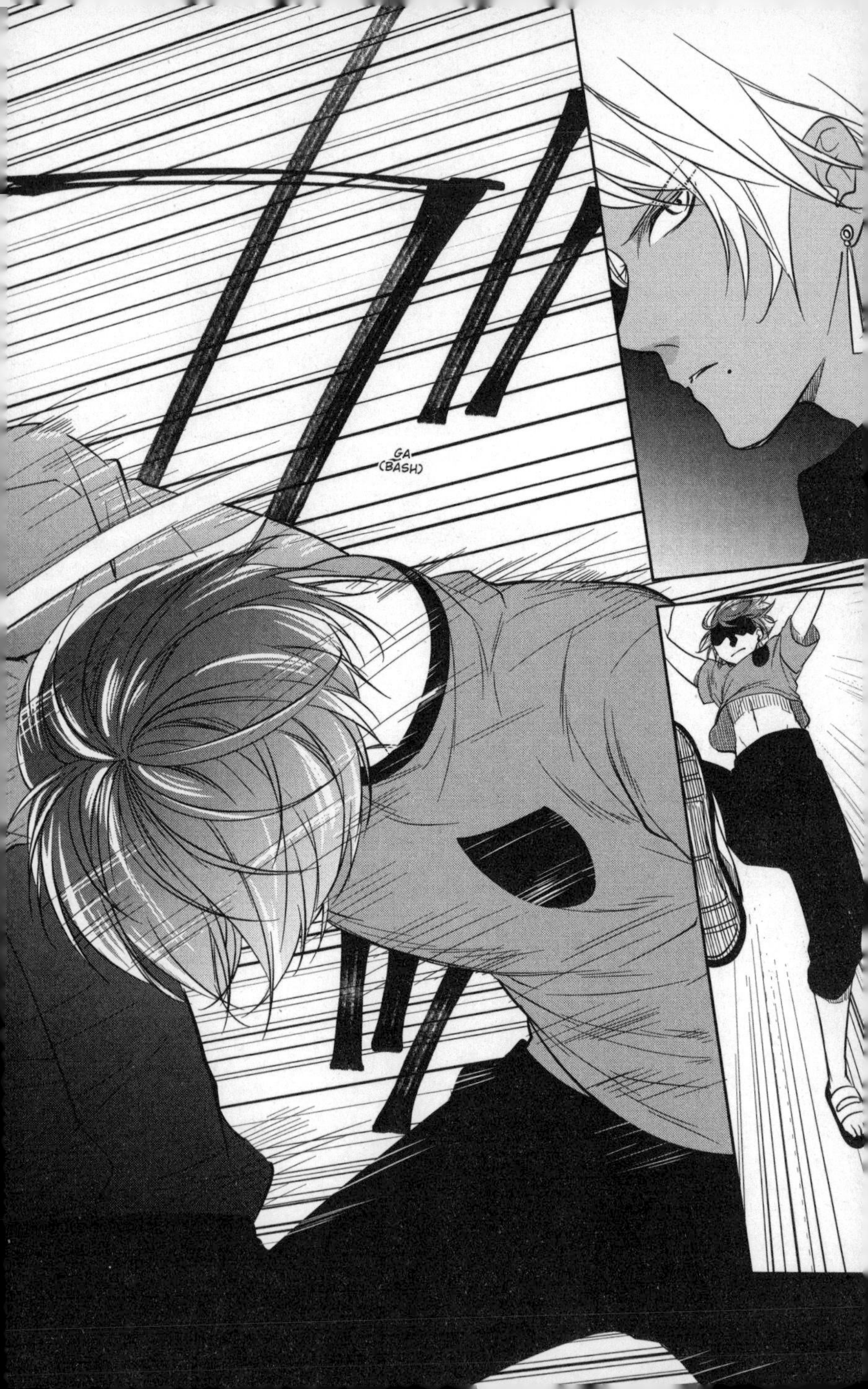
GA
(BASH)

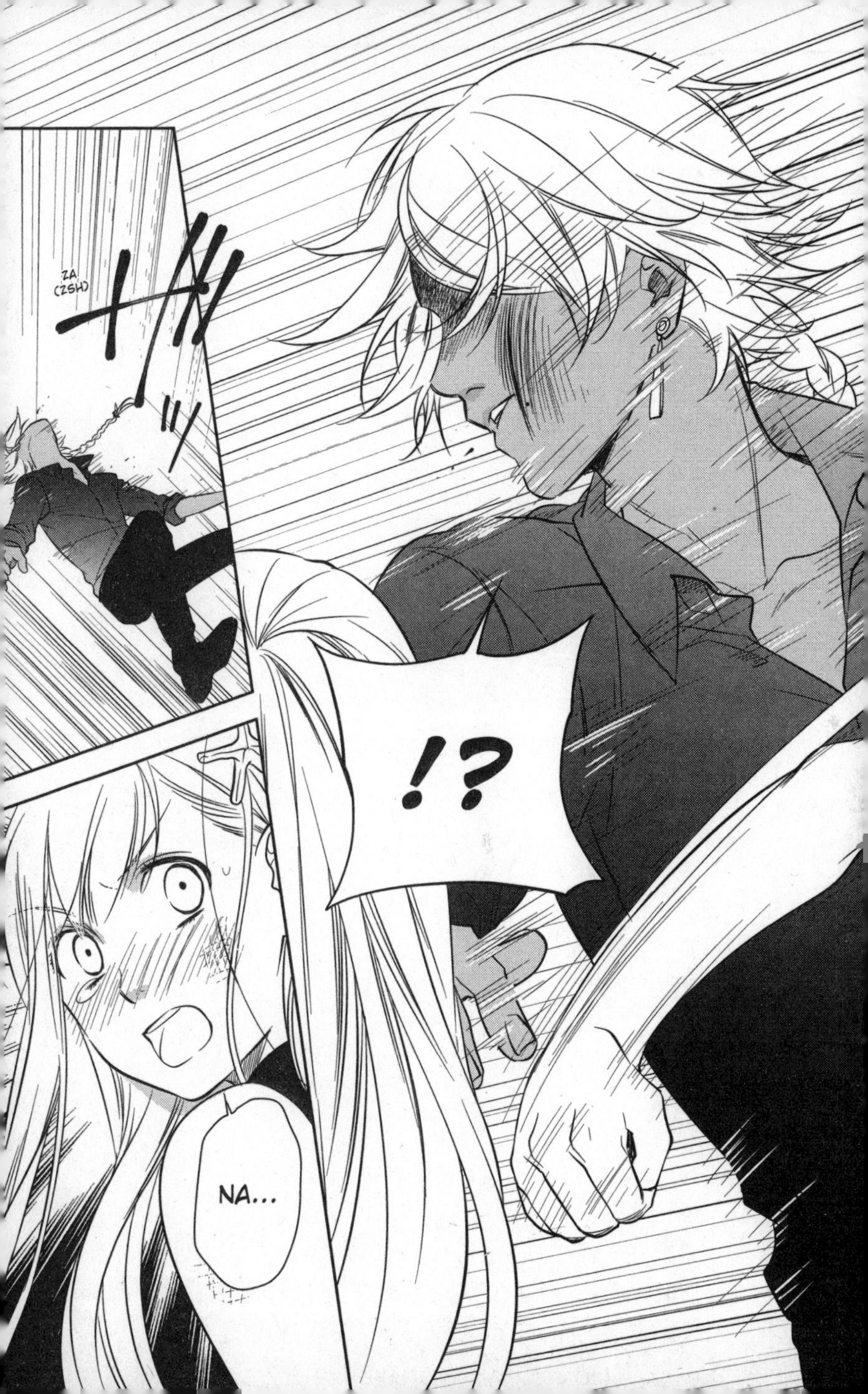
ZA (ZSH)
!?
NA...

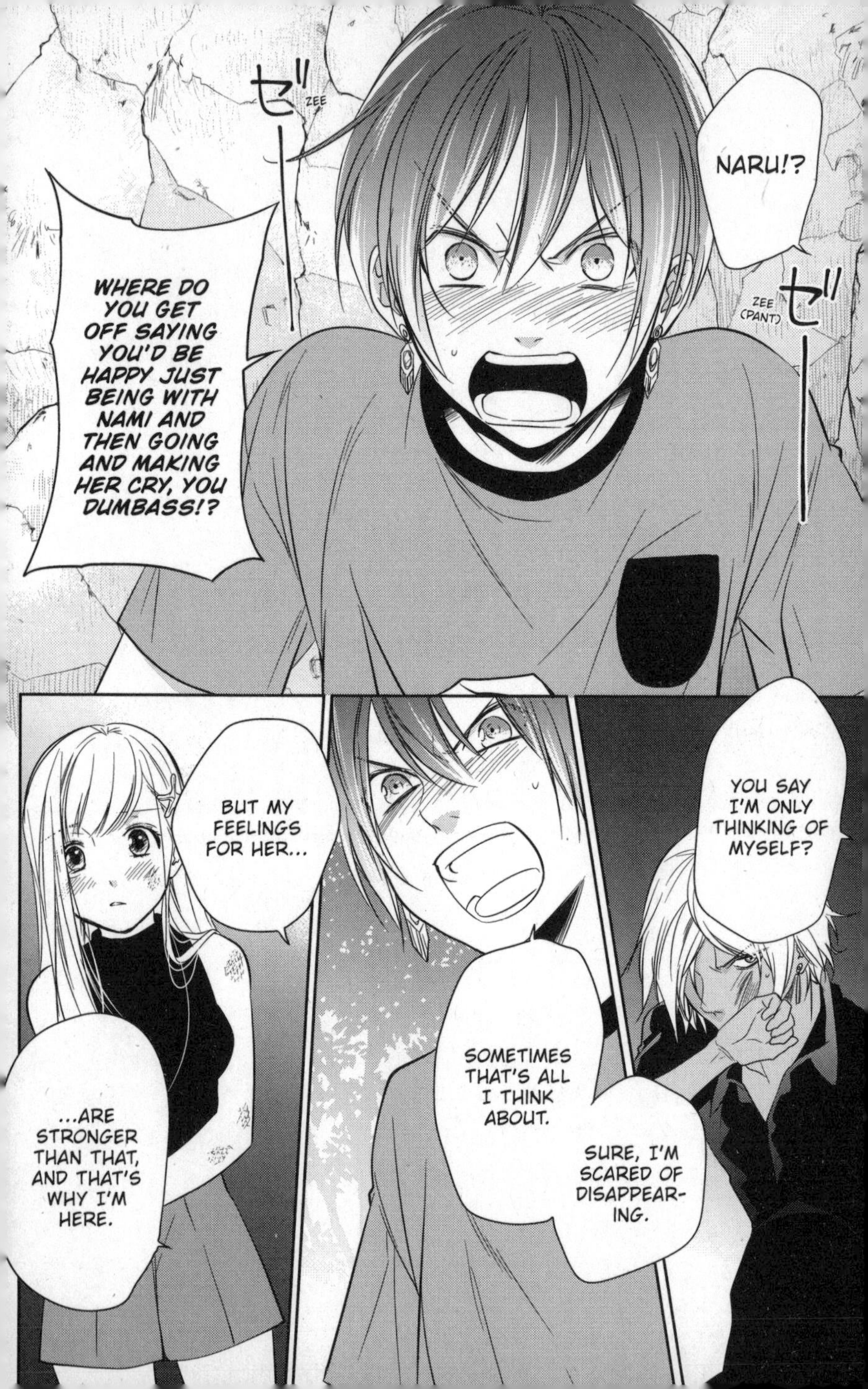
NARU!?
ZEE (PANT)
ZEE
WHERE DO YOU GET OFF SAYING YOU'D BE HAPPY JUST BEING WITH NAMI AND THEN GOING AND MAKING HER CRY, YOU DUMBASS!?
YOU SAY I'M ONLY THINKING OF MYSELF?
SURE, I'M SCARED OF DISAPPEAR-ING.
SOMETIMES THAT'S ALL I THINK ABOUT.
BUT MY FEELINGS FOR HER...
...ARE STRONGER THAN THAT, AND THAT'S WHY I'M HERE.

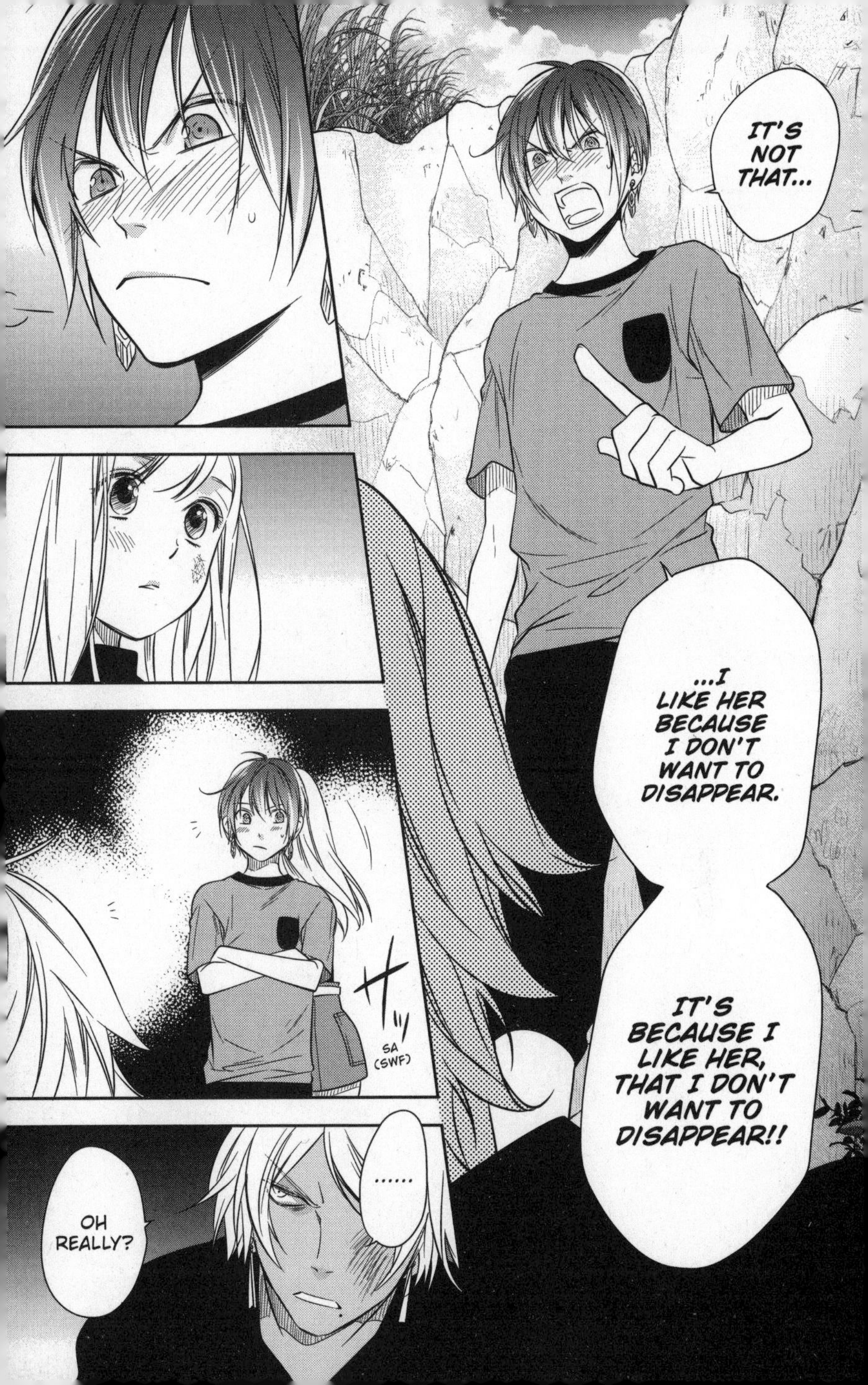
IT'S NOT THAT...
...I LIKE HER BECAUSE I DON'T WANT TO DISAPPEAR.
IT'S BECAUSE I LIKE HER, THAT I DON'T WANT TO DISAPPEAR!!
SA (SWF)
......
OH REALLY?

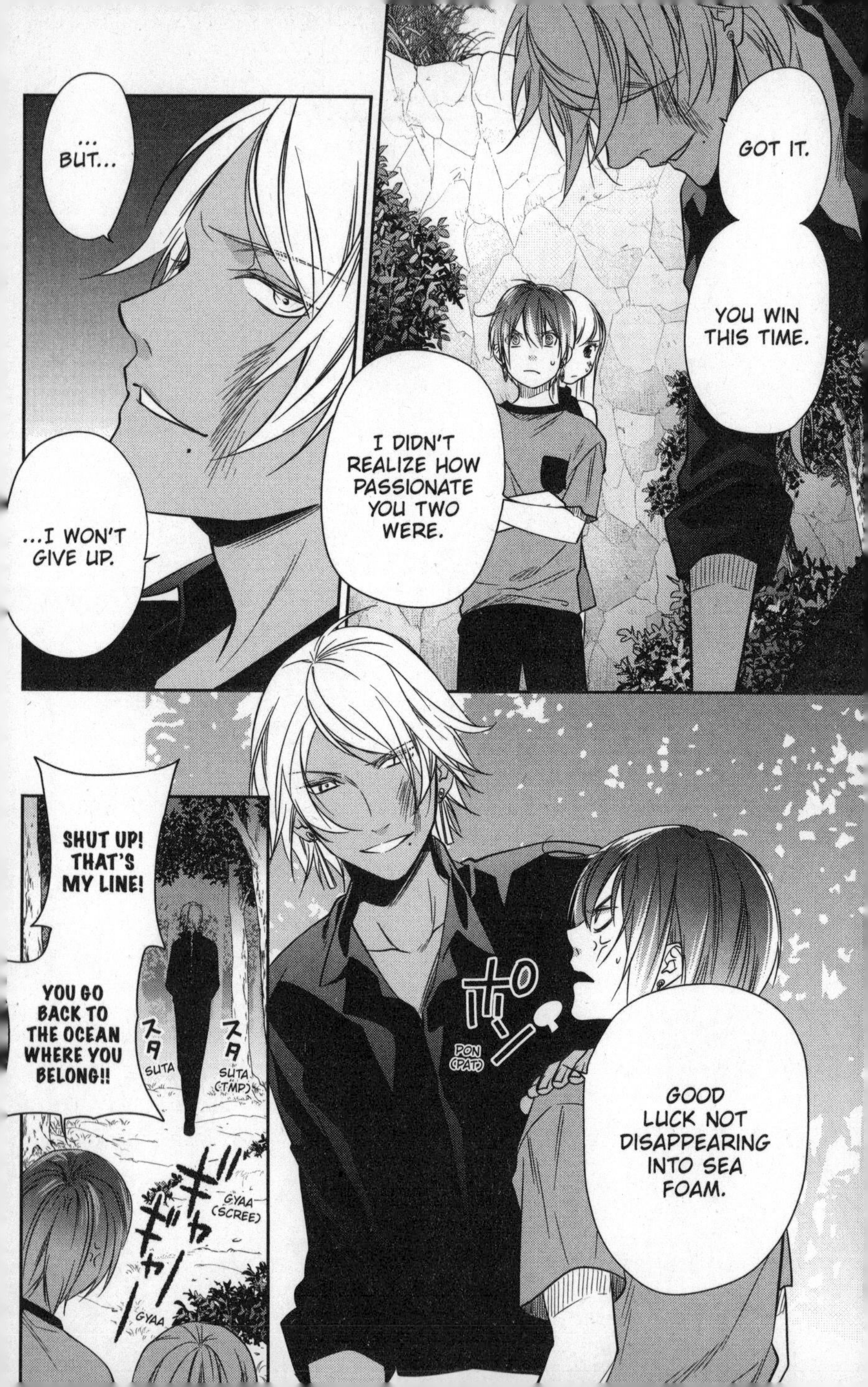
GOT IT.
YOU WIN THIS TIME.
I DIDN'T REALIZE HOW PASSIONATE YOU TWO WERE.
... BUT...
...I WON'T GIVE UP.
ポン
PON (PAT)
GOOD LUCK NOT DISAPPEARING INTO SEA FOAM.
SHUT UP! THAT'S MY LINE!
YOU GO BACK TO THE OCEAN WHERE YOU BELONG!!
スタ
SUTA (TMP)
スタ
SUTA
ギャ
GYAA (SCREE)
ギャー
GYAA

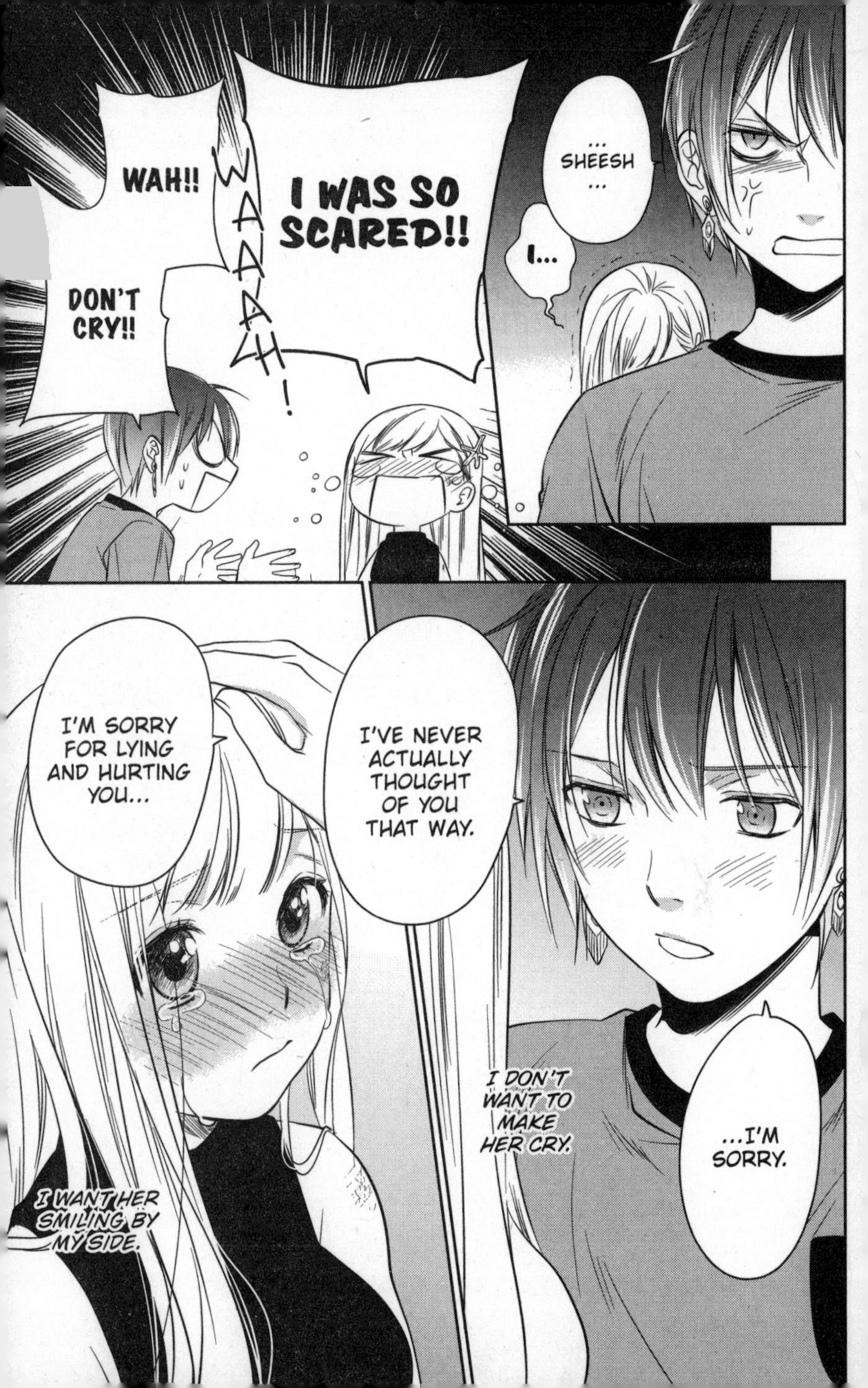

... SHEESH ...
I...
I WAS SO SCARED!!
WAAAAH!
WAH!!
DON'T CRY!!
I'VE NEVER ACTUALLY THOUGHT OF YOU THAT WAY.
...I'M SORRY.
I DON'T WANT TO MAKE HER CRY.
I'M SORRY FOR LYING AND HURTING YOU...
I WANT HER SMILING BY MY SIDE.

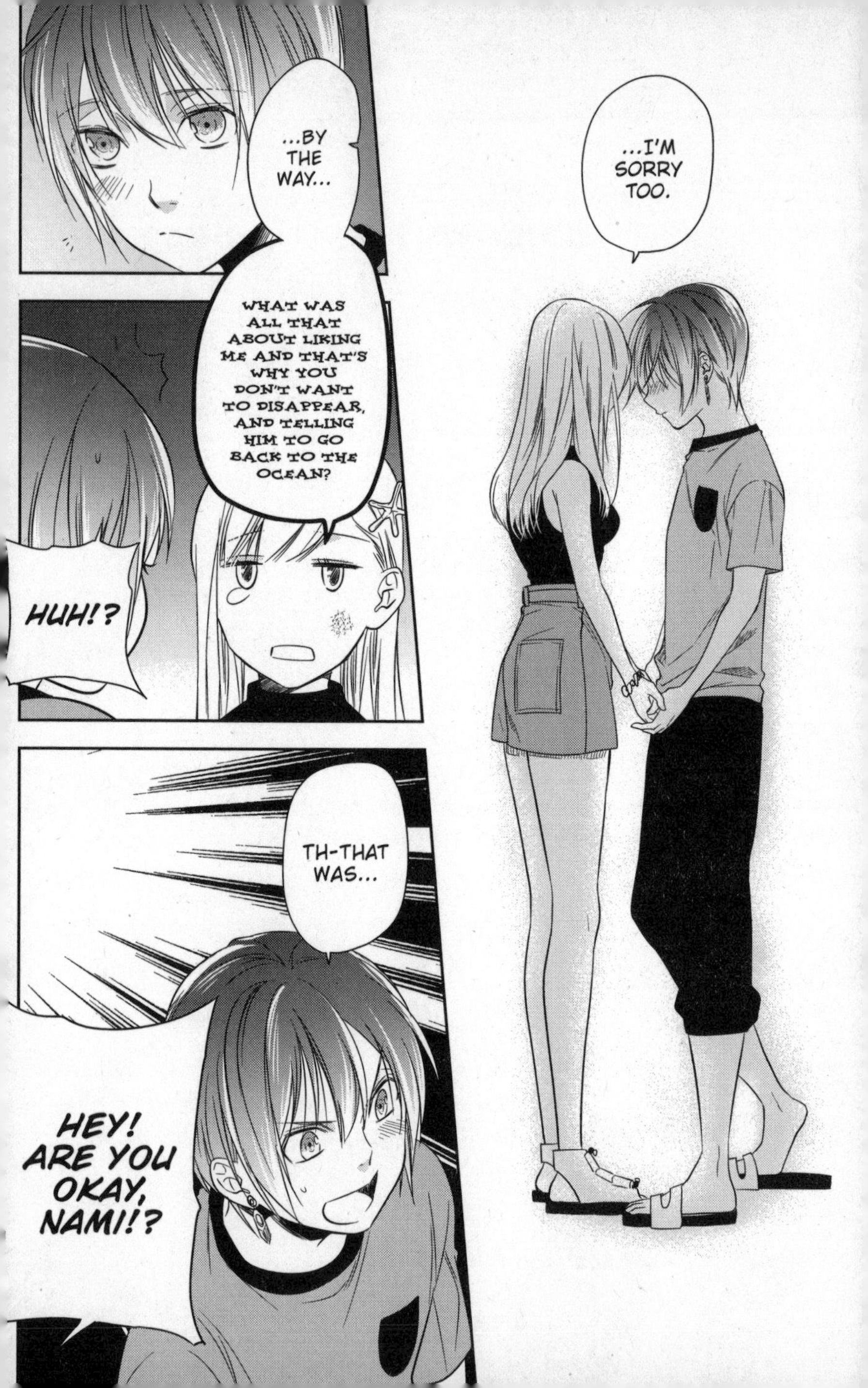
...I'M SORRY TOO.
...BY THE WAY...
WHAT WAS ALL THAT ABOUT LIKING ME AND THAT'S WHY YOU DON'T WANT TO DISAPPEAR, AND TELLING HIM TO GO BACK TO THE OCEAN?
HUH!?
TH-THAT WAS...
HEY! ARE YOU OKAY, NAMI!?

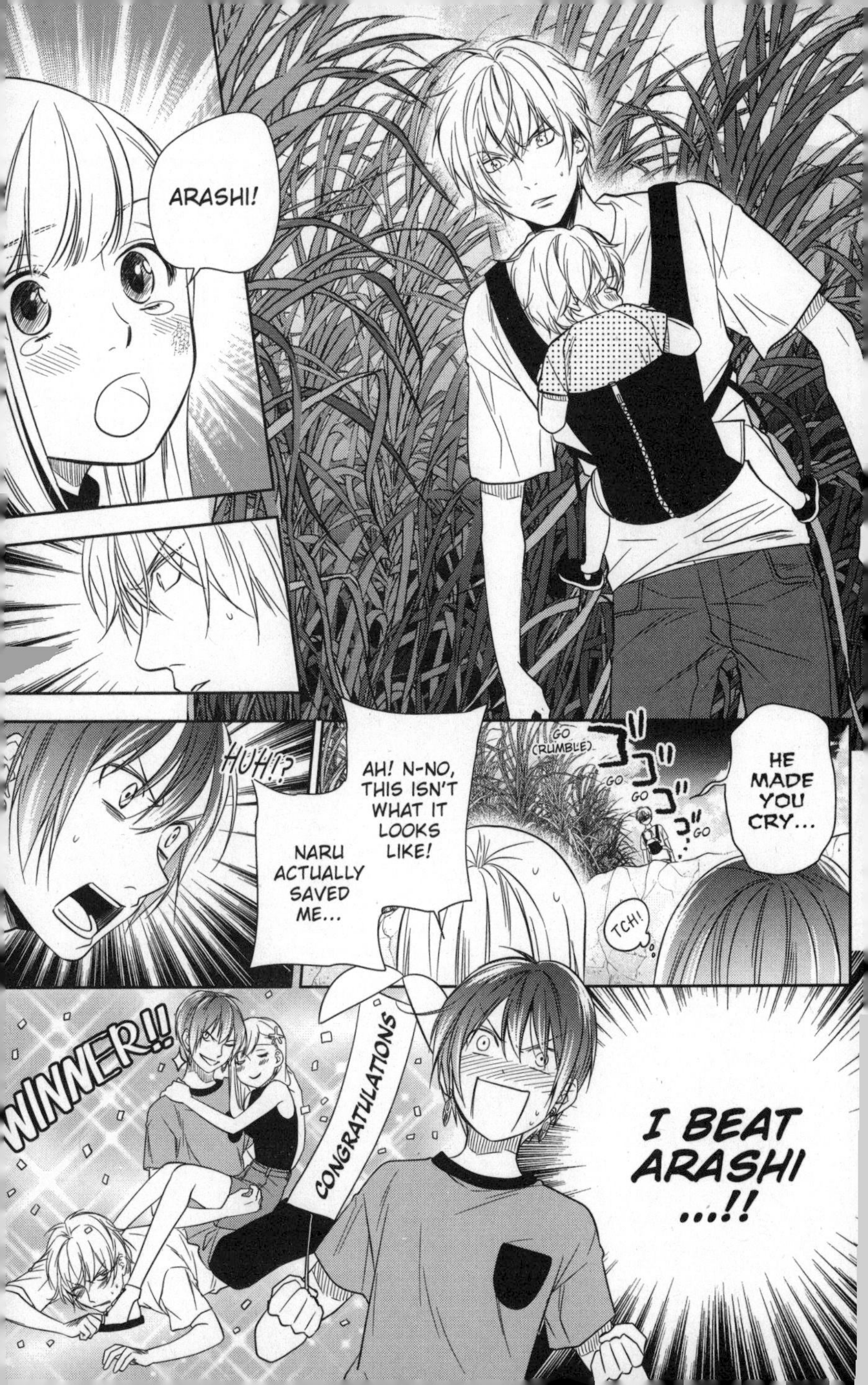

ARASHI!
HE MADE YOU CRY...
GO (RUMBLE) GO GO GO
TCH!
AH! N-NO, THIS ISN'T WHAT IT LOOKS LIKE!
HUH!?
NARU ACTUALLY SAVED ME...
I BEAT ARASHI ...!!
CONGRATULATIONS
WINNER!!

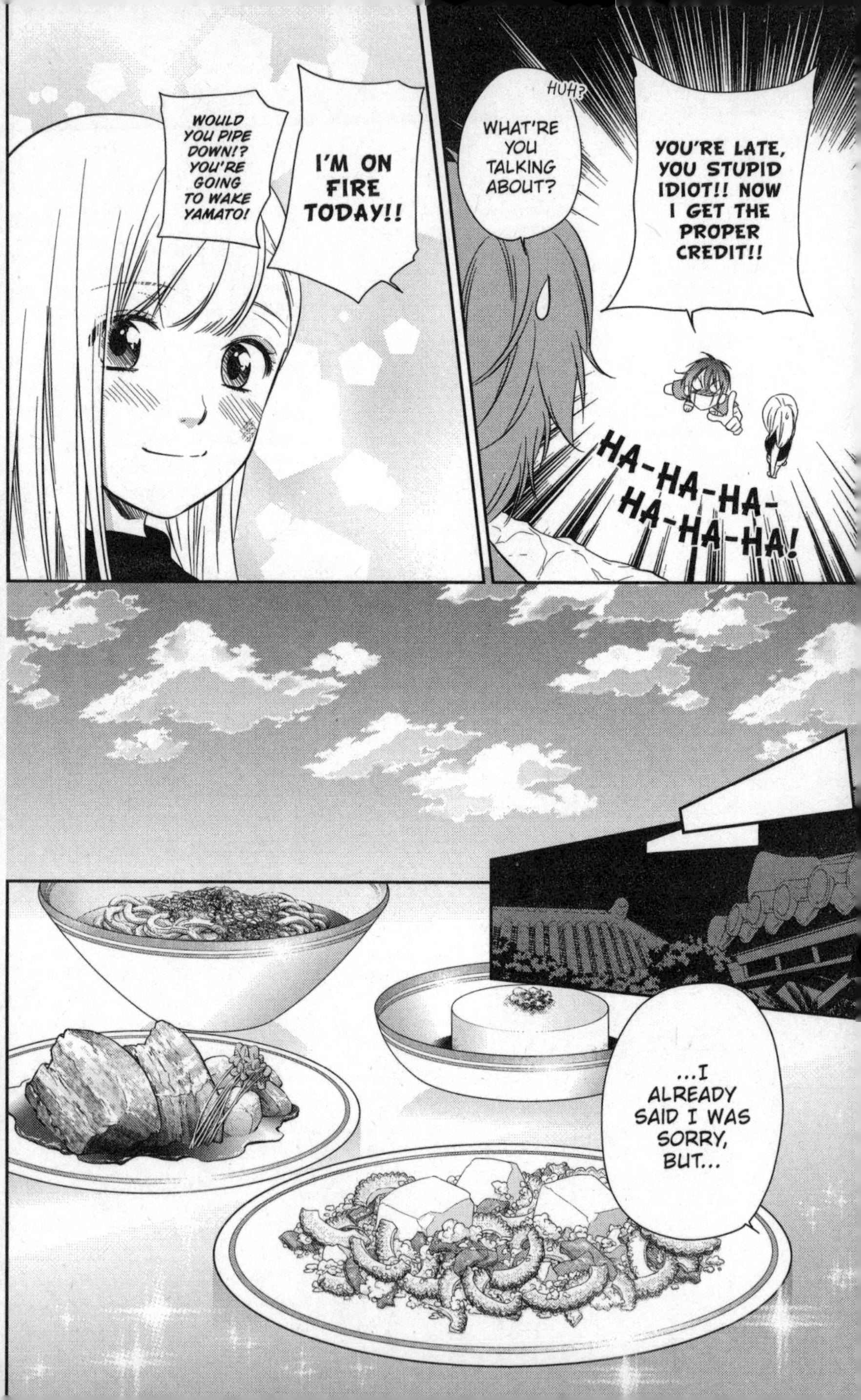
YOU'RE LATE, YOU STUPID IDIOT!! NOW I GET THE PROPER CREDIT!!
HUH?
WHAT'RE YOU TALKING ABOUT?
HA-HA-HA-HA-HA-HA!
I'M ON FIRE TODAY!!
WOULD YOU PIPE DOWN!? YOU'RE GOING TO WAKE YAMATO!
...I ALREADY SAID I WAS SORRY, BUT...

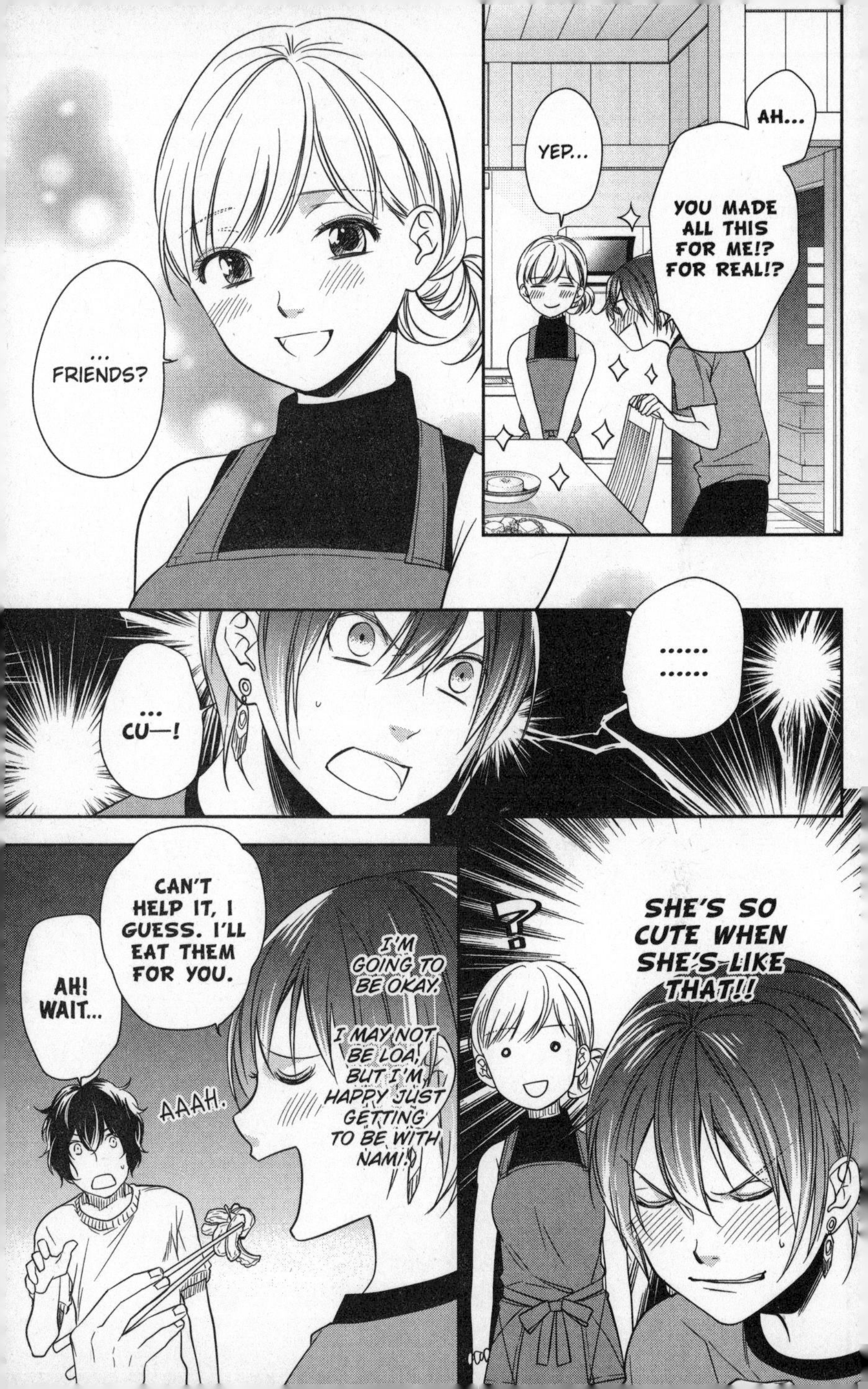
AH...
YOU MADE ALL THIS FOR ME!? FOR REAL!?
YEP...
... FRIENDS?
....
... CU—!
SHE'S SO CUTE WHEN SHE'S LIKE THAT!!
?
CAN'T HELP IT, I GUESS. I'LL EAT THEM FOR YOU.
I'M GOING TO BE OKAY.
I MAY NOT BE LOA! BUT I'M HAPPY JUST GETTING TO BE WITH NAMI!
AH! WAIT...
AAAH.

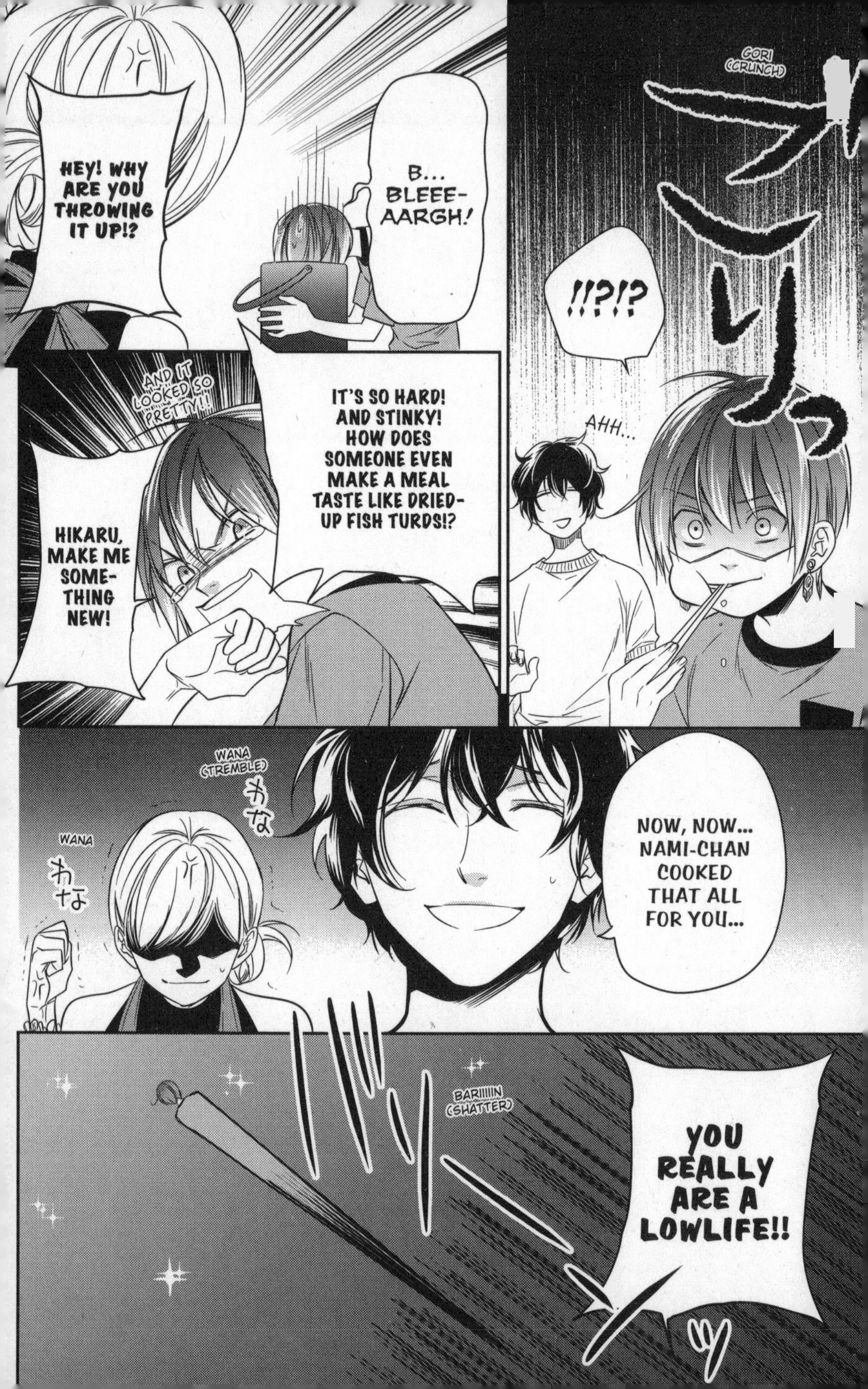
GORI (CRUNCH)
!!?!?
AHH...
B... BLEEE-AARGH!
HEY! WHY ARE YOU THROWING IT UP!?
IT'S SO HARD! AND STINKY! HOW DOES SOMEONE EVEN MAKE A MEAL TASTE LIKE DRIED-UP FISH TURDS!?
AND IT LOOKED SO PRETTY!!
HIKARU, MAKE ME SOME-THING NEW!
NOW, NOW... NAMI-CHAN COOKED THAT ALL FOR YOU...
WANA (TREMBLE)
わな
WANA
わな
YOU REALLY ARE A LOWLIFE!!
BARIIIIN (SHATTER)

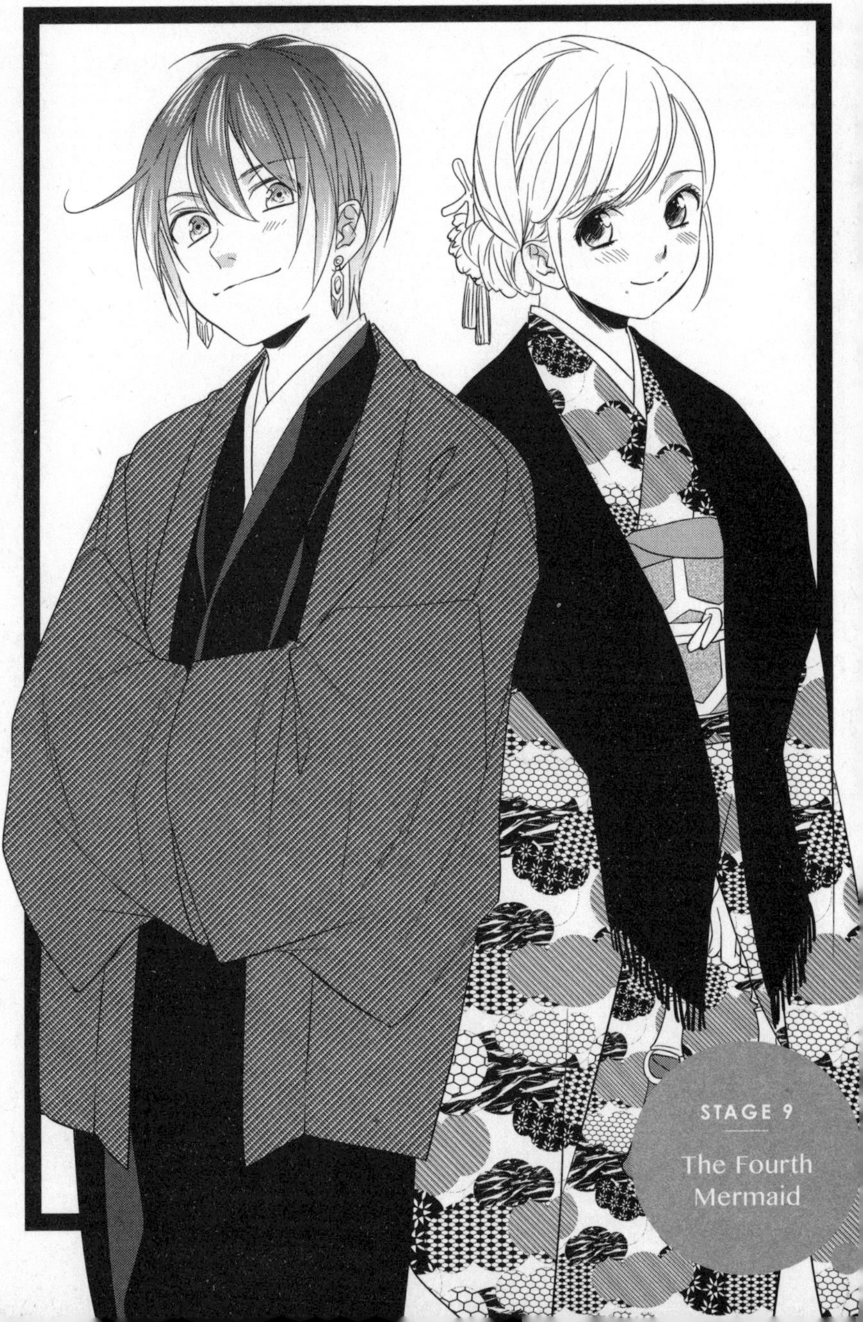
STAGE 9
The Fourth Mermaid

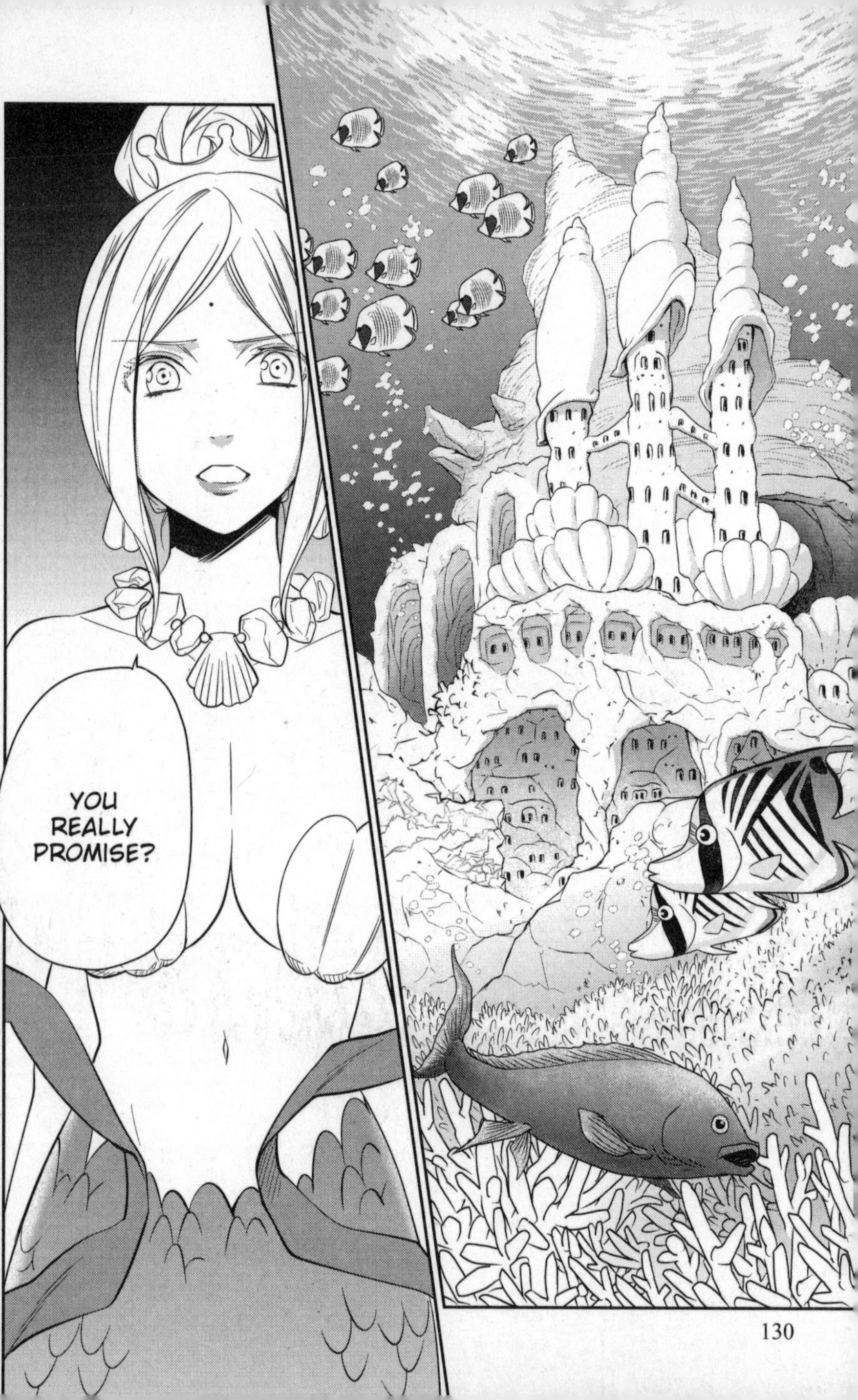
YOU REALLY PROMISE?

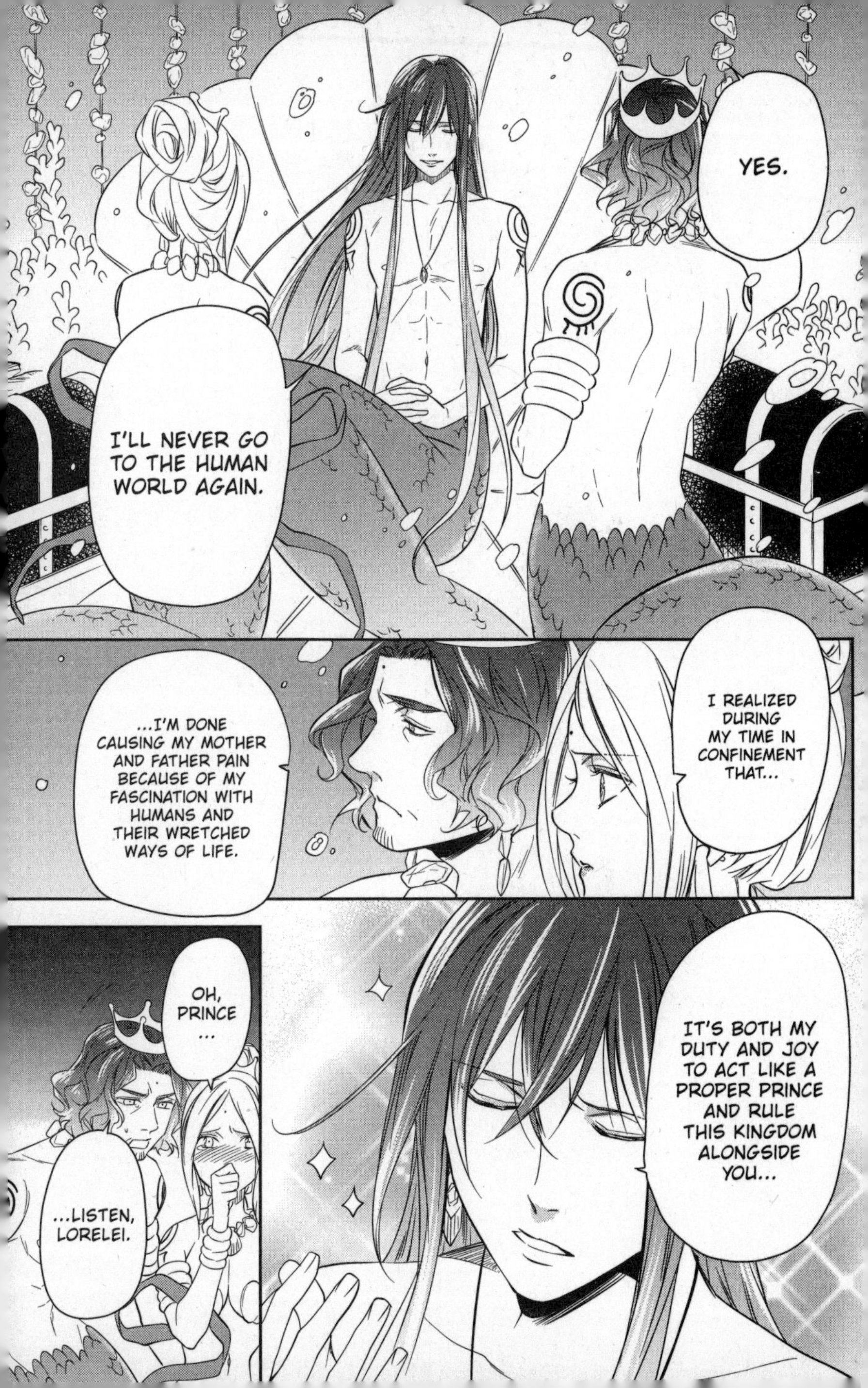
YES.
I'LL NEVER GO TO THE HUMAN WORLD AGAIN.
I REALIZED DURING MY TIME IN CONFINEMENT THAT...
...I'M DONE CAUSING MY MOTHER AND FATHER PAIN BECAUSE OF MY FASCINATION WITH HUMANS AND THEIR WRETCHED WAYS OF LIFE.
IT'S BOTH MY DUTY AND JOY TO ACT LIKE A PROPER PRINCE AND RULE THIS KINGDOM ALONGSIDE YOU...
OH, PRINCE ...
...LISTEN, LORELEI.

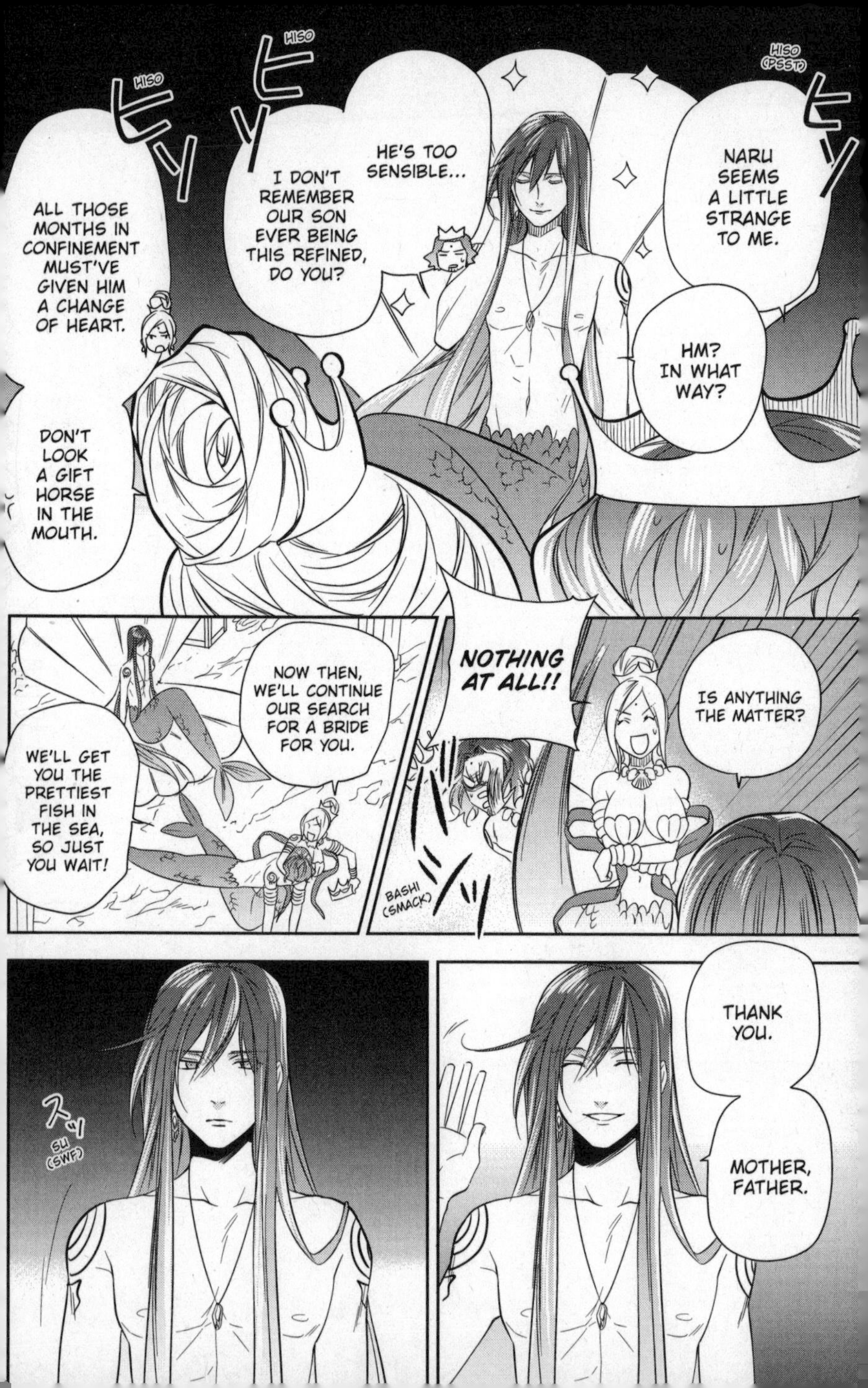
HISO (PSST)
ヒソ
NARU SEEMS A LITTLE STRANGE TO ME.
HM? IN WHAT WAY?
HISO
ヒソ
HE'S TOO SENSIBLE...
I DON'T REMEMBER OUR SON EVER BEING THIS REFINED, DO YOU?
HISO
ヒソ
ALL THOSE MONTHS IN CONFINEMENT MUST'VE GIVEN HIM A CHANGE OF HEART.
DON'T LOOK A GIFT HORSE IN THE MOUTH.
IS ANYTHING THE MATTER?
NOTHING AT ALL!!
BASHI (SMACK)
NOW THEN, WE'LL CONTINUE OUR SEARCH FOR A BRIDE FOR YOU.
WE'LL GET YOU THE PRETTIEST FISH IN THE SEA, SO JUST YOU WAIT!
THANK YOU.
MOTHER, FATHER.
スッ
SU (SWF)

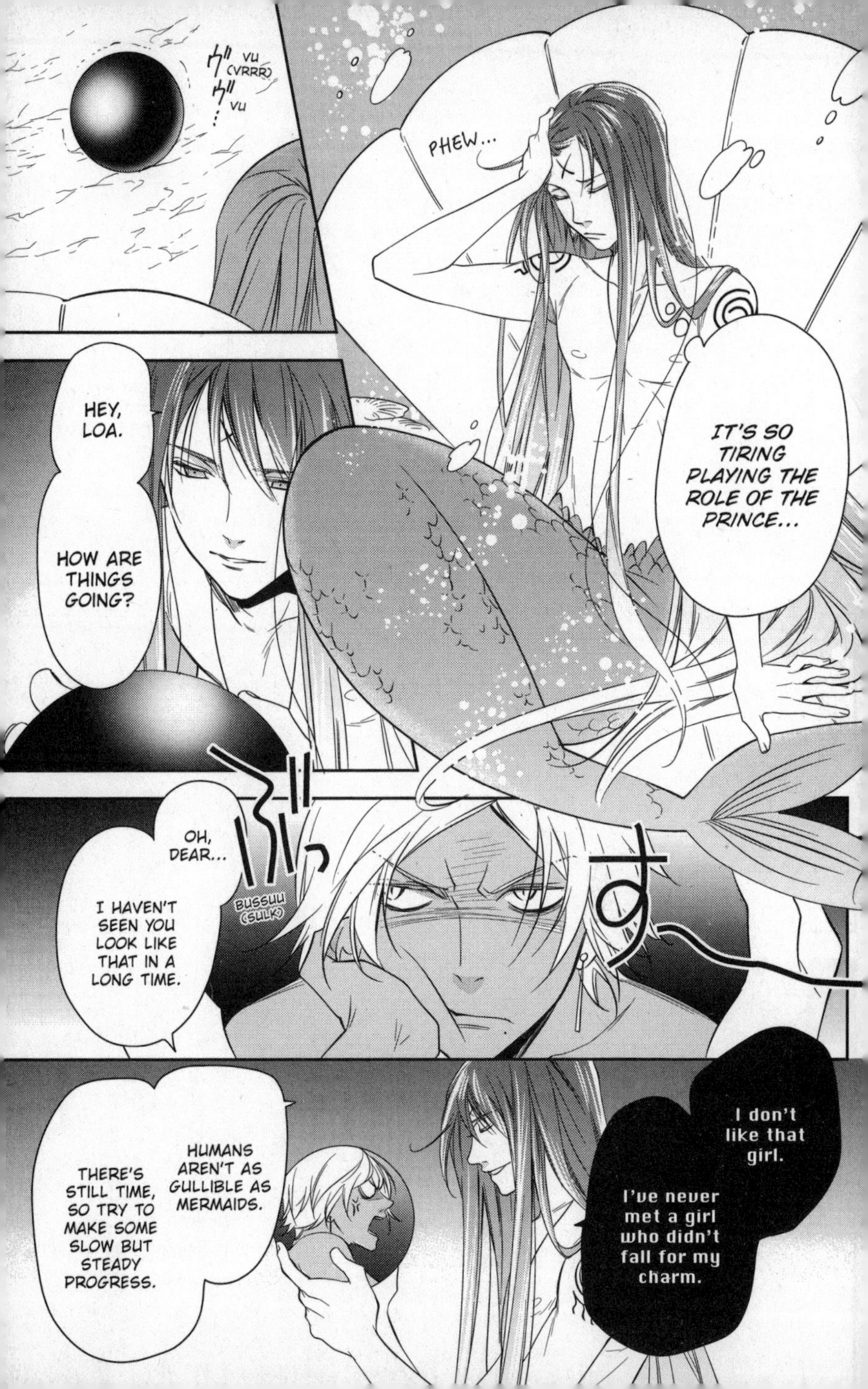
PHEW...
IT'S SO TIRING PLAYING THE ROLE OF THE PRINCE...
ヴ" VU (VRRR)
ヴ" VU
HEY, LOA.
HOW ARE THINGS GOING?
すー
ぶすっ BUSSUU (SULK)
OH, DEAR...
I HAVEN'T SEEN YOU LOOK LIKE THAT IN A LONG TIME.
I don't like that girl.
I've never met a girl who didn't fall for my charm.
HUMANS AREN'T AS GULLIBLE AS MERMAIDS.
THERE'S STILL TIME, SO TRY TO MAKE SOME SLOW BUT STEADY PROGRESS.

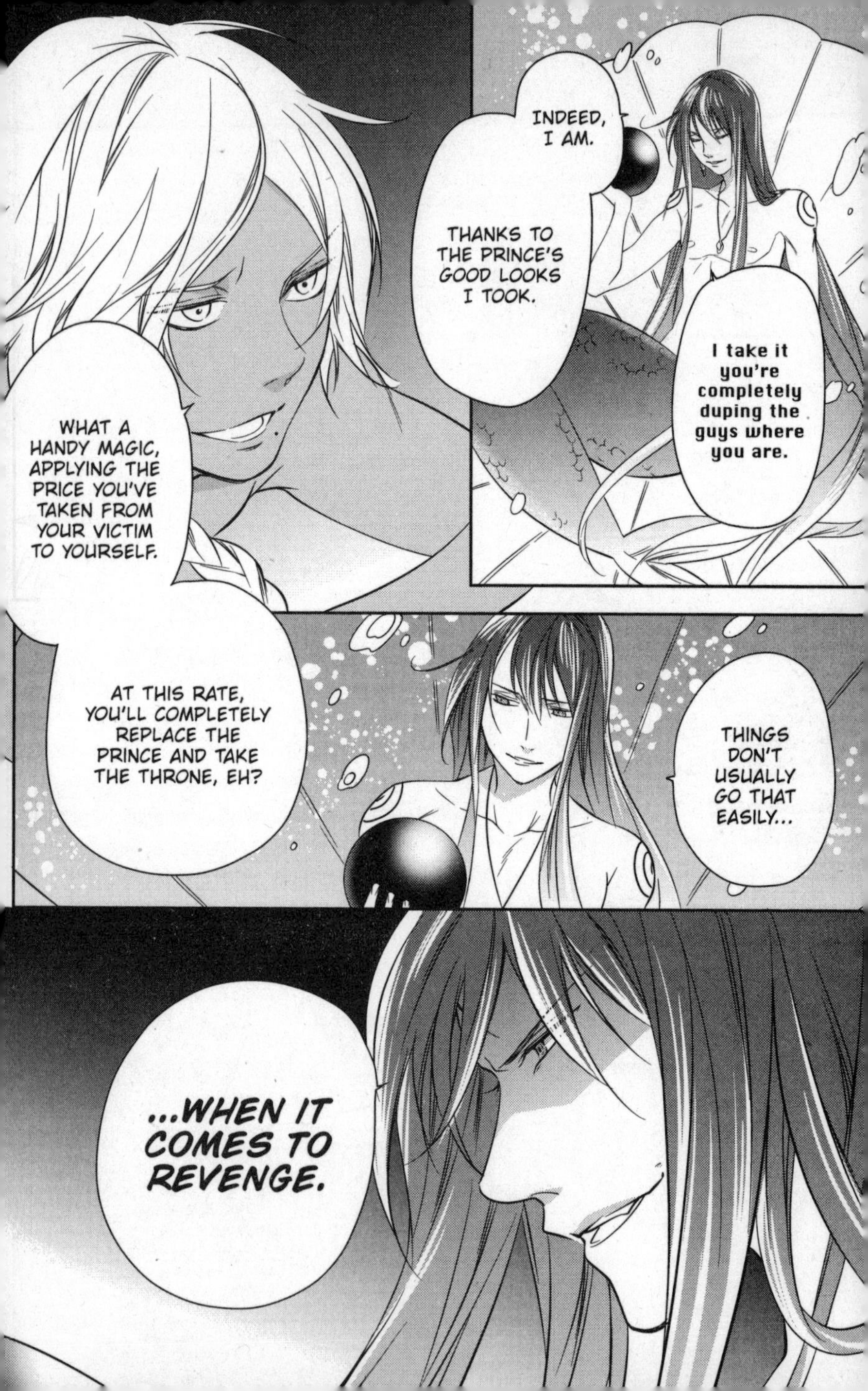

I take it you're completely duping the guys where you are.
INDEED, I AM.
THANKS TO THE PRINCE'S GOOD LOOKS I TOOK.
WHAT A HANDY MAGIC, APPLYING THE PRICE YOU'VE TAKEN FROM YOUR VICTIM TO YOURSELF.
AT THIS RATE, YOU'LL COMPLETELY REPLACE THE PRINCE AND TAKE THE THRONE, EH?
THINGS DON'T USUALLY GO THAT EASILY...
...WHEN IT COMES TO REVENGE.

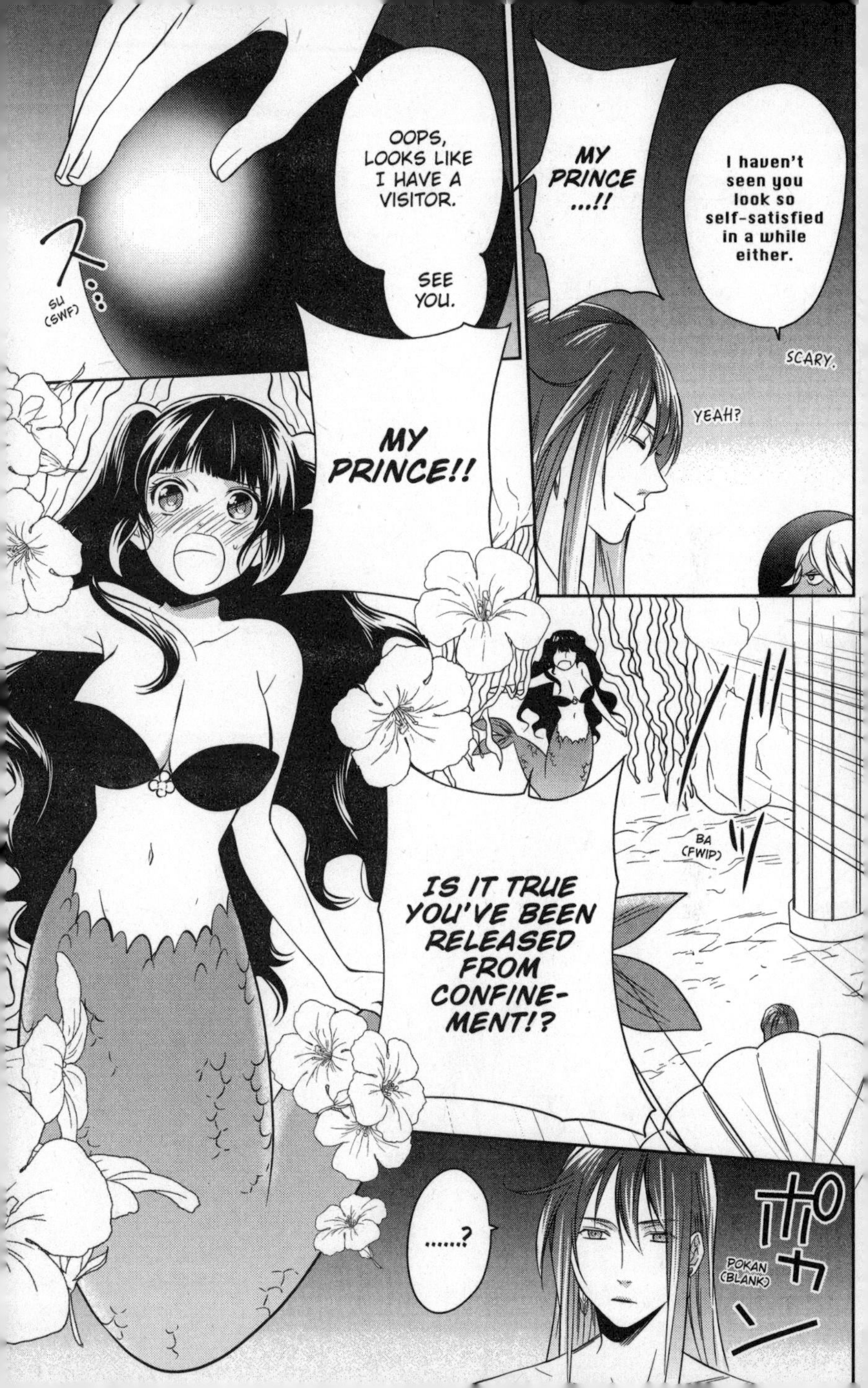
I haven't seen you look so self-satisfied in a while either.
YEAH?
SCARY.
MY PRINCE ...!!
OOPS, LOOKS LIKE I HAVE A VISITOR.
SEE YOU.
SU (SWF)
MY PRINCE!!
BA (FWIP)
IS IT TRUE YOU'VE BEEN RELEASED FROM CONFINE-MENT!?
POKAN (BLANK)
......?

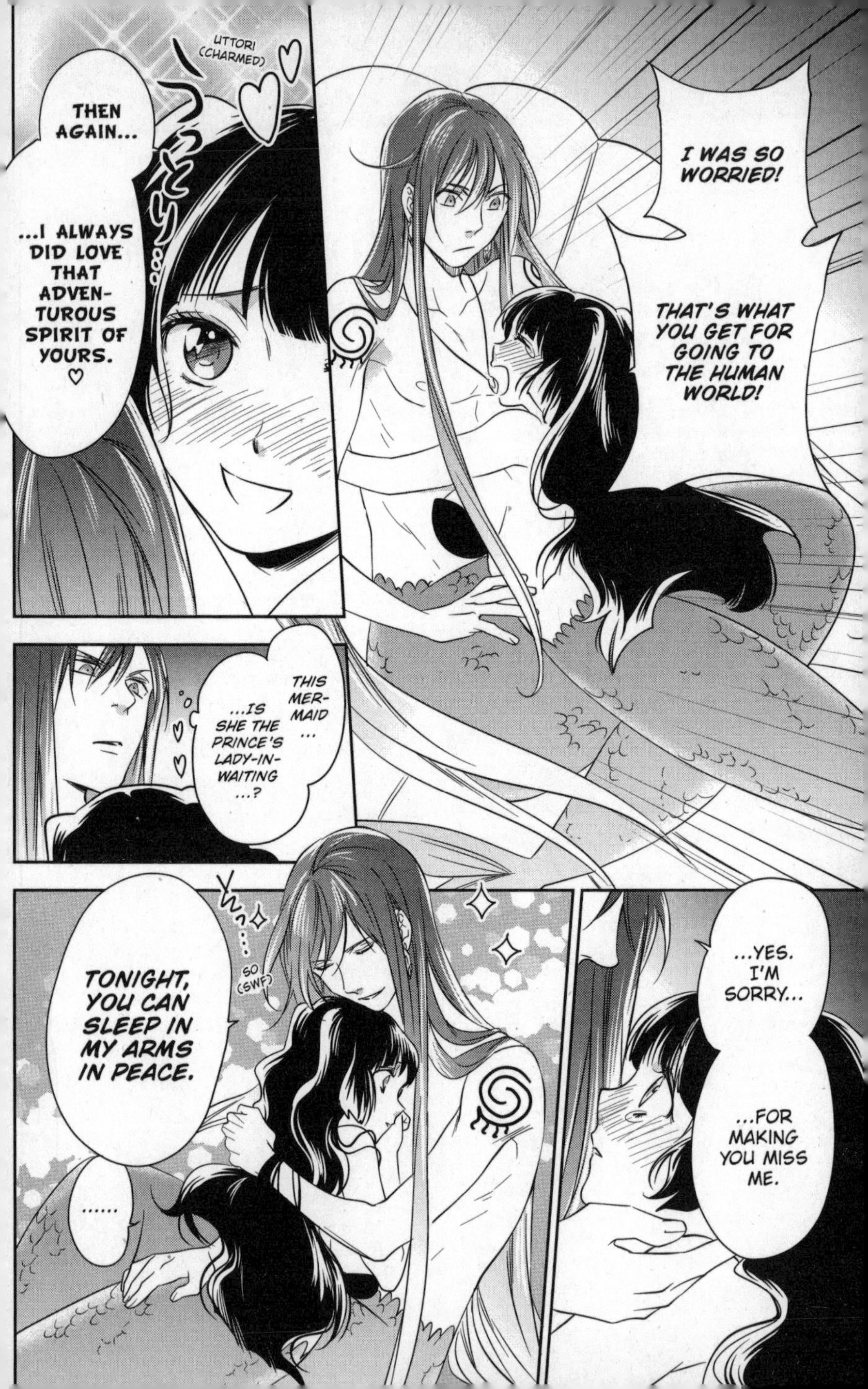
I WAS SO WORRIED!
THAT'S WHAT YOU GET FOR GOING TO THE HUMAN WORLD!
UTTORI (CHARMED)
THEN AGAIN...
...I ALWAYS DID LOVE THAT ADVEN-TUROUS SPIRIT OF YOURS. ♡
THIS MER-MAID ...
...IS SHE THE PRINCE'S LADY-IN-WAITING ...?
...YES. I'M SORRY...
...FOR MAKING YOU MISS ME.
SO (SWF)
TONIGHT, YOU CAN SLEEP IN MY ARMS IN PEACE.
......

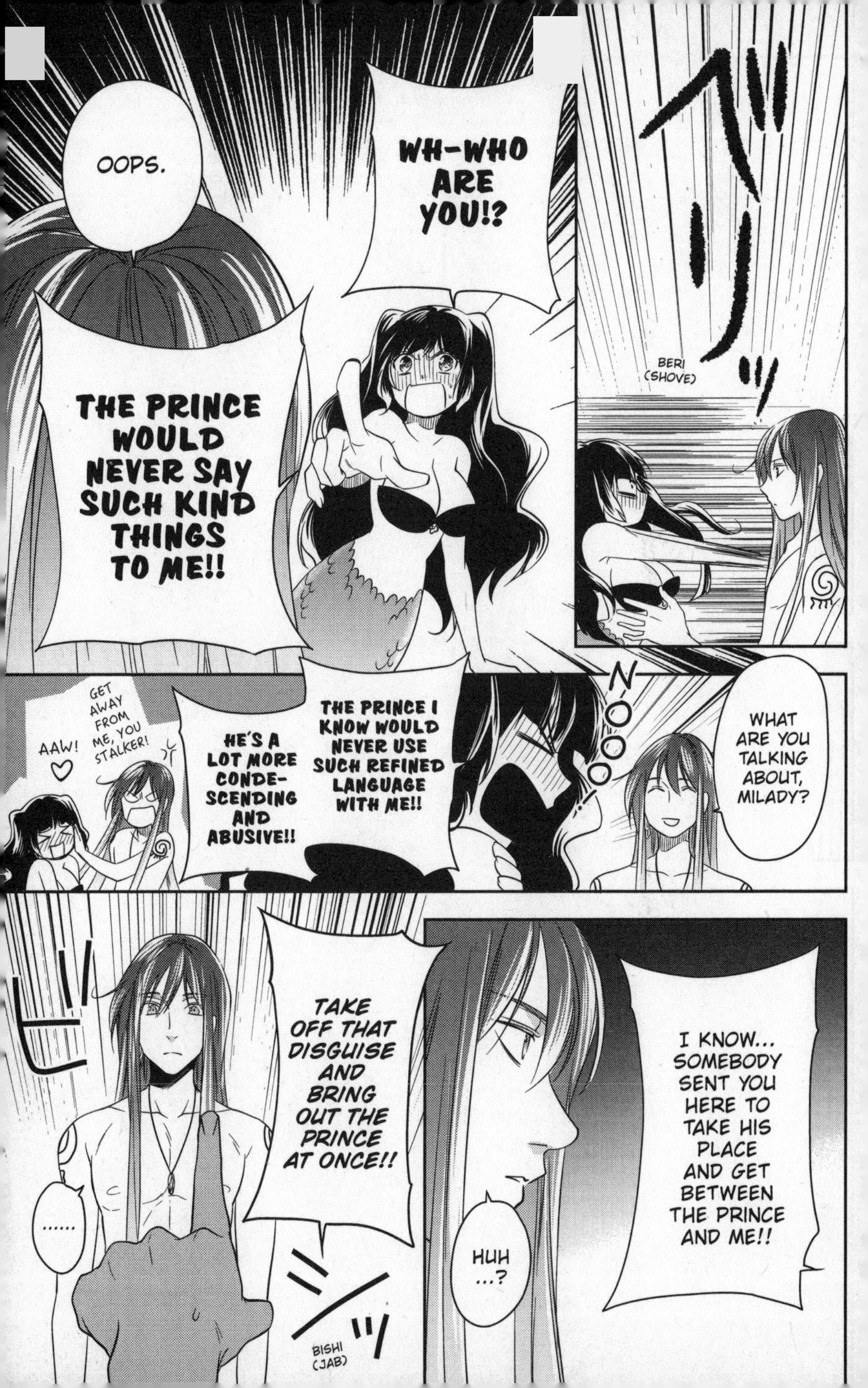
BERI (SHOVE)
WH-WHO ARE YOU!?
OOPS.
THE PRINCE WOULD NEVER SAY SUCH KIND THINGS TO ME!!
WHAT ARE YOU TALKING ABOUT, MILADY?
NOOOO
THE PRINCE I KNOW WOULD NEVER USE SUCH REFINED LANGUAGE WITH ME!!
HE'S A LOT MORE CONDE-SCENDING AND ABUSIVE!!
GET AWAY FROM ME, YOU STALKER!
AAW! ♡
I KNOW... SOMEBODY SENT YOU HERE TO TAKE HIS PLACE AND GET BETWEEN THE PRINCE AND ME!!
HUH ...?
TAKE OFF THAT DISGUISE AND BRING OUT THE PRINCE AT ONCE!!
BISHI (JAB)
......

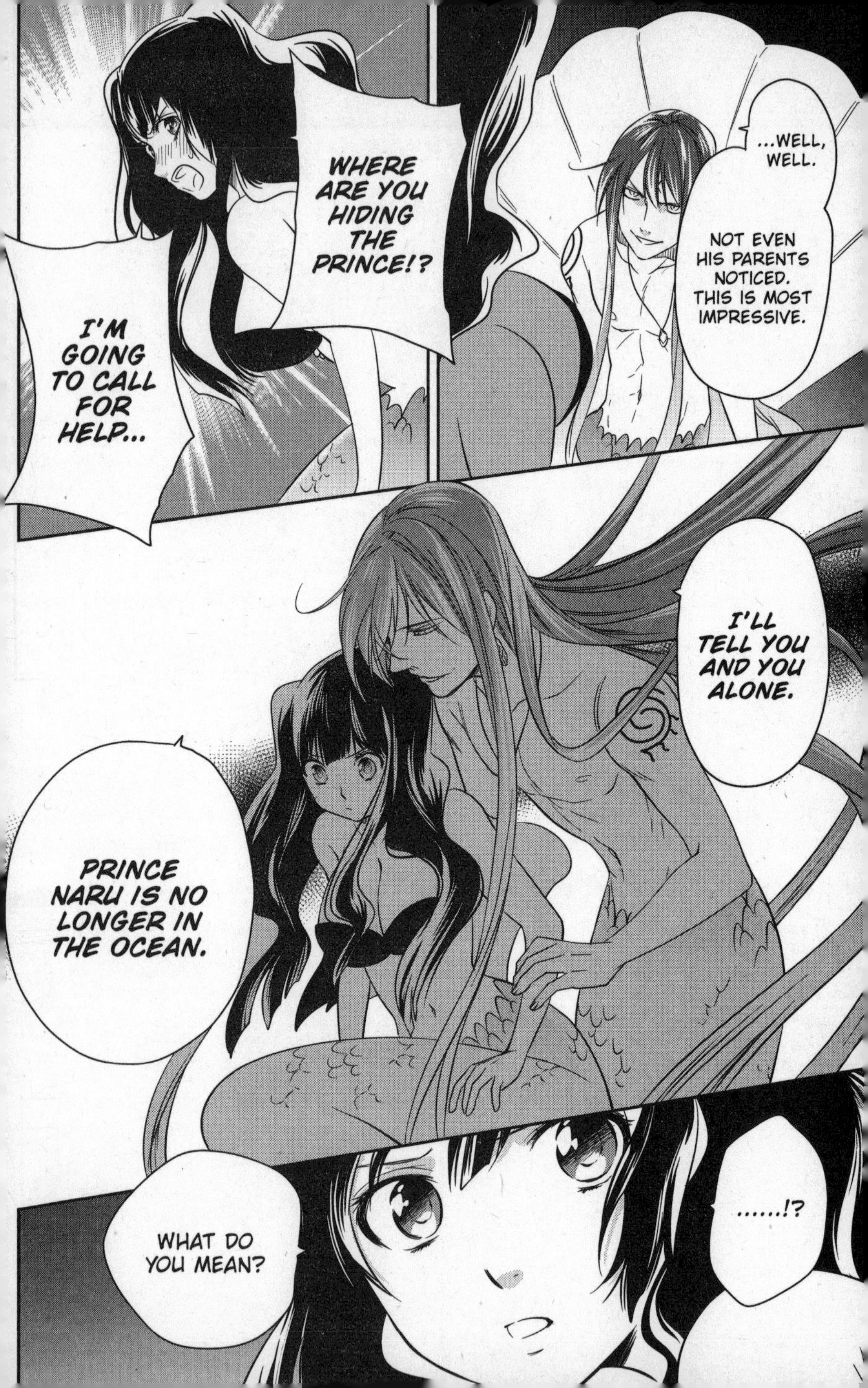
...WELL, WELL.
NOT EVEN HIS PARENTS NOTICED. THIS IS MOST IMPRESSIVE.
WHERE ARE YOU HIDING THE PRINCE!?
I'M GOING TO CALL FOR HELP...
I'LL TELL YOU AND YOU ALONE.
PRINCE NARU IS NO LONGER IN THE OCEAN.
......!?
WHAT DO YOU MEAN?

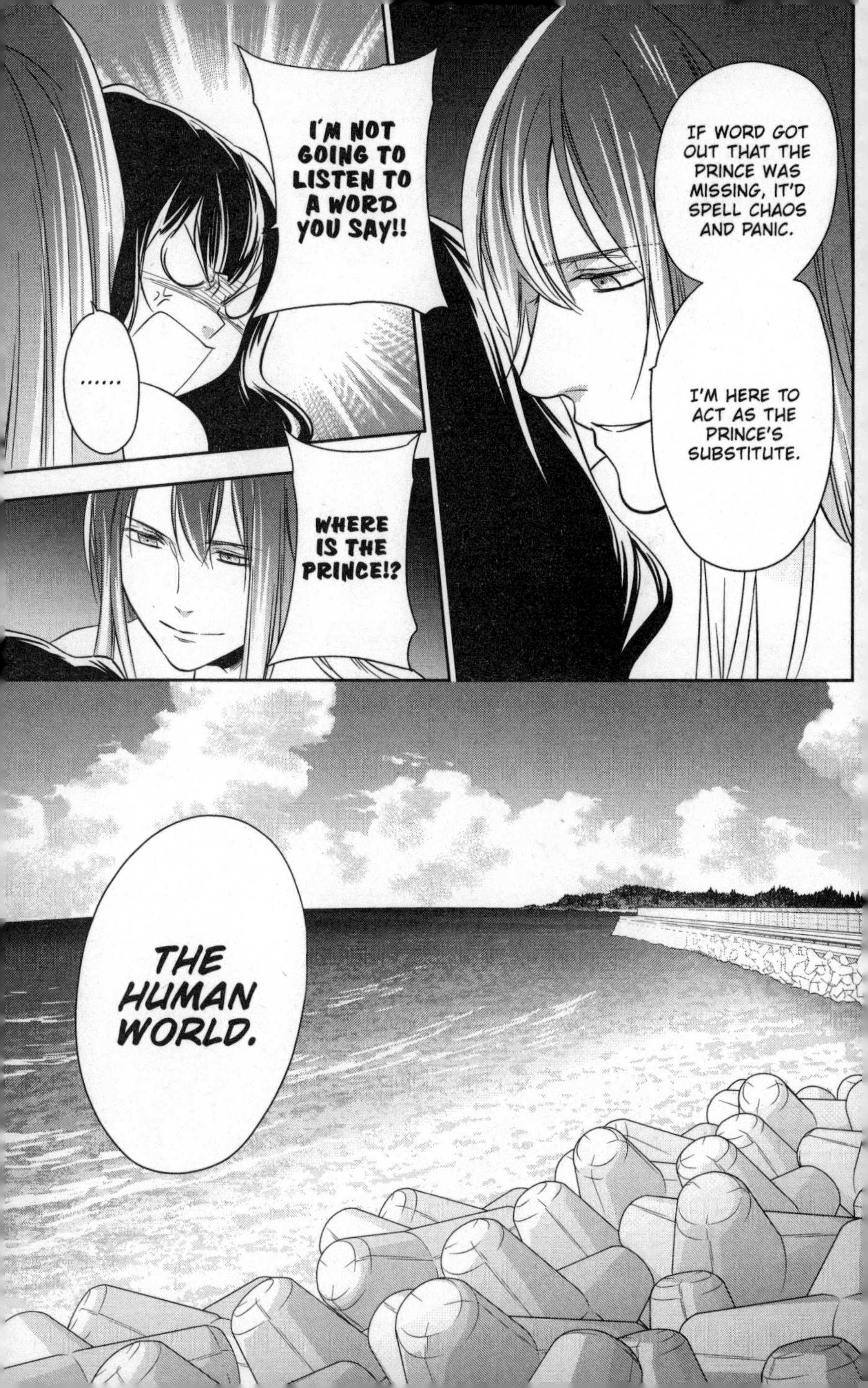
IF WORD GOT OUT THAT THE PRINCE WAS MISSING, IT'D SPELL CHAOS AND PANIC.
I'M HERE TO ACT AS THE PRINCE'S SUBSTITUTE.
I'M NOT GOING TO LISTEN TO A WORD YOU SAY!!
......
WHERE IS THE PRINCE!?
THE HUMAN WORLD.

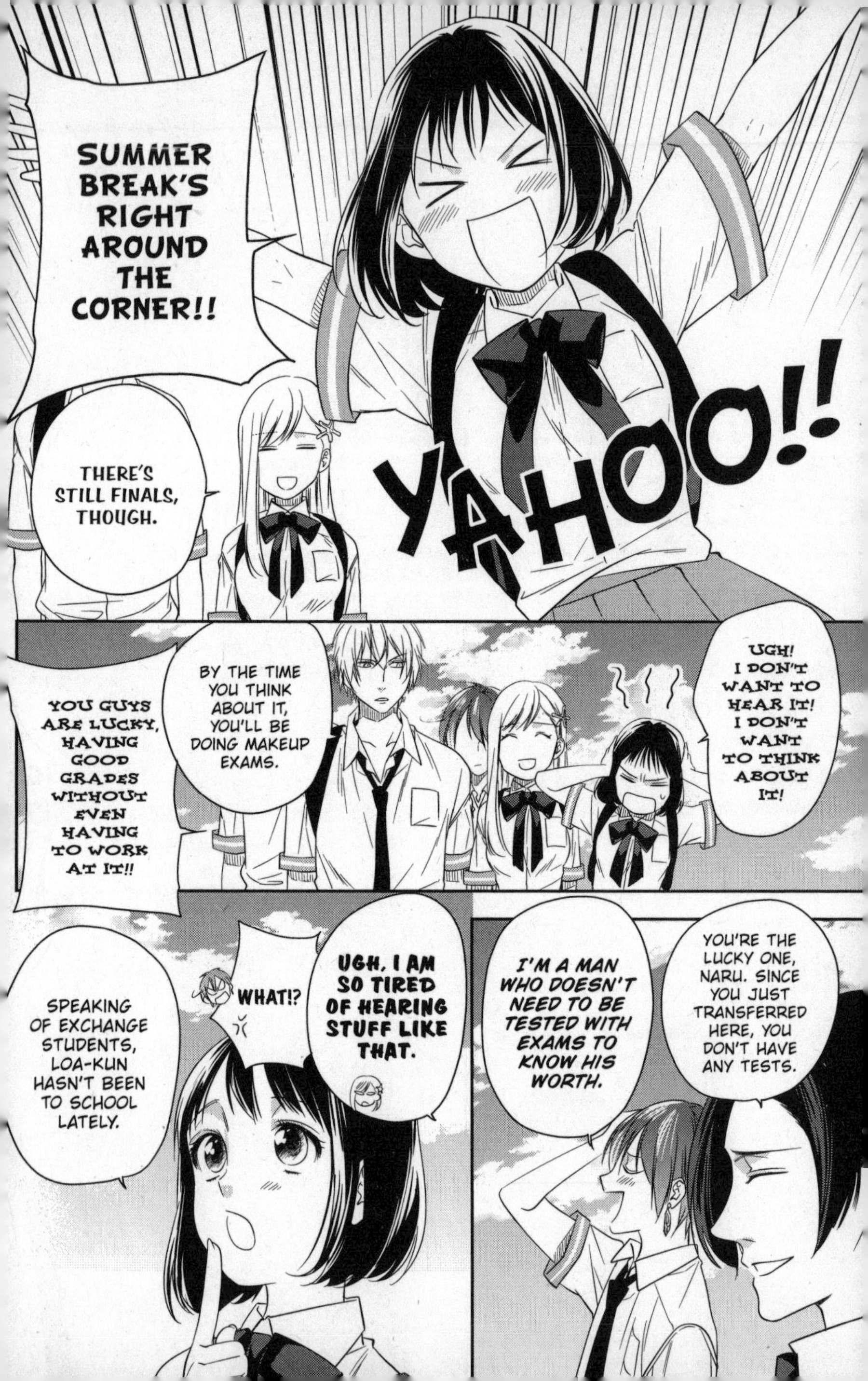
SUMMER BREAK'S RIGHT AROUND THE CORNER!!
YAHOO!!
THERE'S STILL FINALS, THOUGH.
UGH! I DON'T WANT TO HEAR IT! I DON'T WANT TO THINK ABOUT IT!
BY THE TIME YOU THINK ABOUT IT, YOU'LL BE DOING MAKEUP EXAMS.
YOU GUYS ARE LUCKY, HAVING GOOD GRADES WITHOUT EVEN HAVING TO WORK AT IT!!
YOU'RE THE LUCKY ONE, NARU. SINCE YOU JUST TRANSFERRED HERE, YOU DON'T HAVE ANY TESTS.
I'M A MAN WHO DOESN'T NEED TO BE TESTED WITH EXAMS TO KNOW HIS WORTH.
UGH, I AM SO TIRED OF HEARING STUFF LIKE THAT.
WHAT!?
SPEAKING OF EXCHANGE STUDENTS, LOA-KUN HASN'T BEEN TO SCHOOL LATELY.

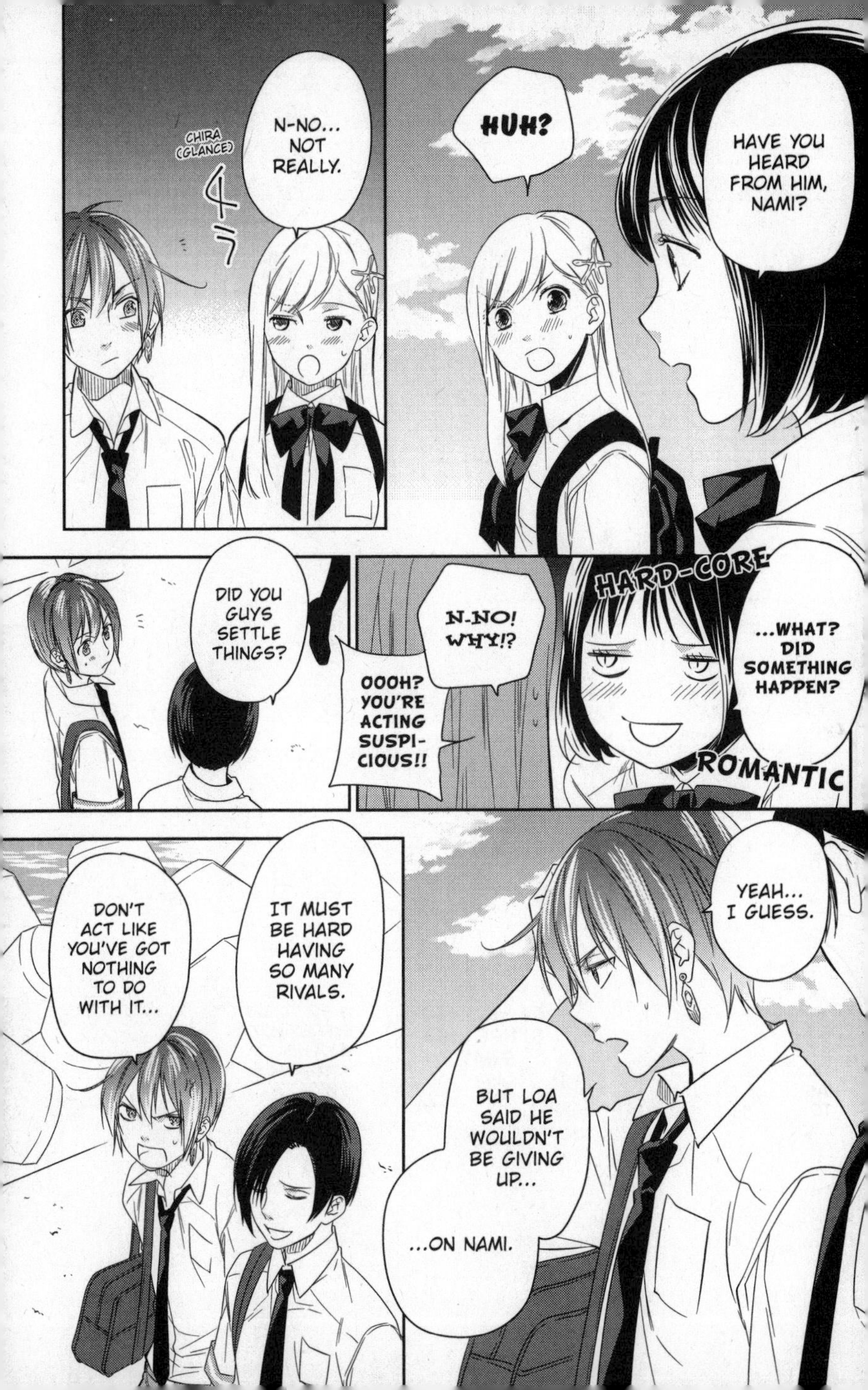
HAVE YOU HEARD FROM HIM, NAMI?
HUH?
N-NO... NOT REALLY.
CHIRA (GLANCE)
...WHAT? DID SOMETHING HAPPEN?
HARD-CORE
ROMANTIC
N-NO! WHY!?
OOOH? YOU'RE ACTING SUSPICIOUS!!
DID YOU GUYS SETTLE THINGS?
YEAH... I GUESS.
BUT LOA SAID HE WOULDN'T BE GIVING UP...
...ON NAMI.
IT MUST BE HARD HAVING SO MANY RIVALS.
DON'T ACT LIKE YOU'VE GOT NOTHING TO DO WITH IT...

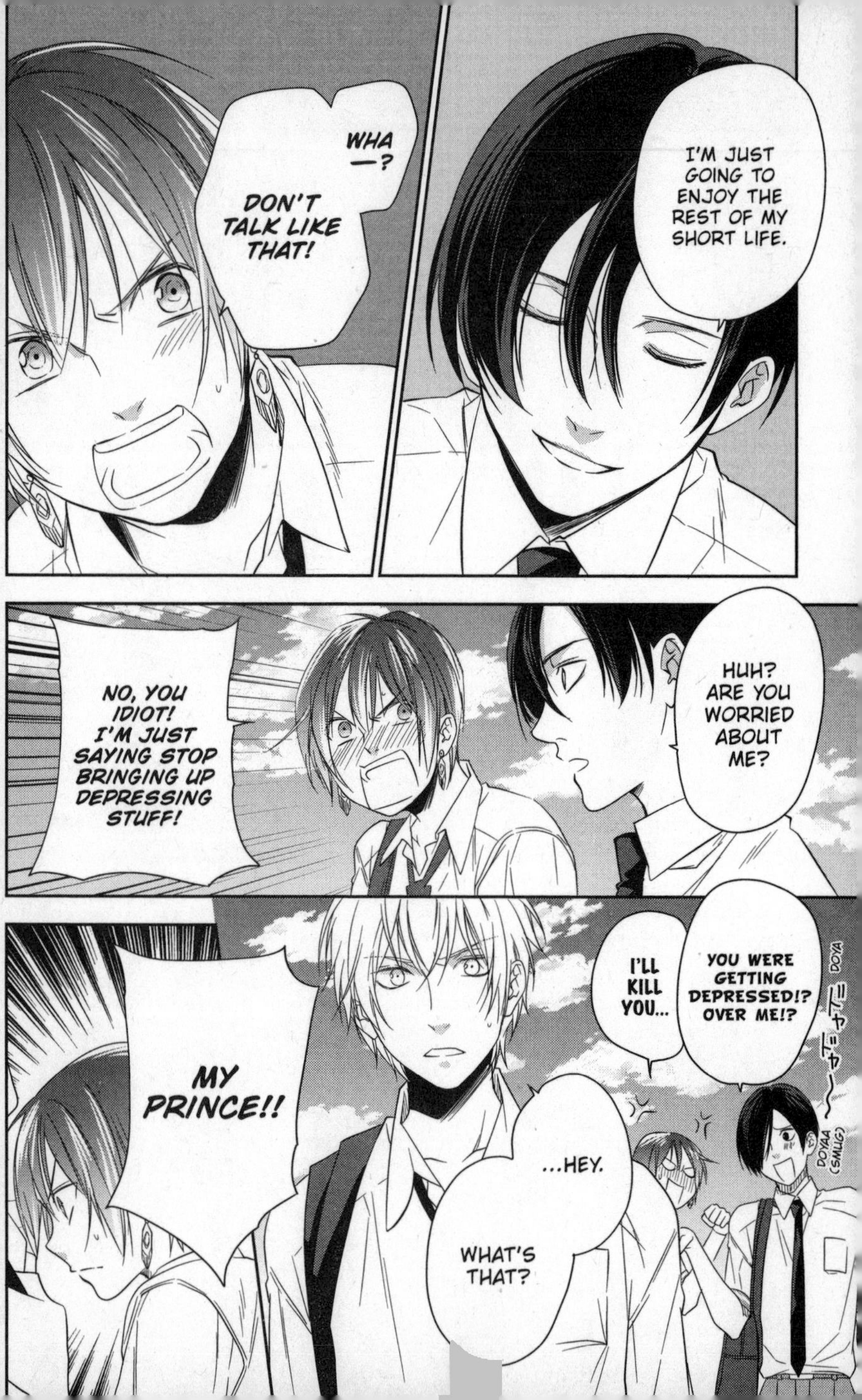
I'M JUST GOING TO ENJOY THE REST OF MY SHORT LIFE.
WHA—?
DON'T TALK LIKE THAT!
HUH? ARE YOU WORRIED ABOUT ME?
NO, YOU IDIOT! I'M JUST SAYING STOP BRINGING UP DEPRESSING STUFF!
DOYA
YOU WERE GETTING DEPRESSED!? OVER ME!?
I'LL KILL YOU...
DOYAA (SMUG)
MY PRINCE!!
...HEY.
WHAT'S THAT?

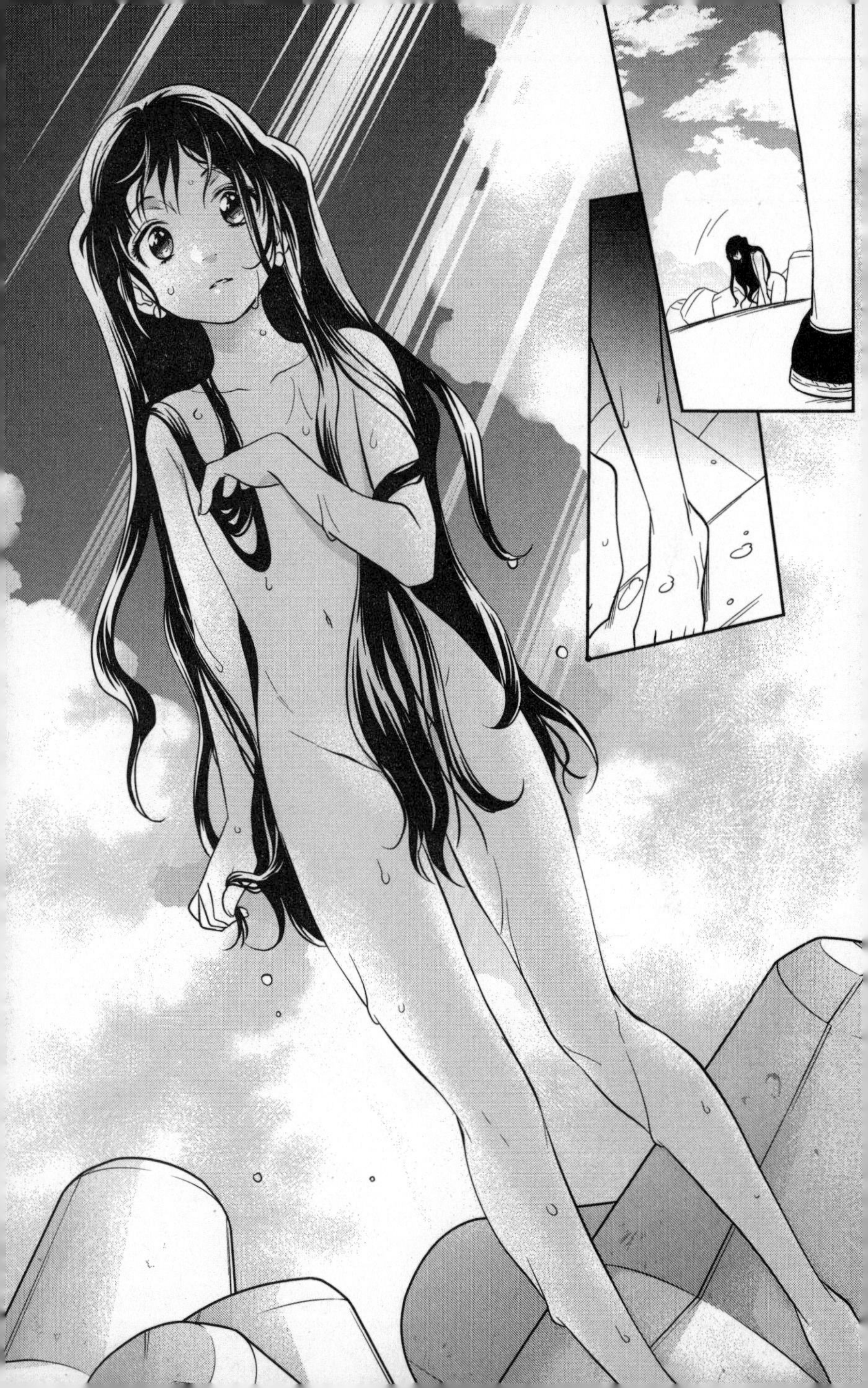

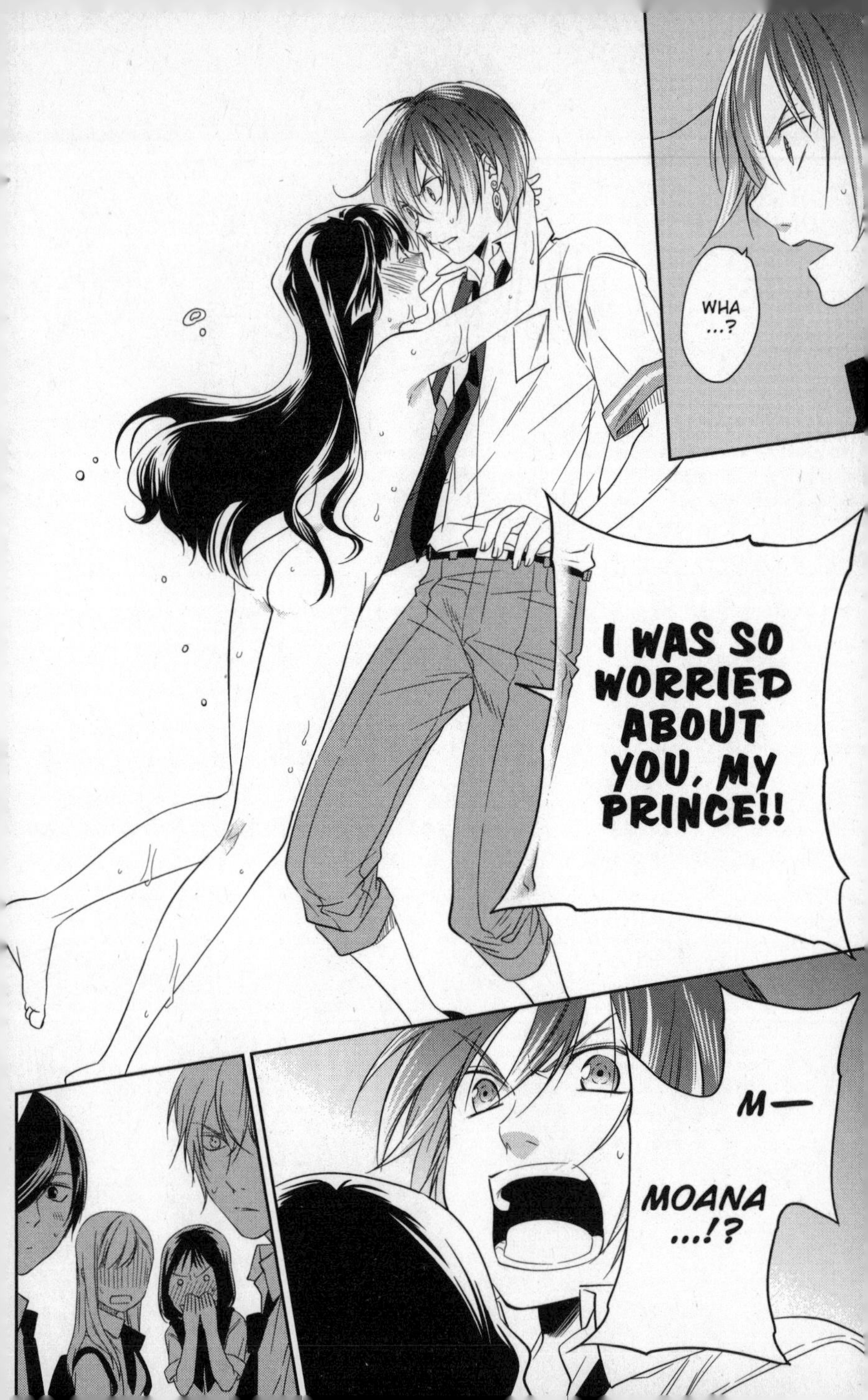
WHA ...?
I WAS SO WORRIED ABOUT YOU, MY PRINCE!!
M— MOANA ...!?

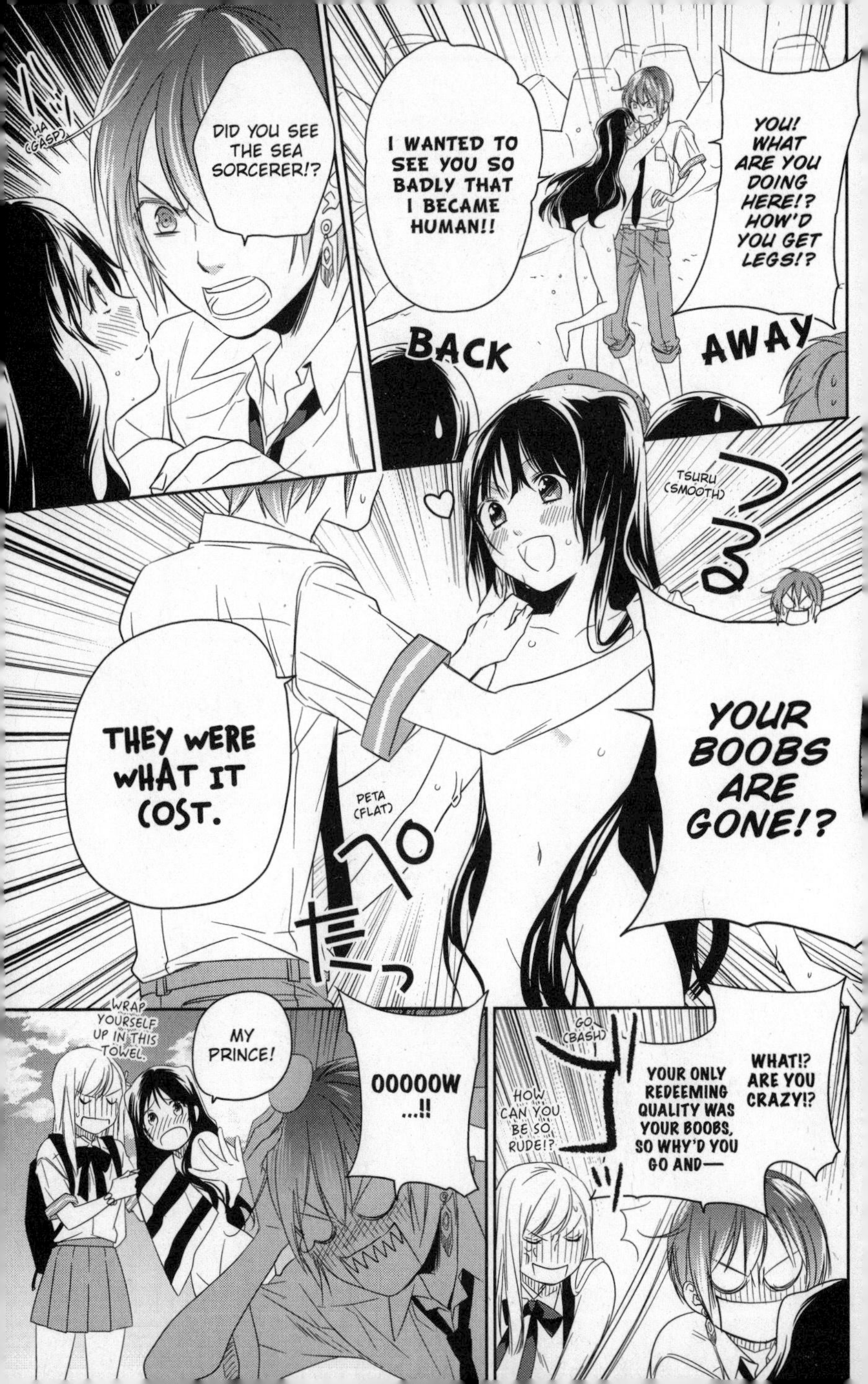
YOU! WHAT ARE YOU DOING HERE!? HOW'D YOU GET LEGS!?
I WANTED TO SEE YOU SO BADLY THAT I BECAME HUMAN!!
HA (GASP)
DID YOU SEE THE SEA SORCERER!?
BACK
AWAY
TSURU (SMOOTH)
YOUR BOOBS ARE GONE!?
THEY WERE WHAT IT COST.
PETA (FLAT)
WHAT!? ARE YOU CRAZY!?
YOUR ONLY REDEEMING QUALITY WAS YOUR BOOBS, SO WHY'D YOU GO AND—
GO (BASH)
HOW CAN YOU BE SO RUDE!?
OOOOOW ...!!
MY PRINCE!
WRAP YOURSELF UP IN THIS TOWEL.

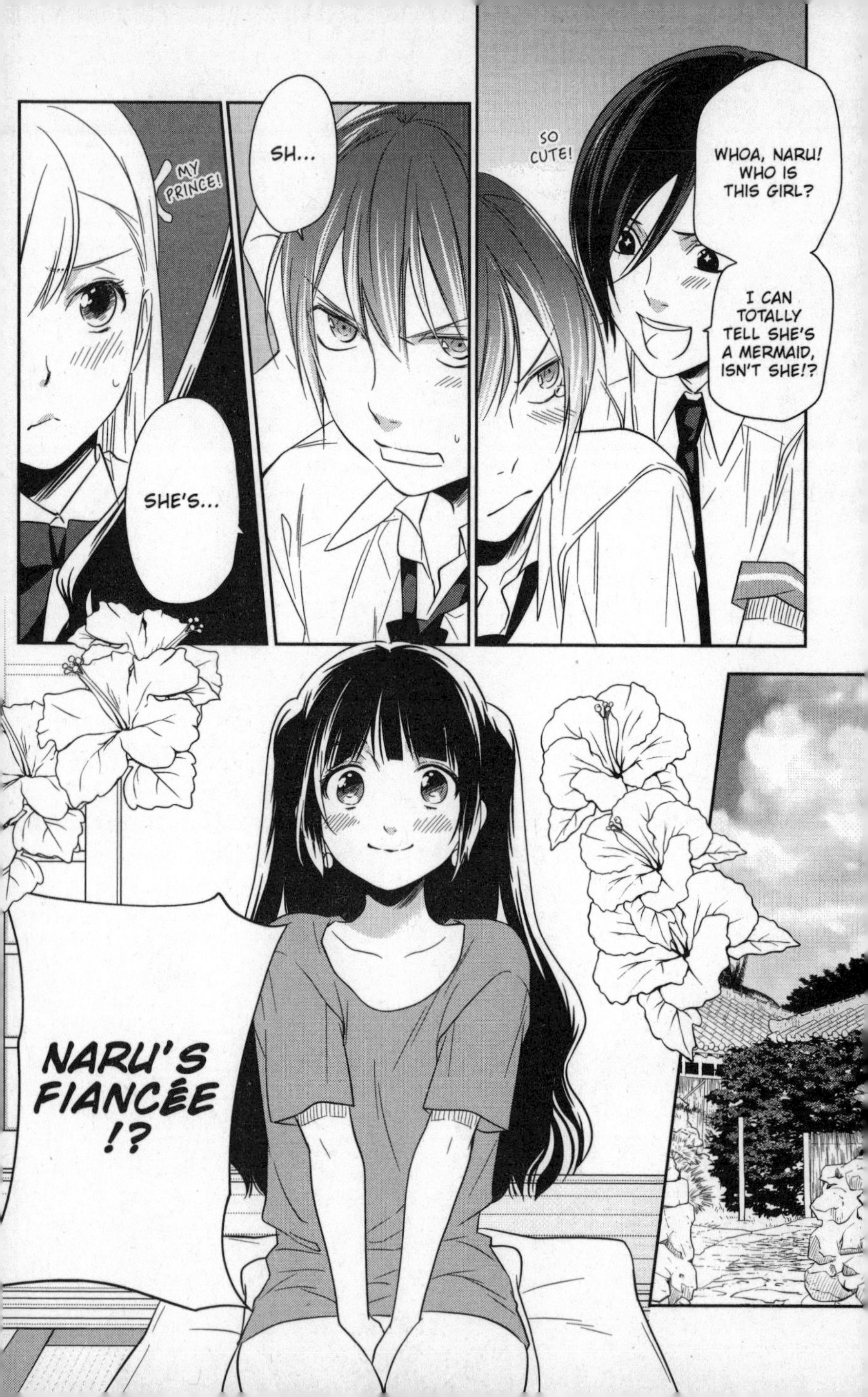
WHOA, NARU! WHO IS THIS GIRL?
I CAN TOTALLY TELL SHE'S A MERMAID, ISN'T SHE!?
SO CUTE!
SH...
MY PRINCE!
SHE'S...
NARU'S FIANCÉE!?

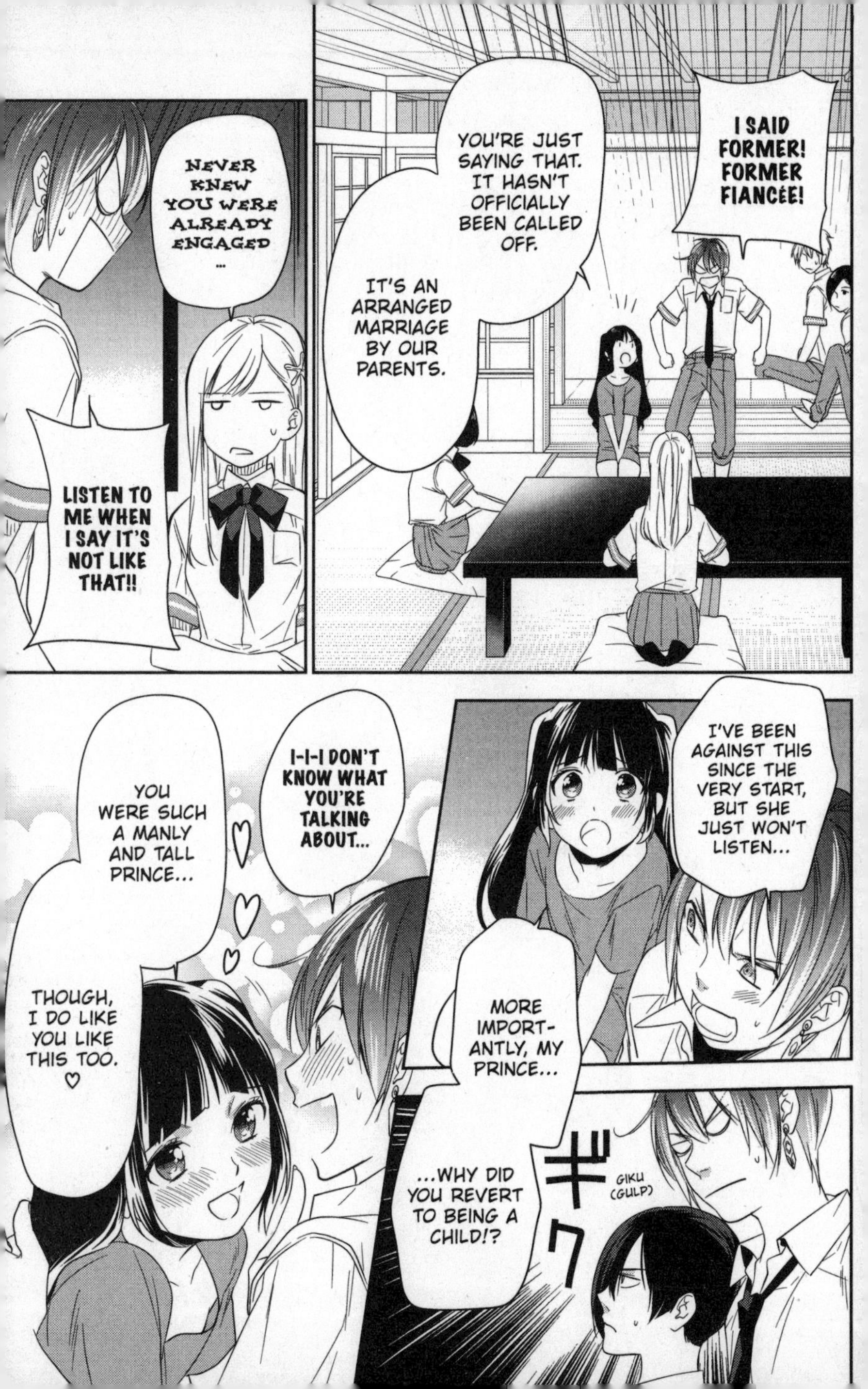
I SAID FORMER! FORMER FIANCÉE!
YOU'RE JUST SAYING THAT. IT HASN'T OFFICIALLY BEEN CALLED OFF.
IT'S AN ARRANGED MARRIAGE BY OUR PARENTS.
NEVER KNEW YOU WERE ALREADY ENGAGED ...
LISTEN TO ME WHEN I SAY IT'S NOT LIKE THAT!!
I'VE BEEN AGAINST THIS SINCE THE VERY START, BUT SHE JUST WON'T LISTEN...
MORE IMPORT-ANTLY, MY PRINCE...
...WHY DID YOU REVERT TO BEING A CHILD!?
GIKU (GULP)
I-I-I DON'T KNOW WHAT YOU'RE TALKING ABOUT...
YOU WERE SUCH A MANLY AND TALL PRINCE...
THOUGH, I DO LIKE YOU LIKE THIS TOO. ♡

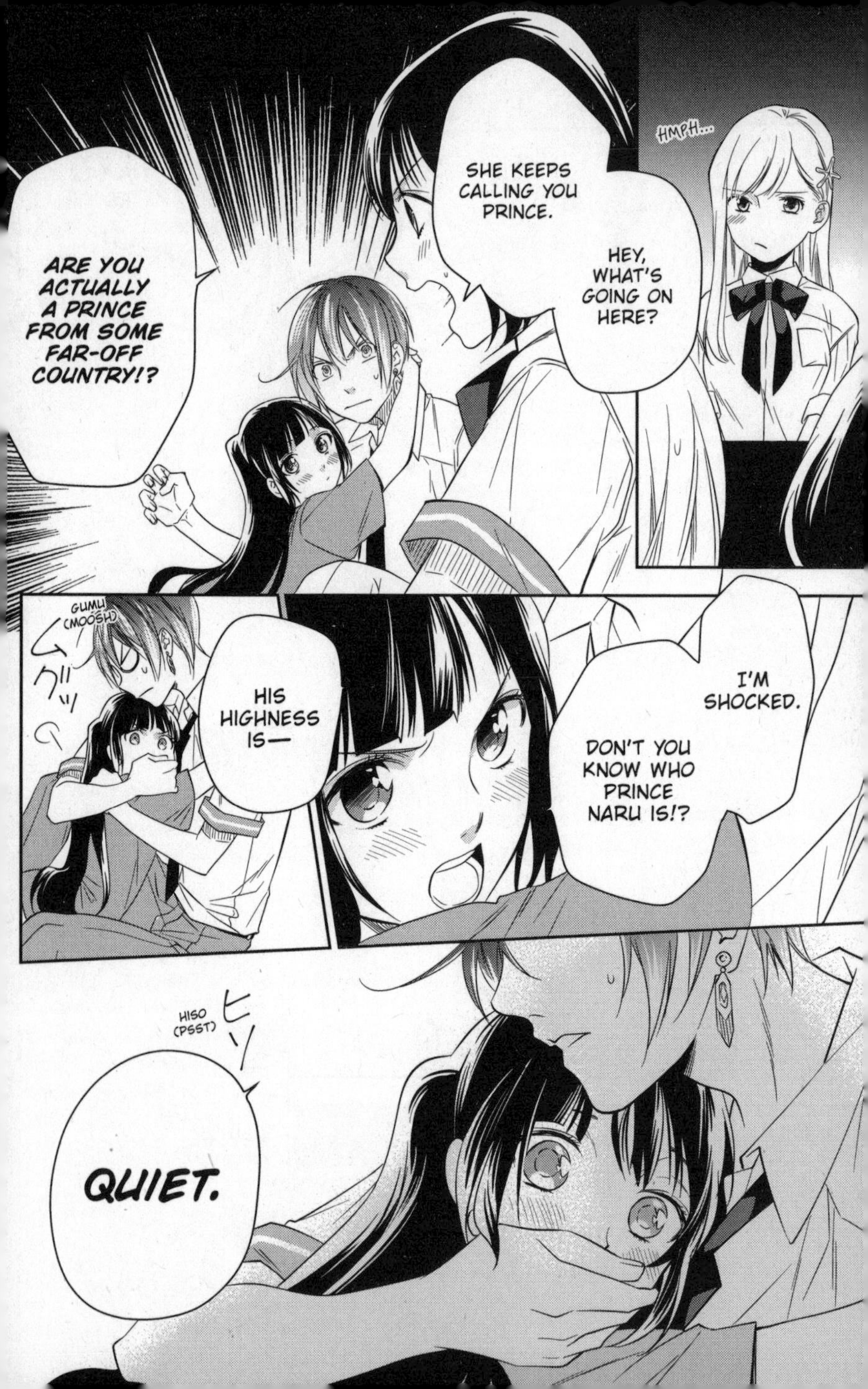
HMPH...
SHE KEEPS CALLING YOU PRINCE.
HEY, WHAT'S GOING ON HERE?
ARE YOU ACTUALLY A PRINCE FROM SOME FAR-OFF COUNTRY!?
I'M SHOCKED.
DON'T YOU KNOW WHO PRINCE NARU IS!?
HIS HIGHNESS IS—
GUMU (MOOSH)
HISO (PSST)
QUIET.

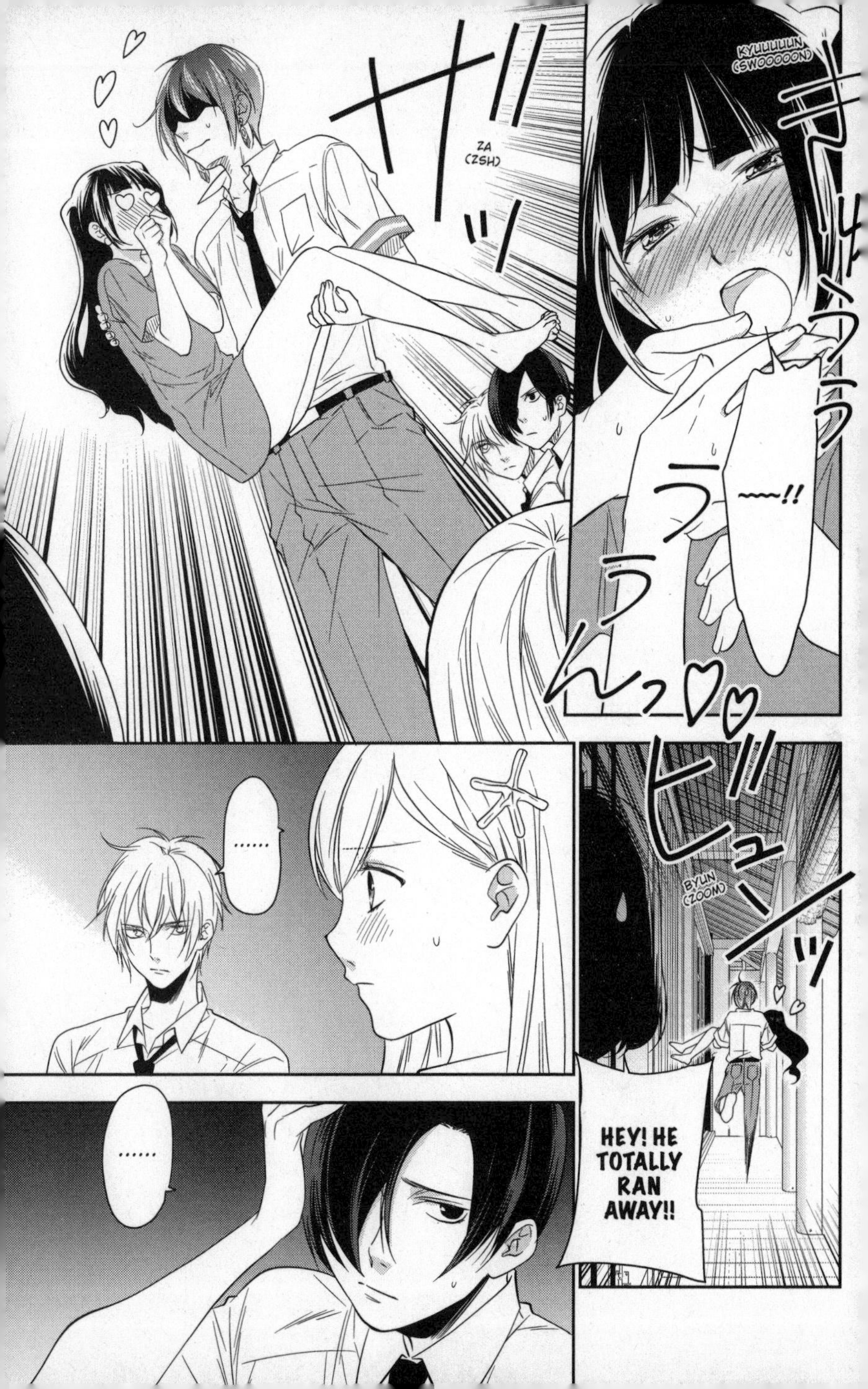
KYUUUUUUN (SWOOOOOON)
~~~!!
ZA (ZSH)
BYUN (ZOOM)
HEY! HE TOTALLY RAN AWAY!!
......
......
~~~

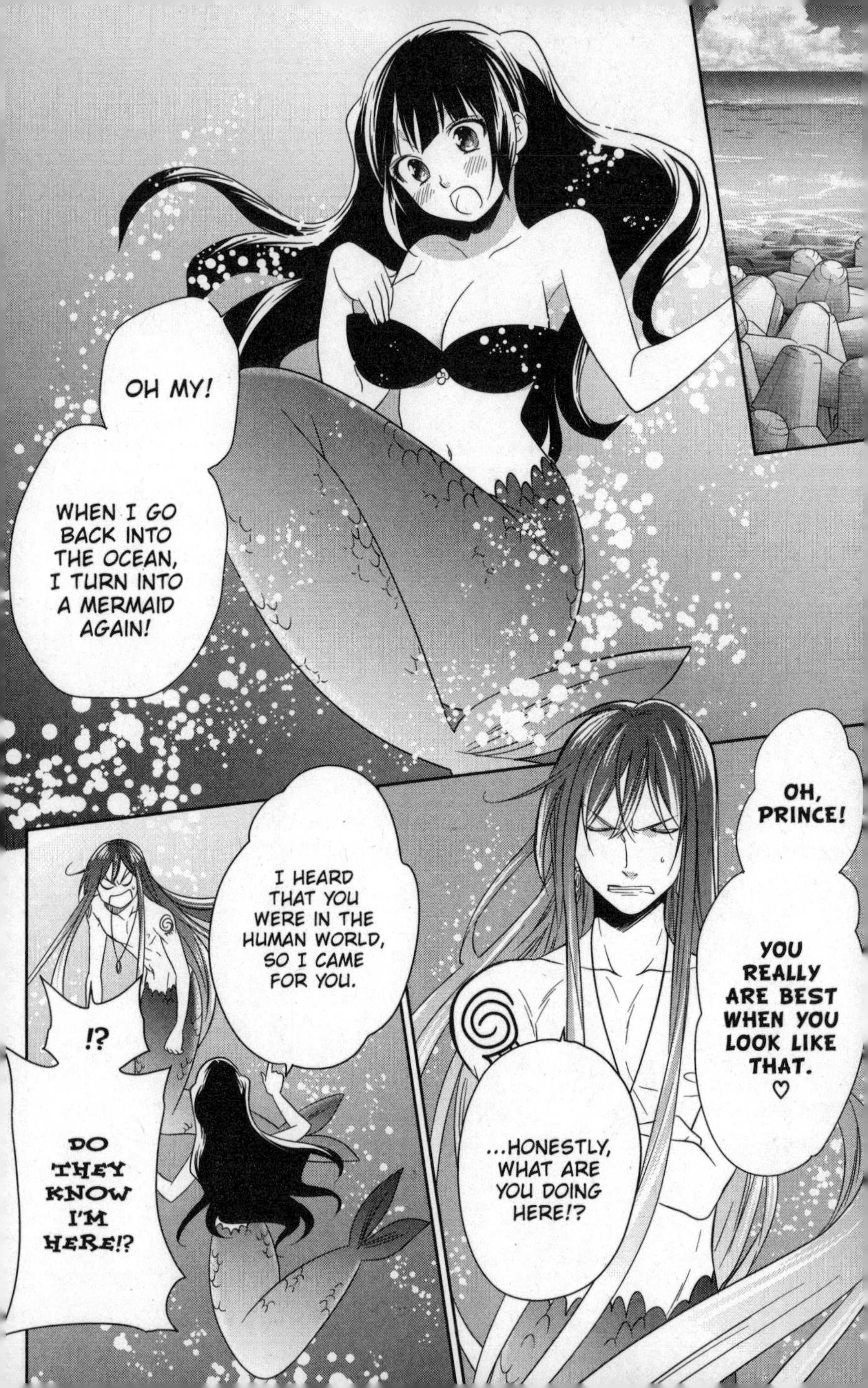
OH MY!
WHEN I GO BACK INTO THE OCEAN, I TURN INTO A MERMAID AGAIN!
OH, PRINCE!
YOU REALLY ARE BEST WHEN YOU LOOK LIKE THAT. ♡
...HONESTLY, WHAT ARE YOU DOING HERE!?
I HEARD THAT YOU WERE IN THE HUMAN WORLD, SO I CAME FOR YOU.
!?
DO THEY KNOW I'M HERE!?

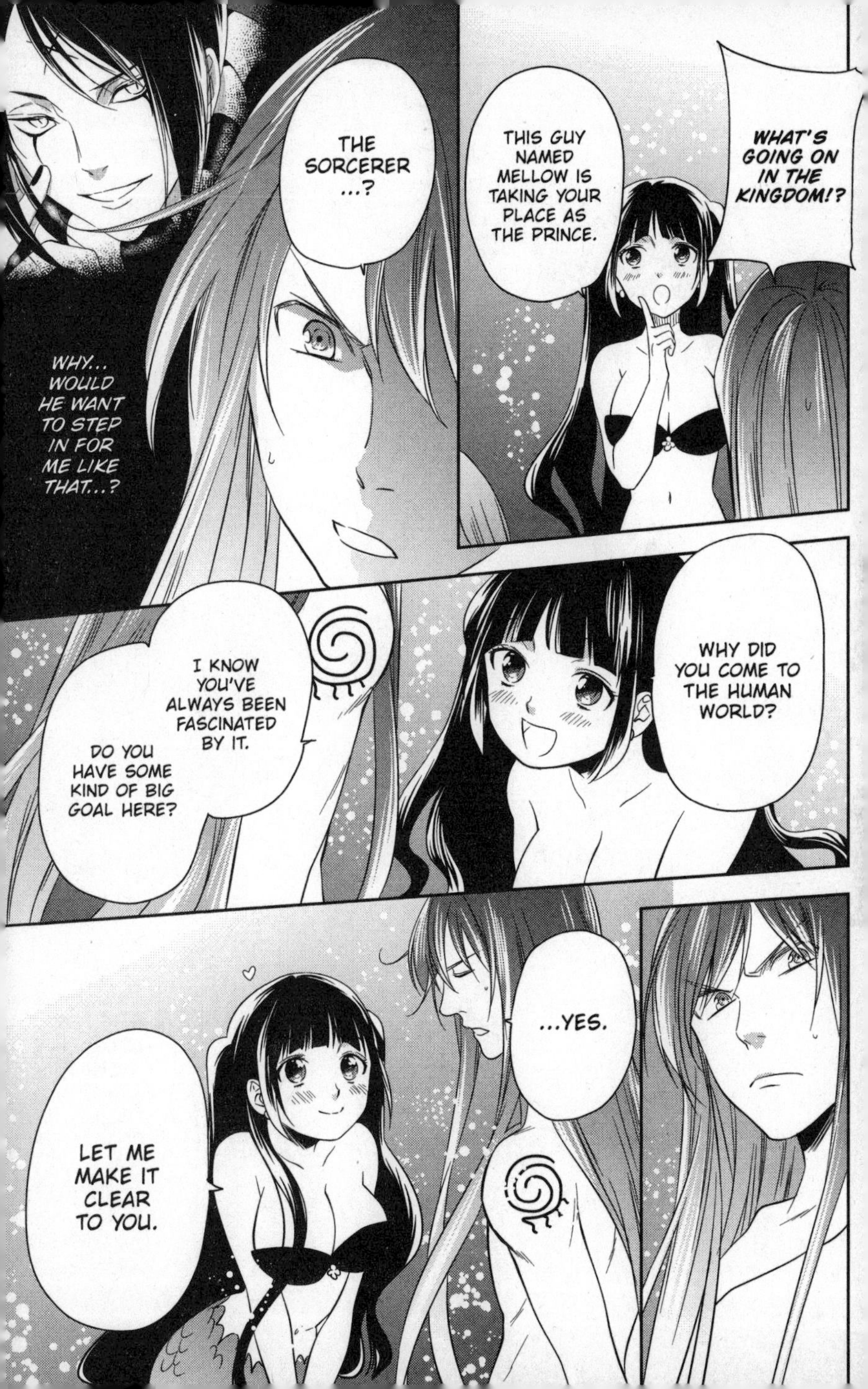
WHAT'S GOING ON IN THE KINGDOM!?
THIS GUY NAMED MELLOW IS TAKING YOUR PLACE AS THE PRINCE.
THE SORCERER ...?
WHY... WOULD HE WANT TO STEP IN FOR ME LIKE THAT...?
WHY DID YOU COME TO THE HUMAN WORLD?
I KNOW YOU'VE ALWAYS BEEN FASCINATED BY IT.
DO YOU HAVE SOME KIND OF BIG GOAL HERE?
...YES.
LET ME MAKE IT CLEAR TO YOU.

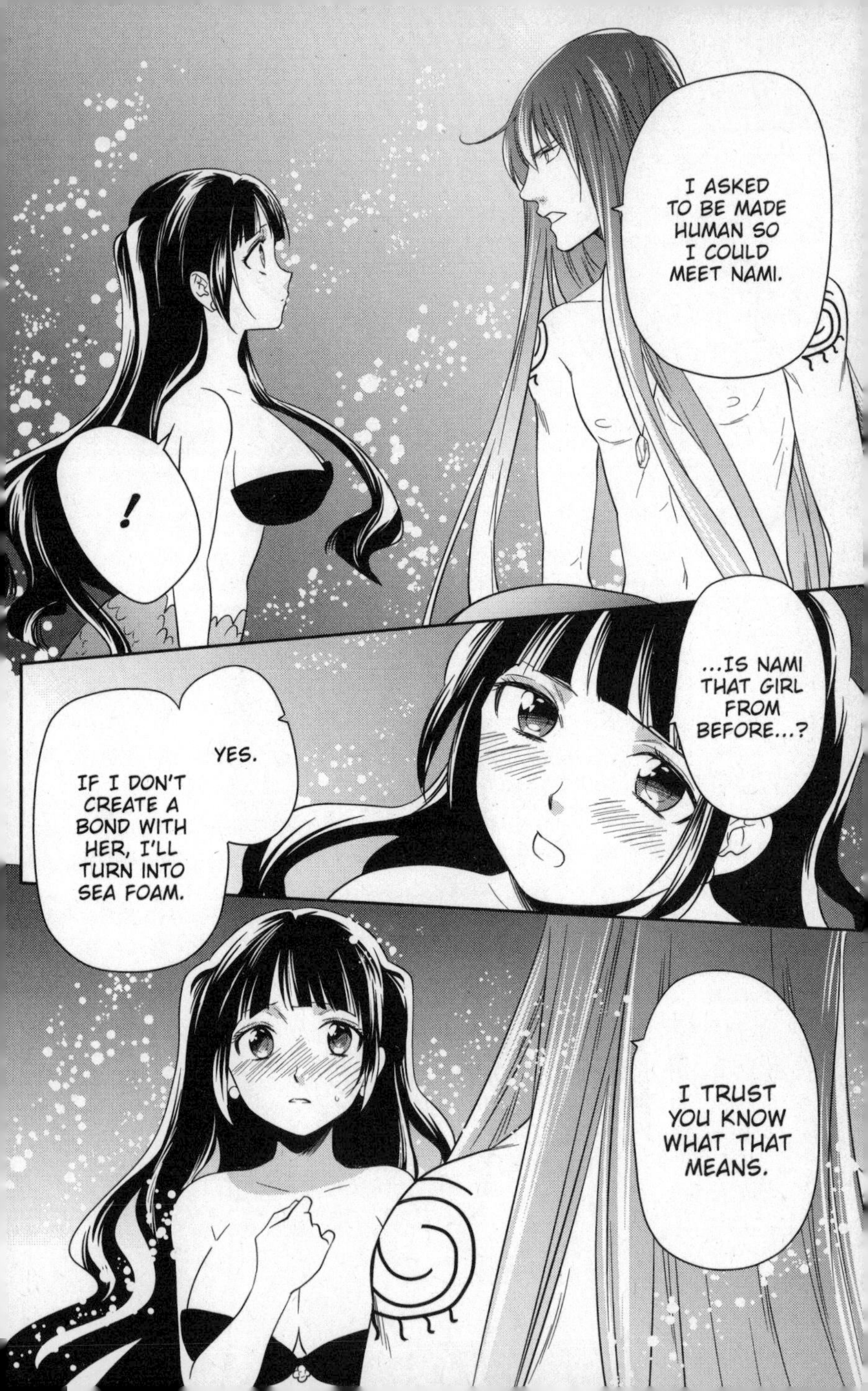
I ASKED TO BE MADE HUMAN SO I COULD MEET NAMI.
!
...IS NAMI THAT GIRL FROM BEFORE...?
YES.
IF I DON'T CREATE A BOND WITH HER, I'LL TURN INTO SEA FOAM.
I TRUST YOU KNOW WHAT THAT MEANS.

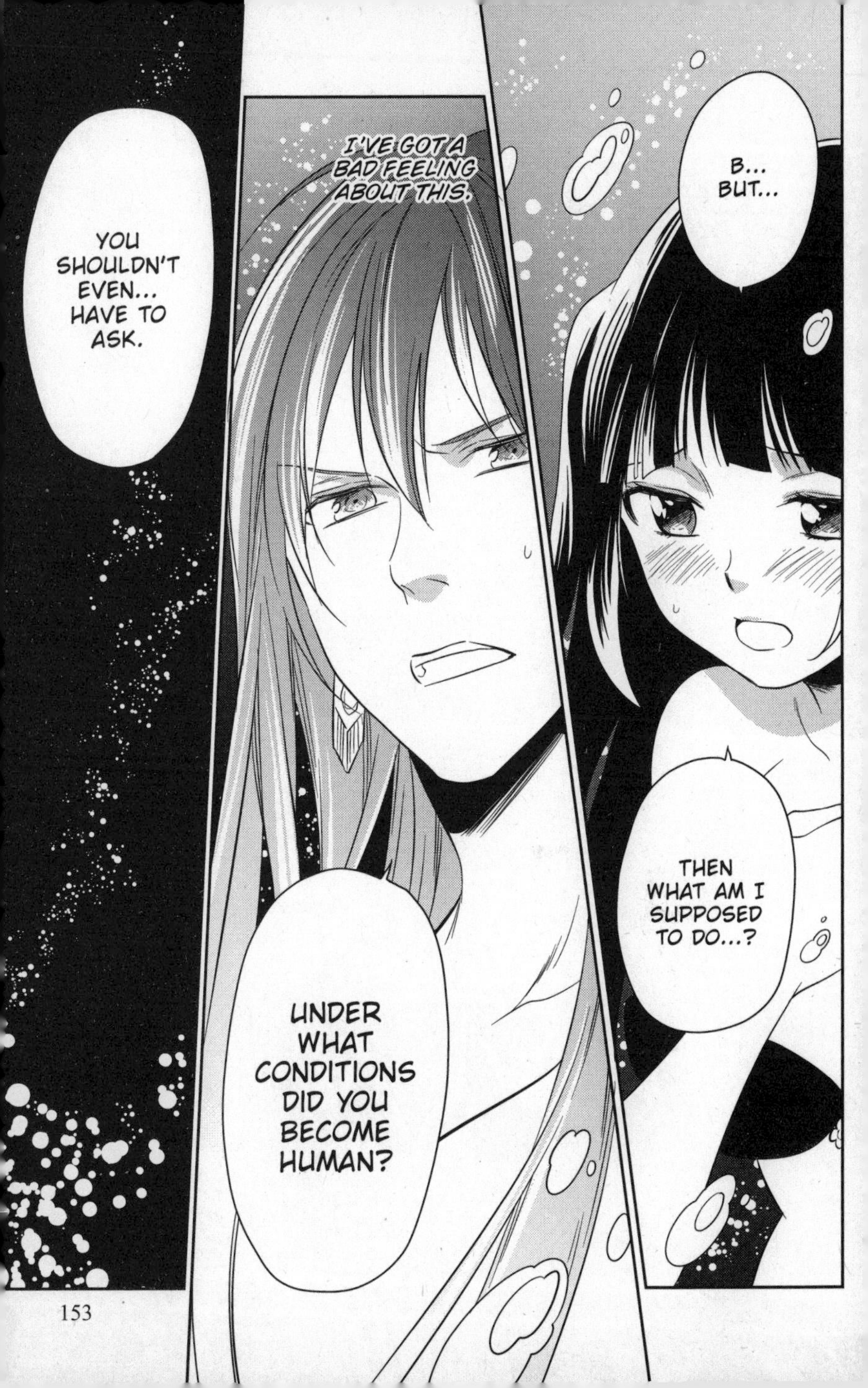
B... BUT...
THEN WHAT AM I SUPPOSED TO DO...?
I'VE GOT A BAD FEELING ABOUT THIS.
UNDER WHAT CONDITIONS DID YOU BECOME HUMAN?
YOU SHOULDN'T EVEN... HAVE TO ASK.

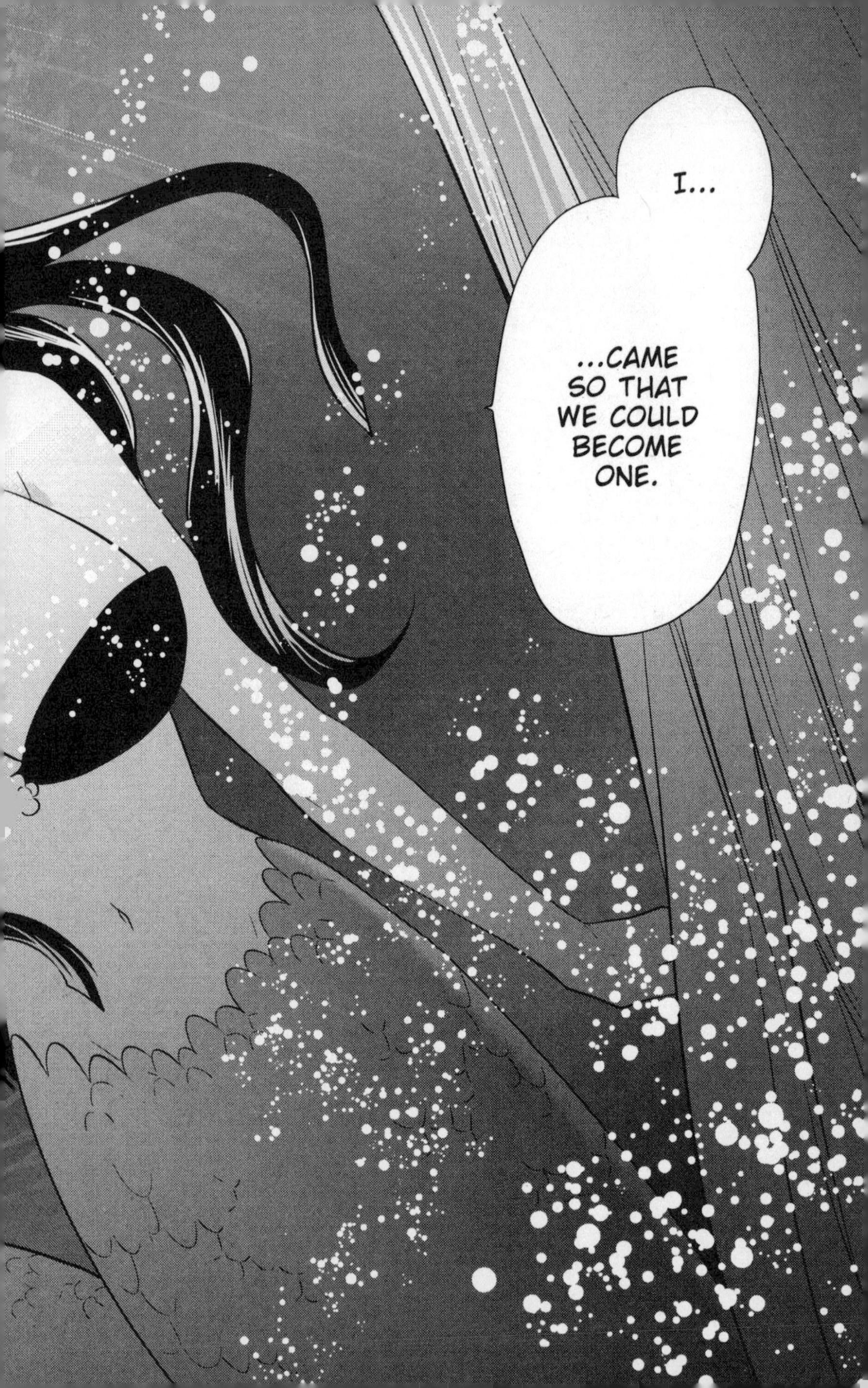
I...
...CAME SO THAT WE COULD BECOME ONE.

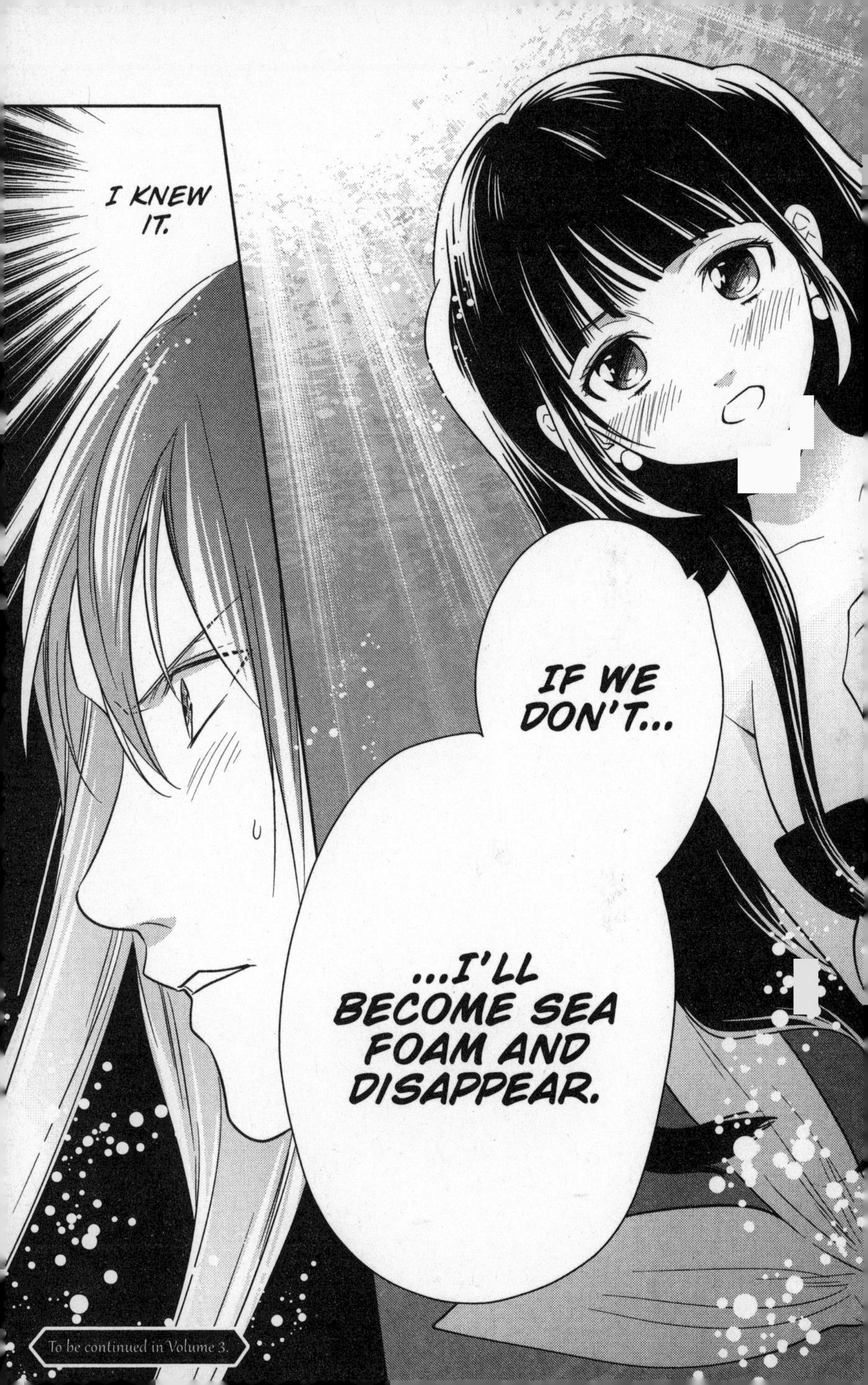
IF WE DON'T...
...I'LL BECOME SEA FOAM AND DISAPPEAR.
I KNEW IT.

To be continued in Volume 3.

MERMAID BOYS

Character Profile ②

Nami Sakuragai

- Born and lives in Miyako Island in Okinawa.

- 16 years old, Born August 22
- 5'1" tall, 93 lbs.
- Blood type: A

- Favorite food: Rice bowl topped with seafood
- Favorite kind of boy: Gentle, broad-minded guys
- Favorite place: Tetrapod
- Hates: Scary stories
- Affiliated flower: Dogwood

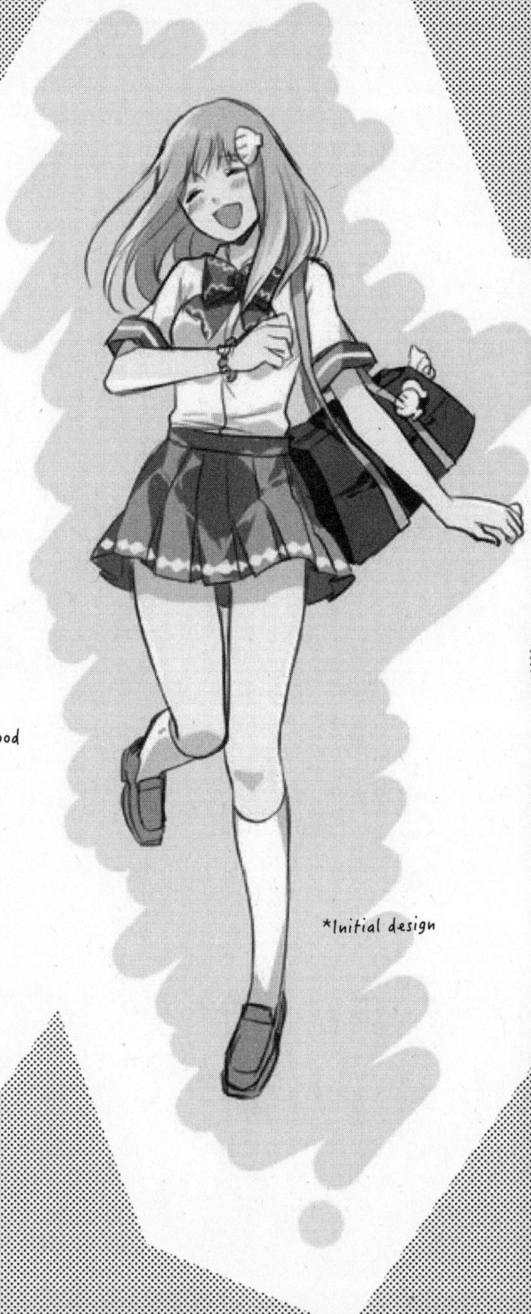

*Initial design

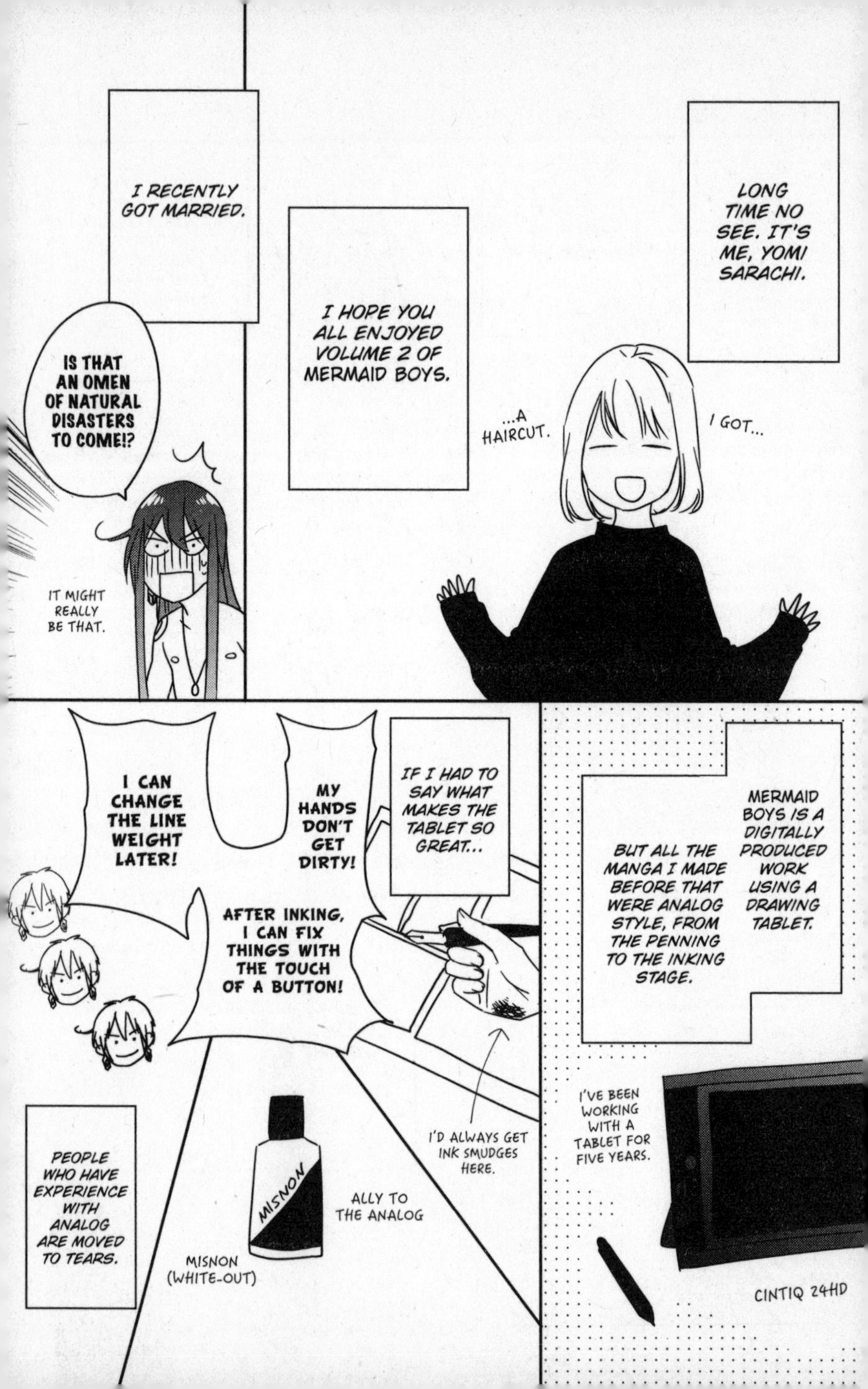
LONG TIME NO SEE. IT'S ME, YOMI SARACHI.
I HOPE YOU ALL ENJOYED VOLUME 2 OF MERMAID BOYS.
I GOT...
...A HAIRCUT.
I RECENTLY GOT MARRIED.
IS THAT AN OMEN OF NATURAL DISASTERS TO COME!?
IT MIGHT REALLY BE THAT.
MERMAID BOYS IS A DIGITALLY PRODUCED WORK USING A DRAWING TABLET.
BUT ALL THE MANGA I MADE BEFORE THAT WERE ANALOG STYLE, FROM THE PENNING TO THE INKING STAGE.
I'VE BEEN WORKING WITH A TABLET FOR FIVE YEARS.
CINTIQ 24HD
IF I HAD TO SAY WHAT MAKES THE TABLET SO GREAT...
MY HANDS DON'T GET DIRTY!
I CAN CHANGE THE LINE WEIGHT LATER!
AFTER INKING, I CAN FIX THINGS WITH THE TOUCH OF A BUTTON!
I'D ALWAYS GET INK SMUDGES HERE.
ALLY TO THE ANALOG
MISNON
MISNON (WHITE-OUT)
PEOPLE WHO HAVE EXPERIENCE WITH ANALOG ARE MOVED TO TEARS.

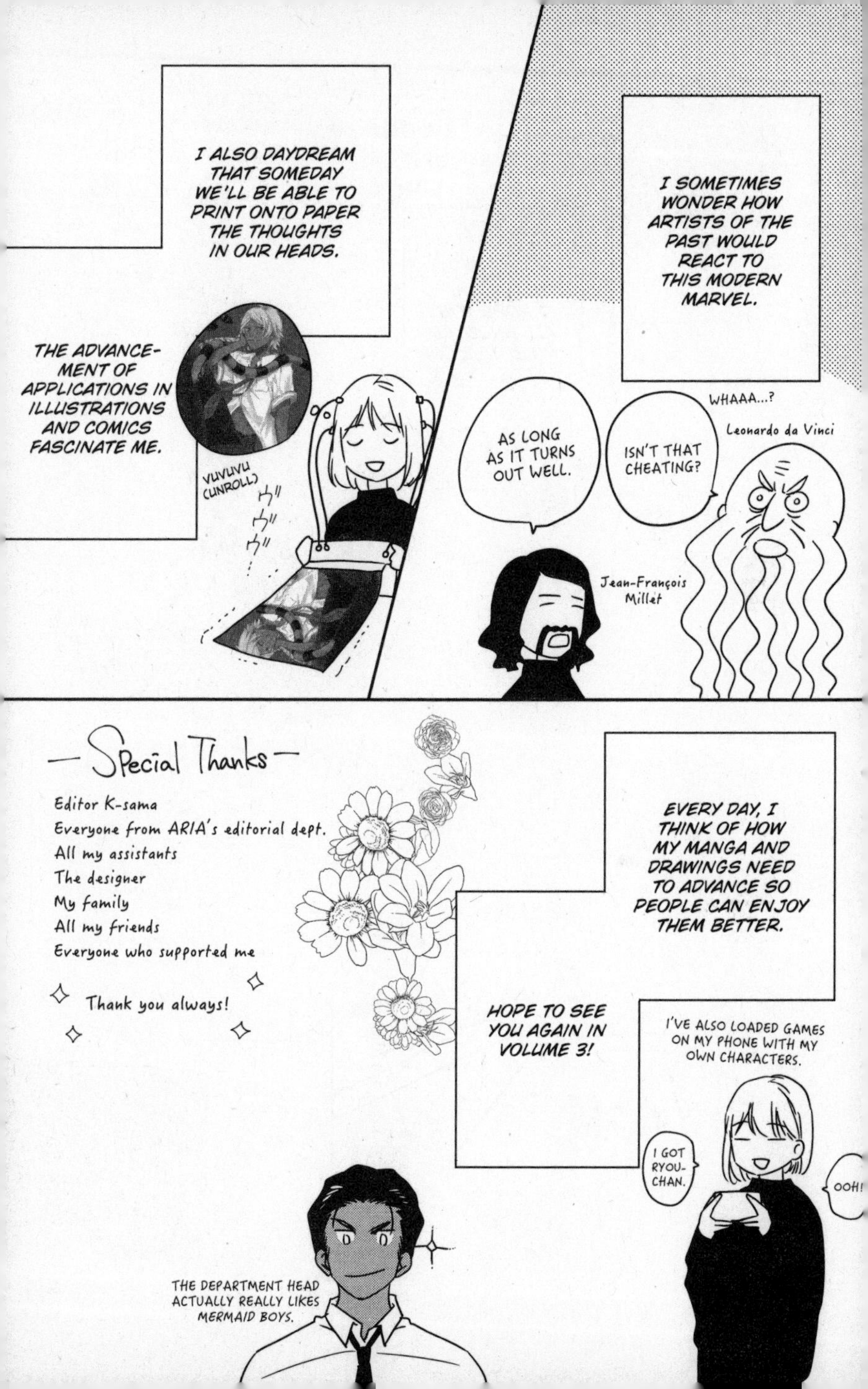
I SOMETIMES WONDER HOW ARTISTS OF THE PAST WOULD REACT TO THIS MODERN MARVEL.
WHAAA...?
ISN'T THAT CHEATING?
Leonardo da Vinci
AS LONG AS IT TURNS OUT WELL.
Jean-François Millet
I ALSO DAYDREAM THAT SOMEDAY WE'LL BE ABLE TO PRINT ONTO PAPER THE THOUGHTS IN OUR HEADS.
THE ADVANCEMENT OF APPLICATIONS IN ILLUSTRATIONS AND COMICS FASCINATE ME.
VUVUVU (UNROLL)
ヴヴヴ
EVERY DAY, I THINK OF HOW MY MANGA AND DRAWINGS NEED TO ADVANCE SO PEOPLE CAN ENJOY THEM BETTER.
HOPE TO SEE YOU AGAIN IN VOLUME 3!
I'VE ALSO LOADED GAMES ON MY PHONE WITH MY OWN CHARACTERS.
I GOT RYOU-CHAN.
OOH!
—Special Thanks—
Editor K-sama
Everyone from ARIA's editorial dept.
All my assistants
The designer
My family
All my friends
Everyone who supported me
Thank you always!
THE DEPARTMENT HEAD ACTUALLY REALLY LIKES MERMAID BOYS.

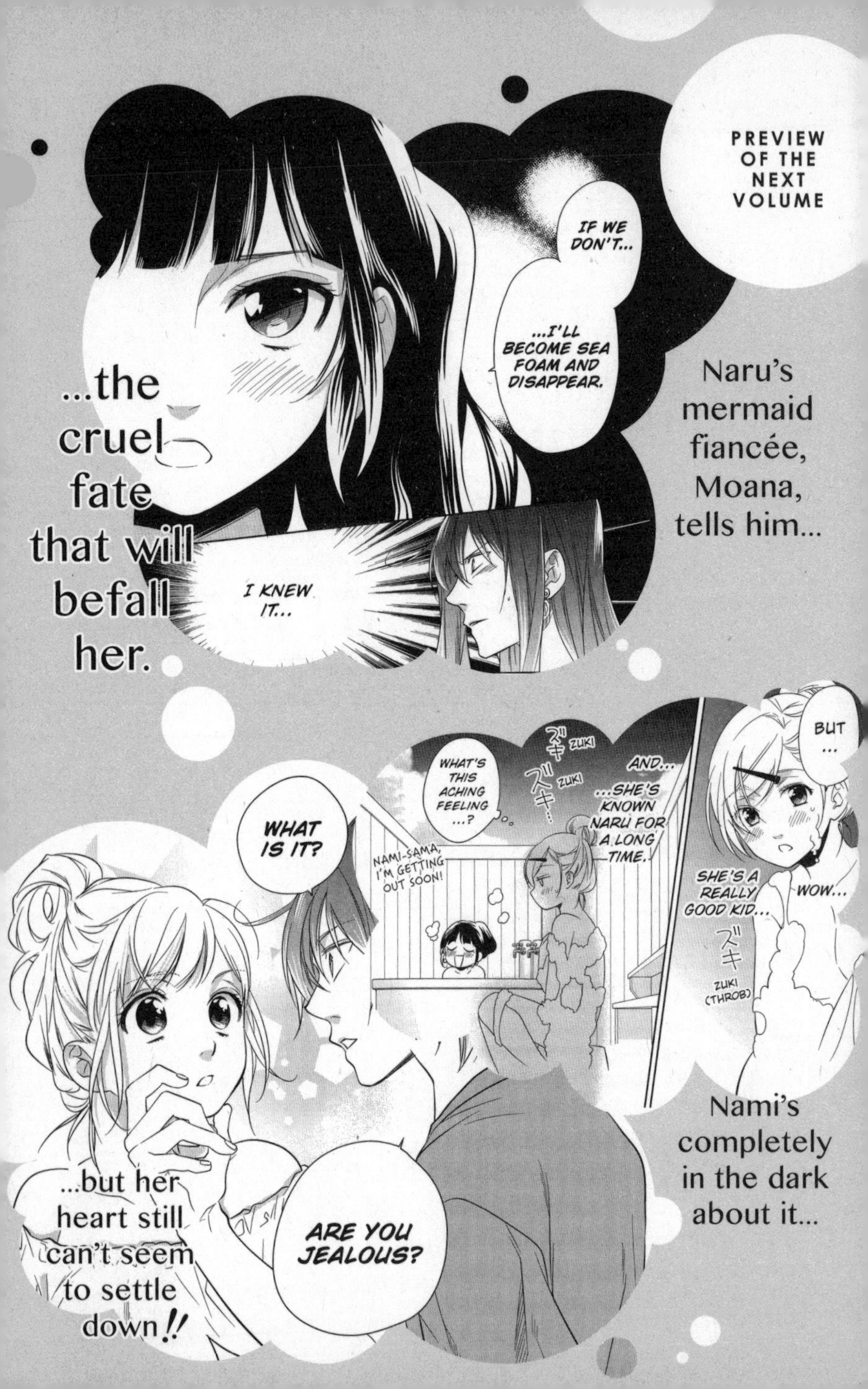
PREVIEW OF THE NEXT VOLUME
Naru's mermaid fiancée, Moana, tells him...
IF WE DON'T...
...I'LL BECOME SEA FOAM AND DISAPPEAR.
...the cruel fate that will befall her.
I KNEW IT...
Nami's completely in the dark about it...
BUT ...
WOW...
SHE'S A REALLY GOOD KID...
ズキ ZUKI (THROB)
AND... ...SHE'S KNOWN NARU FOR A LONG TIME.
ズキ ZUKI
ズキ... ZUKI
WHAT'S THIS ACHING FEELING ...?
NAMI-SAMA, I'M GETTING OUT SOON!
WHAT IS IT?
ARE YOU JEALOUS?
...but her heart still can't seem to settle down!!

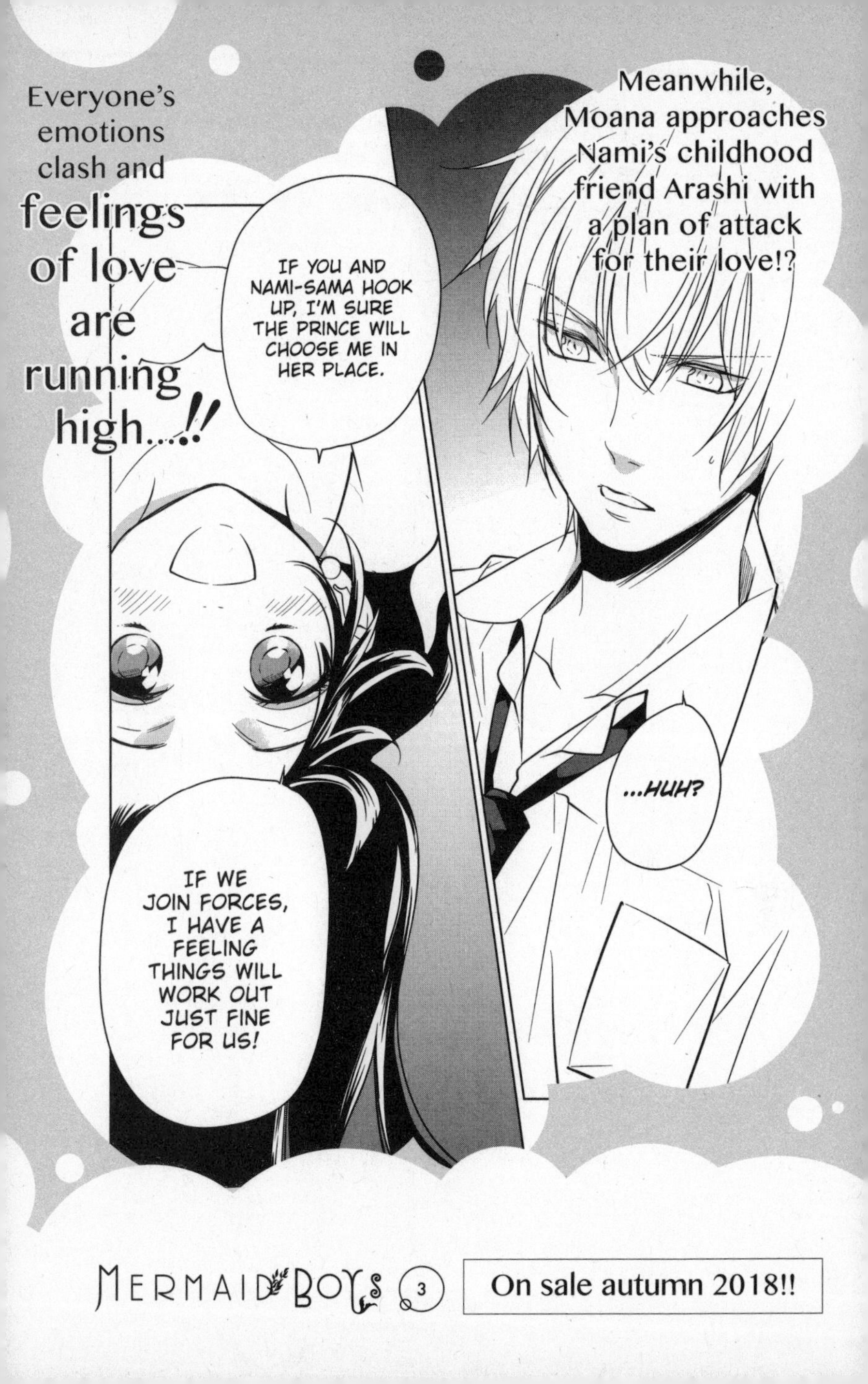
Everyone's emotions clash and feelings of love are running high...!!
IF YOU AND NAMI-SAMA HOOK UP, I'M SURE THE PRINCE WILL CHOOSE ME IN HER PLACE.
IF WE JOIN FORCES, I HAVE A FEELING THINGS WILL WORK OUT JUST FINE FOR US!
Meanwhile, Moana approaches Nami's childhood friend Arashi with a plan of attack for their love!?
...HUH?
MERMAID BOYS 3
On sale autumn 2018!!

MERMAID BOYS 2

Yomi Sarachi

Translation: CHRISTINE DASHIELL 🦑 Lettering: ALEXIS ECKERMAN

MERMAID BOYS
© 2017 Yomi Sarachi. All rights reserved.
First published in Japan in 2017 by Kodansha Ltd., Tokyo. Publication rights for this English language edition arranged through Kodansha Ltd., Tokyo.

English translation © 2018 by Yen Press, LLC

Yen Press
1290 Avenue of the Americas
New York, NY 10104

Visit us at yenpress.com
facebook.com/yenpress
twitter.com/yenpress
yenpress.tumblr.com
instagram.com/yenpress

First Yen Press Edition: June 2018

Yen Press is an imprint of Yen Press, LLC.
The Yen Press name and logo are trademarks of Yen Press, LLC.

Library of Congress Control Number: 2017963580

ISBN: 978-0-316-48097-0

10 9 8 7 6 5 4 3 2 1

WOR

Printed in the United States of America